**MODERN
ENGLISH
IN ACTION**

Modern English in Action

Henry I. Christ

D. C. HEATH AND COMPANY
Lexington, Massachusetts   Toronto

Illustrators: Bill Oakes, Plynn E. Williams, Walter Fournier, Eileen Palmer

Cover design: Robert and Marilyn Dustin

Preface

"Move ahead to basics!" is the slogan of this edition of *Modern English in Action*. "Back to basics" has the sound of retreat, but there is nothing regressive about a concern with basic skills. They provide the underpinning of successful and effective communication. If we fail to provide basic skills, we build our educational castles on quicksand.

There is no denying the very real gains in methodology, content, and organization during the past years. But in the rush toward trying out new programs, schools have sometimes overlooked many important elements. Basic skills in writing and reading throughout the country have faltered. A countrywide sense of disappointment with scholastic achievement has brought about a reevaluation of curricula.

Modern English in Action has always had as its philosophy the inculcation of basic language skills in a sound and stimulating way. A glance at the pages themselves will reveal a very real concern with student interests and the psychology of motivation.

Writing. Teachers have requested books with rich writing programs. To meet this need, *Modern English in Action* provides student writing activities in *all* of the first seventeen chapters. In addition it provides a substantial writing unit (pages 48–183) designed to lead the student from writing a simple sentence to handling more sophisticated writing assignments with confidence.

Chapter 4, "Building Paragraphs," puts students to work composing simple sentences, which later are used as topic sentences of paragraphs. The transition from sentence to paragraph is simple and logical. Then follow thirty pages of step-by-step instruction in writing paragraphs, along with more than twenty-five helpful models. Nothing is taken for granted. Abundant drill is provided, with cumulative instruction in paragraph organization and strategy.

Because the paragraph is the basic unit in most writing, Chapter 5 continues the study of the paragraph. For convenience in providing review as well as new applications, Chapter 5 studies expository, narrative, descriptive, and argumentative paragraphs. The goal throughout is not a mechanical awareness of *types* but a strengthened ability to write a sound paragraph by being exposed to a great variety of paragraphs. Again many models are provided to guide students in their development. The chapter concludes with writing compositions of several paragraphs.

Chapters 6 through 8 provide abundant practice in writing more extended compositions—narration, description, and exposition. Chapter 9 provides assistance in writing reports. Chapter 10, the letter-writing chapter, provides standards for both friendly and business letters, while encouraging students to write both types. Chapter 11, "Publishing a Class Newspaper," may be optional for some classes, but for others it may provide a practical outlet for writing energy.

These are all covered: paragraph writing, pages 49, 52–107, 138, 141, 225, 245; joining paragraphs into a longer theme, pages 103–107; friendly letter, pages 155–162; business letter, pages 163–167, 179; summary, pages 81, 199–200; description, pages 91–94, 120–129; narration, pages 95–97, 108–119; autobiography and personal experience, pages 117–118, 182–183; short story, pages 119; explaining, pages 84–90, 130–141; reporting, pages 142–153; persuasion, pages 98–100, 178–179, 244–245; minutes, page 235; dialog, pages 115–116; writing for publication, pages 168–183; answering questions, pages 79–81; writing poetry, pages 216–219; and reviewing, pages 205, 207.

In addition, in each word-study activity there is practice in composing single sentences. The chapters in the Handbook of Grammar, Usage, and Style amplify and round out the writing instruction with many additional writing activities.

Language Study. *Modern English in Action* provides a sound language-centered program—for example, word study, pages 2–13; context, pages 17–19; dictionary study, pages 20–24; synonyms, pages 24–25; etymology and roots, pages 25–27; vivid words, pages 28–29, 114, 126; conciseness, pages 30, 134, 363, 456–459; thinking, pages 228, 236–245; pronunciation, pages 223–225; figurative language, pages 212–213; and semantics, pages 38–47.

To complement these materials there are word-study activities at the end of most of the first eighteen chapters. Here, as elsewhere, the text itself is used as a laboratory for further study of the language arts.

Handbook of Grammar, Usage, and Style. This section presents a full, rounded program of language elements geared to the needs of young people. The purpose of this section is twofold: to provide a ready reference handbook, conveniently organized for individual student use, and to provide a program of basic skills for explanation, drill, and habituation. The goal of the Handbook is not merely to give knowledge *about* language but to improve the use of language. Sections labeled "Applications in Speaking and Writing" in the Teacher's Manual keep the focus on more effective writing and speaking.

Although the work is so arranged that a teacher may concentrate upon traditional elements in English grammar, *Modern English in Action* introduces a number of generally approved concepts derived from modern research in grammar and linguistics. The Teacher's Handbook suggests ways of effectively combining modern and traditional elements. Sample lesson plans supplement material in the text and are cross-referenced in the overprinted Teacher's Edition. Every effort has been made to incorporate sound current thinking in these books.

At the very end of the text a 32-page supplement provides a comprehensive review of materials met in the Handbook of Grammar, Usage, and Style. This review adds an extra dimension to the language study. The supplement is cross-referenced to appropriate sections in the text. In addition, students are given specific training in the kinds of questions presented on college-entrance examinations.

Activity Code Letters. For easy identification and review, all activities in the first eighteen chapters are labeled with code letters. These identify at a glance the type of activity: W (writing), O (oral), R (reading), L (listening), T (thinking), S (study and research), and V (vocabulary and word study). In the Handbook those practices which include work other than grammar or usage drill are also identified by code letter. Diagraming practices, which always include an alternative to diagraming, are identified by D. For ways in which diagraming may fit into a modern English program, consult page ii and page 28 of the Supplementary Teacher's Manual.

Spiral Skills. The inclusiveness of writing and language skills has been detailed above, but other skills are treated throughout the text. Reading, for example, is treated as a major skill in Chapter 12; but reading skills are also emphasized in Chapter 7 (pages 121–122), Chapter 9 (pages 143–144), Chapter 16 (pages 227–235), Chapter 18 (pages 247–256), and elsewhere.

Teacher Aids. *Modern English in Action* provides direct assistance to the teacher by furnishing (1) complete answers, overprinted where possible; (2) a manual of teaching suggestions, overprinted where possible; and (3) a Teacher's Handbook section, a concise textbook of practical methodology. Aims, lesson plans, samples of corrected compositions, syllabi—aids like these make teaching more effective and more manageable.

The In-Action Principle. The philosophy of *Modern English in Action* is embodied in the words *in action*. Its strategy emphasizes flexibility and a many-sided attack. Numerous, interesting student activities, with ample provision for individual self-teaching, constitute an important part of the book. More than 250 activities in Chapters 1 through 18 alone guarantee abundant student activity. The work is enticing, functional, challenging, and student-oriented.

Acknowledgments. It would be impossible to list the many people who made this edition of *Modern English in Action* possible, but even in a distinguished company, certain names stand out. Ruth L. Lutze, senior project editor at D. C. Heath and Company, was deeply involved in the preliminary preparations for this edition. J. Smongeski and David Libby of the D. C. Heath Design Department played especially prominent roles in the design and illustration of the books. Robert H., William G., and Thomas F. Christ contributed materials, clippings, insights, and many practical suggestions. Milton Blatt, former colleague at Andrew Jackson High School, St. Albans, New York, made many helpful suggestions concerning the college-entrance materials.

Marianna Frew Palmer, senior project editor at D. C. Heath and Company, made specific contributions, guided the books through the many stages of production, and was largely responsible for tying the many threads together.

Brian K. McLaughlin, executive editor of the Language Arts Department at D. C. Heath and Company, played a major role in helping to determine the direction of this edition and to decide changes of emphasis. In addition, he supplied materials and suggestions. Above all, he provided help and encouragement at every stage of the project.

For the typing and preparation of the manuscript; for the reading of the books in their entirety; for many valuable suggestions and usable materials; and above all for her unwavering and optimistic support, I am, as always, deeply indebted to my wife, Marie E. Christ.

HENRY I. CHRIST

Contents

Unit Three—Reading

Unit Four—Speaking

Unit Five—Resources

Handbook of Grammar, Usage, and Style

Unit One — *Words*

1   *Words: The Lighter Side*

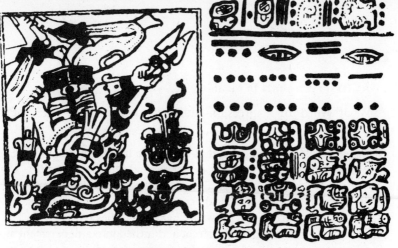

The Mayan script is being deciphered by the use of computers. Above is a sample of the system of dots, dashes, and hieroglyphic symbols the Mayans used for numerical and calendrical notations.

Two neighbors got into a quarrel across the back fence. They couldn't agree because they were arguing from different premises.

A great deal of humor grows out of a play on words. To understand this kind of humor, you have to know how words are used. You must also have a good enough vocabulary to understand the wordplay. In the sentence above, for example, the humor turns on the different meanings of the word *premises*. *Premises* means "some land with a building on it" or "propositions in logic."

PUNS

A common form of wordplay is the pun.

A very old gentleman was admitted to the hospital. Because of his age he was put on the critical list. When he heard about it, he objected. "I'm not critical at all. I like this hospital."

This play on the meanings of the word *critical* ("faultfinding" or "full of danger") is typical of puns. If a word has more than one meaning, it's a prime candidate for the punster. When you use a word in a humorous way to suggest two different meanings at the same time, you are making a pun.

People who look down on others are probably living on a bluff.

This contains a double-barreled pun. *Look down on* may mean "despise" or it may mean "look at someone from a higher spot." *Bluff* may mean a "cliff" or a "deception." Here the speaker makes a telling point about conceited people in a clever way.

3

What word or expression shifts its meaning in each of the following?

1. When a customer objected that the car he had bought couldn't climb even a little hill, the used-car dealer replied, "I told the truth. I said, 'On the level this a good car.' "
2. If you wish to retire in Florida comfortably, buy our mattress.
3. In our front yard, grass grows by inches and dies by feet.
4. The magician walked up the street and turned into a department store.
5. The soccer player used his head and averted a goal.
6. When you go over the budget each week, make a resolution not to go over it.
7. Ricardo has had dramatic experience. His leg was in a cast.
8. Small children can't wait to see flowers come up — roots and all.
9. My cat winters in the house, summers in the woods, and springs at mice.
10. I just saw a man eating fish in the restaurant.

Advertising signs often use wordplay to attract attention. Point out the word or expression that shifts its meaning in each of the following:

1. *Sign in a garden store:* Give an insect an inch and it'll take a yard.
2. *In a trailer park:* We deal in wheel estate.
3. *On a wrecker:* We meet by accident.
4. *On a truck carrying window blinds:* A blind man is driving this truck.
5. *In a watch store:* We give you a good time.
6. *In a garage:* Invite us to your next blowout; we won't leave you flat.
7. *In a tennis shop:* Play the only game where love is guaranteed.
8. *In a discount store:* Prices are born here and raised elsewhere.

THE SOUND OF PUNNING

The stout man sneaked onto the scale and quietly stole a weigh.

Words that sound alike encourage puns. *Way* and *weigh* are different words with different meanings. The punster takes advantage of the similarity of sound and plays with the meanings.

Ireland must surely be the richest country in the world because its capital is always Dublin.

This example puns on the double meaning of *capital:* "wealth" and "seat of government." Then it goes further and puns on the sound of *Dublin*. It likens *Dublin* to "doublin'."

Because of the oddities of English spelling, puns are fairly easy to make up in English. Though puns are sometimes called "the lowest form of humor," most persons secretly and slyly enjoy a good pun — particularly one of their own.

Puns have a long and honorable history. In Shakespeare's time, the pun was commonly used. Shakespeare's plays have many examples. In *Romeo and Juliet* the dying Mercutio says that tomorrow he will be a "grave man." The English poet Thomas Hood is responsible for one of the most famous of all puns: "They went and told the sexton, and the sexton tolled the bell." According to one story, the playwright Richard Brinsley Sheridan was asked to pay a tailor's bill, or at least the interest on the bill. He replied, "It is not in my interest to pay the principal, nor my principle to pay the interest."

ACTIVITY 3 Studying Puns   V

Point out the punning word or words in each of the following:

1. A wedding ring is actually a one-man band.
2. An actor would rather have a small role than a long loaf.
3. When the patient covered up his arm so the doctor could not inject the needle, the doctor said, "Grin and bare it."
4. If something goes without saying, let it.
5. Texas triplets inherited a ranch. They called it "Focus" because it was where the three sons raise meat (sun's rays meet).
6. Christmas is for giving, not for getting.
7. "Son, now that you are taking accounting, I want you to account for that dent in the car's front fender."
8. "What are assistants to Santa Claus called?"
   "Subordinate Clauses, of course!"

HUMOROUS DEFINITIONS

A bore is a person who talks when you wish him to listen.
— AMBROSE BIERCE

All of us enjoy a clever, unexpected definition. In his *Devil's Dictionary*, Ambrose Bierce devised a bookful of unusual definitions like the one quoted. Mark Twain, too, enjoyed bitter-sweet definitions, like his definition of *cowardice:* "The surest protection against temptation."

Sometimes humorous definitions help us to see something in a new light.
Laugh: A smile that burst.
Peacock: A chicken in bloom.

Fanatic: Someone who can't change his opinion but won't change the subject.

Yesterday: The tomorrow that got away.

Cranberries: Grapes with high blood pressure. — ROBERT BENCHLEY

Sometimes the definition contains a pun.

Mamalogue: A scolding by your mother. (What is a monologue?)

Coincide: What you do when it starts raining.

Young children often make up clever definitions. A boy called a period "a comma that has curled up and gone to sleep." Another said that a comma is a "period with a tail."

ACTIVITY 4   Studying Humorous Definitions   V

Which of the following humorous definitions do you like best? Why? Has it helped you to look at something in a new way? Explain.

1. *A secret:* Something that everybody tells everybody else in a whisper.
2. *A luxury:* An unnecessary something that masquerades as a necessity.
3. *Inventor:* A man with wheels in his head.
4. *Ignorance:* The art of relying on experts.
5. *Expert:* A man who has stopped thinking. — FRANK LLOYD WRIGHT
6. *Home:* The place where, when you have to go there, they have to take you in. — ROBERT FROST
7. *Extravagance:* The way the other fellow spends his money. — HARRY THOMPSON
8. *Experience:* The wonderful knowledge that enables you to recognize a mistake when you make it again. — THOMAS LA MANCE
9. *Happiness:* The absence of pain. — CHINESE SAYING
10. *Nets:* Holes surrounded by pieces of string.

ACTIVITY 5   Writing Definitions   VW

Using the examples above as a guide, make up a humorous definition for one of the following or for a word of your own choice:

1. A puppy	6. Oatmeal
2. A question mark	7. A popular song
3. Inflation	8. A homework assignment
4. A football player	9. A crew
5. Thrift	10. Acting

ACTIVITY 6   Having Fun with Words   VW

Read the following examples of fun with words. Then prepare

to present a similar example of your own. It may be a suitable sentence taken from a newspaper, magazine, or store sign. Or you may prefer to try an original one of your own.

1. Don't cook the noodles too long — not over three feet.
2. "He left by midnight."
   "Oh, I thought he left by automobile."
3. "Where was the Declaration of Independence signed?"
   "At the bottom."
4. The child returned to the scene of the grime.
5. He's all right in his own way, but he always wants it.
6. The baby who gets picked up is a howling success.

BONERS

Typhoid fever can be prevented by fascination.
Robespierre lost his head during the French Revolution on the gelatine.
Romeo and Juliet were two French explorers of the Mississippi.
A skeleton is a person with his insides out and his outsides off.

These statements, taken from actual composition papers, arise from faulty information or clumsy expression. To enjoy them, you need some background and a good vocabulary. The first two examples confuse words. *Fascination* is confused with *vaccination* and *gelatine* with *guillotine*. The third sentence confuses *Marquette and Joliet* with *Romeo and Juliet*. The fourth is a courageous but unsuccessful attempt to define. These errors, sometimes called "boners," are often found in student compositions. The humor lies in the unexpected appearance of an inappropriate idea, like *gelatine* for *guillotine*.

Sometimes the contrast is absurd. At dinner a mother said to her complaining child, "Now shut your mouth and eat!"

When the error involves a more difficult word that has been used for a simpler word, the error is called a "malapropism." Mrs. Malaprop is a character in *The Rivals*, a play by Richard Brinsley Sheridan. She is forever making errors, talking, for example, about "allegories on the banks of the Nile" instead of *alligators*. A good rule is this: If you don't know the meaning of the more difficult word, use a simpler one.

ACTIVITY 7   Pointing Out Boners   V

What words are misused in the following?

1. The customs of the prairie prayed on Beret's mind.
2. Godfrey got angry slowly but surly.

3. By some insight the copy of the catalogue was not sent to me.
4. The boy has an extinguished ability in math and science.
5. To revive a fainting person, put his head down until conscience returns.
6. The equator is a menagerie lion running around the earth.

ACTIVITY 8   Pointing Out Newspaper Boners   v

The following errors appeared in various newspapers throughout the country. Errors of this type are usually printers' errors. Explain the error.

1. The directors took office in June, and the treasurer took off in July.
2. Wanted: Experienced housekeeper. Good wages. Two in family — good referee essential.
3. Refreshments of cake squares, iced in pink and glue, were served.
4. The band director has prepared an appalling program.
5. A lake in the water pipe flooded the church cellar.

WORD SHAPES

Another type of wordplay is to make the shape of a word suggest or reflect its meaning. Here are some examples:

REVERSALS

A great many English words make other meaningful words when spelled backwards. *Ten* spelled backwards is *net; desserts* becomes *stressed; drawer* becomes *reward.*

ACTIVITY 9   Studying Reversals   v

1. What word is formed when each of the following is spelled backwards? What does the new word mean?

parts	spools	deliver	time
live	spoons	gnat	spots

2. How many reversals can you think of? Start with easy ones like *nap*, *tool*, and *snip*.

ANAGRAMS AND PALINDROMES

Many words can be scrambled to produce other words. Thus, *smash* is an anagram of *shams* and *untied* is an anagram of *united*. Many word games, like Scrabble, depend on the player's ability to scramble and unscramble words.

Sometimes whole phrases can be scrambled to come up with interesting anagrams. Thus, *nine thumps* is an anagram of *punishment*. Here are some famous anagrams:

The eyes	The countryside
They see.	No city dust here
A decimal point	William Shakespeare
I'm a dot in place.	We all make his praise.

Reversals are specialized anagrams. Even more specialized anagrams are palindromes like *label*, *radar*, and *noon*. These words read the same backwards and forwards. Some palindromes are whole sentences, such as the following tribute to Major General George W. Goethals, who directed the building of the Panama Canal:

A man, a plan, a canal — Panama!

ACTIVITY 10 Writing Anagrams V

Select a word, a name, or a phrase and make up an anagram using all the letters of the original.

EXAMPLES   vile — evil   canoe — ocean

               starch — charts   door — odor

ACROSTICS

Paul's a boy with lots of pep.
Always gay and light of step;
Understanding, free from pride,
Loyal, carefree, true when tried.

If you read the boldface letters down, you have the name *Paul*. The acrostic is a verse in which the first letters of the lines in sequence combine to form a name or other significant word.

Try an acrostic with the first name of a friend of yours. First write his or her name down, with each letter as a first letter of a line or verse. Then make up a verse about your friend.

CONCEALING MESSAGES

During World War II, Navajo Indians played a major role in sending and receiving secret messages. The Navajo language is a difficult one for outsiders to understand. But the Navajo soldiers in the American army made the job even more difficult by using a special coded alphabet of 38 symbols plus an additional vocabulary of 411 other terms. Experts call the Navajo system unbreakable. Thus even if the enemy intercepted a coded message, he could not make sense of it no matter how hard he tried.

People sometimes try to conceal messages from others — and not only in wartime. Parents often try to communicate without a child's understanding the message. Here's a sample, with explanations in brackets:

"Did that certain friend of yours [our youngest child] continue to make satirical comments about [make fun of] his elder sibling's [older brother's] budding romance?"

Sometimes a parent will say, "Watch your language. Little pitchers have big ears!" [The young child is trying to understand what you are saying!]

Sometimes parents spell out words if the child is too young to spell:

"We weren't able to buy the p-u-p-p-y [spelled out]."

As children grow older and wiser, these secret ways of talking become less effective, and parents must wait for more suitable situations to talk privately.

One way of concealing messages, as we saw, was by using big words. But the dictionary can always be used to unlock the secret. For more effective concealment, other methods must be used.

Concealing messages is usually managed by *codes* and *ciphers*. These two words are sometimes confused, but many authorities make a distinction between them. *Code* is the overall term applied to a system of symbols designed to keep the real meaning of messages from anyone who does not know the key to the symbols. Different types of systems are given different names. One type is merely called *code*. Another is called *cipher*.

CODES

In the type called *code*, a convenient word is arbitrarily chosen to stand for another. To interpret this type, you must know what each symbol stands for. You cannot convey any message without using symbols or code words that have been previously agreed upon. In a code a single word may stand for a word, an expression, or a sentence. The parent who used "that certain friend of yours" to mean "our youngest child" was using a kind of code.

ACTIVITY 12 Using Codes V

Translate the message in B, using the code dictionary supplied in A. (This is simplified, of course, but it suggests how a code works.)

A.
no = a	seventy = most
buffaloes = children	happy = secret
pie = code	wish = stage
swallow = go through	

B. Seventy buffaloes swallow no happy pie wish.

ACTIVITY 13 Using Codes V

Using a portion of the code in Activity 12, write the following message in code. To do so, expand the code dictionary supplied in Activity 12.

Young children send each other secret messages with mysterious words and symbols.

CIPHERS

"53‡‡†305)) 6*;4826)4‡.)4‡) ;806*;48†8¶60))85;1‡(;:‡*8†83
(88) 5*†;46(;88*96*?;8)*‡(;485) ;5*†2:*‡(;4956*2(5*—4)8¶
8*;4069285);)6†8)4‡‡;1(‡9;48081;8:8‡1;48†85;4)485†528806*
81(‡9;48;(88;4(‡?34;48)4‡;161;:188;‡?;"

The above communication taken from Edgar Allan Poe's short story "The Gold Bug" is one of the most famous messages written in cipher, or cryptogram, in the world. At first glance, it seems impossible to decipher this message without having the key. Legrand, the leading character in the story, does not have a key, however. He works with the clues provided by the arrangement of symbols and letters. How he deciphers the message and how he is rewarded are fascinatingly told in the story.

Unlike a code, a cipher is not limited to the words or expressions

in any code book.   A cipher can put into words any message at all.
In a cipher the letters of the original message are represented by
letters, figures, or symbols.

For instance, you might set up a cipher alphabet like the following:

a — t	g — q	m — 0	t — u
b — w	h — 5	n — (	u — m
c — 2	i — &	o — #	v — 4
d — $	j — 8	p — a	w — r
e — @	k — x	q — ¢	x — v
f — g	l — z	r — y	y — w
		s — p	z — *

It is then a simple matter to substitute one symbol for another.
The message "I enjoy using ciphers" would read: & @(8#w mp&(q
2& a5@yp. The word *cryptogram* would look like this: 2ywau #qyt0.

For someone who knows the key, deciphering a message in cipher
is relatively easy. For someone who doesn't know the key, deciphering may take a great deal longer, but it usually can be done. Getting
the meaning from a message in code, however, is practically impossible without the code book.

Codes used in war and diplomacy are so involved that they require
code books to decode them. Traditionally, the world's navies use
code books. If a ship is sunk or about to be captured, the code book
must be destroyed, usually by dropping it overboard in its lead jacket.
Armies tend to use ciphers, for armies are subject to sudden ambush.
Also, heavy code books are often impractical for carrying in land
campaigns.

ACTIVITY 14   Studying the Cryptogram   V

Change the following message to a cryptogram, using the symbols
given just above.

Solving cryptograms can be fun.

SOLVING CIPHERS

How can a cipher be solved without a key? The key can usually
be worked out from the language in which the cipher is written.
Suppose you were to see the following combination of symbols over
and over again in a message: x&%. If the cryptogram is a message
in English, you might guess that the three symbols stand for *the*,
since the word *the* occurs constantly in English. On a trial basis
you might substitute *t* for *x* wherever it appears, *h* for *&*, and *e* for
%. These substitutes might give you clues to other words. You

might be wrong, but trial and error eventually narrows down the possibilities.

The frequency of letters in a language might also be a clue. The letter *e* appears on the average about 600 times in 1000 words. If you know the most frequently used letters, you can make intelligent guesses. But really difficult cryptograms conceal the usual frequencies. They are set up to be confusing. The letters may not only be disguised, but they may also be shifted, in accordance with an agreed-upon pattern. These *transposition ciphers* are much more difficult than the *simple-substitution* cipher of "The Gold Bug."

ACTIVITY 15 Studying Letter Frequencies   V

Recently, a new keyboard was suggested for the common type-writer. What is probably the basis for this new keyboard?

ACTIVITY 16 Solving a Simple Cryptogram   V

Using all the helps previously given, try your hand at deciphering the following simple cryptogram. This is a single-substitution cipher. Each letter is represented by another letter. No words have been run together. There are no tricks. Because this may be your first crypto-gram, one clue is provided: one of the words in the message is the word *special*.

Uijt jt b dszquphsbn gps uif cfhjoofs up tpmwf. Ju ibt op tqfdjbm ps vovtvbm qspcmfnt. Ju jt b tjnqmf dszquphsbn.

The solution to this cryptogram is on page 37.

ACTIVITY 17 Word Study   **VW**

The following words were used in this chapter. The page number is after each word. What does each word mean in the sentence in which it appears? Use each word in a sentence of your own. Check your spelling.

premises	3	arbitrarily	11
deception	3	interpret	11
inappropriate	7	convey	11
absurd	7	ambush	12

2 *Building a Vocabulary*

According to legend, an ancient Egyptian king asked the great Euclid for an easy way to learn geometry.

"Sire," replied Euclid, "there is no royal road to learning!"

There is no royal road to vocabulary building, either, but the road may be pleasant and stimulating. If you start now to use some of the suggestions in this chapter, you will develop the habits that assure an effective vocabulary. As you enlarge your vocabulary, you will find better tools for reading and listening; for thinking, speaking, and writing.

Modern English in Action doesn't limit vocabulary building to this chapter. If you apply the suggestions in this chapter as you use the rest of the book, you will notice a substantial increase in your word power.

VOCABULARY TEST (From *The Adventures of Tom Sawyer* by Mark Twain) V

In each of the following sentences look at the italicized word. Then find in the next line or lines a word or expression that means the same or almost the same as the italicized word. On your paper write the numbers of the sentences in a column, place a period after each number, and then write the correct word.

1. Tom gave up the brush with *reluctance* in his face.
   1 agreeableness, 2 a sly grin, 3 relief, 4 unconcern, 5 unwillingness
2. Tom sought *desolate* places that were in harmony with his spirit.
   1 brilliant, 2 cheerful, 3 lonely, 4 inhabited, 5 picturesque
3. He *clamored* up the home stretch.
   1 fell, 2 hurriedly climbed, 3 came noisily, 4 sneaked, 5 tiptoed
4. All trials bring their *compensations*.
   1 curiosity-seekers, 2 decisions, 3 difficulties, 4 rewards, 5 uncertainties
5. Aunt Polly paused, *perplexed*.
   1 angry, 2 annoyed, 3 aroused, 4 puzzled, 5 unhappy
6. Tom carried his *exploits* to Becky's immediate vicinity.
   1 favorite toys, 2 firecrackers, 3 news, 4 striking deeds, 5 supplies
7. Tom was *gratified*.
   1 pleased, 2 provoked, 3 quieted, 4 stirred, 5 upset
8. The poodle's *anguish* grew with his progress up the aisle.
   1 agony, 2 anger, 3 confusion, 4 coolness, 5 uncertainty
9. But Peter *signified* that he did want it.
   1 blurted out, 2 doubted, 3 indicated, 4 said harshly, 5 wrote
10. Huck and Tom threw their tools into a corner and made the *ascent*.
    1 agreement, 2 climb down, 3 climb up, 4 noise and confusion, 5 sign

11. The knife was a sure-enough Barlow, and there was inconceivable *grandeur* in that.
    1 guarantee, 2 honesty, 3 magnificence, 4 quality, 5 service
12. Aunt Polly felt a sudden pang of *remorse.*
    1 curiosity, 2 headache, 3 indigestion, 4 regret, 5 uncertainty
13. The sun rose upon a *tranquil* world.
    1 busy, 2 peaceful, 3 sleepy, 4 stormy, 5 troubled
14. Would Aunt Polly heave one little sigh to see a bright young life so rudely *blighted?*
    1 begun, 2 misunderstood, 3 prolonged, 4 ruined, 5 shamed
15. The search for the bodies of the boys had been a *fruitless* effort.
    1 cheerless, 2 solemn, 3 useless, 4 untiring, 5 valuable
16. The villagers began to gather, *loitering* a moment in the vestibule.
    1 assembling, 2 chatting, 3 lingering, 4 reading notices, 5 rushing back and forth
17. Tom generally began Monday with wishing he had had no intervening holiday; it made the going into captivity so much more *odious.*
    1 disappointing, 2 hateful, 3 permanent, 4 sudden, 5 unexpected
18. They sat together on an *eminence* and conducted field operations.
    1 high spot, 2 rock, 3 tree limb, 4 wagon, 5 wooden bench
19. Tom watched with interest emphasized by *anxiety.*
    1 attentiveness, 2 courage, 3 curiosity, 4 indifference, 5 uneasiness
20. Tom was a trifle *disconcerted.*
    1 absentminded, 2 annoyed, 3 confused, 4 discontented, 5 overburdened
21. Becky thrust the peach away again, but with less *animosity.*
    1 concern, 2 directness, 3 enthusiasm, 4 hostility, 5 vigor
22. Tom withered Joe with *derision.*
    1 a ducking, 2 a look, 3 a suggestion, 4 hatred, 5 ridicule
23. Tom and all his comrades had always looked upon the superstition as *infallible.*
    1 a source of amusement, 2 unfailing, 3 misleading, 4 unfair, 5 unyielding
24. There was something in Aunt Polly's tone that made Tom *apprehensive.*
    1 enthusiastic, 2 fearful, 3 happy, 4 impatient, 5 unwilling
25. And then Aunt Polly *diluted* the compliment.
    1 avoided, 2 denied, 3 expressed, 4 weakened, 5 withdrew

STEPS IN VOCABULARY BUILDING

Enlarge your own experiences. Read widely in many fields. Listen attentively to skilled speakers. Enrich your life and you will find words to describe or manage the new experiences.

2. Use some of your new words appropriately in speaking and writing, but remember that your recognition vocabulary will always be larger than your use vocabulary.
3. When you meet a new word, notice whether the surroundings give you a clue to its meaning. *Context* is a convenient term for a word's surroundings.
4. Look for other clues: little words inside big ones — for example, *forest* in *reforestation*.
5. Become familiar with the dictionary and use it frequently — to check guesses and to look up new words.
6. Learn to group words for easy recall: words of similar meaning (pages 24, 25); words associated in some way (page 25); words with the same roots (pages 25, 26).
7. Become word curious. When you meet a new word, try to learn not only its meaning and its pronunciation but something of its history and its close relatives.
8. Acquire a feeling for words. Be especially alert to vigorous verbs and specific nouns. Use appropriate, effective adjectives. Don't waste words.
9. For easy recall keep a word notebook for the new words you meet.
10. Choose the exact word. Don't confuse *accept* and *except*, for example.

Steps 1 and 2 are up to you. This chapter will help you with all the other steps.

CLUES IN CONTEXTS

A word's context is its surroundings, its background, its environment.

PHYSICAL CONTEXT "Try some of these macaroons." (If the hostess hands you a tray of coconut cookies, you soon learn what a macaroon is.)

WORD CONTEXT "Although I had intended to make three different kinds of cookies, I had time only for the macaroons." (The surrounding words clearly tell you a macaroon is a kind of cookie.)

You have acquired your present vocabulary largely through understanding contexts. You have had to look up few common words in the dictionary, although you are sometimes surprised to find, when you do check, that you have had an inaccurate idea of a word's meaning, either through faulty contexts or through your own misinterpretation.

1. A directly explanatory word, phrase, or clause

   The transistor, a tiny electronic device with unique conductive properties, has revolutionized radio design. (New words, technical words, and words which the author wishes to emphasize are often conveniently explained thus in the text.)

2. A comparison

   The *purple finch* is like a sparrow dipped in grape juice. (This vivid comparison tells us a great deal about the purple finch.)

3. A contrast

   Although the slopes seemed too *precipitous* for even a toehold, the climbers surprisingly reached the summit with ease. (The easy climb is contrasted with the apparently *precipitous*, or steep, slope.)

4. The sentence as a whole

   When the sandbags gave way, the *rampaging* river *inundated* the surrounding countryside. (What do *rampaging* and *inundated* mean?)

ACTIVITY 1   Studying Clues in Contexts   SV

As you read the paragraph, select from the list at the end the best meaning for each italicized word. After finishing the exercise, check your choices with the dictionary.

The lowly cricket is no ordinary insect. Although most insects are *loathed*, the cricket has many friends. For centuries the Chinese and Japanese have kept crickets as pets in elaborate and *luxurious* cages. Some *belligerent* crickets are even chosen as *antagonists* in cricket fights. *Adherents* of the cricket admire his *melodic* fiddling, the pleasant music of a late summer evening. This admiration is not *unanimous*, however. Isaac Stern, famous violinist, was once momentarily *vanquished* by a tiny competitor. He delayed a concert five minutes while attendants *feverishly* tried to find the tiny fiddler, who was happily *nestled* in a potted palm.

careless	disliked	of one opinion	supporters
costly	excitedly	opponents	tuneful
defeated	happily	settled	warlike

ACTIVITY 2   Providing Context Clues   VW

Complete each of the following sentences so that your additional words provide the necessary clue to the word's meaning. If you do not now know the meaning of the word, look it up.

EXAMPLE   If you have an *impetuous* nature, . . .
     If you have an impetuous nature, count ten before acting.

1. The unsuccessful salesman tried to *supplement* his income by . . . .
2. Although I am not usually *susceptible* to colds, . . .
3. In complete *perplexity* I just . . . .
4. We could tell the pole was not absolutely *perpendicular* because . . . .
5. He *waddled* across the room like . . . .

COMMON WORDS WITH UNCOMMON MEANINGS

Context helps us to learn new words. It also helps us to discover when familiar words are used in new and unfamiliar ways. "In *Men of Iron* the bachelors, though pledged to the highest ideals of knighthood, frequently bullied the younger boys." *Bachelors* here has not the usual meaning of "unmarried men," but the far less common meaning of "men in training for knighthood." Familiar-looking words can often cause trouble because we think we understand what we actually do not.

ACTIVITY 3 Studying Words with Uncommon Meanings SV

What does the italicized word in each sentence mean? Check your guess by looking up each word in a good dictionary.

1. As our boat leaves the dock, *pay* out more of the line.
2. I groaned as my dog crashed into the beautiful new *highboy*.
3. There was an *electric* excitement in the air as Jeanne quietly entered the room.
4. Mrs. Perkins wore her *boa* with grace and dignity.
5. The *knight* unexpectedly *checked* the *king*.
6. Gold *leaf* is generally about 1/250,000 of an inch thick.
7. The strawberry plants increased by *runners*.
8. That *horse* is too rickety to support the scaffold.
9. To enable the bees to survive the winter, we did not remove all the *combs*.
10. Because of the pitcher's nervousness, the runner on third base was able to *steal* home.

OLD FRIENDS IN DISGUISE

Imposing-looking words like *incomparable* and *reinvigorate* are not too difficult if you can "see the little word in the big word." If you can see the common words *compare* and *vigor* inside the longer words, you can guess at the meaning of the big words more easily: *incomparable* = *in*, not + *compare* + *able*, able to = "not able to be compared."

In each of the following words look for the small common word which is a part of the longer word. Write down what you think each word means; then check your guess by looking up the words in a good dictionary.

consultation	practical	ruinous	tumultuous
dishearten	ratification	supremacy	undeniable

WHAT'S IN THE DICTIONARY

To look up word meanings where contexts are not helpful and to check guesses about words in context, you will still need that most useful tool, the dictionary. Do you know how to use it?

When you turn to the word *empty* in the *Webster's Students Dictionary*, here's what you will find. The numbers in color are keyed to the points as numbered in the explanation below. (For an explanation of abbreviations see the key in the front of your dictionary.)

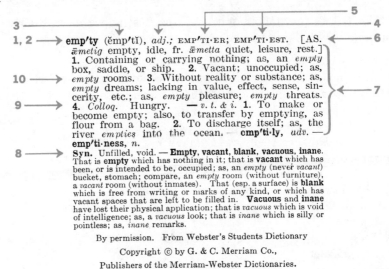

emp'ty (ĕmp'tĭ), *adj.;* EMP'TI·ER; EMP'TI·EST. [AS. æmetig empty, idle, fr. æmetta quiet, leisure, rest.] **1.** Containing or carrying nothing; as, an *empty* box, saddle, or ship. **2.** Vacant; unoccupied; as, *empty* rooms. **3.** Without reality or substance; as, *empty* dreams; lacking in value, effect, sense, sincerity, etc.; as, *empty* pleasure; *empty* threats. **4.** *Colloq.* Hungry. — *v. t. & i.* **1.** To make or become empty; also, to transfer by emptying, as flour from a bag. **2.** To discharge itself; as, the river *empties* into the ocean. — **emp'ti·ly,** *adv.* — **emp'ti·ness,** *n.*

Syn. Unfilled, void. — **Empty, vacant, blank, vacuous, inane.** That is **empty** which has nothing in it; that is **vacant** which has been, or is intended to be, occupied; as, an *empty* (never *vacant*) bucket, stomach; compare, an *empty* room (without furniture), a *vacant* room (without inmates). That (esp. a surface) is **blank** which is free from writing or marks of any kind, or which has vacant spaces that are left to be filled in. **Vacuous** and **inane** have lost their physical application; that is *vacuous* which is void of intelligence; as, a *vacuous* look; that is *inane* which is silly or pointless; as, *inane* remarks.

1. Spelling and Capitalization. When a word may be spelled in two ways, the preferred form is first: *col'or, col'our.* A word which should be capitalized is printed with a capital.

2. Syllabication. Syllables are separated by hyphens, centered dots, or accent marks. In *Webster's Students Dictionary* a hyphen needed in the spelling of a word is indicated by a single hyphen, and the syllables of the word are separated by centered dots or an accent mark: *wide' a·wake'.* In the Funk and Wagnalls *Standard* dictionaries a hyphen needed in the spelling of a word is indicated by a double hyphen, and the syllables are separated by a single hyphen or by an accent mark: *self=con'scious*.

3. Pronunciation. The pronunciation is given in parentheses directly after the word. The key at the bottom or the top of the page explains the diacritical marks. The main accent is indicated by a heavy mark (′), and a secondary stress by a lighter mark (′) or by two marks (″). If two pronunciations are given, both are correct, but the first may be more widely used: *ē′thĕr; ī′* —. The dash takes the place of *thĕr*, which is the same as in the preceding example.

4. Part of Speech. The part of speech is indicated by an abbreviation after the pronunciation. The abbreviations (*adj.* for *adjective, n.* for *noun,* etc.) are explained in the front of the dictionary. If a word is used as different parts of speech, the abbreviation applies to the definition or definitions immediately following it.

Empty is defined first as an adjective, and then as a verb.

5. Irregular Forms. Plurals of nouns, principal parts of verbs, and comparatives and superlatives of adjectives are given if they are irregular or troublesome. Because the comparative and superlative (page 376) of *empty* might cause difficulty, the forms are given.

6. Derivation. The history of the word is in brackets. *Empty* comes from the Anglo-Saxon *aemetig,* meaning "empty" or "idle." *Aemetig* in turn comes from *aemetta,* meaning "quiet" or "leisure" or "rest." This interesting word history suggests that the early Anglo-Saxons felt that *leisure* might lead to *idleness.*

7. Meanings. The word *empty* has four meanings listed for the adjective definition and two for the verb definition. When you look up a word, consider which meaning applies in the sentence you are reading or writing.

8. Synonyms. The words *empty, vacant, blank, vacuous,* and *inane* have similar meanings, but like all related words they differ in use. The brief explanation shows how these words differ. Some dictionary entries include antonyms too.

9. Levels of Usage. Definition 4 is marked *Colloq.* The dictionary makers suggest that this definition is acceptable in conversation, informal writing, friendly letters, and informal speech, but not in formal speaking and writing. By such labels as *Slang, Colloq., Obs.,* and *Dial.* the dictionary indicates the present standing of words. A word like *beteach,* labeled *Obs.* (obsolete), has passed out of the language. *Dial.* (dialectal) after a word like *dabster* indicates that a word or expression is used in only one section of the country and should be avoided in general use.

10. Use. Some dictionaries include a phrase or a sentence to show how the word is used. The first three definitions of *empty* include illustrative phrases — "an *empty* box, saddle, or ship."

ACTIVITY 5   Alphabetizing   **SV**

A. Arrange these words in alphabetical order: *hammock, hawthorn, habitual, harrow, harvester, harpy, harpsichord, handiwork, haughty, hack, hamper, hale, hail, hackneyed, halcyon, hayloft, haunt, harpoon, harmonious, haft.*

B. Look up the meaning of any unfamiliar word in the preceding list.

GUIDE WORDS

If you wish to find *dejected* in the dictionary, don't stumble through aimlessly. Check the guide words at the top of each page. *Degree* and *delicate* at the top will tell you that *dejected* appears on that page.

                                                                    SV
ACTIVITY 6   Using Guide Words Efficiently

1. Below are listed guide words used in *Webster's Students Dictionary* together with the pages on which they appear.

216. decimal — decorate   219. deferentially — degree
217. decoration — deep   220. degree — delicate
218. deepen — deferential   221. delicately — demagoguery

Using these guide words, decide on what pages of the dictionary the following words may be found. Copy the list of words on your paper and write after each word the number of the page in *Webster's Students Dictionary* on which it appears.

EXAMPLE   delegation, p. 220

delete	decrepit	default	decipher
defeatism	defer	deference	decree
deluge	delta	decode	defray
declaim	deity	deck	delirium

2. In a good dictionary find a common meaning of each of the above words. Add the new words to your vocabulary.

GUIDES FOR USING THE DICTIONARY

1. Open the dictionary to the approximate location of the word. If your dictionary has a thumb index, turn to the proper letter of the alphabet. Then use the guide words to find the exact page.
2. Know what you are after. Are you looking for the spelling of a word, its syllabication, its meaning?

3. To figure out the pronunciation of a word, use the key at the top or the bottom of the page. Then say the word aloud several times to fix the correct sounds in your mind.
4. If you want to find the meaning, notice how the word is used in the sentence in which you found it. Then choose the definition that fits the context. Notice the part of speech.
5. Realize that dictionaries arrange meanings differently. The Merriam-Webster dictionaries list meanings in historical order. Most other dictionaries give the commonest meaning first.
6. Use the dictionary appropriate to your purpose. Although a small pocket-size dictionary may be useful in emergencies, you should own a good desk dictionary.

ACTIVITY 7 Using the Dictionary sv

Now let's get quickly from a dictionary accurate information about words. As you look these words up in the dictionary, learn the meanings of all unfamiliar words. You will be tested on these.

1. Which words should usually be capitalized: *autumn, baptist, chinaware, french horn, friday, prussian blue, november?*
2. Which of these words need hyphens: *classroom, greatgrandfather, halflife, PanAmerican, selfappraisal, textbook?*
3. Divide these words into syllables and put in the accent marks: *absolutely, comparable, infamous, invalidate, involuntary, nondescript.*
4. Show how these words are pronounced: *ascertain, athletic, chimney, eighth, height, progress* (noun).
5. As what part of speech is each of these words generally used: *altar, comely, dessert, devastate, give-and-take, idol, keenly, lose, principle?*
6. As what parts of speech may each of the following be used: *caricature, compliment, dredge, garnish, libel, paper, today, where, yoke?*
7. Find the plural of each word: *alto, alumnus, deer, leaf, passerby, piano, sally, sheaf, sheep, volley.*
8. From what language is each word derived: *chauffeur, cobra, eye, genus, mustang, robot, Sabbath, tulip, zephyr, zero?*
9. In the following sentences what dictionary definition best explains the italicized words?

The *sedan* was carried by four servants.
Border guards stopped the traveler to check his *papers.*

10. Find at least one synonym for each of the following: *catch, deceit, device, fantastic, hide, ingenious, new, refer, revere, surprise.*
11. Find an antonym for each word: *gentle, hopeless, ignore, lean.*
12. Find an example of a dialectal word, a slang word, and an obsolete word in your dictionary. List the meaning for each.

ACTIVITY 8   **Testing Word Meanings**   **V**

How well do you recall the meanings of the words used in the preceding activity?

A. Write 1–10 on your paper.   Match numbers and letters. There will be two letters left over.

1. nondescript	a. decorate
2. epitome	b attractive
3. comely	c. hard to classify
4. garnish	d. breeze
5. devastate	e. witty retort
6. zephyr	f. deprive of legal force
7. feign	g. summary
8. invalidate	h. pretend
9. genus	i. classification in biology
10. mustang	j. destroy
	k. wild horse
	l. tycoon

B. List the definitions of five additional words selected by your teacher from the words in Activity 7.

LEARNING WORDS IN GROUPS

Learning words in groups is an economical, efficient, and pleasant way of adding to your vocabulary.   There are at least three important types of word groups: *synonyms, associated words,* and *words with similar prefixes and roots.*

SYNONYMS

English is incredibly rich in synonyms.   In this automotive age you can talk about streets, avenues, drives, roads, boulevards, thoroughfares, highways, expressways, parkways, turnpikes, freeways, and thruways.   Because no two words are actually exactly alike in connotation and denotation (pages 43–46), you can choose the exact word you want.   Some differences are regional.   You will use the *freeway* in Los Angeles and the *parkway* in New York City. Other differences involve connotation.   *Boulevard* suggests a broad, tree-lined street.   *Expressway* suggests speed and efficiency.   *Drive* suggests scenic attractiveness.   Still other differences may have practical bases.   In some cities *streets* run east and west; *avenues* run north and south.

When you meet a new word, look up some of its brothers and first cousins.   There is no better way of increasing your word power.

In a good standard dictionary or a book of synonyms, look up the word group assigned to you. How do the words differ from each other?

1. dream, vision, reverie
2. strange, peculiar, eccentric, odd, quaint, outlandish
3. frank, candid, open, plain, naive
4. jocular, merry, jovial, joyful, blithe
5. play, game, sport, recreation

Using a synonym dictionary, find a group containing at least four synonyms. How do the words differ from each other?

ASSOCIATED WORDS

The stamp collector soon learns words like *imperforate*, *mint*, *precanceled*, and *plate block*. The football fan becomes familiar with *forward pass*, *touchback*, *clipping*, and *defensive holding*. The cook learns *simmering*, *basting*, *dicing*, and *deep frying*. When·you become interested in a field of activity, be alert to the words associated with the activity. If your father has a sailboat, learn *tiller, boom, tack,* and *jib*. The actual experience may be unnecessary, for a book may serve as well. If you read *Treasure Island*, pick up some of the nautical vocabulary.

Choose a sport, a hobby, a favorite recreation, or some other activity. List the words you associate with the activity. Compare your list with your classmates'. Be ready to define unfamiliar terms on your list.

SIMILAR PREFIXES AND ROOTS

Meet the *Port* family. There's *import* and his wife *export*, their children *transport* and *passport*, and numerous nephews and cousins: *portable*, *porter*, *portfolio*, even *port* arms. Although the family members vary in meaning, they all have the common idea of "carry." This stately old Latin family has enriched English.

Port is only one of the hundreds of Latin roots commonly found in English words. You cannot expect to memorize them all, but you can become alert to related words with similar roots. If you meet *cent, centennial, percent, century, centimeter,* and *centigrade,* you will notice the resemblance and be glad to know that the Latin root, *cent,* means "a hundred."

Learning prefixes and roots will help when you meet an unfamiliar word. If you know that *re* means "back" and *pel* means "drive," you can make an intelligent guess at the meaning of *repel.* Many Latin words, however, have been English citizens for centuries and have taken on meanings far removed from the original meanings. *Auditor,* which meant originally only a listener, now also means "a person authorized to examine accounts." The dictionary is always a useful check on your guesses about words.

SEVEN HELPFUL LATIN VERB ROOTS

ROOT	MEANING	EXAMPLE	DEFINITION
jac, ject	throw, cast	re*ject*	*throw* back
mov, mot	move	de*mote*	*move* down
pon, pos, posit	place, put	de*posit*	*place* down
port	carry, bear	*port*able	able to be *carried*
rupt	break	e*rupt*	*break* out
spec, spect, spic	look, see	*spect*acle	something to *look* at
vert, vers	turn	a*vert*	*turn* away

ACTIVITY 12   Studying Latin Roots   VW

Fill the blank in each sentence by supplying the missing prefix or root in the incomplete word. The figure in parentheses at the end of the sentence tells how many letters are to be supplied. After you have written the missing prefix or root, write the whole word.

EXAMPLE

> The procedure of *look*ing inside oneself is called intro—ion. (5)
> spect, introspection

1. *Turn* back; put the car into re—. (5)
2. A shell *thrown* forward is called a pro—ile. (4)
3. Don't *break* this conference up and dis— the proceedings. (4)
4. The —ators *looked* with amazement at the seventy-yard run by the rookie quarterback. (5)
5. The ex—er arranged to have the goods *carried* by air. (4)
6. Something *thrown* back is re—ed. (4)
7. A pre—ion is usually *placed* before its object. (5)
8. Something that *moves* one to action is a —ive. (3)
9. To *turn* a river from its course is to di— it. (4)
10. Something that can't be moved is im—able. (3)

WORD CURIOSITY

The word *turnpike,* mentioned in the road list on page 24, has an interesting history. Many early roads were toll roads. As travelers came to a toll gate, or *pike,* they paid their toll, turned the pike, and went on. When New Jersey set up its famous toll road, it called the road, appropriately, the New Jersey Turnpike, even though drivers no longer actually turn pikes along the route.

Some travelers long ago tried to avoid the toll roads. They earned the name *shunpikers.* The word survives today for a traveler who prefers the slower, more colorful back roads to the swift but often dull turnpikes.

Words have fascinating histories. If you acquire the dictionary-browsing habit, you'll increase your vocabulary and have fun in the process.

ACTIVITY 13 Satisfying Word Curiosity SV

Use your dictionary to find the history of each of the following words. Review #6 on page 23.

aftermath	index	ink	preposterous	vegetable
crestfallen	infant	jot	senate	verdict

A FEELING FOR WORDS

The difference between the right word and the almost right word is the difference between lightning and the lightning bug. — MARK TWAIN

With some pairs of words the difference is one of connotation (pages 43–46). *Dog* and *doggie* refer to the same animal, but *doggie* is a word used by young children, not by adults speaking to each other. This difference in connotation makes "We raise show doggies" sound ridiculous.

A *fib* and a *lie* are both untruths, but a *fib* is a falsehood about a trivial matter. There is a great difference, too, between a sentence like "That's a lie!" and "Isn't that statement inaccurate?" Knowing the word to use is an important skill in working with others.

ACTIVITY 14 Noticing Shades of Meaning SV

In each of the following sentences choose the expression which answers the italicized question. If you need help, consult the dictionary or a book of synonyms.

1. Jack was (lazy, sluggish) in class this morning.
Which word suggests that Jack's condition was temporary?

2. That's (a newfangled, an up-to-date) idea.
   Which word suggests that the writer probably disapproves the idea?
3. That's a (lovely, good-looking) coat you're wearing.
   Which expression is more likely to be used by a woman than by a man?
4. In dress and in the care of her room Caroline is quite (neat, prim).
   Which word suggests that Caroline may be too fussy?
5. Janet (blubbered, wept) as she told her story to her mother.
   Which is more dignified?
6. Jud offered an (apology, excuse) for his action.
   Which word tends to justify the action?

FRESH, ACCURATE, VIVID WORDS

When you overwork words, you wear out both the words and your listeners. Slang may be effective at times, but no one wants to listen to a speaker who calls everything "swell" or "terrific" or "awful." If you overwork any of the following, give the worn-out words and expressions a long rest: *see, say, listen, you know, don't you know, you know what I mean, and everything like that, by the way, as a matter of fact, awfully, great, grand, nice, fine, lovely, now, well, why, so, and, swell.*

FORCEFUL VERBS

flounced

All eyes turned to Marilyn as she ~~walked~~ into the room.

What a different picture the vigorous verb, *flounced*, makes here! The verb is the heart of a statement. Knowing strong, colorful verbs will help you to express yourself more forcefully. (See also pages 264–265.)

ACTIVITY 15 Choosing Forceful Verbs   SV

Complete each sentence by selecting a verb from the following list. Check your answers by looking up each word in the dictionary. There will be two verbs left over.

clutched	glimmered	murmured	thwarted
feigned	grumbled	spattered	whetted
floundered	infuriated	subsisted	writhed

1. The weary party —— in the waist-high snow until they reached the safety of the highway.
2. After being struck by a fast ball, the batter —— in pain.
3. As the little passenger left the plane by herself, she —— her doll to her for comfort.

4. "Why can't Bill change the blade when he uses my razor?" Dad ——.
5. The smell of roast turkey —— our appetites.
6. To get an interesting effect on the porch floor, Dad —— the floor with paints of different colors.
7. When the hunters came near the nest, the grouse fluttered off and —— a broken wing.
8. As we gazed from the Connecticut shore at dusk, the lights —— along the bluffs of Long Island.
9. A majority of the glee club members —— the efforts of a vocal minority to hold a picnic instead of a boat ride.
10. Without adequate provisions Major Rogers' men —— on what they were able to hunt by night.

ADJECTIVES WITH PUNCH

Is a weary, careworn person likely to look *austere* or *haggard*? The correct descriptive adjective creates an effective picture. (See also pages 356-357.)

ACTIVITY 16 Choosing the Right Adjective SV

Consult the dictionary to help you find the answer to each of the following questions. Add new words to your word list.

1. Does an *evasive* answer (1) give the facts, (2) arouse hope, or (3) fail to satisfy?
2. Is a man with a *squat* build likely to be (1) pudgy, (2) lithe, or (3) flexible?
3. Is a *squeamish* person likely to be (1) insensitive, (2) callous, or (3) easily upset?
4. If you were offered *squalid* living quarters, would you be likely to (1) accept, (2) be indifferent to, or (3) reject them?
5. Are *edible* mushrooms (1) safe for eating, (2) poisonous, or (3) tasteless?
6. Is a *prevalent* idea accepted (1) widely, (2) by a few people, or (3) not at all?
7. Is *ominous* news likely to be (1) reassuring, (2) frightening, or (3) slightly annoying?
8. Would a poor child looking at a well-stocked store window be likely to have (1) a *sinister*, (2) a *grotesque*, or (3) a *wistful* expression?
9. Is a vase in a *precarious* position likely to (1) fall, (2) be admired, or (3) be criticized?
10. Is a *brazen* person likely to (1) care what the neighbors think, (2) enroll in an adult-education course, or (3) annoy others by his shameless boldness?

DON'T WASTE WORDS

The right word is the effective word, the vigorous word, the word that cuts out useless explanations. Why beat about the bush and say in a half dozen words what one word would express more pointedly?

ACTIVITY 17 Using Word Shortcuts SV

Each word in the following list means the same or almost the same as the italicized expression in one of the sentences. Substitute the right word for each of the italicized expressions. If some of the words are unfamiliar to you, turn to the dictionary for help.

EXAMPLE Isn't Laurie a clever *person who can imitate the speech and actions of another?* mimic

bequeath	incentive	speculate	stark	transparent
cascade	solace	spurn	traditional	variable

1. Johnny Tremain found *an easing of grief* in hard work.
2. There stood the old pine tree, *standing out in sharp outline* against the sky.
3. The president of the New York Stock Exchange warned new and inexperienced investors not to *buy unknown stocks with the hope of making quick and easy profits.*
4. Each *small, steep waterfall* in the series was a splendid sight in the morning sun.
5. Grandmother promised to *leave by last will and testament* her china to Sally.
6. Many of our family's Christmas activities are *of a nature handed down from generation to generation.*
7. To encourage Ed to maintain his excellent grades, Mr. Dane offered him a trip to Lake Louise as an *offer which would spur him on to action.*
8. Though Norman tried to change his original statement, his lie was *easily seen through.*
9. Today's weather prediction promises strong west winds which may become *changeable from one direction to another* by morning.
10. Did General McAuliffe *reject with scorn and contempt* the German general's offer?

KEEP A WORD NOTEBOOK

In your daily listening and reading you will probably find a great many words that may be new to you. In reading Poe's story "The Purloined Letter," for example, you will find words like *doggerel, expedient, prodigious,* and *scrutinizing.* To add such words to your vocabulary, look them up in a dictionary, enter them with their definitions in a section called "My Word Bank," and then use them in your speaking and writing.

ACTIVITY 18 Beginning a Word Notebook SVW

Begin a list of the interesting new words that you hear used by parents, teachers, schoolmates, or other speakers, or that you see in your daily reading. Give the following information for each word: (1) the source — that is, where you found or heard it; (2) the context; (3) the dictionary definition or synonym that fits the context; and (4) the correct use in a sentence of your own.

At the end of one week compare your list with those of your classmates. Perhaps at the end of the term the teacher will give extra credit for notebooks with a large number of words fully and accurately entered.

EXAMPLES

1. During the last decades of the nineteenth century, America broke out in a *luxuriant* growth of holiday retreats. — HORIZON

   luxuriant — characterized by rich and extravagant ornamentation; growing abundantly and vigorously

   My sentence: Preferring simplicity of design, much modern furniture avoids luxuriant ornamentation.

2. The letter was addressed in a *diminutive* hand to the minister.

   diminutive — small, tiny

   My sentence: The puppets played their parts on a richly decorated diminutive stage.

ACTIVITY 19 Studying Word Meanings SV

According to one study the following words should have been mastered by the end of the ninth year. You've probably met them all in your reading. If you have neglected to look them up in the dictionary before, look them up now. Add to your vocabulary notebook new words and all the words that you are not completely sure of.

abyss	deficient	frustrate	perceptible	stark
accessible	demeanor	futile	perplexity	stigma
advisable	derision	humiliation	pervade	strew
appall	diminutive	hypocrisy	pestilence	tawny
audacity	dissension	impetuous	plaintive	terminal
austere	eccentric	inaugurate	prudent	usurp
authentic	enhance	incessant	relinquish	variable
brazen	exasperate	mercenary	repute	venom
curtail	ferment	oblivion	retard	wan
defer	fidelity	pensive	shimmer	weld

TROUBLESOME WORDS

Do you know a person who has a well-stocked wardrobe but never looks right? Perhaps he chooses the wrong clothes for the occasion or combines colors that clash; at any rate, he is never well dressed.

So it is with words. In addition to having a good store on hand, you must know how to use them. The following list is one to master.

accept, except To *accept* means "to take something offered" or "to approve something suggested." *Except* is usually a preposition meaning "but."

The members *accepted* all the amendments *except* one.

affect, effect To *affect* means "to influence." *Effect* is usually a noun meaning "result."

Although I am not usually *affected* by a hot, dry day, I feel the *effects* of high humidity combined with heat.

amount, number Use *amount* for quantity — anything that is measured or weighed. Use *number* for things that can be counted.

We served a surprisingly large *amount* of lemonade although we had a small *number* of visitors to the fair.

beat, won You can *beat* an opponent and *win* a game or a prize. "We won the Cubs in a close game" sounds as though you are taking the opposing players home with you.

Although we *won* the game, we *beat* the other team by only one run.

learn, teach To *learn* is "to gain knowledge or skill." To *teach* is "to instruct" or "to show how."

This chapter *teaches* you how to acquire new words painlessly. Have you *learned* how?

lend, loan, borrow To *lend* is "to give the use of"; to *borrow* is "to get something with the understanding that it must be returned." *Loan* is ordinarily a noun but may be used as a verb.

If you *borrow* books from friends, be prepared to *lend* them yours in return.

Many small personal *loans* carry excessive rates of interest.

new, knew; no, know Don't carelessly confuse these pairs.

No, I don't *know* whether Dad *knew* about my *new* dog.

quiet, quite   *Quiet* means "free of noise."   *Quite* means "completely, wholly, really."

The children are too *quiet* in the next room.   Are you *quite* sure they're not up to some mischief?

stayed, stood   *Stood* is the past tense of *stand; stayed*, of *stay.*

I should have *stayed* home today.   I have a fever.
Because the theater was crowded, we *stood* throughout the first half of the picture.

than, then   *Than* is a conjunction used in comparisons.   *Then* is an adverb meaning "at that time" or "next."

Tree-ripened fruit is usually sweeter *than* fruit picked green.
Then we saw the wasps' nest — too late!

OTHER PAIRS

Because many writers and speakers distinguish between words in the following pairs, you should be aware of the distinctions that are frequently made.

between, among   *Between* is regularly used with two objects.   *Among* is used for three or more considered collectively as a group.

Divide the cake *between* the twins.
For breakfast we divided the cantaloupe *among* the rest of us.

bring, take   To *bring* ordinarily requires motion toward the speaker; *to take*, away from the speaker.

Take the set of *Modern English in Action* to the bookroom and *bring* back the book truck.

in, into   Although *in* is often used for *into*, *into* is often reserved for motion from one place to another — diving board to water, for example.

From the barn roof Tim jumped *into* the haystack and rolled around happily *in* the hay.

latest, last   *Last* is frequently used for *latest*.   Theodore M. Bernstein declares, however, "*Last* has the connotation of final.   Make it *latest*."   Reserve *latest* for "most recent."

My *latest* water color may well be my *last*.   I'm thinking of painting only in oils.

leave, let   To leave is either "to go away" or "to let stay." To be sure, use *let* when you mean "permit."

Dad will *let* me go if I *leave* for home at eleven.

ACTIVITY 20   **Using Troublesome Words Correctly**   V

In each of the following select the word in parentheses in accordance with the suggestions in this chapter.

1. The winter woods were (quiet, quite) except for the occasional cry of a jay.
2. Mother told me to (accept, except) the C.O.D. package when it came.
3. Central (beat, won) us in both basketball games this year.
4. During my attack of flu I (stayed, stood) in bed three days.
5. How will the omission of the third question (affect, effect) your mark?
6. The father divided his estate (among, between) his many heirs.
7. The bad weather actually decreased the (amount, number) of accidents over the holidays, for many drivers remained at home.
8. Jeri said that I could (borrow, have the lend of) her dance records.
9. Although I (knew, new) the escape velocity of an orbiting satellite, I carelessly omitted one zero in my answer.
10. Everyone at the picnic (accept, except) Dan enjoyed the chicken sandwiches.
11. All of us were (quiet, quite) happy to learn that we'd have an extra day's vacation at Easter.
12. Please (learn, teach) me how to throw a forward pass.
13. Did the tree spraying have any bad (affect, effect) on the bird population of your woods?
14. Has anyone ever estimated the (amount, number) of ice cream sodas the average teen-ager can consume in a week?
15. As a sovereign state tiny San Marino is much older (than, then) Italy.
16. Dad, may I (borrow, have the lend of) your binoculars for the bird walk Saturday?
17. Mom, please (leave, let) me go to Washington with my class.
18. The baby-sitter (stayed, stood) all day with the child until the parents came home.
19. Our oak trees seem more susceptible to disease (than, then) do our maples.
20. I don't (know, no) why television has so few good comedy shows.
21. Will you (bring, take) this mimeograph paper to the printing room?
22. Mrs. Atkins (learned, taught) us how to use the *Readers' Guide.*
23. While in Andrew Jackson High School, Dad (knew, new) Bob Cousy.
24. Webster opened the outside door and strode (in, into) the house.
25. Plants are (affected, effected) by the number of hours of sunlight.

26. Sue thinks that football is a more exciting sport to watch on television (than, then) baseball.
27. Mrs. Brewster (accepted, excepted) Joe's explanation, but she insisted he replace the broken window.
28. May I (borrow, have the lend of) an eraser, please?
29. Mother (learned, taught) me how to change a tire.
30. I hope that Coach Rhodes will (leave, let) Woody play shortstop.
31. Do you find algebra easier (than, then) arithmetic?
32. Have you read Carlota's (last, latest) short story? She is now working on another one.
33. The rain had little (affect, effect) on the high spirits of the hikers.
34. A large (amount, number) of accidents occur on little-used country roads.
35. Please (bring, take) this reel of film to the audio squad in the projection booth.
36. Jan just won't (accept, except) a new idea.
37. At the farm we used to jump from the barn loft (in, into) a pile of sweet-smelling hay.
38. Don't forget to (bring, take) your gym suit to school today.
39. Will your parents (leave, let) you go to the firefighters' bazaar?
40. Despite the increase in the cost of living, the charge for electricity is considerably less (than, then) it was many years ago.

V

MASTERY TEST 1A Correct Word

In each of the following select the word in parentheses in accordance with the suggestions in this chapter. On your paper after the number of the sentence write your choice.

1. I want to (learn, teach) you how to plan a garden.
2. I like ravioli better (than, then) manicotti.
3. The committee will (accept, except) your proposals.
4. A large (amount, number) of people attended the town meeting.
5. Fearlessly she dived (in, into) the freezing water.
6. There are more girls (than, then) boys on the gymnast team.
7. Chef Diane (learned, taught) the audience how to prepare crêpes last night on television.
8. My parents are going to (leave, let) me house-sit this summer.
9. The new eligibility requirements will (affect, effect) the team.
10. I want you to (take, bring) these boxes to the dump.
11. (Let, Leave) me tell the whole story.
12. May I (borrow, loan) some of your records for the party?

13. (Take, Bring) these books to the library.
14. Please (leave, let) me plan the field day.
15. I want you to (bring, take) these plants to the porch.
16. The (affects, effects) of the drought will be felt for many years.
17. Will you (bring, take) these pies to the fair for me?
18. We divided the responsibilities (among, between) all the members.
19. My tomato plants have a large (amount, number) of flowers on them.
20. I dropped my watch (in, into) the pool by mistake.

MASTERY TEST 1B   Correct Word

Follow the directions for Mastery Test 1A

1. If you don't want to eat this sandwich here today, you can (bring, take) it to school tomorrow for lunch.
2. I want to (bring, take) these cookies to the picnic.
3. The rain had a bad (affect, effect) on the roads.
4. The principal did not (accept, except) our excuse for being late.
5. I did not (accept, except) the collect phone call.
6. The policemen (let, left) us park our bikes along the bridge to watch the fireworks display.
7. We (left, let) our dogs play in the water.
8. I enjoyed Ray Bradbury's (last, latest) book and am glad that he plans another.
9. Terry has promised to (learn, teach) me how to do needlepoint.
10. (Bring, Take) the food from the kitchen to the car for our picnic.
11. I dropped a quarter (in, into) the wishing well.
12. He will (leave, let) me take his bike.
13. The supplies were divided equally (among, between) all the hikers.
14. Bob offered to (bring, take) my dog to the vet.
15. I like pies better (than, then) cakes.
16. Salt water is often colder (than, then) fresh water in the North.
17. A great (amount, number)of hurricanes occur every year.
18. Ms. Barberi (learned, taught) us how to use the new computers.
19. Is foil better (than, then) plastic for freezing?
20. The dry weather had a terrible (affect, effect) on my garden.   **VW**

ACTIVITY 21   Word Study

The following words were used in this chapter. The page number is after each word. What does each word mean in the sentence in which it appears? Use each word in a sentence of your own. Check your spelling.

stimulating	15	inundated	18	centennial	26
assure	15	pledged	19	auditor	26
context	17	appropriate	23	trivial	27
misinterpretation	17	connotation	24	flounced	28
precipitous	18	denotation	24	austere	29
rampaging	18	regional	24	haggard	29

SOLUTION TO THE CRYPTOGRAM IN ACTIVITY 16 ON PAGE 13

This is a cryptogram for the beginner to solve. It has no special or unusual problems. It is a simple cryptogram.

(Did you notice that each letter in the original message is represented by the following letter in the alphabet: a = b, b = c, etc.?)

3 *The Power of Words*

```
 NEW  NAME  HELPS
4TH.  AVE.  SEGMENT

  Business Improvement Is
  Noted in Park Ave. South
  Over Four Months [1]
```

When New York City changed the name of a part of Fourth Avenue to *Park Avenue South,* there were sudden and dramatic results. Real estate boomed. Vacant offices were rented. Business in the area spurted. Merchants in the area were proud of their "new" address. Property owners decided to improve the appearance of their stores in keeping with the dignity of the new name. Business groups sought new zoning laws to prevent their "new" area from encouraging careless tenants. All these changes resulted from a single act: the replacement of one name with another.

What had really happened? The street itself didn't suddenly become a new street when the mayor signed the bill authorizing the new name. The change was in words — and in people. Business people began to think of the street differently. Their new attitude had profound effects on the street itself.

ACTIVITY 1   Studying a Quotation   OT

Read and think about the following quotations. Be ready to discuss in class what you think they mean.

A. Compare these two quotations.

1. "What's in a name? That which we call a rose
   By any other name would smell as sweet."
2. "Who steals my purse steals trash; . . .
   But he that filches from me my good name
   Robs me of that which not enriches him,
   And makes me poor indeed."

B. Give an example or two to demonstrate the truth or falsity of these quotations.

ACTIVITY 2   Studying Newspaper Reports   OT

The following are condensed reports of news items in the public press. Discuss the importance of *naming* in each example.

---

[1] Headline from the *New York Times*. Reprinted by permission.

1. For a while the National Weather Service used the term *Discomfort Index* to indicate the relationship of temperature and humidity. (A Discomfort Index of 75 means that approximately half the people will feel uncomfortable.) City business people objected violently, however, and the Weather Service decided upon Temperature-Humidity Index as a substitute. A high "Discomfort Index" hurt sales, but a high "Temperature-Humidity Index" had little effect.

2. Residents of Briar Park on Long Island fought bitterly to have their postal address "North Wantagh" instead of "Levittown." Though Briar Park is surrounded by Levittown, the residents of this smaller area felt that the North Wantagh address had more prestige.

3. When the first monkeys were sent into space to test the ability of living things to withstand the acceleration, the scientists called the two little monkeys "Able" and "Baker." As names, *Able* and *Baker* merely mean *A* and *B*. The scientists avoided common names for the animals because they didn't want them to acquire personalities and seem like pets, rather than nameless laboratory animals.

WORD MAGIC

Folk tales are filled with magic, and much of the magic deals with words. In a famous story, the sorcerer's apprentice says the magic words and almost drowns when he cannot undo the charm. In another story, a miller's daughter wins power over the dwarf Rumpelstiltskin when she learns his real name. By means of magic words enchantresses turn princes into frogs and frogs into princes.

"Ridiculous nonsense!" you say, but are you aware of word magic in everyday life? Advertisers use slogans, charms, and even "magic" words like *hexachlorophene*. Political speakers use the magic of oratory to spellbind listeners. Even *you* try a little word magic when you try to persuade your dad to let you go to the county fair.

WORDS AND BEHAVIOR

In explaining the benefits of a life-insurance policy, an agent often says, "If there is a claim." He doesn't say bluntly to the client, "If you die." Many people don't like to hear unpleasant words like *death*, *heart disease*, or *cancer* because they feel the word may bring the real thing. "Speak of the devil and he's sure to appear" is an old expression that indicates how strongly people believe in the power of words.

Words influence you and your actions as they influenced the merchants on Park Avenue South. Don't call a boy a "delinquent,"

for he may live up to the name. On the other hand, if you praise a
boy, he will probably try to live up to the good opinion. Words make
you look at things differently. Real estate agents call a broken-down
wreck of a house a "Handyman's Special." The name takes away
some of the misery and adds a touch of positive glamour.

You may like or dislike a person on first sight because she has a
name with pleasant or unpleasant associations for you. You may
buy one brand of toothpaste with *britone* because you are impressed
by the name of the "secret ingredient." You may support one
candidate for student court justice because someone has called him
"a regular fellow." You may be impressed by cars with "custom
styling," shampoos that impart a "miracle sheen," hats with "that
exclusive touch." In editorials, advertising, radio and television
discussions people are trying to persuade you to support a policy,
see a movie, or buy a product. In response to these appeals do you
act thoughtfully and deliberately, or hastily and emotionally?

ACTIVITY 3   Talking about "Word Magic"   OT

Think of an experience in which words played an important role
in your life. Tell the class how your actions were influenced by the
choice of a word or a name.

ACTIVITY 4   Studying Persuasion in Advertising and Editorials   S

From your newspaper and magazine reading or your television
and radio listening, select and list in your notebook at least three
persuasive sentences. Underline the words with an emotional
appeal.

EXAMPLE

In any group the man who stands out wears a Weareeze suit.

Who stands out appeals to our natural desire to be noticed and recognized. We are being urged to try the suit so that we too may
"stand out."

WHAT'S IN A NAME?

In Viennese families the name *Adolf* had always been popular.
Before 1938 about a hundred boys a year were named *Adolf*. From
1938–1945 about 340 a year were given the name. During the first
few postwar years not a single Viennese baby was named *Adolf*. The
name itself consisted of the same five letters, but its association with
Adolf Hitler made it at first very popular and then a word to avoid
altogether.

Names play an important role in human affairs.   Many names like *Bill*, *Jim*, *Joe* are acceptable masculine names.   But a boy named *Archibald*, *Percy*, or *Montmorency* may have to struggle against ridicule.   Yet generations ago these were respected "fighting names." For example, the Hotspur in Shakespeare's *Henry IV* was a Percy.

Football teams prefer fighting names like *Panthers*, *Tigers*, or *Wolverines*, to suggest courage, strength, endurance.   Real-estate developers prefer colorful names like *Sunnyacres* and *Forestgreen* because the words suggest beauty, tranquillity, or gracious living. Even a barren, rocky development seems to take on a little charm if it is called *Stonehurst*.

ACTIVITY 5   Studying Pairs of Names   OT

In each of the following pairs of words or phrases which is the more attractive name?   Why?   If there is disagreement among class members, discuss reasons for the disagreement.

1. Ermine coat — white weasel coat
2. Leafy Grove Estates — Miller's housing development
3. Morris's Motel — Timberpoint Lodge
4. Sixth Avenue — Avenue of the Americas
5. cypress lagoon — cypress swamp
6. picture window — large window

ASSOCIATION WITH NAMES

Why do you like certain names and dislike others?   Usually the explanation is simple: an unhappy experience with a Charles may make you dislike the name *Charles*.   There is nothing unpleasant in the word itself.   Writers sometimes choose character names that they feel will fit their characters.   In Dickens' novel, for example, the Cheeryble brothers are good-natured and pleasant.   In real life there is nothing to prevent a Mr. Cheeryble from being an unhappy miser.

ACTIVITY 6   Studying Character Names   T

Four of the following play villainous roles in the novels of Charles Dickens.   Which four would you judge them to be?   Keep in mind, though, that in real life such associations are accidental.   (The answers are at the bottom of the next page.)

Betsy Trotwood	Wackford Squeers
Edward Murdstone	Tommy Traddles
Daniel Quilp	Thomas Gradgrind

SUGGESTION IN WORDS

In addition to their dictionary definitions words convey something extra. It is this something extra that makes the difference between *ermine* and *weasel, house* and *home, Montgomery* and *Monty, dog* and *doggie. Home* suggests the warmth of family life; *house* does not. *Monty* suggests a friendly familiarity; *Montgomery* is more formal. *Doggie* suggests a child's speech; *dog* can be used by the most dignified old gentleman. The difference between words in these pairs is not a matter of definition.

DENOTATION AND CONNOTATION

The *denotation* of a word is its dictionary definition; the *connotation* is what the word suggests because of the way it has been used. Denotations are easily checked in the dictionary; connotations vary widely, from situation to situation, from person to person.

Both *beautiful* and *handsome* mean "pleasing to the eye," "good to look at," but we wouldn't call a man beautiful. Why not? The answer lies in use. The word *beautiful* is applied to paintings, music, architecture, scenery, girls, and women — but not men. Foreigners learning English make many mistakes because of connotation.

Because of connotation, words develop personalities of their own. Some words — *mother, friend, brother, country, meadow* — tend to have pleasant associations. Others — *snake, trap, fear, want, sly* — may have unpleasant associations.

Unfortunately, our feelings about words sometimes lead us astray. Because *snake* tends to have unpleasant associations for most of us, unthinking persons kill black snakes, garter snakes, and milk snakes. All these help people by killing large numbers of disease-carrying, destructive rodents. "There's a snake in that pile of rocks" needn't arouse unpleasant emotions. The word *snake* covers good and bad. Just so, the words *American, Briton,* and *Canadian* include good and bad representatives. Words may suggest dignity (*cathedral, sovereign, gracious, majestic, altar, arch*); humor (*giggle, waddle, strut, tumble, yokel, antics*); strength (*vigor, steel, oak, beams, captain*); beauty (*dawn, dusk, sunset, glade, grove*); and a host of other qualities. The person sensitive to connotation never says, "The grizzled sea captain giggled at the landlubber's foolish question." The person says "roared with laughter." *Giggled* clashes in connotation with *grizzled sea captain.*

Answers to Activity 6:
(Evil roles are played by Murdstone, Quilp, Squeers, and Gradgrind.)

In the list preceding the sentences, find the word that has a connotation more appropriate than that of the italicized word in each sentence. On your paper write the word after the number of the sentence. There will be ten words left over.

adorable	chariot	feed	ma	toddler
animals	child	good-looking	mother	wagon
bunny rabbits	energy	hand	paw	wailing
cats	exercise	lunch	rabbits	weeping

1. Two *pussycats* were howling and fighting in the backyard.
2. A *kiddie* has a different outlook on life from an adult.
3. The conference was recessed for *chow*.
4. Phaëthon, son of Apollo, once drove the golden *vehicle* of the sun.
5. The white-haired old lady didn't seem to have the *pep* to leave her cozy rocker by the fire.
6. Near the millpond stands a fine old *crying* willow.
7. As they walked down the road, Albert bashfully took Sue's *fist* in his.
8. The senator introduced his *mom* to the assembled guests.
9. "That's a *darling* new car you have," Grandfather gruffly told Dad when we met.
10. When does the hunting season for *bunnies* open?

ACTIVITY 8   **Studying Pairs of Sentences**   **OT**

Explain how the sentences in the following pairs differ from each other and convey different messages, though the denotations are somewhat similar.

1. a. The debris from the wedding cluttered the small, crowded room.
   b. The cozy reception room was decked with rose petals fallen from the wedding bouquets.
2. a. You have a point, but don't you think this may be another way of looking at the problem?
   b. You liar! You're completely misrepresenting the facts.
3. a. The miserable jalopy wheezed down the street, gasped its last breath in front of our house, and disgorged a disreputably dressed future juvenile delinquent.
   b. The old car came down the street and stopped at our house. A casually dressed teen-ager stepped out.
4. a. I had nothing to do anyway, so I thought I'd grind out a reply to your last letter.
   b. I've been looking forward to replying to your last letter; so here goes.

5. a. The weather-beaten flimsy shack at the edge of the swamp sagged
in the moonlight as though it intended to sink into the ooze.
   b. The picturesque cabin at the edge of the bayou showed its uneven,
jagged lines against the bright moonlight.

STEREOTYPES

Sometimes the associations that cluster around a word harden
and form a highly inaccurate picture. Because some teen-agers are
immature, cartoons, television skits, and the movies often picture
the typical teen-ager as giddy, emotionally unbalanced, and down-
right silly. Such inaccurate generalized pictures are called *stereotypes*, a term meaning "plates used in printing." People in real life
are infinitely varied; stereotypes don't change. Don't think or talk
in stereotypes.

ACTIVITY 9   Studying Stereotypes   T

Listed below are typical stereotypes. Match the quality in B
usually associated with the person in A. Why are these associations
misleading?

A	B
1. bride	humorless
2. American father	kindly
3. grandfather	absent-minded
4. Englishman	scatterbrained
5. journalist	dominated by his wife
6. lady driver	unskilled in cooking
7. landlord	fast-talking
8. professor	hard-hearted

GOOD AND BAD LABELS

"Sam's a pest." "Susie's a drip." "Paula's a conceited snob."
"Julie's a tattler."

Too many of us go carelessly through life, attaching labels to
people. Sometimes a label tells more about us, the users, than about
our victims. *Pest*, *drip*, *snob*, and *tattler* are unflattering labels, but
they may reflect merely the prejudice of the speaker. Before you
use a label, hesitate; ask yourself, "Is this fair? Upon what evidence
do I assign such a label?" There is a common saying, "Sticks and
stones may break my bones, but names will never hurt me." This
is, of course, untrue. Words of unfavorable connotation, sometimes

called "loaded words," may seek to substitute emotion for fact. The gossip who wishes to discredit an acquaintance may call her a *conceited, self-centered, selfish busybody*. Listeners have a right to say, "What do you mean by these labels? Prove your assertions."

Pal and *go-getter* are labels rich in pleasant connotations. They are approving labels, but they may also be inaccurate. Some words or phrases with pleasant associations are called "prestige words" — for example, *progress, positive approach, broad program of improvements*. Speakers may use these to cast a pleasant glow of approval over their program or party. But the words themselves may mean little.

ACTIVITY 10   Studying a Check on Harmful Gossip   OT

Be ready to discuss how the following three questions can eliminate harmful gossip.

1. Is it true?   2. Is it kind?   3. Is it necessary?

ACTIVITY 11   Studying Good and Bad Connotation   RT

Pick out the "loaded" words in the following passage. Tell whether they are words of good or bad connotation. Point out how these words may substitute emotion for fact.

My candidate is a patriotic statesman whose main concern is the good and welfare of all the people. He presents a positive program of legislation designed to bring the golden benefits of prosperity to every home in this glorious state of ours. The opposition candidate, my friends, is a meddling politician whose spendthrift policies can lead only to disaster. Though he is stingy with money himself, he has no reservations about plunging the state into bankruptcy.

A FEELING FOR CONNOTATION

Unfortunately, since connotation cannot usually be checked in the dictionary, everyone must be alert to the use of loaded words to sway judgments. Frequently, highly emotional words carry little content. *Trustworthy* and *unreliable* give us somebody's judgment, but we may need the facts to judge adequately for ourselves.

ACTIVITY 12   Finding Words with Good and Bad Connotation   RT

From the editorial page of a newspaper, from the reporting of political talks, or from advertising, find three examples of words with favorable connotation and three with unfavorable connotation. Explain how each is used to persuade the reader or listener to action.

EUPHEMISMS

Sometimes we try to gloss over the harsh realities of life by choosing words of pleasant connotation. *Euphemism* is the substituting of a mild, indirect, or less distasteful word for another. *Pass away* and *go West* are old euphemisms for *die*. *Lubritorium* is a euphemism for *grease pit*.

Because certain occupations are felt to have more prestige than others, some employees adopt euphemisms to give status to their jobs. In *The American Language* H. L. Mencken listed many of these: *mortician* for *undertaker*, *aisle manager* for *floorwalker*, and *beautician* for *hairdresser*.

ACTIVITY 13   Studying Euphemisms   V

Can you match the occupation at the left with the euphemistic title at the right? Answers are at the bottom of the page.

A	B
1. tax collector	assistant treasurer
2. house wrecker	demolition engineer
3. junior box-office clerk	director of internal revenue
4. press agent	public relations counsel
5. trash collector	sanitary engineer

ACTIVITY 14   Challenging Your Ingenuity   W

How many of these words can you weave into a forceful, meaningful paragraph? Compose your own topic sentence.

suggestion in words	labels	slogans	feelings
connotation	names	euphemisms	thinking

ACTIVITY 15   Word Study   VW

The following words were used in this chapter. The page number is after each word. What does each word mean in the sentence in which it appears? Use each word in a sentence of your own. Check your spelling.

segment	39	slogan	40	prestige	46
authorizing	39	deliberately	41	spendthrift	46
profound	39	tranquillity	42	sway	46
apprentice	40	prejudice	45	adequately	46

Answers to Activity 13:
 1 — B3, 2 — B2, 3 — B1, 4 — B4, 5 — B5

Unit Two — *Composition*

4   *Building Paragraphs*

Good paragraphs make writing easier to read and understand. Each indention tells the reader, "Now here's another point," or "Wait till you hear this part of the story," or "Somebody else is going to talk." If you are not sure about how to compose paragraphs, this chapter will help remove your uncertainties.

THE SENTENCE—BASIS OF ALL WRITING

Before you can compose a good paragraph, however, you must be able to write a good sentence. A teacher of writing once told his students, "Don't worry about writing the great American novel. Forget about composing long and brilliant articles. First learn to write a simple, clear, direct English sentence!"

"That's no problem," you say. "Anyone can at least write a good sentence. What could be easier?"

The job is not so simple as it seems. Paragraphs sometimes fail because the sentences within them are dull or carelessly written. Before you attempt the paragraph, try your hand at the English sentence. Can you write a single, strong sentence right now?

ACTIVITY 1 Writing a Sound Sentence   **W**

What are you planning to do this evening? Write a single sentence—ONE sentence—telling clearly and directly what your plans are.

EXAMPLE This evening I plan to finish *Poirot Investigates,* replace a string on my guitar, and watch the *Mystery Movie* on television.

ACTIVITY 2   Evaluating Sentences   S

As each classmate in turn puts a sentence on the chalkboard, ask the following questions.

1. Is the sentence grammatically correct, with a subject and a verb?   (Review pages 259–277.)
2. Does the sentence convey a clear message?   If not, how can it be improved?
3. Does the author use any unnecessary words?   If so, which words or expressions can be shortened, compressed, or omitted?

Get to the Point

A sentence should read as if its author, had he held a plough instead of a pen, could have drawn a furrow deep and straight to the end.—HENRY DAVID THOREAU

Good sentences don't ramble.   They waste no words.   They come to the point swiftly and directly.   They allow the reader to follow the thought without possible confusion.   (See also pages 454–461.)

RAMBLING AND DULL   If you have some ideas about writing, whether it is now or perhaps in the future, it seems to me you'll have to keep on writing.

TO THE POINT   If you wish to be a writer, write.—EPICTETUS

ACTIVITY 3   Studying a Quotation   S

What does the quotation by Henry David Thoreau mean to you? Does he offer sound advice about writing?   Explain.

ACTIVITY 4   Studying Sentences   S

What does each of the following sentences mean to you?   Is the meaning in each conveyed clearly and concisely?

1. Your disposition, not your position, determines happiness.
2. Often the last key on the ring opens the door.
3. Learn to disagree without becoming disagreeable.
4. Triumph is just "umph" added to "try."
5. The bigger a man's head gets, the easier it is to fill his shoes.

ACTIVITY 5   Writing Concise Sentences   W

Experienced air travelers learn to travel with as little baggage as possible.   Write each of the following sentences as simply and as directly as you can. Cut out all extra baggage. Save your sentences. You may wish to use one or more later.

1. A sentence beginning with the words *Last summer* or *Last winter*
2. A sentence presenting your viewpoint on a particular sport
3. A sentence about part-time jobs
4. A sentence telling something about soap operas or your favorite TV program
5. A sentence about the recent or coming elections

ACTIVITY 6   Writing a Challenging Sentence   **W**

Have you ever been puzzled by life, by people, or by things that happen? Have you ever thought, "Isn't it strange that. . . ?" Try to recapture one of these thoughts and express it in a good, sound sentence. Save your sentence for possible use later.

EXAMPLE   If the common dandelion were rare and expensive, how it would be praised for its matchless beauty!—JOHN KIERAN

Develop the Writing Habit

Inch by inch, life is a cinch. Yard by yard, life is hard.

A mile runner doesn't run long distances at first. He trains and works up to the longer distance. The same truth holds for writing. If you are frightened by the idea of writing a long composition, go into training. Write a very little at a time, but write often. One excellent method is training yourself to write a sentence a day—about anything. Writing the sentence is the important step. You will soon find that the idea of the paragraph is manageable. Then the longer theme will seem less forbidding. But begin with the sentence. A single sentence can carry a message all by itself.

ACTIVITY 7   Writing a Daily Observation   **W**

Each evening for a week, write a single sentence presenting some idea you had during the day. Share these sentences with your classmates next week. Save your sentences for possible use later.

EXAMPLES

Tuesday—For the first time I realized today that I do my best work before noon.

Friday—The green of the maple is strikingly different from the green of the dogwood.

Sunday—Unlike television, books can be enjoyed at any hour and in any place without disturbing others.

From the Sentence to the Paragraph

Now that you have tried your hand at a number of good, concise sentences, you are ready for the next step: the paragraph. The paragraph has been called "the rounded development of a single idea."

"How shall I go about writing a paragraph?" you ask. "How do I know when to stop? How long should a paragraph be, anyway?"

One student invented what he considered a foolproof method. He merely counted his sentences and started a new paragraph after every five sentences! His method made his compositions look good —from a distance. But his paragraphs were a little confusing. There is more to paragraphing than counting sentences.

How Long Should a Paragraph Be?

The length of a paragraph depends upon how many sentences you need in order to develop a particular point or part of a subject. In written conversation a paragraph may be only a sentence or even a single word. In most compositions, however, you will need from 100 to 200 words to make each major point clear to the reader. As a rule, begin a new paragraph

> with an explanation—when you go on to a new idea or a new step.
> with a description—when you change the mood or the point of view.
> with a story—when you change the time, the place, or the action.
> with written conversation—when you change the speaker.

ACTIVITY 8   Studying Paragraphs   **S**

Examine paragraphs in books, magazines, and newspapers you are reading. What is the average length of each?

WHAT MAKES A GOOD PARAGRAPH?

A good paragraph has only one main idea. The sentences in the paragraph support or explain this idea.

Decide on a Topic

There should be no problem in deciding upon topics for paragraphs. If you have completed the sentence activities in this chapter, you already have many topics for paragraphs. Your sentences for

Activities 5, 6, and 7 will lead smoothly into paragraphs. These sentences, based upon observation, reflection, and experience, are filled with paragraph ideas.

The possibilities are limitless. Here's another way to get started. List five of your major interests—for example, sports, music, dancing, reading, and knitting. Then choose one of these and list additional areas of interest within the larger topic. In music, for example, you might list these: the ragtime of Scott Joplin, the songs of Joni Mitchell, the dulcimer, the early Beatle records. Don't stop there. Narrow your choice still further. For the dulcimer you might list these: special qualities of the dulcimer, history of the dulcimer, the place of the dulcimer in folk music.

Now, by choosing one of these, you are in the proper range for a topic sentence. You might create this topic sentence: "Because it is hauntingly beautiful to listen to and yet fairly easy to learn, the dulcimer has become one of the most popular instruments among young people." By emphasizing its sound and its simplicity, you can then develop your paragraph.

Finding a topic and then working down to a topic sentence is like working with an inverted pyramid.

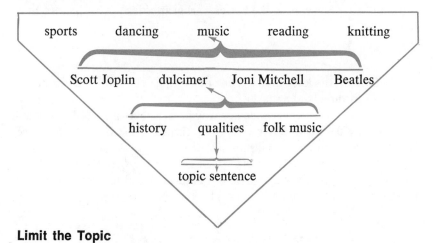

Limit the Topic

Only a narrow topic can be developed in one paragraph. If you're a spelunker, or cave explorer, you'll need five or more paragraphs to tell something about your hobby. But in one paragraph you can tell about one of these topics: the appeal of cave exploration, the equipment needed, the hazards of and safety precautions for cave explorers, the rewards of your hobby, or your feelings when you explored your first cave.

ACTIVITY 9 Studying Two Paragraphs

Each of the following paragraphs deals with sports, but one of the writers has failed to limit the topic. Point out the paragraph that is too broad. Show how the better paragraph deals with a more limited topic.

1

In football the knee injury is one of the most common and one of the most serious threats to a player's career. A ball carrier may be hit from two directions, twisting his knee in a way nature never intended. A quarterback may be hit off balance as he is throwing the ball. If his knee buckles under him, he may sustain a serious injury. A lanky end may be tackled while he is still in the air. If he falls in the wrong way, his knee may suffer. Even a sturdy tackle or guard may find his knees painfully twisted at the bottom of a pile-up. The knee is a fragile part of the body.

2

The knee is a delicate apparatus. Under certain conditions of stress it may be injured. Injuries in sports are threats to the careers of players. A baseball player, a football player, or a soccer player relies upon his legs. Even in tennis a player may twist a knee, an ankle, or a calf muscle. Golfers may develop other leg problems under the strain of putting. Basketball players are in constant motion, putting tremendous pressure on their legs.

ACTIVITY 10   Narrowing the Topic

Choose three of the following subjects.   For each, think of three or more topics that are narrow enough to be handled in one paragraph.   Be prepared to tell your classmates why your topics would be suitable for one-paragraph themes.

Camping	Housecleaning	Safety
Earning money	Modern inventions	Saturday chores
Family fun	My hobby	A school club
Fishing	My pet	Water sports
Gardening	Racing	Woodworking

State Your Idea in a Topic Sentence

To be sure the particular point you want to make about your topic is clear, state it in a topic sentence.   Although the topic sentence comes first in many paragraphs, it may be in the middle or at the end.   If the first sentence is the topic sentence, then the last sentence, often called the *clincher,* usually repeats the main idea in different words.

Although the topic sentence may be omitted in paragraphs of essays, stories, or novels, generally the main idea is clearly implied. In your compositions, reports, and essay tests, however, beginning with a topic sentence will help you to stick to the topic.   Be specific.

Catch your reader's attention by using vivid, action-packed words.

NOT   There are some hazards in cave exploring.

BUT   One slip of a rope, one loose piton, or one careless member of the group can spell disaster for cave explorers.

Look at Your Sentences

At this point your practice in writing good, sound sentences will come in handy. The topic sentence has to be a good, effective, concise statement if it is to do its job properly. Look over the sentences you wrote for Activities 5, 6, and 7. You may find some good topic sentences there.

Whether you choose a sentence you wrote earlier or prefer to write a new topic sentence, be sure to limit your subject so that you can handle it in a single paragraph. After you have written your topic sentence, your paragraph will begin to write itself.

ACTIVITY 11   Comparing Topic Sentences   S

Which sentence in each of the following pairs seems to you a more vivid, effective topic sentence for a paragraph? Why? Point out the effective words in the sentence you consider superior. Use the preceding example as your guide.

1. a. Big-league baseball players seldom cheat, but they may sometimes stretch the rules a bit.
   b. Big-league baseball rules are sometimes hard to apply uniformly and effectively.
2. a. The dogwood is a very beautiful tree for lawn or garden at every season of the year—from spring, through summer and autumn, to winter.
   b. For beauty of flower in spring, leaf in autumn, and tree outline in winter, there is no finer tree than the dogwood.
3. a. The secret of making money in the stock market is summed up in four words: *buy low; sell high.*
   b. To make money in the stock market, the wise investor must study market trends and act accordingly.
4. a. Power tools are remarkable work savers if users remember these tools cut *anything!*
   b. Power tools are good to have, but users must take all safety precautions and watch out for the tools' dangerous cutting abilities.
5. a. Many different kinds of people partake of the facilities of the Community Center.
   b. Students and executives, artists and lawyers, men and women, senior citizens and teenagers—all use the Community Center.

ACTIVITY 12   Writing a Topic Sentence   W

For one of the topics you selected in Activity 10, write a topic sentence. The class will judge it on these points: (1) Is it specific? (2) Does it arouse interest in the topic? (Be guided by the discussion based on Activity 11.)

Support the Topic Sentence

To make your meaning clear, be generous with your facts and ideas. Not all paragraphs are developed in the same way. "Basketball is a better spectator sport than soccer" suggests that you give reasons to prove your statement. "Our boxer pup Rocky has many lovable qualities" calls for examples. There are a number of ways to develop paragraphs. Here are some suggestions.

1. Give examples. The topic sentence "I've had some hair-raising experiences in caves" needs the support of one or more examples. Specific examples arouse your reader's interest and help explain what you are stating in your topic sentence.

Notice how S. I. Hayakawa uses examples to prove his statement that interpreting words is a constant task for every citizen.

(1) The interpretation of words is a never-ending task for any citizen in modern society. **(2)** We now have, as the result of modern means of communication, hundreds of thousands of words flung at us daily. **(3)** We are constantly being talked at, by teachers, preachers, salesmen, public officials, and moving-picture sound tracks. **(4)** The cries of the hawkers of soft drinks and soap chips pursue us into our very homes, thanks to the radio—and in some houses the radio is never turned off from morning to night. **(5)** Daily the newsboy brings us, in large cities, from thirty to fifty enormous pages of print, and almost three times that amount on Sundays. **(6)** The mailman brings magazines and direct-mail advertising. **(7)** We go out and get more words at bookstores and libraries. **(8)** Billboards confront us on the highways, and we even take portable radios with us to the seashore. **(9)** Words fill our lives.—s. i. HAYAKAWA, *Language in Action*	**(1) Topic Sentence** **(2) Example** **(3) Example** **(4) Example** **(5) Example** **(6) Example** **(7) Example** **(8) Example** **(9) Clincher Sentence**

ACTIVITY 13 Studying Development by Examples S

The preceding paragraph was written before television became the number one entertainment medium. Would S. I. Hayakawa's conclusions be true today? Explain.

ACTIVITY 14 Studying Development by Examples RS

Read the following paragraph and then point out the examples introduced by Richard Murray-Shelley to support his statement that man has used helps in calculating.

Throughout time man has augmented his natural calculating ability by one means or another. First he counted on his fingers—doubtless the reason why the most commonly used number system is based on ten. Then came simple calculating devices such as the ancient abacus, which

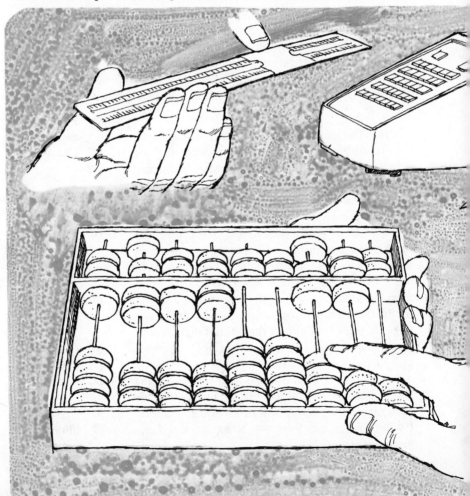

still finds universal use. Desk calculating machines and the slide rule all led inevitably to the modern digital computer, which in the last few years has caused such a revolution in computing methods.—RICHARD MURRAY-SHELLEY, *Computer Programming*

2. Fill in details. The topic sentence "It was the first time I'd ever been in a cave" calls for details about the experience. What did you see or fail to see? What were your feelings? What is the inside of a cave like? The more details you provide, the more your reader will share your experience.

Buenos Aires, Argentina

Read the following paragraph and then point out the details used by Gerald Durrell to support his statement that Buenos Aires, decked out for spring, was looking her best.

Buenos Aires, decked out for spring, was looking her best. The tall and elegant buildings seemed to gleam like icebergs in the sun, and the broad avenues were lined with jacaranda trees covered with a mist of mauvy blue flowers, or *palo borracho,* with their strange bottle-shaped trunks and their spindly branches starred with yellow and white flowers. The spring-like atmosphere seemed to have infected the pedestrians, who fled across the road through the traffic with even less caution than usual, while the drivers of the trams, buses and cars vied with each other in the time-honoured Buenos Aires game of seeing how close they could get to each other at the maximum speed without actually crashing.—GERALD DURRELL, *The Whispering Land*

Facts and statistics are forms of detail. A paragraph may be developed by marshaling facts to prove a statement and support a topic sentence. Point out how facts are used in the following example to support the statement that flextime is an aid to production and a booster of employee morale.

Flextime, a plan whereby employees set their own working hours, is becoming more popular every day. The record of this method, which allows employees to distribute their eight-hour working day with only a few limitations, is astounding even its supporters. In Europe more than five million workers are under the new system. More than ten percent of workers in West Germany and more than a quarter of the workers in Switzerland are on some version of flextime. People in the United States are accepting the idea more and more. In California, Blue Cross–Blue Shield has all its employees on flextime. Other companies using flextime are the John Hancock Life Insurance Company, Continental Telephone, and Exxon. More than 30,000 United States Government employees are on flextime, and the number is growing. It looks as though flextime will eventually be commonplace in industry in the United States.

3. Compare.   The topic sentence "Going down into a cave is a little like going into the cellar of an abandoned house on a cloudy, dark night" calls for paragraph development by comparison. Why is the cave like the cellar? What similarities (darkness, unfamiliarity, quiet) can be pointed out?

Read the following paragraph and then point out the use of comparisons to support the statement that a person's character is like the seed of a plant.

A person's character is like the seed of a plant. No matter what quality a seed possesses or what kind of structure it displays, it will not survive unless the ground in which it is planted is fertile. It must have the warmth of sunshine and the freshness and moisture of falling rain. The surroundings in which we live, like the soil and rain for a seed, help determine how character will develop.—STUDENT WRITER

For easier teaching and simpler presentation, various ways of developing paragraphs are presented individually. Fully developed paragraphs may, however, combine some of these methods for greater effectiveness. But even paragraphs developed in this way usually display a particular order and stick to the single topic.

What point is the writer of the following paragraph trying to make? How does the paragraph use facts to support his basic comparison? How does his clincher sentence partly restate his topic sentence?

Compared with many other peoples, people in the United States do not live very long. Though the United States leads the world in most measures of material success—personal income, production, profits—in life expectancy it ranks only twenty-fourth for men and ninth for women. Men in the United States live an average of 67.1 years, and women 74.6 years. Men survive longer in most Western European nations, as well as in Japan, Israel, Greece, East Germany, Australia, and some other countries. Indeed, in Norway, Denmark, and The Netherlands, men live longer than 70 years on the average; in Sweden, the world's leader, male longevity is 71.9 years—almost five years more than in the United States. While women in the United States do appreciably better, they still rank behind women in Sweden, The Netherlands, Iceland, Norway, Denmark, France, Canada, and Britain.—*Time*

4. Use contrast. The topic sentence "The average cave explorer is quite different from the person who watches television all weekend" calls for paragraph development by contrast.   Why is the cave explorer different from the television watcher?   How do the active demands of cave exploration differ from the more passive demands of watching television?   Developing a paragraph by contrast emphasizes differences.

ACTIVITY 19   Studying Development by Contrast   **RS**

Read the following paragraph and then point out George R. Stewart's use of contrast to support his statement that summer weather tends to be a local affair, while fall, winter, and spring weather is more international.

Fall, winter, and spring are international in their weather controls; summer, we may say, is isolationist.   In the three other seasons, most of all in winter, New Yorkers and Chicagoans can be severely affected by a storm that starts over the Gobi Desert or the Sea of Okhotsk.   But in summer the weather is largely determined by the give-and-take between the surface of North America and the nearby seas.   Some of the weather is much more local even than that.   Although a winter storm sweeping down from the Canadian Northwest pays little attention to any local features except the higher mountains, in summer a county may breed its own thunderstorm and that storm may die out before it even gets over the county line.—GEORGE R. STEWART, "The Bad Old Summer Time," *New York Times Magazine*

5. Compare and contrast.   The topic sentence "In some ways exploring caves is like any exploration, but there are certain real differences" calls for paragraph development by both comparison and contrast.   This method is more common than development by either comparison or contrast alone.   When we make comparisons, we also tend to point out important differences as well.   For example, football is like soccer in many ways, but there are significant differences that make each sport unique.   A paragraph would point out both similarities and differences.

There are at least three ways to handle comparison and contrast.

1. Describe football's major points, then soccer's, following the same order of points.
2. Discuss the likenesses first and then the differences.
3. Compare football to soccer point by point.

ACTIVITY 20   Studying Development by Comparison and Contrast   **RS**

Read the following paragraph and then point out George Stewart's use of comparison and contrast to distinguish between "a historical event" and "a dramatic event."

The difference between "a historical event" and "a dramatic event" is well illustrated by the stories of the Stevens Party and the Donner Party. The former is historically important, and the pioneers who composed it brought the first wagons to California and discovered the pass across the Sierra Nevada that serves still as the chief route for railroad, highway, telephone, and airline. The Donner Party, however, is of negligible importance historically, but the story has been told and retold, published and republished, because of its dramatic details of starvation, murder, heroism, and disaster. Against every American who knows of the one, a thousand must know of the other. As a kind of final irony, the pass discovered by the Stevens Party has come to be known as Donner Pass.—GEORGE R. STEWART, "The Smart Ones Got Through," *American Heritage*

ACTIVITY 21   Studying Paragraph Development   **RS**

Read the following two paragraphs and "Kachina Dolls" on page 75. Answer these questions.

1. Does each paragraph have a topic sentence? If so, what is it?
2. Which paragraph is developed principally by details? What are the main details in that paragraph?
3. Which paragraph is developed by giving examples? What examples are used?
4. Which paragraph is developed by comparison and contrast? Which of the three ways is used? What likenesses are pointed out? What differences?
5. What words and expressions paint the most vivid pictures?
6. Do any paragraphs have clincher sentences? If so, what are they?

HOW DO THE ARTERIES DIFFER FROM THE VEINS?

Arteries and veins are both hollow tubes through which the blood flows. The two differ, however, in three important respects. The work of an artery, first of all, is to carry blood rich in oxygen from the heart to the various organs of the body. The work of a vein, on the other hand, is to return to the heart blood laden with carbon dioxide. In structure, too, veins and arteries differ markedly. Although the walls of both are composed of three coats of tissue, the veins are thinner than the arteries and less elastic. A third point of difference is the way the blood moves within the two types of vessels. Propelled by the force of the heartbeat, the blood rushes through the arteries, which expand and contract to push it forward in spurts. In the veins, however, the blood flows slowly and smoothly.

FOLKLORE TO THE RESCUE

People's imagination has produced many colorful interpretations for the sudden silence that sometimes befalls a group. Probably of German origin is the remark "An angel flew through the room" or "An angel just passed over the house." The Irish version is, "The angels are changing guard." If someone of Dutch ancestry is present, he or she may say, "The pastor is passing by." From still another member of the group may come, "It must be twenty past." This expression may have arisen out of the assassination of Lincoln at 8:20 p.m. or the time of Christ's death on the Cross. On the other hand, it may have originated when watchmakers followed the custom of setting their sign clocks at a permanent 8:20. Thus people often draw on folklore to fill the lull in conversation, for remarks about twenty past, the angels, or the pastor are but imaginative interpretations of an experience.

ACTIVITY 22   Studying Paragraph Development   **RS**

What method of paragraph development is used in each of the following paragraphs? Point out the topic sentence of each.

A

An English sparrow is quite different from a white-throated sparrow. While the English sparrow is bold and brash, the white-throat is shy and retiring. The English sparrow will nest anywhere, even on top of a neon sign, but the white-throat nests away from the haunts of people. The English sparrow chirps and scolds. The white-throat sings its sad, melodious cry, one that its hearers never forget. The English sparrow has spread throughout the country, rubbing elbows with a variety of animals and with people. The white-throat, less aggressive, stays in the background. The male English sparrow has a handsome black vest, but the white-throat's lovely white bib is even prettier. These cousins are indeed quite different in habit and appearance.

B

In rare moments tennis players approach the unthinking spontaneity of the leopard. These moments seem to occur most frequently when

players are volleying back and forth at the net. Often the exchange of shots at such short quarters is so rapid that action faster than thought is required. These moments are exhilarating, and the players are often amazed to find that they make perfect placements against shots they didn't even expect to reach. Moving more quickly than they thought they could, they have no time to plan; the perfect shot just comes. And feeling that they didn't execute the shot deliberately, they often call it luck; but if it happens repeatedly, one begins to trust oneself and feel a deep sense of confidence.—W. TIMOTHY GALLWEY, *The Inner Game of Tennis*

6. Use analogy. The topic sentence "Studying for an examination is like preparing for a tennis match" calls for paragraph development by analogy. Analogy is an extended comparison, often comparing two things that on first appearance seem unlike. (See also "Painting Word Pictures," pages 211–212, and "Similes and Metaphors in Everyday Language," pages 212–213.)

ACTIVITY 23 Studying Development by Analogy RS

What two things are being compared in the following paragraph? What are some of the similarities between the two? Does the final sentence continue the analogy, or comparison, or does it drop the point made in the topic sentence?

Learning mathematics is like the path up a very high mountain. Mountain climbers tell of reaching one false peak after another, each time seeing a new one beyond. And as one reaches new peaks, there comes again and again a sudden illumination—and a reorganization of old familiar ideas—as the patterns of the foothills stand out more clearly. Just so in mathematics. The mountain of mathematics has built up for many centuries; its size matches its age. Yet, like all of science, less than half of the labor that has gone into mathematics is more than ten years old, and it grows faster today than ever before.—JOHN W. LUKEY, *Listen to Leaders In Science*

7. Give reasons. The topic sentence "Our school should have a soccer team" calls for paragraph development by giving reasons. Why do you think your school should have a soccer team? What reasons can you offer?

ACTIVITY 24　Studying Development by Reasons　　RS

In the following paragraph what reasons does Bradley Smith provide for saying that the Acadians are a stubborn people?

The Acadians are a stubborn people. Theirs was the first French colony to survive in Canada. For 45 years after Britain seized Acadia in 1710 and renamed it *Nova Scotia,* the conquered race refused to give the oath of allegiance to the British king. Finally, in 1755, an impatient British governor ruthlessly uprooted them. Their houses were burned and their lands seized. Six thousand of them were herded onto ships and scattered throughout America. But they would not stay scattered and give up their culture. Almost four thousand of them surmounted endless hardships to find their way to Louisiana, then still a French possession, and reestablish their lives.—BRADLEY SMITH, "Acadia Country," *American Heritage*

8. Define. The topic sentence "Philately is more than merely accumulating postage stamps" calls for paragraph development by defining. What is philately? How does it go beyond merely collecting stamps?

ACTIVITY 25　Studying Development by Defining　　RS

How does the following paragraph make clear the meaning of the word *philately?*

Philately is more than merely accumulating postage stamps. Philately suggests learning as well as collecting, studying as well as pasting stamps in albums.   It includes postal history, postmarks, methods of printing, and kinds of paper.   It deals with stamp topics and personages, current events and ancient history.   It is concerned with errors and oddities, freaks and rarities.   It involves envelopes and postal cards, as well as postage stamps.   There is a great deal more to philately than most people realize.

Stick to the Point

If your topic sentence is "The rewards of spelunking far outweigh the dangers," don't be sidetracked into telling about safety measures or the hazards of skin diving.   Discard every sentence that doesn't support or explain your topic sentence.

ACTIVITY 26   Studying Unity in the Paragraph   RS

Three sentences in the following paragraph do not stick to the topic and should be eliminated.   Pick out these three sentences and tell why you think they do not support the topic sentence.

Whenever I fail to select my television programs in advance, I'm always disappointed.   I sit hypnotized at the set and watch many things I don't really enjoy.   A week ago I watched an old movie that creaked and sputtered to its dreary conclusion.   My brother likes old movies, however.   Saturday I was trapped into watching a variety show that had neither variety nor showmanship.   Some variety shows feature top stars in top acts.   Sunday evening I napped through a discussion program on a topic that was remote from my experiences and interests.   Discussion programs are the most important programs on television.   Last night's situation comedy was funny the first time I saw it, but it lost some of its charm on the second run-through.   My New Year's resolution will be: Plan my television viewing in advance!

Arrange Material in Order

How should you arrange your paragraph?   What order should you follow?   There are a number of ways in which you can arrange the material in the paragraph.

1. Time Order.   This order is usually followed in a narrative paragraph (page 95), but it is used in other types of paragraphs as well.   Tell what happened first, then next, and next.   Keeping time order makes your paragraph easier to follow.   Jumping around is confusing.

ACTIVITY 27   Studying Time Order   RS

Read the following paragraph and then point out how time order
is used in the development of the paragraph.

In early evening the lake was at its most appealing.   The warm setting sun cast its waning beams across the quiet water.   A breeze stirred
the pine tops and carried the scent of pine needles through the moist air.
Then, as the breeze grew stronger, a few ripples were stirred into life,
lapping quietly against the banks.   As at a signal, a miniature orchestra
began to tune up.   Crickets formed the string section, and bull frogs were
the bass drums.   The brighter hues and harsher noises of day were lost
in the serenity of evening.—STUDENT WRITER

2. Space Order.   This order is commonly used in a descriptive
paragraph, but it may be used in other kinds of paragraphs as well.
Be consistent as you support your topic sentence.   Don't jump around
haphazardly.   Proceed from left to right or right to left; farthest to
nearest or nearest to farthest; surroundings to center or center to
surroundings.

ACTIVITY 28   Studying Space Order   RS

Read the following paragraph and then point out how space order
is used in the development of the paragraph.

If you visit my sister in her room, enter at your peril.   There is a
battered old rocker at the left of the door, with its rungs occasionally
sticking into the walking space.   Directly ahead there is a half-made ship
model on the floor, waiting to be finished.   Just to the right of the model
debris, you will notice half a dozen books, all open to various pages of
interest to my sister and no one else.   Continuing to look to the right, be
especially on guard.   Here are two rickety crates, piled high with ice
skates, old tennis sneakers, a skateboard, and a basketball.   Uncertain
equilibrium marks this collection for a fall some day.   If it should fall as
you enter, be prepared!

3. Order of Importance.   If you wish to leave your reader with
something to remember, save your punch line till the end.   Lead up
to it and then conclude with a vivid point.

ACTIVITY 29   Studying Order of Importance   RS

Read the following paragraph.   How does the author conclude
his paragraph?   Is it vivid, memorable?   Explain.

Sky City Mission at Acoma, New Mexico

When you look back at them, many of the fundamental discoveries of science seem so simple, too absurdly simple. How was it men groped and fumbled for so many thousands of years without seeing things that lay right under their noses? So with microbes. Now all the world has seen them cavorting on movie screens; many people of little learning have peeped at them swimming about under lenses of microscopes; the greenest medical student is able to show you the germs of I don't know how many diseases. What was so hard about seeing microbes for the first time?— PAUL DE KRUIF, *Microbe Hunters*

ACTIVITY 30   Rearranging a Scrambled Paragraph   S

The sentences in the following paragraph have been scrambled. Decide in what order the sentences should be presented. Then answer the questions at the end.

ACOMA, CITY OF THE SKY

1. The massive rock is four hundred feet above the plateau surrounding it. 2. On festival days, ceremonial dances take place and all the color of ancient days is revived. 3. This old settlement has earned its name, for it is located on a sheer rock mesa. 4. Even if there are no festivals, however, visitors drive up the sandy road between the cliffs and enjoy their visit to the sky city. 5. About sixty miles west of Albuquerque, New Mexico, lies the Acoma Indian Pueblo, ancient city in the sky. 6. From this neighboring valley visitors may come to the top, especially on days of religious festivals.

1. Which sentence is the topic sentence?
2. Is the paragraph developed by giving details, by giving examples, by giving reasons, or by comparing?
3. Which words and phrases give clues to the order of the paragraph?

4. Reverse Order. As you have seen, most paragraphs begin with a general statement and then supply details, examples, or comparisons to develop the general statement, or topic sentence. Sometimes this order is reversed. The paragraph plunges right into details or examples; the generalization, or topic sentence, comes at or near the end of the paragraph. In this arrangement the punch line and the topic sentence may be one and the same.

ACTIVITY 31   Studying Reverse Order   RS

Read the following paragraph. Where does the topic sentence occur? Is this arrangement effective? Explain. What advantages may be gained by occasionally writing paragraphs with this structure?

One rather special fruit tastes like a cross between a peach and a cantaloupe. It is delightful and appetizing, a favorite around the world for centuries. It can be used in a great many ways, from a delightful relish to a main meal at breakfast, from an appetizer to a dessert. It grows all over the tropical and subtropical world, including our own Florida, but it is almost unknown to inhabitants of temperate regions. If problems of shipping and storing are solved, the delicious mango may become as popular in the North as the avocado, or even the orange.

5. Order of Restatement. Sometimes a paragraph states the topic in an opening topic sentence and then restates the topic in the closing sentence, often with some expansion of the original statement. This device provides a strong clincher (page 55) and reminds the reader of the topic. "Tell 'em and tell 'em again" is sometimes held up as a rule for dramatists and playwrights. It's good advice for writers, too.

ACTIVITY 32   Studying Order of Restatement   **RS**

Read the following paragraph. What is the topic? Where is it first stated? Where is the topic restated? How does this restatement strengthen the paragraph? How do the middle sentences illustrate the point the author is trying to make?

A simple experiment will distinguish two types of human nature. Gather a throng of people and pour them into a ferryboat. By the time the boat has swung into the river, you will find that a certain proportion have taken the trouble to climb upstairs in order to be out on deck and see what is to be seen as they cross over. The rest have settled indoors to think what they will do upon reaching the other side or perhaps to lose themselves in apathy and tobacco smoke. But leaving out those apathetic or addicted to a single enjoyment, we may divide all the alert passengers on the boat into two classes—those who are interested in crossing the river and those who are merely interested in getting across.—MAX EASTMAN, *The Enjoyment of Poetry*

Use Connectives

To help the reader follow your paragraph development, use connectives to show the relationships among your sentences.

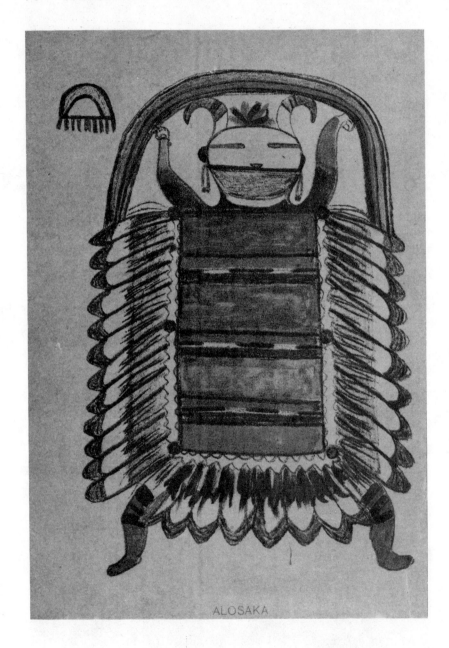

ALOSAKA

ACTIVITY 33   Studying Connectives   **RS**

A. Study the following paragraph.   Note the various kinds of connectives that are used as bridges from one sentence to the next. (Numbers refer to the list following.)

KACHINA DOLLS

Kachina dolls are unusual forms of native American art.   *They* are wooden images of spirits in the Hopi Indian religion.   *Some* have human characteristics; *others* represent animal gods or the elements of nature. True Kachina *dolls* are always carved from cottonwood roots that have been waterlogged and then sun-dried.   The *roots* are cut into three lengths—two to three inches, six to eight inches, and twelve inches—and then carved into one of the more than 250 types of Kachinas.   *Finally* a coat of whitewash is applied, and symbolic designs are painted in green, blue, yellow, white, red, or black.   *Usually* the smallest dolls are sold to tourists.   The medium- and large-sized *dolls* are generally made for the Kachina ceremonial dances.   *At that time* the dolls are given to Hopi children as part of their religious instruction.   Since *they* are the most authentic and the best made, the ceremonial *dolls* are prized by collectors.

1. A personal pronoun whose antecedent (page 396) is in the preceding sentence
2. Another word that refers to a word in the preceding sentence
3. A noun from a preceding sentence repeated
4. A phrase that repeats an idea from the preceding sentence
5. An adverb telling where, when, what, how, or why in relation to the preceding sentence

B. Connective adverbs and phrases like those in 4 and 5 are valuable words for keeping your ideas flowing smoothly.   Here are additional examples: *just then, secondly, on the other hand, besides, in addition, next, meanwhile.*   Suggest at least five others.

C. Look again at the paragraph examples in Activity 21. Point out the connectives that link the sentences together.

ACTIVITY 34　Completing a Paragraph　　　　W

Part of a topic sentence and the connectives of a paragraph are given below. Develop the paragraph by filling in the gaps.

At the end of the term our class should . . . . My principal reason for making this suggestion is that . . . . Furthermore, I feel . . . . Of course, . . . On the other hand, . . . Despite . . . . I believe . . . . For these reasons I urge the class to . . . .

ACTIVITY 35　Writing a Paragraph Step by Step　　　W

Write an original paragraph, following one of the sets of directions below. Use connectives to carry the reader from one sentence to the next.

A. 1. Copy this as your topic sentence: *Students perform many valuable services in* . . . . (Name your school.)
2. In your second sentence name one such service by students.
3. In your third sentence mention another example.
4. In your fourth sentence describe what you consider the most outstanding example of student service to your school.
5. In your fifth sentence conclude your paragraph, telling why you consider the services performed by students valuable.

B. 1. Copy this as your topic sentence: *So far this year our most outstanding assembly program has been* . . . . (Complete the sentence.)
2. In your second sentence describe one feature that made the program outstanding.
3. In the third sentence mention another.
4. In the fourth sentence add still another.
5. In the fifth sentence conclude your paragraph, telling why you found the program so outstanding.

Make a Plan

To make sure your paragraph sticks to the subject and presents material in good order, follow a plan. First write your topic sentence. Then list all the points you intend to use to support the topic sentence. Arrange these points in the best possible order, crossing out any that don't belong.

ACTIVITY 36   Studying a Plan   **RS**

Study this plan for "Folklore to the Rescue" on page 65.   Then read the paragraph again and be ready to answer these questions.

1. What details does the writer add to each point in the plan?
2. Why does the writer repeat details in the last sentence?

TOPIC SENTENCE   People's imagination has produced many colorful interpretations for the sudden silence that sometimes befalls a group.

PLAN   The Germans refer to an angel.
The Irish also talk about angels.
The Dutch say something about the pastor.
Someone may say, "It's twenty past."
All are examples of how folklore fills the lull in conversation.

ACTIVITY 37   Planning and Writing a Paragraph   **W**

Using the topic sentence you wrote for Activity 12, plan a paragraph to be developed by details, examples, or comparison.   Then write the paragraph.   After you have written your first draft, test your paragraph with the following questions.   If an answer is "No," revise where necessary.   When your paragraph meets the test satisfactorily, copy it neatly and hand it in with your plan.

CHECKLIST FOR A PARAGRAPH

1. Is the topic small enough to be treated adequately in one paragraph?
2. If there is a topic sentence, does it announce the topic of the paragraph clearly and interestingly?
3. Does the paragraph stick to the subject?
4. Are the sentences arranged in sensible, easy-to-follow order?
5. Does the paragraph say anything?   Do the details and examples add fresh, new information to what the topic sentence says?
6. Has the paragraph a forceful ending?
7. Have you written complete sentences?   (Refer to Chapter 32.)
8. Do the words express your ideas exactly and vividly?   (Refer to pages 28, 29, 264–266, and 361.)

ACTIVITY 38   Completing a Paragraph   **W**

1. For a special challenge, select one of the statements in Activity 4 and use it as a topic sentence.   Write a paragraph supporting the topic sentence by using one of the methods suggested in this chapter.

2. Select one of the sentences you wrote for Activity 5, 6, or 7 and use it as the topic sentence. Using the models in this chapter as a guide, write a paragraph supporting the statement.

ACTIVITY 39 Writing a Paragraph with Details and Examples **W**

Complete one of the following beginnings for a topic sentence. Then make a plan for developing your topic sentence in a paragraph. Choose details and examples from your observation and experience. Make sure your paragraph passes the checklist before you hand it in.

1. One chore I really enjoy is . . .
2. The longest day of my life was . . .
3. It was the first time I'd . . .
4. Have you ever tried . . .
5. The car parked across the street . . .
6. That was the most exciting . . .
7. Some of my dreams . . .
8. The greatest obstacle in understanding football is . . .
9. Dad was . . .
10. What would we do if we didn't have . . .

ACTIVITY 40 Writing a Paragraph Using Comparison and Contrast **W**

For one of the following write a carefully thought-out topic sentence and have your teacher approve it. Plan and write a paragraph that clearly shows the likenesses and differences in what you are comparing.

1. Compare two of your classmates as to their temperaments, likes and dislikes, or theories of meeting school problems.
2. Compare a typical summer day at home with a day you've spent at the beach or in the mountains.
3. Compare your radio or television interests with those of another member of your family.
4. Compare your present school with one you attended in the past. Limit yourself to the two or three most important or interesting points of comparison.
5. Compare first-aid treatment for sunstroke with the treatment for heat exhaustion.

ACTIVITY 41   Writing a Paragraph Giving Reasons   **W**

Complete one of the following topic sentences and write a fully developed paragraph expanding the idea of the topic sentence.   Use the paragraph in Activity 24 as a guide.   Provide reasons for supporting the topic sentence and conclude with a summarizing statement.   Use connectives.

1. I wish our family lived in . . .
2. In the past year I have completely changed my attitude toward . . .
3. In reading, I prefer . . .
4. My favorite television program is . . .
5. For me the best season of the year is . . .
6. One school regulation that should be changed is . . .
7. The three things I look for in a friend are . . .
8. The most important training a school can give is . . .
9. In comparison with large high schools, small schools are . . .
10. The best ways to improve our marking system would be . . .

ACTIVITY 42   Writing a Paragraph Definition   **W**

Select one of the following subjects and write a topic sentence for a paragraph, fully defining the subject you have chosen.   Then write a well-planned paragraph supporting the topic sentence.   Use the model in Activity 25 as a guide.   Refer to magazines, textbooks, or reference books as helps, if you wish, but use your own words.

EXAMPLE OF TOPIC SENTENCE   In cosmetic surgery the doctor is interested not primarily in alleviating pain or bettering health but in improving appearance.

artificial respiration	pocket calculator
crewel	recycling
etching	supersonic airplane
holography	ten-speed bicycle
numismatics	vitamins

ANSWERING QUESTIONS

How do you answer a question like "What is one use of chemical products on the farm?"   Do you plan your answer as a paragraph with a clear topic sentence and good details?   You should.   In an answer to a question, a good topic sentence repeats the important words of the question: *One use of chemical products on the farm is to replace food elements taken from the soil by plants.*   But don't stop here.   Support the topic sentence with details and examples.

ACTIVITY 43   Studying an Answer to a Question   **RS**

The following paragraph is an answer to the question about chemicals on the farm.   Read it and be ready to answer these questions.

1. What words of the question are repeated in the topic sentence?
2. What details support the topic sentence?

One use of chemical products on the farm is to replace food elements taken from the soil by plants.   Continual drain of nutritive elements from the soil, especially in one-crop states like Iowa, has produced a need for more concentrated and balanced plant-food mixtures.   Today test-tube products are widely used for fertilizers.   In no time even poor soil can be made more productive.   According to the National Planning Association the yield of corn, hay, wheat, or other crops can be increased from 50 to 200 percent when chemical fertilizers are used.   Although millions of acres of farmland have been turned into land for highways, homes, and factories, the use of chemical fertilizers makes it possible to reap larger harvests on fewer acres.

ACTIVITY 44   Writing a Paragraph Answer to a Question   **W**

As an answer to one of the following questions, write a good paragraph with a definite topic sentence.   In the topic sentence repeat the key words of the question.

If you need to, check your facts in your science or social studies textbook, but close the textbook before you begin to write.

1. How did the main character in one of the stories you read this term influence another character?
2. How does jet propulsion work?
3. What causes the aurora borealis?
4. What is a major cause of traffic accidents?
5. What does a program of reforestation include?
6. What are the steps in the life cycle of a clothes moth?
7. What causes rain?
8. What can you do to prevent fire in your home?
9. Why is crop rotation essential?
10. How are jurors in your local courts selected?

ACTIVITY 45   Drawing Conclusions from Your Reading   **OR**

On the basis of what you have read in this chapter, state in your own words a one-sentence definition for the following: a paragraph, a topic sentence, a clincher sentence, a spelunker, and folklore.

ACTIVITY 46   Writing a Summarizing Paragraph   **W**

Review the points made in this chapter and write a paragraph with the following topic sentence: *There are certain key suggestions to keep in mind when writing a paragraph.*

ACTIVITY 47   Word Study   **VW**

1. What is the derivation of the word *paragraph?*
2. The following words were used in this chapter. What does each mean in the sentence in which it appeared?   (The page number is after each word.)

furrow	50	elastic	65	equilibrium	69
inverted	53	retiring	65	cavorting	71
hazards	53	haunts	65	ceremonial	71
precautions	56	aggressive	65	throng	72
augmented	58	spontaneity	65	apathetic	72
appreciably	62	exhilarating	66	prized	75
negligible	64	surmounted	67	nutritive	80

5 *Paragraphs for Every Purpose*

True ease in writing comes from art, not chance.—ALEXANDER POPE

ON A YOUTHFUL PORTRAIT OF
ROBERT LOUIS STEVENSON

A FACE of youth maturing; a mouth of tender,
    Sad human sympathy yet something store
In clasp of lip: wide eyes of calmist splendor,
    And brow severely ample and heroic;—
The features—all—lit with a soul ideal....
    O visionary boy! what were you seeing,
What hearing, as you stood thus midst the real
    Ere yet one master-work of yours had being?

Is it a foolish fancy that we humor—
    Investing daringly with life and spirit
This youthful portrait of you Ere one rumor
    Of your great future spoke that men might hear it?—
Is it a fancy, or your first of glories,
    That you were listening, and the camera drew you
Hearing the voices of your untold stories
    And all your lovely poems calling to you?

— James Whitcomb Riley.

You learn to ski by skiing. You learn to swim by swimming.
In the same way you learn to write by writing. There is no substitute
for practice. Don't think you haven't the experiences or the knowledge. Willa Cather once said, "Most of the basic material a writer
works with is acquired before the age of fifteen."

Perhaps you are overwhelmed by the thought of writing long
compositions. One antidote for this fear is practicing on shorter
units: sentences and paragraphs. Chapter 4 introduced ways of developing paragraphs and suggested devices for making your paragraphs more effective. This chapter will provide additional help in
writing typical short paragraphs. Then it will move on to the longer,
more involved paragraph. After this you will be shown how to link
your paragraphs together, how to create a block of paragraphs.
With this groundwork, later writing assignments in the text will be
more manageable.

WHY WRITE?

The desire to write grows with writing.—ERASMUS

Why bother taking time to acquire writing skills?   Logan Pearsall Smith wrote, "The great art of writing is the art of making people real to themselves with words."   Writing can help you deepen your own experiences, sharpen your observations, understand yourself better, and share your experiences with others.   Very often you do not know what you think until you have to write your thoughts down.

Of course, writing has vocational value as well.   Many jobs require some ability to put ideas and experiences on paper.   Letters, reports, notices, memoranda—these are all common in many jobs. Practice in writing is a must for college-bound students too.   There is no better way to practice than to work with paragraphs.

KINDS OF WRITING

Writing is sometimes divided into four major areas: exposition (or explanation), description, narration (or storytelling), and argumentation.   These divisions are convenient for talking about writing, but few compositions are wholly of one type or another.   Categories frequently overlap.   A good story often includes description or explanation.   A good argument often uses explanation.   A longer composition may include all four types of writing.   Still, for talking about writing, the categories are useful.   They remind us of the basic aims and purposes of writing.

The previous chapter explored ways of developing paragraphs— by use of details, examples, comparisons, and other methods.   This chapter shows how different kinds of paragraphs can be developed by one or more of the methods previously studied.

EXPOSITORY PARAGRAPHS

Expository writing seeks to inform.   It presents ideas and facts, situations and problems.   It often increases the reader's knowledge about some person, process, or area of living.   Chapter 8 deals with the longer explanation, but shorter units are worth examining too. Even a single paragraph can be a complete explanation, informative and challenging.

The following examples of expository paragraphs provide variety in development, but all of them seek to inform.   They suggest the possibilities and diversity of the expository paragraph.

1

To form a good bridge in holding the cue stick in pool, wrap your left index finger around the top of the cue, then set your left hand down firmly on the table. Your curled index finger and thumb should now touch. Spread the other three fingers out on the table. Be sure the heel of your left hand rests on the table, and you have a good solid bridge. This bridge supports the cue which moves through it. The tension of your curled index finger should not be so tight that the cue jams, nor so loose that the cue wobbles. Try it too tight, then too loose, then just right. Some players apply a thin dusting of talcum powder to the fingers of the left hand so the cue slides smoothly.—WALTER W. ARNDT, *Modern Maturity*

2

An autumn weekend without football is like a Fourth of July without fireworks. One might say that football is the trademark of fall in the United States. From early September, when the last blast of summer has passed, till January, when the barren trees have had their first taste of snow, everyone, male and female, young and old, is affected by the inescapable spirit of the sport. Whether it be high school, college, or professional, the excitement, tension, and pageantry are ever present and distinguish it from other sports in the United States. All fans look forward to the crisp autumn weekend when they can pile into a car and drive off to their favorite campus or stadium.—STUDENT WRITER

3

Once you begin to study it, all nature is equally interesting and equally charged with beauty. I was shown a picture by Cezanne of a blank wall of a house, which he had made distinct with the most delicate lights and colors. Now I often amuse myself when I am looking at a wall or a flat surface of any kind by trying to distinguish all the different colors and tints which can be discerned upon it, and considering whether these arise from reflections or from natural hue. You would be astonished the first time you tried this to see how many and what beautiful colors there are even in the most commonplace objects, and the more carefully and frequently you look the more variations do you perceive.— WINSTON CHURCHILL, *Thoughts and Adventures*

4

There is a cheap literature that speaks to us of the need of escape. It is true that when we travel we are in search of distance. But distance is not to be found. It melts away. And escape has never led anywhere. The moment a man finds that he must play the races, go to the Arctic, or make war in order to feel himself alive, that man has begun to spin the strands that bind him to other men and the world. But what stretched strands! A civilization that is really strong fills man to the brim, though he never stir. What we are worth when motionless is the question.— ANTOINE DE SAINT-EXUPÉRY, *Flight to Arras,* translated by Lewis Galantiere

5

As soon as you begin to take yourself seriously and imagine that your virtues are important because they are yours, you become the prisoner of your own vanity and even your best works will blind and deceive you. Then, in order to defend yourself, you will begin to see sins and faults everywhere in the actions of other men. And the more unreasonable importance you attach to yourself and to your own works, the more you will tend to build up your own idea of yourself by condemning other people. Some of the most virtuous men in the world are also the bitterest and most unhappy because they have unconsciously come to believe that all their happiness depends on their being more virtuous than other men.—THOMAS MERTON, *Seeds of Contemplation*

ACTIVITY 1   Studying Expository Paragraphs   S

After reading the preceding paragraphs, be ready to answer these questions.

Paragraph 1

1. Is the explanation presented in understandable order? Could you pick up a cue stick and hold it properly after reading the paragraph? Point out examples of good explanation.
2. What is a bridge as defined in the paragraph?

Paragraph 2

3. Does the writer present a favorable picture of the football season? Point out words and expressions to prove your case.
4. How does the clincher sentence support the topic sentence?

Paragraph 3

5. What examples does Winston Churchill supply to support his topic sentence?
6. Has this paragraph suggested to you a new way of looking at things? Explain.

Paragraph 4

7. Which sentence of the paragraph seems to you the better topic sentence, the first or the last? Explain.
8. What examples does Saint-Exupéry include of activities he does not consider essential to living?

Paragraph 5

9. How can a person become a "prisoner of his own vanity"? What is Thomas Merton's attitude toward those who condemn other people? How can virtuous people be unhappy?
10. Explain in your own words what the first sentence means to you.

ACTIVITY 2   Writing an Expository Paragraph   W

Using one or more of the paragraphs discussed in Activity 1 as a guide, write a clear, informative expository paragraph. Plan your paragraph (pages 76–77). Be sure it sticks to its subject. You may use one of the topic sentences on the following page or one from an activity in Chapter 4.

1. We need friends as much as we need food and air.
2. If you want to know what someone is like, notice how that person spends money (drives a car, plays a game, or speaks to younger people).
3. The weakest part of a modern automobile is . . .
4. The best way to plan for an examination is to relax.
5. I have a secret recipe for making great . . .
6. I have three recommendations for a rainy day.
7. If your garden is less than forty square feet, you can still grow some vegetables successfully.
8. Serving food at a fast-food chain is a marvel of efficiency.
9. The problems of surf-casting are different from those of fishing from a boat.
10. The basic plan of football (or some other game) is not difficult to understand.

ACTIVITY 3   Writing a Paragraph on a Proverb   W

Proverbs are folk wisdom, derived from the experiences of generations of people. They express general truths, but truth can be

elusive.   Proverbs may conflict: "Many hands make light work."
"Too many cooks spoil the broth."   Still, they often make excellent
topic sentences for expository paragraphs.

Choose one of the following lesser-known proverbs as a topic
sentence.   Using the checklist on page 77 as a guide, write a paragraph supporting the topic sentence you have chosen.

1. The brightest of all things, the sun, has its spots.
2. A little neglect may breed great mischief.
3. The winds and the waves are always on the side of the ablest navi-
   gators.
4. True merit is like a river: the deeper it is, the less noise it makes.
5. A false friend is worse than an open enemy.
6. A good word costs no more than a bad one.
7. If you don't have what you like, you must like what you have.
8. Nothing is positively certain but uncertainty.
9. Wise men change their minds, fools never.
10. Understand your opponent before you answer him.

ACTIVITY 4   Writing a Paragraph on a Quotation   **W**

Like proverbs, famous quotations often make good topic sentences.   Choose one of the following quotations as a topic sentence and write a paragraph supporting the sentence you have chosen.

1. Education is that which remains after one has forgotten everything he learned in school.—ALBERT EINSTEIN
2. The only way to have a friend is to be one.—RALPH WALDO EMERSON
3. He who has never learned to obey cannot be a good commander.— ARISTOTLE
4. Nothing is particularly hard if you divide it into small jobs.—HENRY FORD
5. Laugh, and the world laughs with you; weep, and you weep alone.— ELLA WHEELER WILCOX
6. The only thing sure about luck is that it will change.—BRET HARTE
7. Repetition does not transform a lie into a truth.—FRANKLIN D. ROOSEVELT
8. Too often we enjoy the comfort of opinion without the discomfort of thought.—JOHN F. KENNEDY
9. The love we give away is the only love we keep.—ELBERT HUBBARD
10. To me, faith means not worrying.—JOHN DEWEY

Humorous Paragraphs

Expository paragraphs need not be grimly serious.   There is plenty of room for fun and wry observation, as this example by G. K. Chesterton demonstrates.

Roughly speaking, there are three kinds of people in this world.   The first kind of people are People; they are the largest and probably the most valuable class.   We owe to this class the chairs we sit down on, the clothes we wear, the houses we live in, and, indeed (when we come to think of it), we probably belong to this class ourselves.   The second class may be called for convenience the Poets; they are often a nuisance to their families, but, generally speaking, a blessing to mankind.   The third class is that of the Professors or Intellectuals, sometimes described as the thoughtful people; and these are a blight and a desolation both to their families and also to mankind.   Of course, the classification sometimes overlaps, like all classification.   Some good people are almost poets, and some bad poets are almost professors.   But the division follows lines of real psychological cleavage.   I do not offer it lightly.   It has been the fruit of more than eighteen minutes of earnest reflection and research.— G. K. CHESTERTON, "On Running After One's Hat"

ACTIVITY 5   Studying a Humorous Paragraph   S

Look once again at the Chesterton paragraph and prepare to answer these questions.

1. What is the topic sentence?
2. What three types of people are there according to Chesterton?
3. What humorous touches reveal the author's intention—not to be taken seriously?
4. How does the final sentence clinch the humorous tone of the paragraph?

ACTIVITY 6   Writing a Humorous Paragraph   W

Try your hand at a humorous paragraph, using one of the following topic sentences as a starter.   Be sure to support your topic sentence with examples, details, comparisons, or some other technique (pages 57–68).

1. Roughly speaking, there are three kinds of dogs (cats, athletes, newscasters, movie stars, students, or some other) in this world.
2. Worrying can be good for you.
3. When I was young, I always thought that . . .
4. New brooms sweep clean, but they also raise a lot of dust.
5. People watchers have more fun.
6. Who said a dog's life is all that bad?
7. Dishwashing can be a fine art.
8. Who's afraid of horror movies?
9. Among the devil's inventions the alarm clock must rank very high.
10. Choosing a hat (dress, suit, sport jacket, skirt, pair of slacks, pair of shoes, or some other) can be hard on the nervous system.

DESCRIPTIVE PARAGRAPHS

Descriptive writing seeks to recreate reality by drawing a picture in words.   It may be of two kinds: informational and technical or imaginative and fictional.   The former resembles a snapshot.   The latter resembles a painting.

Informational and technical description may be found in catalogs, textbooks, court records, and news accounts.   Imaginative description may be found in creative writing of all kinds: personal essays, novels, short stories, and plays.   Both kinds of description have their place. Chapter 7 deals with observing and describing in the longer composition, but descriptive paragraphs provide excellent preparation for these later assignments.

The following examples of descriptive paragraphs provide variety in development, but all of them seek to present a picture.

1

There is another sort of day which needs celebrating in song—the day when spring at last holds up her face to be kissed, deliberate and unabashed. On that day no wind blows either in the hills or in the mind; no chill finds the bone. It is a day which can come only in a northern climate, where there has been a long background of frigidity, a long deficiency of sun.—E. B. WHITE, *One Man's Meat*

2

Nowhere in all the sea does life exist in such bewildering abundance as in the surface waters. From the deck of a vessel you may look down, hour after hour, on the shimmering disks of jellyfish, their gently pulsating bells dotting the surface as far as you can see. Or one day you may notice early in the morning that you are passing through a sea that has taken on a brick-red color from billions upon billions of microscopic creatures, each of which contains an orange pigment granule. At noon you are still moving through red seas, and when darkness falls the waters shine with an eerie glow from the phosphorescent fires of yet more billions and trillions of these same creatures.—RACHEL L. CARSON, *The Sea around Us*

3

Wellington, the capital of New Zealand, in the North Island, was no more than a frontier settlement a hundred years ago, a scattering of wooden huts at the western edge of the deep, hill-encircled harbor. Today a vigorous young city stretches along the narrow foreshore and climbs the Tinakori Hills behind. Sections of the waterfront have been built on reclaimed lands. Trams rattle along the quays almost in the shadow of the overseas liners. Warehouses—baled wool and crated butter—overtop the tide; and where the Town Hall now stands, old wharf-piles have been discovered.—GEOFFREY GRIGSON and CHARLES HARVARD GIBBS-SMITH (eds.), *Places*

ACTIVITY 7 Studying Descriptive Paragraphs S

Select one of the model descriptive paragraphs and be ready to answer these questions.

1. What is the topic sentence? Is it a good guide to the paragraph? Does the paragraph support the topic sentence?
2. What vivid, picture-making words does the writer introduce?
3. Does the paragraph present a striking picture? Explain.

A description of a person is sometimes called a "character sketch." Magazine articles and book-length biographies try to capture someone's personality in words. The short, paragraph-length character sketch is a challenge of a different kind. The subject of a character sketch may be an actual person or a fictional character.

Note how each of the following paragraph sketches tries to capture a personality in a short space.

1

Small, ugly, vital, with keen blue eyes, Turner* was the son of a London barber and of a butcher's daughter of ungovernable temper, which brought her to the madhouse. As a boy Turner was "singular," "silent," "exclusively devoted to his drawing," intolerant of society, indifferent to theatres or music, and with no "faculty for friendship." As a man he took care that little should be known of his private life: he was secretive, lonely (he never married), sharp-tongued in self-defense, stingy, and always immensely active, energetic, and productive.—GEOFFREY GRIGSON and CHARLES HARVARD GIBBS-SMITH (eds.), *People*

2

Huckleberry was cordially hated and dreaded by all the mothers of the town, because he was idle and lawless and vulgar and bad—and because all their children admired him so, and delighted in his forbidden society, and wished they dared to be like him. Tom was like the rest of the respectable boys, in that he envied Huckleberry his gaudy outcast condition, and was under strict orders not to play with him. So he

*Joseph Mallord William Turner, famous English painter (1775–1851)

played with him every time he got a chance. Huckleberry was always dressed in the cast-off clothes of full-grown men, and they were in perennial bloom and fluttering with rags. His hat was a vast ruin with a wide crescent lopped out of its brim; his coat, when he wore one, hung nearly to his heels and had the rearward buttons far down the back; but one suspender supported his trousers; the seat of the trousers bagged low and contained nothing; the fringed legs dragged in the dirt when not rolled up.—MARK TWAIN, *The Adventures of Tom Sawyer*

ACTIVITY 8   Studying Character Sketches   S

Reread the character sketches and be ready to answer these questions.

1. What kind of person was Joseph Turner? What words best reveal his personality?
2. What contradictory personality traits did Turner seem to have according to the writer of the paragraph?
3. Why was Huckleberry Finn so appealing a companion to the other boys in town?
4. What specific details does Mark Twain introduce to show Huckleberry Finn to you?

ACTIVITY 9   Writing a Descriptive Paragraph   W

Using the model descriptive paragraphs as a guide, write a descriptive paragraph of your own. Perhaps the following verse or one of the topics on the next page will give you an idea for a paragraph.

> I have a feeling of contentment
> As I look up to the sky,
> Because I'm filled with turkey
> And also pumpkin pie.—STUDENT WRITER

1. What a meal!
2. Thanksgiving (Christmas, Fourth of July, or other holiday)
3. My brother (sister, mother, father, aunt, or any other relative)
4. My grandmother's house (or another place)
5. A favorite room (automobile, pet, TV program, school subject, or hobby)

NARRATIVE PARAGRAPHS

When something happens, we use narration to tell about it. Narration is the reporting of incidents and experiences as in storytelling (Chapter 6). Narrative paragraphs tend to be shorter than expository or descriptive paragraphs.

The narrative paragraph may have a topic sentence, as in the following opening paragraph of a short story. The first sentence sets the mood of the paragraph.

I hurriedly put one arm in my khaki raincoat, opened the front door, ran out, and slammed it. I rushed down our multicolored flagstone walk. I angrily groped for the other sleeve of my raincoat and ran faster as I crossed the street at the corner. I went through the stately, wrought iron gate of Memorial Park, my haven in times of anguish.—STUDENT WRITER

ACTIVITY 10   Writing a Narrative Paragraph

Choose one of the following topic sentences, and write a narrative paragraph, including examples and details to support your topic sentence. Keep your paragraph simple and brief. Stick to the topic. Don't branch out and include experiences not suggested by the topic sentence.

1. What I meant to say didn't come out the way I intended.
2. I'll never forget one special moment on my trip to Arizona (or some other place).
3. I rolled up my sleeves and began to work.
4. Last week I experienced a very strange coincidence.
5. I planned to relax all morning, but something upset my plans.
6. The rain kept coming down, and we kept getting more nervous.
7. When the doorbell rang, I wasn't ready for what happened next.
8. I thought the game was lost, but suddenly everything changed.
9. I spilled the glass of water, and the fun began.
10. Last Monday (or other day) was a disaster (constant joy) from breakfast to bedtime.

Starting a New Paragraph

Since narrative paragraphs are usually links in a longer story, they often do not have topic sentences. The writer begins a new paragraph when she changes the time, place, action, or speaker, but she seldom constructs a narrative paragraph as formally as an expository or descriptive paragraph. Turn to page 116 and notice where the author of "Earthquake" begins each new paragraph.

Notice, too, how a student tells the following short story with three vivid paragraphs. She begins her second paragraph when the narrator approaches the stallion. She begins her third paragraph as the narrator swings into the saddle.

The red stallion tossed his head in terror. He jerked back and half bucked. The two men who held his head stood firm. The stallion trembled, his eyes rolling, lather running down his flanks. The rest of the men mounted the corral fence.

I walked up to the stallion, gathered the reins in my hand, and stepped into the stirrup. I had decided to ignore the warnings of the men. Usually I checked the cinch strap, but that time I hadn't. It was the worst mistake I ever made.

I swung into the saddle easily and gave the signal to the men. They loosened their hold on the bridle and raced to the fence. As the red began rearing, I took off my dusty grey stetson and began fanning him. The raucous cries of the men filled the air when suddenly I heard, or rather felt, the cinch snap. The saddle slipped a little, but I held tight to it. My stetson flew through the air, and I soon followed it.—STUDENT WRITER

Dialog Paragraphs

Some narrative paragraphs consist entirely of dialog. For the sake of clarity a new paragraph begins with each new speaker, as in the following example.

"Mom, please tell Mike to get out of the bathroom. I've got to brush my teeth. By the way, Mom, will you press my blue dress right away? This green one looks utterly decrepit; and besides, Jane has one just like it. Mike, get out of there!"

"All right. I'll get out . . . for a dime, but I have to see the dime first."

"Mom, will you make the little monster get out?"

"All right, Mike, get out of the bathroom so Lou can brush her teeth before Bill comes. You've had your fun."

"O.K. Here I come. Out of the way!"

"Mike, you monster. Just wait till I can get my hands on you. Bill will be here in a minute, and I haven't brushed my teeth . . . Mom, something dreadful has happened!"

"What's wrong, dear?"

"I just washed my mouth with bubble bath. Ohh, Mike, you've done it again!"—STUDENT WRITER

ACTIVITY 11   Studying Dialog Paragraphs   S

Reread the preceding dialog and be prepared to answer the following questions.

1. How many characters are there in the short dialog? How do you know?
2. How can you tell when each one begins to speak?
3. What happens in this narrative? How can you tell?

Identifying the Speaker

The preceding brief story consists entirely of dialog without actually identifying the speakers. Usually in narrative, speakers are identified. Often other explanatory material is included. The student might have expanded the third paragraph from the end in the following way.

"Mike, you monster. Just wait till I can get my hands on you. Bill will be here in a minute, and I haven't brushed my teeth."
Lou goes into the bathroom and begins to brush her teeth. Her face suddenly shows disbelief and annoyance. She cries out in anguish, "Mom, something dreadful has happened!"

The original version omits explanations and relies on the reader to set the stage himself. A good general rule is be clear, but be simple. The fewer words you need to tell your story and get the effect you want, the better.

ACTIVITY 12   Writing Dialog Paragraphs   W

Listen to a conversation in school, at home, in a public place, or on television and record four or five paragraphs of dialog. Begin a new paragraph when you change speakers. Review correct punctuation of quotations (pages 298–300). Be tactful in reporting the dialog.

ARGUMENTATIVE PARAGRAPHS

Argumentation seeks to persuade and to convince by presenting the writer's opinions. It often takes a position on some topic and urges its readers to take some action. It usually relies on facts, evidence, examples, and reasons. Argumentation, of course, often requires explanation.

The following paragraphs present the writers' viewpoints.

1

If you'd like an exciting, informative, fairly inexpensive hobby, collect autographs. The chase is part of the fun as you try to get the signature of a television star, an outstanding athlete, or a prominent government official. You will be gaining knowledge and some surprises too. You will learn, for example, that signatures of some early Presidents are more common than signatures of some recent Presidents. You needn't spend a fortune on your collection, however. Most of the signatures can be gained right now with a little persistence, ingenuity, and luck. For many people, autograph collecting beats collecting stamps, coins, or minerals.

2

The United States needs a consistent, long-range energy plan. Oil shortages and price increases have demonstrated how dependent the United States is on energy. Supplies of oil are not unlimited. Even if the United States were to become independent of other oil-producing countries, the specter of depletion would remain. Other forms of energy must be explored: greater use of coal, use of solar energy, and more efficient harnessing of natural forces like tides and rivers. Even the great question of nuclear energy must be grappled with. We must look ahead— ten, twenty, fifty years, or longer. We cannot, in any case, afford to drift.

ACTIVITY 13   Studying Argumentative Paragraphs   S

1. What reasons does the first paragraph give for collecting autographs? Does the paragraph make a strong case for the hobby? Explain.
2. Why, according to the second paragraph, does the United States need a long-range energy plan? How does the final sentence return to the topic sentence?
3. Look at the first two paragraphs of this chapter (page 83). How does the first paragraph support the topic sentence (the third sentence of the paragraph)? What suggestions does the second paragraph make for learning to write longer compositions?

ACTIVITY 14   Writing an Argumentative Paragraph   W

Do you have strong feelings about some law, procedure, custom, regulation, point of view, or governmental policy? State your opinion in a topic sentence and then write the paragraph supporting your topic sentence. Plan your paragraph (page 76). Use connectives (pages 72–76). Stick to your topic (page 68).

EXAMPLE   Pay television is (or is not) the direction in which television in the United States must move.

ACTIVITY 15   Writing an Argumentative Paragraph   W

Using the model paragraphs as guides, plan and write a composition using one of the following topic sentences. Be sure to support the topic sentence with details, examples, reasons, comparisons, or some other device. Stick to your topic.

1. The best kind of hunting is done with a camera.
2. The mountain lion (hyena, Siamese cat, Doberman pinscher, or other animal) deserves a better reputation than it has.
3. The behavior of fans at sporting events needs some improvement.
4. Young and old must work at narrowing the generation gap.
5. Black studies should be included in the school curriculum.
6. School examinations should be more frequent but less important.
7. Teaching students to listen is as important as teaching them to read.
8. Every student should be required to pass a swimming test before graduation.
9. The space program should be expanded, not cut back.
10. The federal government should (or should not) administer the welfare system.

MULTIPURPOSE PARAGRAPHS

The four forms of writing frequently overlap. Often you will be writing a paragraph that may include narration and description, exposition and argumentation, or other combinations. In the following paragraphs, description and exposition combine for the effects sought by the writers. They are developed differently, however. The first paragraph uses details (pages 59–61) to support the topic sentence. The second paragraph is developed by comparison and contrast (pages 63–67).

1

How quiet and in some ways refreshing a rainy Sunday afternoon can feel when there is nobody home and no place to go. Somehow just the thought of all the things you should be doing draws you closer to the rain-streaked window and the colorless sky. You may rest your chin on the window sill and in doing so watch the journey of a raindrop down the pane. How many miles has it traveled? What has it seen? It might have been part of the ocean once, a minute part of the whole. Once it might have nestled in the grasses and listened to the conspiracies against kings. It might have been part of a storm, crippling communities, or the rainfall which ended a drought. It is probable that it has changed whole lives. However, no matter where it has been, it has lived.—STUDENT WRITER

2

A tree in its old age is like a bent but mellowed and wise old man; it inspires our respect and tender admiration; it is too noble to need our pity. We take the fading of flowers very lightly; it is regrettable to see them go, but we know they are not sentient beings; they cannot regret their fresh tints, nor know when the firm fine form begins to droop. But the old age of a butterfly, the fading of its colors, the dog-earing of its brave frail wings, is a pitiful thing, for if the butterfly does not know that it is beautiful, it certainly knows when it is buffeted by the winds, and weighted and abraded by the autumn rains.—DONALD CULROSS PEATTIE, *An Almanac for Moderns*

Methods of developing a paragraph may also be combined. A writer may use details, examples, comparisons, and contrasts—or any combination—within a single paragraph. (Review pages 57–68).

ACTIVITY 16 Studying Multipurpose Paragraphs   S

Read the following paragraphs and be ready to answer these questions.

1. The first paragraph is basically descriptive, but Thoreau also expresses a point of view about nature. What is that point of view? Where is it expressed?
2. *Delicious* is a word usually reserved for taste or smell. How does Thoreau enlarge the meaning of the word? Does he use it appropriately? Explain.
3. What senses does Thoreau appeal to? What sense-arousing words does he use to recreate his experience?
4. How does Moss Hart combine description and exposition in supporting his statement that the first performance of a play is difficult for the playwright?
5. Point out details, examples, and contrast in the second paragraph.
6. Did you find any of Hart's statements humorous? Explain.

1

This is a delicious evening, when the whole body is one sense, and imbibes delight through every pore. I go and come with a strange liberty in Nature, a part of herself. As I walk along the stony shore of the pond in my shirt sleeves, though it is cool as well as cloudy and windy, and I

see nothing special to attract me, all the elements are unusually congenial to me. The bullfrogs trump to usher in the night, and the note of the whippoorwill is borne on the rippling wind from over the water. Sympathy with the fluttering alder and poplar leaves almost takes away my breath; yet, like the lake, my serenity is rippled but not ruffled. These small waves raised by the evening wind are as remote from storm as the smooth reflecting surface. Though it is now dark, the wind still blows and roars in the wood, the waves still dash, and some creatures lull the rest with their notes. The repose is never complete. The wildest animals do not repose, but seek their prey now; the fox, and skunk, and rabbit now roam the fields and woods without fear. They are Nature's watchmen—links which connect the days of animated life.—HENRY DAVID THOREAU, *Walden*

2

The initial performance, the raising of a curtain on a play before its very first audience, is for me at least the worst two hours of that play's existence, whatever its subsequent fate may be. No one really knows anything much about a play until it meets its first audience: not its directors, its actors, its producers, and least of all its author. The scenes he has counted on most strongly, his favorite bits of fine writing—the delicately balanced emotional or comedic thrusts, the witty, ironic summing up, the wry third-act curtain with its caustic stinging last line that adroitly illuminates the theme—these are the things that are most likely to go down the drain first, sometimes with an audible thud. The big scene in the second act, or the touching speech that reflects all of the author's personal philosophy—that cherished mosaic of words on which he has secretly based his hopes for the Pulitzer Prize or at the very least the Drama Critics Award—such things the audience invariably will sit silently but politely through, patiently waiting for the reappearance of that delightful minor character, who was tossed in only to highlight the speech, or for an echo of that delicious little scene which was written only as a transition to the big one.—MOSS HART, *Act One*

ACTIVITY 17 Writing a Multipurpose Paragraph   W

Each of the following sentences may lend itself to mixed development—narration and description, description and exposition, narration and exposition, description and argumentation, or other combination. Choose one of the topic sentences and in a well-developed paragraph support the statement. Follow the suggestions for planning (page 76). Use the checklist (page 77) as a final guide before turning in your paper.

1. I have an idea for a great timesaving invention.
2. Giving the vote to eighteen-year-olds has had some unexpected results.
3. I thought I was being considerate, but my friend did not agree.
4. Green is beautiful—a green thumb, that is.
5. After a particular experience I had had, I vowed I'd never worry again.
6. For a change of taste, try . . . instead of . . .
7. I've had boring evenings before, but last night was the worst.
8. I once thought that airplanes were meant for looking at, not flying in.
9. You don't have to spend a lot of money to have a good time in . . .
10. A most interesting hobby is making useful things out of junk.

WRITING SEVERAL PARAGRAPHS

A writer often needs more than a single paragraph to develop an idea. She will then develop a group of paragraphs, sometimes called the paragraph block, to handle her discussion. You, too, will often find it necessary to develop an idea with several paragraphs.

Just as a good paragraph will have one main idea, so too will a good composition have one central idea. In planning a longer composition, first state your central idea in a sentence. Then list the topics that will help you explain it.   Each topic will become the subject of a paragraph.   For a four-paragraph composition on a school club, for example, the paragraph topics might be listed as follows:

THE PRINTING SQUAD

CENTRAL IDEA   Membership in the Printing Squad will provide fun for the student and service to the school.

PLAN   1. Purpose of the squad   or   1. What the squad is
       2. Membership requirements   2. How you can join
       3. Activities of the squad   3. What the squad does
       4. Advantages of membership   4. Why you should join

Next, plan each paragraph.   Choose topic sentences that will tell the reader what to expect.   Help him to go from one paragraph to the next with expressions like those discussed on page 75.

Read the following composition and try to decide how the student planned and wrote his composition.

I guess almost everyone has a mental quirk of some sort, but I think I discovered an extreme case of imbalance in my own family.   My brother had cyclomania.   He was absolutely nuts about bicycles—not ordinary ones, but a strange species with multiple gears and double chains, adorned with gadgets designed to confuse the layman and send fanatics like my brother into ecstasy.   For a period of almost ten months he talked, slept, and thought bicycles.

It all started innocently enough with a job at a bicycle shop.   "A summer job," he said, "nothing more."   Then it happened!   He was infected with the germ.   For him it was a pleasant disease, but for the rest of the family it was a very odd experience.   After he landed the job at the shop, he would spend almost all of his money on equipment for bicycles.

   After work he would seclude himself in his laboratory, the garage, to create.   Often he would stay there past twelve o'clock, piecing together the gears and parts for a rear wheel or straightening one of five European racing frames.   On occasion I've gone out to the garage to find my demented brother crouching over a pile of fantastic objects, pushing them around on the pavement like an alchemist with an experiment.   Then he'd walk over to one of the partly assembled bicycles and add the apparatus to it.   His greasy hands clutched at the tools as he made adjustments to the thing.   Then, setting down the tools and aiming the bicycle at the open door, he and his creation would flash out into the darkness

for another test. That was almost all he did, not often riding for pleasure, but always working or testing. In a minute or two he'd fly back through the door and screech to a stop.

"The oil cup doesn't drip right and the derailleur cable isn't pulling on gear nine enough to mesh properly. And that," he said, drawing a deep breath, "will ruin my twelve-dollar free-wheel. Hand me the wrench."

To this very day when I go out into the garage, I can see the dormant spores of this rare disease in the form of nuts, gears, and various other parts, waiting for some susceptible being. While in the garage, I walk carefully because I've seen the disease that turns sane people into technical maniacs. I want no part of cyclomania.—STUDENT WRITER

The student probably got the idea for his composition as he thought one day about his brother's interest in bicycles. This was no ordinary interest, so the student decided on the word *cyclomania*. He had to state the theme of his composition, so he wrote the opening two sentences as the topic of the paragraph and of the longer composition to come.

Paragraphing was the next problem. The student summarized the problem in his first paragraph, telling about his brother's ten-month interest in bicycles. Where should the next paragraph begin? Logically enough, it should begin at the beginning. The student used as the first sentence of his second paragraph a statement of how it all began. Why begin the third paragraph at "After work"? This represented a new place, the laboratory, where his brother spent most of his time. The student chose a quotation to begin the next paragraph. The final paragraph was planned as a summary of the composition with a few extra details to make it vivid.

The student used time and place words to tie parts of the composition together: *there, after, then, to this very day, on occasion.* Each paragraph developed as a unit in itself. But each paragraph also became part of the larger whole, with all details contributing to the single effect desired. He avoided extraneous details like the tricycle he had as a child or the time his father won a bike race.

ACTIVITY 18 Writing Several Paragraphs W

On one of the following subjects or another approved by your teacher, plan a composition of several paragraphs. State your central idea in a sentence and then list the topics that will help explain it. Plan the paragraphs and then write the composition. Don't forget the connectives between paragraphs. Check your spelling and punctuation (pages 462–478; 286–303).

1. Science fiction. 2. A science experiment. 3. Being a good school citizen. 4. My favorite magazine. 5. Soapbox derbies. 6. Training of an astronaut. 7. Fun with an aqualung. 8. I'm a collector. 9. My hobby. 10. Lifesaving. 11. Scouting. 12. Jet propulsion. 13. Planting a home vegetable garden. 14. Making a dress. 15. Building a model.

ACTIVITY 19 Writing Several Paragraphs W

Select one of the quotations below as the basis for a longer composition. Plan a composition of several paragraphs using the quotation as your opening statement. Be sure you link your paragraphs together. (You may, instead, use one of the quotations in Activity 4, page 90, if you have not already used it. This will be a much fuller treatment of the subject than in Activity 4.)

1. The art of conversation isn't lost—it's hidden behind the TV set.—
   SIDNEY BRODY
2. Happiness is a way station between too much and too little.—
   CHANNING POLLOCK
3. Music is not a drug, but a diet.—SIR HENRY HADOW
4. Nothing is really work unless you would rather be doing something else.—SIR JAMES BARRIE
5. Anger improves nothing except the arch of a cat's back.—COLEMAN COX

6. Happiness is a form of courage.—HOLBROOK JACKSON
7. Where all think alike, no one thinks very much.—WALTER LIPPMANN
8. If we don't stand for something, we will fall for anything.—IRENE DUNNE
9. A problem well stated is a problem half solved.—CHARLES F. KETTERING
10. Everybody has to be somebody to somebody to be anybody.— MALCOLM S. FORBES

ACTIVITY 20   Word Study   VW

The following words were used in this chapter. What does each mean in the sentence in which it appeared? (The page number is after each word.)

antidote	83	pulsating	92	depletion	99
diversity	84	granule	92	sentient	101
barren	85	quays	92	abraded	101
pageantry	85	secretive	93	imbibes	101
brim	86	perennial	94	congenial	102
blight	90	crescent	94	serenity	102
desolation	90	groped	95	subsequent	102
cleavage	90	raucous	96	quirk	104
unabashed	92	ingenuity	99	seclude	104
shimmering	92	specter	99	dormant	105

6   *Writing Narratives*

Ernest Hemingway, a great storyteller at work

Just as the guest of honor entered, Bud stepped on Princess's tail. Princess let out an anguished screech, and Bud dropped the tray of olives he was carrying. As olives started peppering the furniture and the guests, Wendy rushed to help Bud, upsetting a glass of lemonade. George, seeing Wendy's plight, bounded toward the scene of disaster.

"Watch out for that lamp!" cried Dad.

Wouldn't you like to know what happened next? Have you ever participated in a series of fast-moving events like these?

IT HAPPENED TO ME

You cannot live an ordinary week without having at least one experience worth sharing with others. Can you see the narrative possibilities even in fairly commonplace events? Can you tell your story effectively?

Notice how a student narrates the following vacation experience without wasting words or slowing the pace.

COUNTRY COMFORTS

"There's the hotel," my mother said. "After the long, hot ride, I'll be glad to get into an air-conditioned room."

"A cool shower will feel good too," agreed Dad as we pulled up to the door.

109

We strode confidently to the threshold and then backed away from a blast of hot air. My father looked at my mother and wrinkled his brow. He didn't say a word but walked resolutely into the lobby, followed by two weary females.

I gloomily remembered that glowing advertising folder: "Rest in country comfort in our luxurious air-conditioned hotel."

Dad walked to the desk and began talking to the clerk. Although I could not hear their conversation, I could see my father's face. It was red and getting redder. His eyes were wide and flashing as he rapped his knuckles on the desk. He suddenly turned and came over to us.

"Everything is fine," he said grimly. ."The air-conditioning system has broken down, the pool-filter system is out of operation, and there is a mix-up in our reservations. Every nearby hotel is solidly booked, and we're stuck here with emergency accommodations."

Our "accommodations" consisted of two rooms the size of walk-in closets. As they were just above the kitchen, kitchen heat was added to the accumulated natural variety. The bureau drawers were broken, and the tiny closets had no place for hangers. The poles had rotted and fallen to the floor. We struggled with one of the windows for ten minutes. When we finally pried it open, we found it had no screen. Dad looked thoughtfully at the army of unfriendly mosquitoes buzzing hungrily just outside the dusty window. Then he snapped his fingers and said, "Away from these country comforts and back to the city!"

I never did learn whether there was poison ivy on the lawn. — STUDENT WRITER

GUIDES FOR TELLING A STORY

1. Begin at once. Tell the "who," "what," "when," and "where" of your story, but don't waste words on a lengthy, unnecessary introduction.
2. When possible, arouse curiosity and keep your readers in suspense. Don't give away the point of your story at the beginning.
3. Tell the happenings in order.
4. Include all necessary information.
5. Picture the people, places, and action. Use the names of the people and places.
6. Quote directly. Make conversation lifelike.
7. Keep the story moving swiftly by omitting unnecessary words and details. Conclude briefly.
8. If the story is funny, don't tell how funny it is before you begin. Don't laugh louder than anyone else at the end.

9. Talk to your classmates, and talk in turn to pupils in different parts of the room. Look into their eyes, not at the ceiling or the floor.
10. Stand easily, not stiffly. Don't slouch or wriggle.
11. Speak distinctly. Pause after each sentence. Don't tie sentences together with *and, but, so, and-ur, but-ur,* or *so-ur.*
12. Use a pleasing voice.

ACTIVITY 1 Studying a Story   S

How well does "Country Comforts" follow guides 1–7? Point out effective examples of storytelling.

ACTIVITY 2 Choosing an Experience to Tell About   OS

List six of your experiences that you think might interest the class. Talk over the list with your classmates, and choose the idea that arouses the most interest. Then start thinking about how you will tell your story. These possibilities may suggest experiences.

1. One of your "firsts" — first trip by yourself, first date, first fight, first horseback ride, first part in a play
2. Embarrassing experience — being locked out, being lost, mistaking someone for another, forgetting something
3. Unexpected incident — startling discovery, misunderstanding, humorous accident.

JOT IT DOWN

Jot down everything you can recall on your chosen topic. Don't worry about the possible suitability of the items or the organization of your story. The flow of ideas at the beginning is an important aid to memory. One idea recalls another. Later you can exercise necessary critical judgment.

Now let's follow a story thread from beginning to final writing. This is the beginning of an idea list for a student's personal experience during an earthquake.

1. The weather was unusual.
2. The world suddenly turned to Jell-O.
3. There had been no warning of any disaster.
4. I thought we were being buried under an avalanche.
5. Everyone at the lodge was saved.
6. Some people were camping in the mountains nearby.
7. Our chimney caved in and showered stones on the lawn.
8. Etc.

ACTIVITY 3   Writing Your Idea List   **W**

As preparation for telling the experience chosen in Activity 2, jot down all the points you can remember, using the form just suggested.

PLAN YOUR STORY

"One day I lived through an earthquake. This event occurred two years ago. Or was it three? No, I think it was two because this was the year I went to the lodge. Well, anyway that morning I had played a lot of tennis. Then I had gone swimming. Then I decided to have another game of tennis."

By now you are saying to yourself, "This is one storyteller I'd like to tune out!" You have decided that a dramatic experience doesn't guarantee a dramatic storyteller. Some persons could make a trip to the moon sound dull.

Now that you have the raw materials in your idea list, exercise judgment in choosing details and organizing them.

GUIDES FOR PLANNING A STORY

1. Write a sentence summarizing what your story is about.
2. Jot down all the happenings you expect to cover in your story.
3. Arrange the points in the order things happened.
4. Cross out any happenings that are not needed or do not belong.
5. Add happenings that are needed to make your story complete and clear.

ACTIVITY 4   Planning Your Story   **SW**

Following the guides just given, make a plan for the story you have decided to tell the class (Activity 2).

EXAMPLE OF PLAN

This story is about how my family and I lived through an earthquake.

EARTHQUAKE

1. Bedtime — eerie quality of air
2. Beginning of quake — inside cabin
3. Turmoil outside cabin
4. The moving earth — my fear
5. Warning the others
6. The rest of the night — later tremors
7. The next morning — gigantic slide ten miles away
8. My reaction

CAPTURE YOUR AUDIENCE

Whenever I see Jell-O quivering in a cup, a shiver runs down my spine.

Don't you want to know why an innocent substance like Jell-O can terrify someone? A good storyteller captures attention at once.

A good way to begin is by having a character speak or think, or by showing a character in action. If the setting is particularly important in the story, start with a description that sets the stage. Try occasionally an exclamation or question.

WEAK   I once went to a party that featured a scavenger hunt.

BETTER   "Why in the world could you possibly want a golf club at nine in the evening?" Mother asked me.

ACTIVITY 5   Studying Story Beginnings   S

Which story beginning in each of the following pairs would be likely to attract more listeners? Why?

1. There was a new girl in our class. She had transferred to our school from Roanoke. I wanted to meet her, but I didn't have the courage for a long while. Then one day I was walking with my friend Lew Martin, and I told him I would speak to the girl. When I walked up to her, I was too shy at first to say anything.

"There's that new girl from Roanoke," I told Lew Martin. "I'm going to speak to her." I summoned up all my courage, straightened my shoulders, and strolled over to her. I opened my mouth, but no words came.

2. My grandfather sat hunched over the board, frowning. It was his move, and his king was in check. He stretched out his hand, let it hover for a moment over the threatened king, then drew it back. I sat mouse still, struggling to keep a solemn expression on my face.

Once in a while when my grandfather plays a game of chess with me, he has a pretty hard time of it. Usually he beats me fairly easily. But this one time I remember I managed to get him into a tight corner, and I tried hard not to show my excitement.

ACTIVITY 6   Beginning Your Story   OW

Write two trial beginnings for the story you planned in Activity 4. Use two of these five ways of starting: 1. Have yourself or another character speak or think. 2. Show a character in action. 3. Describe the time or place of the story. 4. Start with an exclamation. 5. Start with a question. When you have written your two story beginnings, read them to your classmates. Find out which they like better and why.

PICTURE ACTION

Let your characters speak and act for themselves. If you want to tell a story about your Aunt Miriam's mania for collecting things, don't just say "My Aunt Miriam loves to collect things." Observe her carefully, and describe what you see and hear in accurate, vivid detail. (See pages 125–127.) Call on your stock of vigorous verbs (page 264) and specific nouns (page 266) to show your aunt coming in from her afternoon walk, pulling pinecones, unusual mosses, feathers, and bits of wood from her coat pockets. Show her in her cluttered living room proudly exhibiting her shell collection. " 'And this is a rare one,' said Aunt Miriam, lifting a gaudy, orange-spotted shell from its cotton-lined box. . . ." Your audience will get the idea. Your aunt collects things!

USE CONVERSATION

Which is more exciting, more natural, and more interesting?

1. The repairman warned us not to go near the puddle of water because a high-voltage cable had come down as a result of the storm. This damage had made the water dangerous.
2. "Don't go near that puddle!" warned the repairman. "There's a high-voltage cable down from the storm. Touching that water would be suicide."

HINTS ON WRITING CONVERSATION

1. Make your conversation realistic. Observe the way you and the people around you talk. Practice imitating the talk of a variety of people. Study the dialog in good stories.
2. Write contracted forms as they are spoken — *I'm, we're, what's, who's, they're, don't, it's, doesn't* (page 475).
3. Do not overuse *said*. Find an accurate, vivid verb — *whispered, squeaked, muttered, croaked, shouted, laughed* — or omit *said* altogether if it is perfectly clear who is speaking.

ACTIVITY 7 Punctuating and Paragraphing Conversation   S

Study the conversation on pages 109–110 and answer these questions.

1. What punctuation marks enclose a direct quotation?
2. What punctuation ordinarily separates a direct quotation from the rest of the sentence?
3. In conversation when is a new paragraph begun?

Rewrite the following imaginary conversation between the captain of the *Titanic* and some of his crew, using dialog (pages 298–301). Begin a new paragraph each time the topic changes or a different person speaks.

EXAMPLE   The captain asked Murdock if the passengers were panicking, and Murdock said that they didn't know yet.

"Murdock," the captain demanded, "are the passengers panicking?" "They don't know yet," he replied.

IT ISN'T UNSINKABLE?

Captain Smith reached the ship's bridge, taking two steps of the ladder at a time.   He asked Murdoch, the First Officer, what had happened.   Murdoch said that they had hit an iceberg.   The captain asked if the bridge had been warned about the berg.   Murdoch explained that he had seen it moments after the forward lookouts had rung the warning bell.   Captain Smith asked what Murdoch had done then.   Murdoch told him that he had brought the ship's wheel hard to starboard and that he had reversed the engines.   Smith told him to stop the engines and to close the watertight doors.   Murdoch reported that both things had already been done.

Smith shouted for Fourth Officer Boxhall.   Boxhall appeared at the captain's side.   Smith told him to find the ship's carpenter and to get him to estimate the damage.   Smith then told him that after he had found the carpenter, he was to bring Thomas Andrews, the ship's designer, to the bridge.   Moments later the carpenter came to the bridge.   He told Captain Smith that the ship was taking water fast.   The carpenter then explained that the first five watertight compartments were flooded.   Andrews arrived on the bridge.   The captain gave him the carpenter's report.   Andrew slowly explained that with five compartments flooded the ship could not float.   Captain Smith thought to himself that it would be a busy night.

Choosing one of the following situations or another, retell a conversation you overheard or in which you took part.

1. Asking directions.   2. On the telephone.   3. At the game. 4. Buying something.   5. Walking down the street.   6. Discussing a new movie.   7. At the dinner table.   8. On the bus, train, or subway.

CHOOSE A GOOD TITLE

The title "Earthquake!" is more likely to arouse interest than "An Unusual Experience." Tailor your title to fit your story. "Lost on Mount Katahdin" is a better, more specific title than the vague "A Climbing Adventure." Arouse curiosity if you can.

ACTIVITY 10 Choosing Titles S

Which title in each of the following pairs is more interesting or, because it is narrower, more suitable for a brief story?

1. An Exciting Game
   Ten Seconds to Go

2. Mustard in the Ice Cream
   An Embarrassing Experience

3. My Canoe Trip
   When We Hit the Rapids

4. Ben and the Blue Ribbon
   At the Fair

Now you are ready to tell your story. Before you do, see how the student has followed the suggestions to create an exciting narrative about the earthquake.

EARTHQUAKE!

Whenever I see Jell-O quivering in a cup, a shiver runs down my spine. It reminds me of an August night in a mountain lodge when the solid earth came apart.

As I went to my cabin for the night, there was an almost eerie stillness in the air. Just before midnight I was suddenly awakened. The cabin had started to twist and buckle. The drawers of my dresser came flying out, and the stovepipe fell. At the same time I heard a horrible roar.

As I rushed from the cabin, I thought at first we were being buried under an avalanche. Then I realized that the rocks rolling across the lawn were from the chimney on the lodge. Every time I tried to take a step, the earth came up to meet me.

"Get out of the cabins!" I screamed. By this time the earth was swaying and buckling so severely I could hardly stand upright.

My parents rushed from their cabin and reinforced my cries: "Get out of the cabins!" Guests stumbled sleepily out onto the lawn.

After a few moments someone suggested, "We'd better stay in the cars the rest of the night." We all heartily agreed. During the night there were tremors, but none as severe as the first two. So the night passed.

The next morning we learned that a gigantic landslide only ten miles from the lodge had created a new lake on the Madison River. Sixty million tons of rock and earth had fallen to form a natural dam.

Although we were told later that the two initial shocks had lasted only two minutes each, I'm sure they had lasted twenty times as long. I know. I was there! — STUDENT WRITER

ACTIVITY 11   Telling Your Story   O

Using the plan you wrote for Activity 4 and the better of the two beginnings you wrote for Activity 6, prepare to tell your story to the class.   Review the Guides for Telling a Story, pages 110–111.   Practice telling your story at home or to friends first.   Then tell it in class.

ACTIVITY 12   Listening to Stories   L

As you listen to your classmates telling stories, rate the storytellers on the basis of the following points.

1. Did the storyteller follow the first seven guides?   Give examples to prove your answer.
2. What words made you see, hear, and feel with the storyteller?
3. Did she speak distinctly in a pleasing voice?   Did she stand easily erect and look at his audience?

ACTIVITY 13   Writing a Story   W

Using one of the following ideas or another idea from the list you considered in Activity 2, make a plan and write a story.   Start writing anywhere, but come back later and write a good beginning.   Lead up to a climax.   Picture the action, use conversation, and pick a good title.   See guides 1–7 on page 110.   Revise thoroughly, copy neatly, and check carefully.   Does every sentence begin with a capital letter and end with a period, a question mark, or an exclamation point (pages 278–285)?   Are the sentences, including direct quotations, punctuated correctly (pages 286–303)?

1. Unexpected victory.   2. One rainy night.   3. Friends to the end. 4. I try ice (or roller) skating.   5. The first money I ever earned. 6. Parent for a day.   7. Are dogs people?   8. Caught in the act. 9. Shopping woes.   10. I don't understand me.   11. My class demonstration.   12. My first day in ——.   13. A day to remember.   14. A lunchroom episode.   15. A camp experience.

WRITING YOUR AUTOBIOGRAPHY

What kind of person are you?   How did you get that way?   Think back.   What is your earliest memory?   What childhood experiences made the deepest impressions on you?   What do you know about your grandparents?   Who was your first real friend?   Were you ever punished unjustly?   What was your earliest ambition?   What has been your greatest disappointment?   Your greatest success?

When you write an autobiography, you write about what you know best — your own life. To make your autobiography entertaining, apply what you have learned about storytelling. Make yourself and your family sound like real people. Picture the action. Be as lively and amusing as you can, but tell the truth. As you think about your past, jot down memories and observations you might use.

Some classes write and bind books which they call "Chapters of Autobiographies," "Our Adventures," "Experiences of Bloomsburg Boys and Girls," or the like. They often illustrate these books with drawings and photographs.

ACTIVITY 14 Writing Your Autobiography   W

Write one or more chapters of your autobiography. Here are some topic suggestions. Activity 2, "Choosing an Experience to Tell About" on page 111 may suggest other topics.

1. My ancestors. 2. My parents. 3. My sisters and brothers. 4. Early school days. 5. Earning my allowance. 6. My first party. 7. Learning to swim. 8. My first pet. 9. My best friend. 10. Family fun. 11. On a farm (or at camp). 12. My hobby. 13. Christmas at our house. 14. When I was sick. 15. The day we moved. 16. Making the team. 17. My greatest achievement. 18. My likes and dislikes.

RETELLING STORIES

For retelling choose a short, simple, to-the-point story that your classmates will enjoy. If you want to tell about a book, a movie, or a play, choose one incident and tell that as fully and as vividly as you can. Don't wear your listeners out trying to tell the whole story.

ACTIVITY 15 Retelling a Story   LO

Prepare to retell one of the following stories or another favorite of yours. Try out your story at home or tell it to a small group of friends. Then tell it in class. Keep the hints on page 110 in mind.

As your classmates are telling their stories, listen carefully. Decide who were the best storytellers and why.

1. A favorite short story
2. An incident from a book, movie, or television play
3. An incident from American history
4. An Old Testament story — for example, Joseph and the coat of many colors, David and Jonathan, or Ruth and Naomi
5. An anecdote — a brief, pointed, entertaining story

6. A tall story, an animal story, or a science-fiction story
7. A myth or legend, folktale or fable
8. An interesting newspaper or magazine story

WRITING SHORT STORIES

The four elements of a short story are character, setting, plot, and theme — the idea behind the story. When you write a short story, start with a character you know. Put him in a setting you can describe accurately and give him a problem you know something about. Put obstacles in his way and work toward a climax in which the character either solves his problem or is overcome by it. Use your imagination, but write as if the story were true. If the character seems real and the plot probable, the story is a success. The reader cares what happens and reads on anxiously to find out.

Personal experiences, the experiences of your friends, a chance remark overheard on the street, and unusual news items provide excellent material for short stories.

Some stories are written in the third person. In others the writer makes himself the main character and tells the story in the first person. The beginner usually finds it easier to write in the first person — to say "I got up . . . I remember . . . I was ready."

ACTIVITY 16 Writing a Short Story   W

1. Have you read the Greek and Roman myths about Apollo, Diana, and Jupiter? Write a myth of your own. If you wish, you may relate another adventure of one of the ancient gods or goddesses.

2. Write an original adventure, mystery, or science-fiction story.

3. Have you heard about the herd of California cattle getting lost in a redwood tree that had been hollowed out? Or about the man who killed a snake by putting its tail in its mouth so that it swallowed itself? Write an original tall tale in which you let your imagination run free. (For more tall tales read "They Have Yarns" in Carl Sandburg's *The People, Yes.*)

ACTIVITY 17 Word Study   VW

The following words were used in this chapter. The page number is after each word. What does each word mean in the sentence or phrase in which it appears? Use each word in a sentence of your own. Check your spelling.

anguished	109	avalanche	111	mania	114
luxurious	110	tremors	112	cable	114
accumulated	110	gigantic	112	narrative	116

7 *Writing Descriptions*

"‍‍Tell me about the Holly Hop," pleads a sick friend.

"I'll expect a play-by-play description of the championship game," writes your camp pal Bill.

Can you make your listener or reader see and hear what you saw and heard? At the end of the conversation or letter, will she feel that she was at the dance or the game with you?

If not, you need to observe more sharply. Waking up to the world around you can fill each day with new and exciting experiences. Your conversations will be livelier, and your letters more entertaining. In fact, all your speaking and writing will improve.

ACTIVITY 1 Testing Your Powers of Observation   **SW**

In class write a description of the items on your desk or study table at home. Before you start studying this evening, look sharply at the top of your desk. Did you omit any items from your description? What details can you add to make the description more vivid and complete?

KEEP A JOURNAL

Have you ever tried keeping a diary? If it sounded like this — "October 3. I got up, washed my face, ate breakfast, went to school" — you probably gave up after a few days. "Life is pretty dull," you concluded.

Keeping a journal of observations is different. Watching for things to write about every day sharpens your powers of observation. The journal, like an artist's sketchbook or a writer's notebook, becomes a valuable source of ideas.

Carry a small notebook and a pen or a pencil in your pocket or handbag. Use those moments before the last passengers board the school bus, before your friends join you at the table in the cafeteria, or before the bell signals the beginning of class to jot down your observations of people and things about you.

See more by looking at less. Study hands one day; shoes, neckties, voices, or puddles another day. Learn to notice differences.

ACTIVITY 2 Studying a Journal Entry   **RS**

Read the following entry from a student's journal. What aspect of the beach does she concentrate on? Through which of the five senses does she receive most of her impressions of the beach at night?

121

THE BEACH AT NIGHT

I went down to the beach tonight. No one else was there. I stood still a moment, listening. The only sound was of the waves lapping against the shore. Then a gull squawked, and I heard the heavy flapping of his wings as he took off in the quiet air. The bird circled away, and again there was the same ghostly silence, broken only by the rhythmic slap-slapping of the waves against the shore. — STUDENT WRITER

ACTIVITY 3   Starting Your Journal   W

Start your journal tonight. Write today's date and give a brief but accurate description of something you observed during the day. Tomorrow watch for something new to write about, or choose a special subject for observation. At the end of two weeks be ready to share some of your most interesting observations with your classmates.

Continue your journal for the rest of the term. In addition to your observations of places and things about you, occasionally include ideas that come to you as a result of your reading.

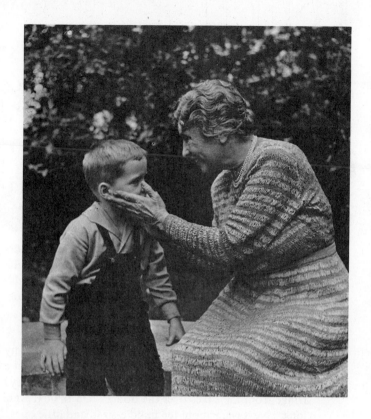

USE ALL FIVE SENSES

Use your ears as the student who wrote "The Beach at Night" did, but use your other senses too — eyes, nose, taste, sense of touch. What did you see in the cafeteria at noon? What did you hear? Laughter when a stack of trays clattered to the floor? What did you smell? Spicy spaghetti sauce redolent with garlic? What did you feel? A sharp elbow jamming into your ribs as you stood in line?

"I have often thought it would be a blessing," wrote Helen Keller, blind and deaf from the age of nineteen months, "if each human being were stricken blind and deaf for a few days at some time during his early adult life. Darkness would make him more appreciative of sight; silence would teach him the joys of sound." [1]

ACTIVITY 4   Seeing Things   OS

On your way home tonight or on your way to school tomorrow morning, pretend that you are about to lose your sight. Choose

[1] From *Three Days to See*, by Helen Keller. Copyright 1933 by Helen Keller, reprinted by permission of Doubleday & Company, Inc.

one picture worth remembering — an object, a person, a happening. As you prepare to describe the picture to your classmates, note the details that will bring it clearly to mind. Then in class describe vividly what you saw. The following is an example of such an observation.

ICICLES

The frozen snow crunched under my boots, and my breath made little transparent puffs in the still morning air. I stopped at the garage for a minute, waiting for Dad. Then I saw the icicles. They hung in a sparkling fringe from the eaves over the doors. On the left were two nearly a foot long. Next were about ten middle-sized and little ones, lined up according to size. Each icicle was slightly larger at the top and tapered in uneven ridges to a spear-sharp point. Glistening against the clean white garage doors, the icicles reflected bits of color — blue sky, red bricks, yellow sun.

Just then Dad hurried out. He didn't see the icicles — just yanked open the door. I watched in dismay as the door swung back. Snapped off cleanly, the icicles fell, shattering into dozens of pieces on the icy driveway. — STUDENT WRITER

ACTIVITY 5 Recording Sense Impressions   W

In your journal entries for the next four days concentrate in turn on each of the other four senses — hearing, taste, touch, smell.

ACTIVITY 6 Using All Five Senses   S

Divide your paper into sections for the five senses. Select one of the topics listed after the following example or a similar topic approved by your teacher. Allow sufficient time for careful on-the-scene observation, and jot down everything you see, hear, smell, taste, and feel. Keep your chart for use in Activity 10.

A CHART OF SENSE IMPRESSIONS ON THE SUBWAY

SIGHT	SOUND	SMELL	TASTE	TOUCH
Signs — "Please keep hands off the door."	Slap of the doors, throbbing hum.	Stale, warm air; peanuts — oily, penetrating.	Slightly sour, gritty taste of subway dirt and dust I've "eaten."	Rough texture of woven, rattancovered seats.
Ads — Golden-brown Downyflake waffles with maple sirup. "While you ride keep refreshed with Wrigley's Spearmint."	Bang and clash getting under way. High hum, sustained roar as train rushes through tunnel.	Chill, dank air as train picks up speed. Hot, smoky, acid smell as train stops at a station.	Scratchy thirst accentuated by Life Savers ad showing happy waterskier splashing along.	Cold smoothness of white pole I grip to steady myself. Rhythmic bounce along a rough stretch of track.
Lights blinking in tunnel. Blur as another car goes by. Blue flash.	Hollow blast of warning whistle. Sudden chuff of brakes — lower hum. Shriek, grind, stop.	Rush of new passengers — a whiff of spearmint gum and heavy perfume.		Violent side-to-side swaying. Forward pitch as train slows. Sharp jerk back.

In the locker room	In our basement
At the amusement park	In the barn
Our living room before dinner	At breakfast
In the movies	While baby-sitting
In the bus, railway, or airlines	At the supermarket
terminal	At the corner of —— and ——
At the skating pond	(two streets in your town or city)
In the school library	On the beach

SHARE YOUR OBSERVATIONS

Can you make others see, hear, smell, taste, and feel what you saw, heard, smelled, tasted, and felt? Here are some suggestions.

1. Choose the important points. Give enough details to make the picture clear but not enough to weary or confuse.

2. Arrange details in easy-to-follow order. What did you notice first?

3. Use connectives. To help your listener or reader put the parts of your description together in his mind, use such connective words and phrases as *in the distance, on my right, somewhat nearer, at my feet;* or *first, five minutes later, after that,* and *finally.*

4. Describe; don't catalog. A list of objects is not a word picture.

NOT   In the cabin were a table, chairs, a cupboard, a bed, and a fireplace.

BUT   Gradually my eyes adjusted to the dim light in the cabin and lighted on a grimy tablecloth carelessly draped over a rickety table. A few daisies drooped in a jelly glass amid a clutter of dirty dishes.

5. Be accurate, specific, vivid. Use words that make your reader see, hear, and feel what you observed. Exact nouns and action-packed verbs bring a description to life. (See pages 264–265.) Use adjectives and adverbs sparingly. (See pages 355, 356 and 360, 361.)

NOT   The *animal went* across the road.
NOT   The *tiny animal went very slowly* across the road.
BUT   The *turtle crawled* across the road.

ACTIVITY 7   Using Specific Nouns and Action-packed Verbs   V

Using the preceding example as a model, substitute a specific noun and an action-packed verb for the italicized word or words in each sentence. Choose words to help the reader see, hear, or feel.

1. The *large vehicle came* to a stop.
2. Breaking through a hole in the center of the line, the Jefferson *player cunningly got away from* the defensive backs.
3. Meowing angrily, the mother *animal moved up* her paw and *very powerfully applied it to* her *offspring.*
4. A *uniformed public servant said vehemently*, "Young lady, you're jaywalking!"
5. The wind *gave a wavy appearance to* the surface of *the body of water.*
6. *A member of the family roughly and quickly took* his briefcase, *loudly said* "Good-by," and *moved rapidly* to the bus stop.
7. A rusty wreck of *an automobile went noisily* down Wychwood Road.
8. Suddenly in that sea of faces I *caught sight of a female relative.*
9. Wearing her mother's high-heeled *footwear*, Cindy *stood unsteadily* in the doorway.
10. The wind *made a noise* in the *trees.*

ACTIVITY 8   Reading a Description of Action   RS

Read the following description. Then list the action-packed words and expressions that help you see, hear, and feel.

THE DEATH OF CRISPUS ATTUCKS

On the night of March 5, 1770, the clanging of the bell in the Old Brick Meeting House aroused Boston patriots. Grabbing fire buckets, they raced into the dimly moonlit streets toward the muffled shouts echoing from the Custom House. There a jeering crowd showered snowballs, chunks of ice, sticks, and stones on a lone British sentry. Leveling his musket at the mob, the redcoat screamed "Guard! Guard!" From the barracks across the square a British captain and seven soldiers battered their way through the menacing crowd to the sentry's side. Led by Crispus Attucks, the patriot mob pressed closer to the bayonet points, booing the soldiers and daring them to fire. Finally the brawny Attucks shouldered his way to the sentry and scuffled with him for his musket. The command "Present!" stilled the mob momentarily, but then the hoots resumed amid another bombardment of snowballs. "Fire!" rang out; a musket cracked. Crispus Attucks slumped onto the snow-covered ground — the first casualty of the Boston Massacre.

6. Use an occasional vivid figure of speech (pages 211–213) to capture a picture.

NOT In the cold morning the cattle's breath was visible.
BUT Droves of cattle were thawing the morning with their smoky breath.
  — CHARLES DICKENS

7. Be objective. Let your reader or listener draw her own conclusions about the atmosphere of a scene or the emotions of a person you are describing. Tell only what you have observed. Use words that appeal to one of the five senses, and your reader will know that Sandra was nervous before the concert or that the basketball game was exciting.

NOT   Robbie has a messy room.

BUT   Every day Robbie blazes a trail from the doorway of his room to the desk in the far corner. Kicking aside the skates he dropped yesterday, he carelessly tosses his cap and jacket at a chair — and misses. Cap and jacket land on a stack of dusty phonograph records and tattered comic books.

ACTIVITY 9   Describing Objectively   **W**

Using the description of Robbie's room as a model, improve three of the following ten descriptions.

Dad was tired.	Mother was annoyed.
I was homesick.	The dog was friendly.
We had a good swim.	It was a perfect day for a picnic.
Tom was disappointed when he wasn't elected class president.	Carol was frightened by the roar. The policeman comforted the lost child.
Aunt Maude is a collector.	

ACTIVITY 10   Describing What You Have Observed   **RW**

Reread the sense impressions you listed for Activity 6, choose the important details, and arrange them in good order. Write a paragraph in which you describe accurately and vividly. Check your finished work for sentence fragments and run-together sentences (pages 442–453).

ACTIVITY 11   Describing a Stranger   **OW**

On a bus or train, at a station, at a game, at a play, or somewhere else observe an interesting stranger. Study her face, her expression, her clothes, and her hands. Look for anything unusual about her. Note her mannerisms, what she is carrying, and any other clues to her personality and occupation. Prepare an oral or a written description that will give your classmates a vivid picture of this stranger.

Read the following example first. Notice the lively descriptive touches, the accurate, vivid verbs. Notice that this description not only tells us what this man looks like but shows him in action.

ON THE BUS

Three big men sat jammed together on the narrow side seat just behind the bus driver. One stared blankly ahead the way early-morning bus riders do, but the other two were wide awake and deep in conversation.

The one on the right did most of the talking. His voice was loud and hearty, rising above the roar and rattle of the bus. As he talked, his right index finger traced a pattern in his left palm, then stabbed the air in a series of exclamation points.

His broad red face was creased with smiles, and his blue eyes were bright with the story he was telling. Then came the laugh. His eyes squinted shut, and he shook all over.

Comfortable in layers of clothes, he looked ready for anything. His khaki windbreaker, worn and frayed at the sleeves, was unzipped, probably because it was too small over the two flannel shirts — black-and-white check cotton over gray-and-blue plaid wool. Big, rather short dungarees covered gray wool pants; and a gray felt hat, too small, battered, but with brim sharply snapped, was perched on his head. White cotton socks drooped around his ankles just above his scuffed black shoes.

"Our stop!" he exclaimed, heaving himself to his feet. His bulk filled the aisle. His two pals straggled after him to the exit.

ACTIVITY 12   Listening to a Description   L

As a classmate reads aloud an original description written for Activity 10 or 11, listen carefully for vivid words. Make note of at least five examples of good description. Compare your list with those of your classmates.

ACTIVITY 13   Word Study   VW

A. In your notebook make five columns, one for each sense. Then list at least five accurate, vivid words for each — words that will help your reader or listener see, smell, hear, taste, and feel what you did. Be prepared to discuss the appropriateness of your choices.

In your reading when you come across a word that appeals especially to one of your senses, add the word to your notebook list.

EXAMPLE

SIGHT	SMELL	SOUND	TASTE	TOUCH
silvery	acrid	moan	sugary	velvety

B. The following words were used in this chapter. The page number is after each word. What does each word mean in the sentence in which it appears? Use each word in a sentence of your own. Check your spelling.

rhythmic 122	redolent 123	objective 127
clattered 123	clutter 126	shuffles 127

8 *Writing Explanations*

"**W**hy should I increase your allowance?" asks your father. "How do you make those delicious brownies?" asks a friend. "What on earth is a T-formation quarterback?" asks Aunt Aggie. "How can I get to the nearest gas station?" asks an unhappy motorist. Every time you answer questions like these, you are explaining. Are your explanations brief, clear, easy to follow?

PLAN YOUR EXPLANATION

Explanations, like buildings, need plans. To build a simple wren house, you might carry your plan in your head. To build a three-room log cabin, you would probably have to draw up some plans on paper. Likewise, you can plan a simple explanation in your head — directing a visitor at the main entrance to the principal's office, for example — but you will need paper to plan a more complicated explanation. A simple list of points to be covered is the first step in making brief, clear, easy-to-follow explanations.

In planning an explanation, think about the following:

1. The Facts to Present. In deciding what to include, take into account what your reader or listener knows about the subject. What facts does she need for a thorough understanding? If you're telling your little sister at her first football game about penalties, explain terms like *holding*, *scrimmage line*, *center*, *clipping*, and *unnecessary roughness*. If you are talking to a teammate, forget about explaining such terms.

2. The Order of Presentation. Give first the facts needed to understand other facts. Lead the reader or listener step by step from what he knows to facts or ideas you wish to make clear.

HOW TO MAKE AN INFORMAL OUTLINE

1. Number the main points 1, 2, 3, 4. Letter any subpoints a, b, c, d, and indent them under the main points. (The formal outline is explained on pages 147, 148.)
2. Study your list of points, consider the amount of material you have on each point, and decide on your paragraphing. Your points may all belong in one paragraph, or you may need several paragraphs. Both oral and written explanations are made up of paragraphs.
3. Decide on a title and make sure that every point in your outline is on your subject.

HOW TO TRAIN YOUR DOG TO OBEY COMMANDS

POINTS TO BE COVERED   The best time to train.   Short commands (sit, stay, here, heel, down).   Ten-minute training periods.   Selecting a spot.   Why teach obedience?   Training needs (six-foot pliable leather leash, chain collar with three-inch free play, dog on left).   Praise obedience. Rebuke disobedience.   Right hand (holds leash, guides). Left hand (regulates leash, pats, pushes, corrects).   Never give food.

INFORMAL OUTLINE

  1. Why teach obedience } ¶ 1
  2. Selecting a spot
  3. The best time to train
  4. Ten-minute training periods
  5. Training needs   ¶ 2
    a. Six-foot pliable leather leash
    b. Chain collar with three-inch free play
    c. Dog on left
  6. Short commands — sit, stay, here, heel, down
  7. Praise for obedience   ¶ 3
  8. Rebuke for disobedience
  9. Never give food
10. Right hand
    a. Holds leash
    b. Guides
11. Left hand   ¶ 4
    a. Regulates leash
    b. Pats and pushes
    c. Corrects

ACTIVITY 1   Arranging Points in Order   S

If you were explaining the following subject, in what order would you arrange the topics?

How to Fix a Bicycle Flat. Applying a thin coat of rubber cement over and around hole and letting cement become cloudy. Wiping off water and cleaning the damaged spot with a metal buffer. Pulling off cloth backing on patch, placing patch over hole, and letting it dry. Pumping up tube and immersing it in water to find the leak. Checking tire for damage before inserting patched tube. Removing tube. Inserting tube. Mounting tire and tube on wheel. Taking tire off the rim. Removing wheel from frame.

ACTIVITY 2   Outlining the Explanation   S

Choose a topic from the following list or choose another topic and have your teacher approve it.   Select something you have done.

Make notes of the points you wish to cover. Include every detail needed to make your explanation clear. Then arrange your points in an informal outline. Keep this outline for use in Activity 4.

1. How to read a weather map or a timetable. 2. How to load a box camera. 3. How to use a slide rule. 4. How to send a money order. 5. How to open a savings account. 6. How to give a home permanent or set hair in rollers. 7. How to prepare a boat for winter storage. 8. How to eat a boiled lobster or an artichoke. 9. How to prepare peas, beans, asparagus, or some other vegetable for the home freezer. 10. How to play punch ball, croquet, checkers, shuffleboard, twenty questions, or any other simple game. 11. How to build an aquarium, a bird feeder, rabbit hutch, tree house, kayak, bookcase, or any other article you have built. 12. How to do mouth-to-mouth resuscitation. 13. How to change a typewriter ribbon. 14. How to put on nail polish. 15. How to make chocolate brownies, fudge, waffles, pumpkin pie, popovers, or candy apples. 16. How to make a box kite. 17. How to row a boat. 18. How to prepare the soil for a vegetable garden. 19. How to study for an examination. 20. How to tie a bowline knot.

EXPLAIN ACCURATELY AND THOROUGHLY

1. Know your subject. If you don't have all the facts necessary for a complete explanation, track them down by investigating, observing, and experimenting. Don't confuse your listener with an explanation like this: "The veins return the blood to the heart, and the arteries carry blood. . . . Wait a minute. Maybe it's reversed. Anyway, one carries blood away and the other returns it."

2. Be a mind reader. When you plan your explanation of how to play shuffleboard, put yourself in your listener's or reader's place. What may confuse or puzzle him? When giving oral explanations, watch for blank or puzzled expressions. Make difficult points clear by explaining them in two or three ways.

3. Use examples and comparisons. Connect your explanation with something your listener or reader already understands. Compare the eye of a hurricane with the hole in a huge doughnut. Or if you're trying to make your audience realize how strong the heart is, say, "The heart generates enough energy in twelve hours to lift a sixty-five ton tank car one foot from the ground." Don't overlook the value of appositives in explanation (page 292). *Shuffleboard, a perfect game for mild exercise, is played. . . .*

4. Use diagrams, pictures, and charts or display the materials needed. Simple diagrams, charts, and maps help to explain myopia, how to build a campfire, or how to reach the nearest service station. To show how to recognize and mount butterflies, show mounted butterfly specimens of your own.

5. Use words your listener or reader understands. If you must use a technical term or other unfamiliar words, stop and explain.

6. Be brief and clear. Cross out repetitions and useless words. Make your sentences more compact by using compound predicates, appositives, and complex sentences for some simple or compound sentences. (Refer to pages 274, 275, 292, 422, 423, and 427–439.)

NOT   The anemometer is an instrument to measure the velocity of the wind. It has four cups. These cups catch the wind, and the wind turns them.

BUT   The four cups of the anemometer, an instrument to measure wind velocity, catch the wind and are turned by it.

7. Be complete. Don't omit important details. If you leave out a step in directions for selecting a campsite, your trusting friend may wake up to find himself and his sleeping bag floating in a lake.

8. Make your explanation smooth. Follow the suggestions in the chapter on paragraphing (pages 48–77). Provide transitional words. Stick to the topic.

ACTIVITY 3   Studying an Explanation   OS

Is the explanation below accurate, brief, clear, and easy to follow? Support your evaluation by telling how the explanation does or does not follow the guides.

HOW TO TRAIN YOUR DOG TO OBEY COMMANDS

Does your dog run the other way when you call? Does he jump all over people and tie you up in his leash like a railway express package? If he does, you have a canine delinquent on your hands. Why not begin right now to teach him what every dog should know?

First pick a spot where you and your dog will have as few distractions as possible. Give your dog his day's lesson before he has eaten, when he is more alert. Keep the lessons businesslike and do not let them run over ten minutes. Use a six-foot pliable leather leash and a chain collar. The collar should be loose enough to leave two or three inches of free play. Remember that the dog always goes on your left.

Keep your commands short — sit, stay, here, heel, down, over. Let your voice show approval, displeasure, shame, and affection. If obedience brings praise and disobedience brings a sharp rebuke, your dog will soon do the right thing. Don't feed your dog during training periods. Let your praise and an affectionate pat be his only rewards.

When training your dog, you will need to use both hands. Use the right hand for holding the leash and guiding. Use the left hand for regulating the leash, patting, pushing, and correcting.

KINDS OF EXPLANATION

Most of your explanations will be in answer to one of these questions: "Why do you think so?" "How do I get there?" "How does it work?" "What is it?" and "How do I do it?"

How Do I Do It?

In explaining a process — how to pitch a tent, how to build a campfire, or how to fix a bicycle flat — arrange the steps in order. Don't omit important steps that you might take for granted — like checking the tire for damage before replacing it.

If you are telling how to make or build something, include the materials needed and perhaps the uses of the finished product. When you explain how to address an envelope or how to tie a slipknot, demonstrate as you talk or ask a friend to demonstrate for you. If you tell how to make a bird feeder or other small article, display the finished product. If it's edible, give your audience a sample.

ACTIVITY 4   Explaining, and Checking Listening   LO

A. Prepare to give in class the explanation for which you wrote an outline in Activity 2. Explain so clearly that everyone in the class will understand. If your topic is how to knead dough or how to throw a curve ball or how to press flowers, make the process clear to everyone.

B. After you have given your explanation to the class, test your listeners' understanding by calling on classmates to answer questions like these: "What was the first step?" "What tools are needed?"

What Is It?

Definition is an important part of explaining. To explain a jet engine to most people, you'll probably need to define such terms as *air intake, turbine, gearbox, side thrust.*

A definition should be clear, accurate, and concise. One of the best ways to define something is to tell (1) what class it belongs to and (2) what its particular qualities are.

NAME	CLASS	PARTICULAR QUALITIES
A box score is	a statistical summary	showing the number of hits and runs in a ball game.
A caisson is	a watertight box	for underwater construction.
A dynamo is	a device	for converting mechanical energy into electrical energy.

AVOID THESE MISTAKES IN DEFINITION

1. Don't put the term you are defining in too broad or too narrow a class.

TOO BROAD   A lifeguard is a person who . . . (Use a broad class like *person*, *man*, or *object* only as a last resort.)

STILL TOO BROAD   A lifeguard is an athlete who . . . (Divers, pitchers, and sprinters are also athletes.)

TOO NARROW   A lifeguard is a boy scout who . . . (Not all lifeguards are boy scouts. There are also women lifeguards.)

BETTER   A lifeguard is an expert swimmer employed at bathing beaches and pools to prevent drownings.

2. Don't begin your definition with *when* or *where*. If you are defining a noun, the word after *is* should also be a noun (the name of the class).

NOT   *Descant* is when a counterpoint or related melody is sung above the main melody.

BUT   *Descant* is a counterpoint or related melody sung above the main melody.

3. When defining a term, do not use the word itself or a word derived from it.

NOT   *Obesity* is the quality or state of being obese.

BUT   *Obesity* is the quality or state of being very fat.

If the dictionary defines *naturalization* as the "act of being naturalized," look up *naturalize*. There you will find the clue to the longer word.

4. Don't define an unfamiliar term with a word more unfamiliar still.

NOT   *Lethargy* is apathy. (What's apathy?)

BUT   *Lethargy* is a dull, sluggish state brought on by illness, great fatigue, overeating, etc.

ACTIVITY 5   Correcting Faulty Definitions   **S**

Correct these faulty definitions:

1. *Myopia* is when a person cannot see distant objects distinctly.
2. A *nostrum* is a panacea.
3. *Courage* is being courageous.
4. An *autocracy* is where one person has unlimited power or authority over others.

5. A *hexagon* is when a figure has six sides.
6. A *grease monkey* is a man who works on automobiles or airplanes.
7. To be *courteous* is to show courtesy.
8. A *Star Scout* is a person who has given at least three months' service as a First Class Scout and has qualified for any five merit badges.
9. A *tourniquet* is when you use a tight bandage to stop bleeding.
10. To *maim* is to mutilate.

ACTIVITY 6 Defining Words   V

Define ten of the following by giving the class and the particular qualities in the form shown on page 135. Give a common definition of the word. Check your definitions in a good dictionary.

amoeba	cartoon	gopher	slide rule
bunt	choke	rodent	strait
bus	corporal	rodeo	umbrella
cacao	dictator	sentry	zipper

Define to Avoid Misunderstandings

Many words mean different things to different people. When you use the word *school*, for example, do you mean a building, the student body, the courses of study, or Lyons Township High School? If you explain just what you mean by words like *American, freedom, socialist, undemocratic,* you will avoid many arguments.

Often such words that refer to ideas you cannot see, touch, hear, taste, or smell cannot be defined clearly and accurately in one sentence. You may need a paragraph or many paragraphs. Make clear what you mean when you use abstract words by giving details, examples, or comparisons. (See Chapter 4, "Building Paragraphs.") Note how the writer of the following paragraph makes his meaning clear.

WHAT IS FREEDOM?

What is this precious heritage of ours? Does freedom mean doing exactly as we please? No, that would soon encroach upon the freedom of others. We may, for example, choose our own television or radio entertainment without fearing that a knock on the door will herald an armed guard come to drag us off to prison for watching a forbidden program. This freedom of choice, however, does not give us the right to turn the volume of our set so loud that we disturb the neighbors — especially after midnight. We are free to assemble in large groups for football and basketball games, but we are not free to hit the spectator in front of us over the head with a pop bottle when we disagree with him. Laws limit our freedom so that the freedom of each citizen is protected. As long as our actions do not hurt others, we are free to act, speak, work, and worship as we please.

ACTIVITY 7 Writing a Paragraph Definition **W**

Using the preceding example as a model, write a paragraph explaining what one of the following terms means to you.

American	Grade B movies	propaganda
courage	happiness	school spirit
a good sport	loyalty	welfare state

How Does It Work?

In telling how something works don't take too much for granted. Explain clearly, concisely, completely.

ACTIVITY 8 Studying an Explanation **S**

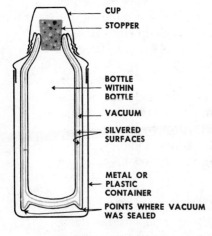

CUP
STOPPER
BOTTLE WITHIN BOTTLE
VACUUM
SILVERED SURFACES
METAL OR PLASTIC CONTAINER
POINTS WHERE VACUUM WAS SEALED

1. Is the following explanation accurate, clear, complete, concise?
2. Of what use is the diagram?

HOW A THERMOS BOTTLE WORKS

When a hot or cold liquid is poured into a thermos bottle (sometimes called a vacuum bottle), the liquid remains at almost the same temperature for as long as twenty-four hours. The construction of the bottle makes it difficult for heat to pass out or in.

The thermos bottle, usually made of metal or of durable plastic, has an inner container made of glass. This inner container is a bottle within a bottle. At the points shown on the diagram, all the air is sucked out of the space between the walls of the two bottles. The resulting vacuum is then sealed and blocks the passage of heat from or to the inner bottle.

The facing walls of the glass bottles are coated with a silvery solution. When heat waves try to escape from or penetrate the inner bottle, these silvered walls turn them back. Some heat does pass through the glass walls and the stopper of cork, rubber, or plastic, but the process is a slow one because glass, cork, rubber, and plastic are poor conductors of heat.

Explain completely the construction and the operation of one of the following. Make clear how the device does its work. A diagram may help you. Use the guides on page 133 in revising your explanation. Spell and punctuate correctly (pages 286–303, 469–485).

accordion	dry cell	incubator	rocket
air brake	electric mixer	iron lung	safety match
air conditioner	escalator	lie detector	siphon
ball-point pen	Ferris wheel	life jacket	steam iron
binoculars	gas meter	microphone	sundial
boomerang	Geiger counter	periscope	telescope
carburetor	helicopter	pinking shears	vacuum cleaner
cream separator	hypodermic syringe	Polaroid camera	water faucet
drawbridge	incandescent lamp	radar	whistling teakettle

How Do I Get There?

Stop and think before you answer a how-do-I-get-there question. Take into consideration how the person will go — walk, drive, or take a bus or subway. Use such specific terms as *first traffic light*, *north, left, at the first fork*. Mention conspicuous landmarks or buildings that will enable the stranger to check his course — the post office, the Chevron service station. Avoid meaningless directions like "Turn at the next-to-last traffic light" or "Get off at the last cross-roads."

With a classmate playing the role of a stranger in front of your home, school, or the post office, act out giving directions to the library, the town hall, a factory, a church, a park, a hotel, a theater, or some other point in your community. Your partner will give you his location and ask, "How do I get from here to the . . .?" Take a moment to think about your answer. Then speak clearly and courteously. Your partner will ask questions if he does not understand any points.

Another member of the class may test your partner on his ability to listen to and remember facts by asking him to repeat the directions.

Why Do You Think So?

Every day you explain why you think as you do — why you think baseball is more fun to watch than basketball, why you read comic books, why you enjoy westerns, why the movie at the State is worth seeing, why your school should adopt the honor system. If you want others to see a subject as you see it, you must give the facts and ideas on which you base your opinion. If you're for something, ask yourself why. Is it practical? Is it interesting? Is it hard? Dull? Unworkable? Useless? Be accurate and be specific.

Give your facts and ideas in an order your readers or listeners can follow easily. In explaining why your allowance should be increased, for example, arrange your points in the order of importance with your best reason last.

ACTIVITY 11   Studying an Explanation   S

1. In the following explanation are the ideas presented in easy-to-follow order?
2. What specific reasons does the writer give for having a juice machine?
3. What do you consider the writer's strongest argument?

NEEDED: A JUICE MACHINE

Every day for gym period we girls go through this exhausting routine: change into our gym clothes, play a hard game of volleyball or what have you, take a hot shower, change into our school clothes. By this time we're thirsty, dry, dehydrated.

Wouldn't it be a pleasure to have a cool, refreshing drink after this tiring ordeal? The boys' gym already provides this small luxury. After gym class a thirsty boy can drop a coin into the juice machine and receive a cup of frosty, vitamin-packed orange, pineapple, or grape juice. The juice not only quenches his thirst but also replaces some of the energy-producing food he has burned up. Refreshed, he goes to his next class.

Why aren't the girls entitled to the same privilege? It's time we too had a juice machine in our gym. — STUDENT WRITER

ACTIVITY 12   Telling How You See It   OW

Choose a topic about which you have a definite opinion. In a speech or a written explanation give clear, specific reasons to support the position you take.

Here are a few suggested topics, but use one of your own if you wish.

1. Why a ninth grader should join a school club, read a newspaper daily, budget time, learn the school rules, eat a well-balanced breakfast, attend home games, or _____.

2. Why I am planning to get a job this summer, to take Spanish or another subject, to go to college, to try out for the school operetta, to learn to dance, to be a fashion designer, or _____.

3. Why we should have a swimming pool, a hockey team, a class magazine, new regulations for the school cafeteria, dances after basketball games, a teen-age recreation center, a language laboratory, or _____.

4. Why I like or dislike Saturday mornings, camping trips, western movies, comic books, television commercials, early-morning disc jockeys, mowing the lawn, baseball, or _____.

ACTIVITY 13 Try Your Skill   W

1. You have persuaded an out-of-town friend to go to the camp you have been attending for the past two summers. He asks what clothing and equipment he will need. Write your reply to his letter.

2. Write an invitation to a friend or relative asking that he spend the weekend with you. Give him full directions for reaching your house by automobile, bus, or train.

3. Have you had difficulty assembling a model airplane, a knocked-down bookcase, an "easy-to-assemble" toy, or some other article because of poor directions? Rewrite the directions so that they are complete and easy to follow. Then write a courteous letter to the manufacturer and enclose your revision of the directions.

4. Write a letter to the editor of your school paper about some condition in your school that needs improvement. Be brief, factual, and courteous. Use as a salutation: To the Editor (give the name of your school paper). Omit the letter closing, but sign your name.

5. Write to your local television station or to a sponsor explaining why you liked or disliked a recent program.

ACTIVITY 14 Paragraph Drill   SW

Review the points made in this chapter and write a paragraph with the following topic sentence: *Good explanations have certain things in common.*

ACTIVITY 15 Word Study   VW

The following words were used in this chapter. The page number is after each word. What does each word mean in the sentence in which it appears? Use each word in a sentence of your own. Check your spelling.

experimenting	133	regulating	134	encroach	137
canine	134	heritage	137	herald	137
delinquent	134	abstract	137	dehydrated	140

9 *Writing Informative Reports*

Would you like to become a highway engineer when you finish school? Do you want to tell the Shutterbugs about methods of enlarging snapshots? Would you like to learn more about the education of a pioneer boy or girl than is in your history textbook? Collecting and sharing information on subjects like these is reporting. To present an informative, interesting report, you have to become an authority on your subject by tracking down information in several sources. Then you must organize your material in easy-to-follow order.

CHOOSING A TOPIC

To do a good job on a report you need a good topic — one that interests you and one you can find plenty of material on. Then ask yourself what you and your classmates or club members would like to know about the topic. The writer of a report on helicopters jotted down these questions: What is a helicopter? How are helicopters used by the armed services? How are they used in civilian life? What is the future of helicopters?

ACTIVITY 1   Choosing a Topic for a Report   SW

Choose one of the following, or find a topic of your own and have your teacher approve it. Then jot down four or five questions you think you should answer in your report.

1. A recent development in weather forecasting (communications, highway safety, airplanes). 2. Safety devices in jet planes. 3. A peacetime use of atomic energy. 4. History of the comic strip. 5. The origin of a folk ballad. 6. The job of a forest ranger (or some other worker). 7. The training of a frogman. 8. The making of animated cartoons. 9. Opportunities for homesteading in Alaska. 10. Water color as a medium of painting. 11. The use of chemicals in farming. 12. Equipment needed in snorkeling. 13. A great engineering project. 14. Qualifying for an Olympic team. 15. Frozen foods. 16. Furniture (or shelter) in colonial times. 17. Teen-agers behind the wheel. 18. One duty of the United States Secret Service (guarding the President, for example). 19. Fighting forest fires. 20. Prefabricated houses. 21. Keeping the air free from smoke. 22. The Coast Guard at work.

FINDING INFORMATION

Even if you already know quite a bit about a subject — for example, snorkeling or painting with water colors — check your facts and add to them to make a good report. Use these sources to supplement your own experience and observation:

1. Encyclopedias. For a bird's-eye view of your subject, look your topic up in two or more encyclopedias (pages 247–250). To find all the material an encyclopedia contains on a subject, track down all cross references. The article on helicopters in the *World Book Encyclopedia*, for example, refers you to these related topics: aerodynamics; Air Force; airplane; autogiro; aviation; convertiplane; Sikorsky, Igor I. At the end of an encyclopedia article you may find also a list of books on the subject.

2. Books. To find books on your subject — helicopters, for example — look in the library card catalog (pages 251–254) under as many related subjects as you can think of — helicopter, airplane, aviation, autogiro. In textbooks and other books use the table of contents and the index. If it's important to have your material up to date, pay attention to the copyright dates.

3. Magazines. To find up-to-date material quickly and easily, use the *Readers' Guide to Periodical Literature.* The *Readers' Guide*, published twenty times a year, is an index of the articles in over a hundred magazines. Here is a sample entry from the *Readers' Guide:*

> HELICOPTERS in insect control
> Massive river spraying project planned. D.
> C. Winston. il Aviation W 100:88-9 Ap 29
> '74

A key at the front of the *Readers' Guide* explains the abbreviations and symbols. Here is an explanation of the preceding entry. The title of the article is "Massive River Spraying Project Planned." The author is D. C. Winston. The article is illustrated. It can be found in *Aviation Week*, volume 100, pages 88–89 of the April 29, 1974 issue.

4. People. Consult an authority for firsthand information about your subject. If, for example, you want to know about secretarial work, ask a secretary. Your parents and teachers also can answer many of your questions.

PREPARING SOURCE CARDS

As soon as you find a book or an article you can use, jot down the following information on a 3 × 5 or 4 × 6 card or paper:
(1) Author's name (If you don't know the author, begin with the title.)
(2) Title of book or article
(3) Publisher or publication, date, pages
(4) Call number of a book so that you can find the book quickly
(5) A number in the upper right corner of the card to identify your source when you are taking notes

FOR AN ENCYCLOPEDIA ARTICLE

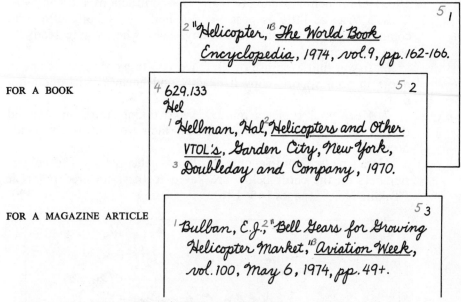

[2] "Helicopter,"[B] *The World Book Encyclopedia*, 1974, vol. 9, pp. 162-166.   [5] [1]

FOR A BOOK

[4] 629.133
Hel
[1] Hellman, Hal,[2] *Helicopters and Other VTOL's*, Garden City, New York, [3] Doubleday and Company, 1970.   [5] [2]

FOR A MAGAZINE ARTICLE

[1] Bulban, E. J.,[2] "Bell Gears for Growing Helicopter Market,"[B] *Aviation Week*, vol. 100, May 6, 1974, pp. 49+.   [5] [3]

The plus (+) on the card above indicates the article is continued on other pages.

The colored numbers are keyed to the points in "Preparing Source Cards" on page 144.

ACTIVITY 2 Finding Material for a Report   S

Find four or more reliable sources on the topic you chose in Activity 1. Use only one encyclopedia article, and include at least one book and one magazine article. List each source on a separate card as shown above. Keep your cards for use in Activities 3–9.

TAKING NOTES

After finding an article or a chapter on your topic, read it through rapidly to see whether it has information you can use. Then read it again, taking notes.

1. Use a separate 3 × 5 or 4 × 6 card or paper for each fact, set of figures, or idea. Write on only one side.

2. At the top left of every card write the subject of the note.

3. In the upper right corner write the number you have assigned to the source from which the note is taken.

4. Write the page number of your source.

5. Take most of your notes in your own words. (Refer to pages 198, 199 for help in summarizing.) Use contractions and abbreviations. Write as little as possible, but make your notes clear and complete enough to make sense days later when you're ready to write your report.

6. If you find a phrase or sentence you think you may want to quote in your report, copy it exactly and enclose it in quotation marks.

7. Keep your topic in mind. Avoid taking notes on material that is off the subject. Don't repeat facts you've already made note of.

Here are two sample note cards on helicopters. The colored numbers on the cards below are keyed to the numbered points in "Taking Notes" (pages 145–146).

Card 1:

3
1

2
Farming

4 p 162

Prev frost damage – Fly
back & forth over orch. & veg.
fields. Rotors stir up warm
air.
} 5

Card 2:

3
3

2
Future

4 p. 556

Lifting device – e.g. house from fac.
to foundation.
} 5

Igor Sikorsky told auth.; "Cargo helicopters
will have no fuselage as we know it
today. They'll simply be flying frames
to lift big loads from one place
to another."
} 6

Using the note card system, take brief, clear, complete notes on the material you found for your report (Activity 2). Be ready to copy one of your cards on the board for class criticism. Keep these cards for use in Activities 5 and 6.

ORGANIZING YOUR MATERIAL

As you read over your notes, look at the subject heading on each card. Which headings go together? Which cards are useless? Decide what the main topics are and arrange your cards in sensible order. Time order is good for a "how to" report or a "history of" report. Space order is good for a topic like "The Climate of the United States." Begin with the west coast (since weather travels east) and move across the country. A report on a man or an organization may follow this pattern: history; achievements; significance for us.

HOW TO OUTLINE

1. First write the title.
2. Number the main topics I, II, III, and letter the subtopics under each main topic A, B, C. Number subtopics under capital letters 1, 2, 3, 4, and letter subtopics under Arabic numerals a, b, c, d. Place a period after each topic number or letter.
3. Limit the number of main topics to five or six. For a short paper three or four will be enough. Be sure each main topic is an important division of the subject, not a subdivision of another main topic.
4. Never write a single subtopic — that is, an A without a B or a 1 without a 2. When there is material for only one subtopic, include the point or fact in the main topic.
5. Begin each subtopic farther to the right than the main topic above it. Keep Roman numerals in a vertical line, capital letters in another vertical line farther to the right, and so on.
6. Write either a topic outline (words or phrases) or a sentence outline (complete sentences throughout), but do not mix the two. Express all topics of the same rank in parallel form. If I is a noun, II and III should be nouns. If A is a prepositional phrase, B and C should be prepositional phrases.
7. Use no punctuation after a topic in a topic outline. Use periods only when writing a sentence outline.
8. Capitalize the first word of each topic and other words that would be capitalized in a sentence.

Here is the outline for the report on helicopters. What are the main points of the report? How many subtopics does each main point have? What details are listed for each subtopic? How does the paragraphing of the report on page 151 follow the outline? Prove that topics of the same rank under the same head are in parallel form.

THE FLYING WORKHORSE

I. Description of the helicopter
   A. Appearance
   B. Unique features
II. Uses of the helicopter
   A. In large cities
      1. Commercial transport
         a. Air taxi
         b. Flying delivery truck
      2. Traffic control
   B. In rescue work
      1. Wartime
      2. Peacetime
   C. In farming
      1. Seeding, fertilizing, spraying, dusting crops
      2. Drying ripe fruit
      3. Preventing frost damage
      4. Herding livestock
   D. In remote areas
      1. Forests
      2. Telephone, power, gas, and oil lines
      3. Offshore oil rigs
      4. Aluminum plant in Canada
III. Helicopters and Tomorrow's Transportation
   A. Economy
   B. Convenience

Outline the report you have taken notes for (Activity 3). Make your topics definite. Avoid vague divisions like "Introduction" and "Conclusion."

WRITING A FIRST DRAFT

1. With your notes and outline before you, plunge right in. Write freely and rapidly, leaving a space between lines. You'll need this space for correction and revision later.

2. Unless a better plan occurs to you, follow your outline.

3. Brighten your report with details and examples. Refer to your own experience.

4. Be accurate. Copy names, dates, and statistics carefully.

5. Give an author credit when you use his exact words or state his original idea in your own words. Enclose his exact words in quotation marks. If you try to pass off someone else's words or ideas as your own, you will be guilty of *plagiarism* — another word for stealing. Follow these forms:

FOR A BORROWED SENTENCE   Describing the sound of a helicopter in an article in the *National Geographic Magazine*, Peter T. White said, "The roaring and whining from above had become louder still, like some monstrous buzz saw."

FOR A BORROWED PHRASE   In a *National Geographic Magazine* article Peter T. White said that a helicopter sounds "like some monstrous buzz saw."

FOR A BORROWED IDEA   In a *National Geographic Magazine* article Peter T. White compared the noise of a helicopter to the buzzing of a large saw.

ACTIVITY 6   Writing the First Draft of Your Report   W

Write the first draft of the report you have outlined (Activity 5). Get down on your paper all the material you intend to include.

REVISING YOUR REPORT

Read your first draft. Correct and revise until you can answer "yes" to all of these questions.

1. Will your beginning interest your reader or listener in your report? Do you get to your first point quickly? Don't waste time on a long introduction.

2. Are the ideas arranged in a sensible, easy-to-follow order? Shift sentences or paragraphs to the point where they belong.

3. Have you made the reader's progress from sentence to sentence and from paragraph to paragraph easy? Refer to pages 72, 75 for examples of good thought-connecting words.

4. Is each idea clearly developed? If there are gaps, fill them in. Omit material that isn't on the subject.

5. Have you enclosed an author's exact words in quotation marks (see pages 298–302) and given an author credit for phrases, sentences, or ideas you have borrowed? (See page 146.)

6. Is your ending forceful? Round off your report in your last paragraph.

7. Are your sentences varied? Don't begin every sentence with the subject. Use appositives and complex sentences. (See pages 292, 293, 427–439.)

*If Y*our parents ~~may~~ move to another city/,

a
A team of helicopters may pick up your house/
and ~~they may~~ move it to a new foundation.

8. Have you used vivid, exact words and expressions? Cross out vague, dull, colorless ones. (See pages 456, 457.)

Marooned victims of floods, fires, snowstorms, and avalanches
~~Many other people~~ have also been rescued, the

picking them up either by landing or by using a cable
helicopter ~~effecting rescue in one of two ways~~.

9. Are there any repetitions or useless words? Look suspiciously at every *which, that, any, and many others, along the lines of, in the field of*. (See pages 456, 457.)

With the wind from its rotors farmers have blown ~~off~~

to
rain from fruit ~~that is~~ (ripe) for ~~the purpose of~~ ~~preventing it from~~ rotting and have mixed the

to
warm upper air with the ground chill ~~so that they~~

~~might~~ prevent damage ~~from~~ (frost).

10. Are your grammar, spelling, and punctuation correct? Watch particularly for careless mistakes and for sentence fragments and run-together sentences.

Ranchers ~~they~~ use helicopters to herd cattle

and round up strays/, A helicopter replacing

e   *s*
eight̬en cowhand̬.

Read the following report.   In what ways does it carry out the suggestions in this chapter?   Use the following key to guide you in your evaluation.

1. The sentence states the theme of the report.
2. The writer plunges into the first point after a brief introduction of only two sentences.
3. These details or examples help develop the topic.
4. The writer gives credit for borrowed ideas and also gives authority for the statements.
5. These sentences round out the report and give the writer's conclusions.
6. The sentence is a bridge from the first main point — description of the helicopter — to the second — uses of the helicopter.
7. This sentence prepares the reader for discussion of one basic use of a helicopter.   What sentences prepare for discussions of the other uses?

THE FLYING WORKHORSE

What World War I did for the airplane World War II did for the helicopter, but the Korean War and the Vietnam War really proved its worth. [1] Since then, the uses of the fragile "whirlybird" have multiplied. [2] Resembling an airplane without wings, the helicopter has one or two overhead rotors.   Each rotor consists of three or four long, flat blades that enable the craft to take off and land vertically, to fly forward, backward, and sideways, or to hover in one spot.   [6] Because of these features the helicopter is more than a means of transport; it is also a flying crane that can drop and pick up people and equipment by the cable technique where there are no roads or landing strips.

[7] Used as a flying taxi, delivery truck, or police car, the helicopter speeds the movement of people and cargo in traffic-clogged cities.   [3] To

avoid traffic jams, the President steps into a helicopter on the White House lawn for a trip to the airport or his country home.   [3] For the same reason some suburban dwellers in Los Angeles take a helicopter when they want to shop downtown.   [3] In many cities airlines use helicopters for shuttle service from airport to the city or to another nearby airport. [3] In New York, Chicago, and Los Angeles the post office uses helicopters to deliver mail to suburban branches.   [3] In Los Angeles flying police cars observe the freeways, direct motorcycle police officers and emergency vehicles to trouble spots by the quickest way, and advise motorists of alternate routes to avoid tie-ups.

Because it can move at a snail's pace or hover almost motionless over one spot, the helicopter is at its best in rescue operations.   [3] During World War II, the Korean War, and the Vietnam War helicopters saved the lives of hundreds of service people.   [3] Marooned victims of floods, fire, snowstorms, and avalanches have also been rescued, the helicopter picking them up, either by landing or by using a cable.   [4] In *The Helicopter,* Jacob Shapiro ranks the craft with important lifesaving devices like the miner's safety lamp.

The farmer has discovered other uses for the helicopter.   [3] The farmer seeds, fertilizes, sprays, and dusts crops from a helicopter.   [3] With the wind from its rotors farmers have blown rain from ripe fruit to prevent rotting and have mixed the warm upper air with the ground chill to prevent frost damage.   [3] Ranchers use helicopters to herd cattle and round up strays, a helicopter replacing eighteen cowhands.

People have put the helicopter to work in many remote areas.   [3] In forests, for example, the craft makes an ideal observation booth for fire detection.   [3] After a fire has been spotted, a ranger can direct fire fighters from a hovering helicopter, drop supplies, or even unroll a hose up a mountainside.   [3] Inspectors of telephone, power, gas, and oil lines use helicopters, which can also land repair people near trouble. [3] Helicopters service the offshore oil drilling rigs in the Gulf of Mexico. [3] One of the most spectacular uses of the helicopter was in the building of an aluminum plant in a remote section of British Columbia.   [3] Not only did the helicopters fly in workers, equipment, and supplies, but they also lifted tower sections into place.

[5] We have not used the helicopter nearly enough.   Congestion around major cities and airports takes a high toll in time, money, energy, and sometimes lives.   [4] In *Helicopters and Other VTOL's*, Hal Hellman suggests ways in which helicopters can further save precious fuel by expanding their short-haul possibilities.   [5] Like other VTOL's (vertical take-off and landing craft), the helicopter is ideally suited for short hops. Unlike the jet, which needs a large sprawling airport, the helicopter needs very little space.   [3] An airport like Kennedy in New York may cover nine square miles or more.   [3] By contrast, a complete

heliport may require only two acres.   [5] The role of the helicopter in public transportation may have just begun to unfold.

ACTIVITY 8 Writing Your Final Draft   **W**

Copy your report neatly and legibly. Follow the instructions on pages 191–192.

PREPARING YOUR BIBLIOGRAPHY

Before you hand in your report, prepare an additional sheet headed "Bibliography." Refer to your source and note cards.
1. List all the sources you used for your report.
2. Alphabetize by the last name of the author or, if the author's name isn't given, by the first important word of the title.
3. Give the number of pages you read in each source.
4. Underline the titles of books and magazines; put quotation marks around the titles of articles.

ACTIVITY 9 Preparing Your Bibliography   **W**

After you have studied the bibliography for "The Flying Work-horse," prepare the bibliography for your report. Where are commas and periods used? Quotation marks? When do you underline?

BIBLIOGRAPHY

"Helicopter," *World Book Encyclopedia*, vol. 9, 1974, pp. 162–166.
"Helicopter Boom Spawns Competition," *Aviation Week*, vol. 101, September 23, 1974, pp. 75–77.
"Helicopters Boost Trauma Unit's Service," *Aviation Week*, vol. ˋ101, November 11, 1974, pp. 67+.
Hellman, Hal, *Helicopters and Other VTOL's*, Garden City, Doubleday and Company, 1970, pp. 70–94.
Winston, D. C., "Massive River Spraying Project Planned," *Aviation Week*, vol. 100, April 29, 1974, pp. 88–89.

ACTIVITY 10 Word Study   **VW**

The following words were used in this chapter. The page number is after each word. What does each word mean in the sentence or phrase in which it appears? Use each word in a sentence of your own. Check your spelling.

| authority | 143 | plagiarism | 149 | technique | 151 | hover | 152 |
| encyclopedia | 144 | shift | 149 | suburban | 152 | marooned | 152 |

10 *Writing Letters*

Janice Collins frowned as she sat at her desk planning her circus party. I'll have to write some letters, she thought. Inviting Sally for the weekend will be easy, but how do I go about ordering those decorations from Dennison's?

What about you? Are you letter-perfect or do you need to brush up on social and business correspondence? Do you write all the letters and notes that courtesy demands?

FRIENDLY LETTERS

Do you miss the gabfests you and Pete used to have before he moved to Cincinnati? You can still have them. Chatting by letter is one way of keeping friendships alive.

WHAT DO YOU WRITE?

What would you tell your friend if you were talking with him? Although there are no set rules for the subject matter of a friendly letter, your friends will look forward to hearing from you if you:

1. Write about the simple, everyday things that have happened to you—basketball tryouts, buying a new suit, the math test, a stirring movie. Your friends and relatives want to hear about *you*.

2. Show your interest in your reader by talking about her experiences, hobbies, family, or work. If she's a shutterbug, for example, tell her about that exhibit of color photographs at the museum.

                                    2931 Fort Boulevard
                                    El Paso, Texas 79900
                                    September 22, 19--

Dear Pete,

   Did you ever eat an ant? Well, I did, and I'm still
alive to write about it. For a few hours, though, I
wondered if I'd ever sing in the Austin Choir.

   Yes, I made the choir. Last Saturday there was a picnic
at Hueco Tanks to initiate the eighteen new members. At
rehearsal we all heard veiled threats about what was in
store for us and were warned to wear old clothes. When
we arrived at the picnic ground, we soon found out the
reason.

   To begin the festivities, we new members were told to
line up, and our hands were smeared with honey. Then
Doug Reynolds, the president, announced, "We're so glad to
have such fine new talent in the choir that we've imported
a special treat for you. Whet your appetites on these
chocolate-covered ants." Some of the girls squealed, and
Al Barta and I exchanged rather sick grins, but we each
swallowed an ant. When Al saw there were only enough ants
for one serving, he smacked his lips and asked for seconds.
Isn't that just like Al--always acting like
a clown?

   The rest of the afternoon was less gruesome. We new
members next had to display our talents. I wish you could
have seen Vic Duron and Howie Wilcox doing the minuet.
They brought down the house.

   The gang all say hello. What's your new school like?
We're all waiting to hear if you were as confused your
first few weeks as a freshman as we were.

                            Your pal,

                            Steve

3. Tailor your topics to fit your reader's interests. If your grandmother doesn't know the difference between a punt and a lateral, tell her about the colorful half-time drills of the bands. Save a play-by-play description for your old friend Roger, the quarterback of the Far Rockaway eleven.

4. Answer your friend's questions if you're replying to a letter. Make your answer so complete that your reader will understand even if he's forgotten his question: "Your question about my plans for the summer reminds me that it's time for Dad and me to check our camping equipment. The first of July. . ."

ACTIVITY 1 Finding Topics to Write About ST

1. List the experiences you've had this week. What have you enjoyed talking about with your family and friends?

2. Think about two people to whom you might write letters— a friend your own age and an aunt, uncle, or other older relative. List the interests of each and then choose three suitable topics from the preceding list. If you select the same topic for each person, what details will you tell one that you won't tell the other?

HOW DO YOUR LETTERS SOUND?

Are you ready to write? Not quite. Organize your thoughts on scratch paper first; then develop them in paragraphs. Think how you will make your letter a conversation with your reader and not just a catalog of events.

1. Begin brightly. Write a lively opening sentence.

NOT   I am glad to hear you like your new home.

BUT   So you and your family are now dyed-in-the-wool Texans!

2. Give details. Tell who, what, where, when, why, and how. Use specific nouns and vivid verbs. (See pages 264–267.)

NOT THIS   I had a good time this weekend. Friday night I went to a party. Saturday we went to the lake. Then on Sunday we played tennis.

BUT THIS   Friday night was the start of a fun-filled weekend. Shirley invited Gloria, Judy, and me to one of her famous slumber parties. The only missing ingredient was you, and your name was constantly popping up. You'll just have to plan to visit us soon so you can sprawl with us on the bearskin rug in front of the fire and munch popcorn while we listen to our favorite records. We'll have to tie up Shirley's brother, though. That little fiend put cornflakes in our beds. Gloria's shrieks awakened the whole house and set Jiggs to howling.

3. Be natural. Write the way you talk.   Use contractions like *aren't, doesn't, don't, I'll, they're,* and *we're.*

4. Be vivid.   Use colorful, original comparisons that will help your reader see, hear, or feel what you are describing.

NOT   Peggy couldn't sit still.

BUT   Peggy was hopping around like drops of water on a hot griddle.

5. Think before you write.   Never use sarcasm; never write secrets or unkind gossip; never write in anger.   If you do write when you are angry, read the letter through the next day, realize you went overboard, and tear the letter up.   Don't joke if there is any possibility of your being taken seriously.   Don't cause needless worry. If you write when you are in the midst of a spell of homesickness, your parents will worry long after you have forgotten all about the night you felt blue.

6. End courteously but briefly.   Make the closing lively and interesting.   Omit unnecessary excuses and apologies.

NOT   This is the end of the paper.   Mom says I have to go to bed now.   I
         guess I'll have to close.

BUT   I hope your holiday was as much fun as mine.   Was it?

ACTIVITY 2   Planning a Friendly Letter   S

Organize the topics you chose for the letter to a friend in the second part of Activity 1.   What will make a good beginning?   A good ending?   What details can you add to each topic to make it come alive?   Save this plan for Activity 3.

HOW DO YOUR LETTERS LOOK?

You may write a rough draft of your letter on composition paper, but good manners demand that every letter you mail be neat, attractive, and arranged according to standard form.   Follow these suggestions to make your letters not only sound interesting but look attractive too.

Paper.   Unruled white paper is always correct.   Paper with a monogram or a printed name and address is always in good taste, as is plain gray or cream stationery.   It may be either single or double sheets.

Writing.   Letters should always be written in ink or typed.   The typewriter may be used for most friendly letters.   Letters of congratulation or condolence should, however, be handwritten.

Margin. Leave a margin of at least a half inch at the left of the page or frame your letter like a picture with a margin of a half inch or more on all sides.

Paging. When you use folded stationery, write the pages of a long letter in the order 1, 2, 3, 4, as if they were pages of a book. Write a shorter letter on the first and third pages. Write on only one side of very thin paper.

Letter Style. There are two styles for arranging your letter. Use the same style—indented or block—in the heading, the closing, the signature, and the addresses on the envelope.

PARTS OF A FRIENDLY LETTER

BLOCK	**INDENTED**
3734 Lilac Lane	*1227 Fourth Street*
Philadelphia, PA 19136	*Graham, TX 76046*
June 2, 19—	*September 30, 19—*

Heading. The heading tells the place and date of writing.

1. Place the heading at least a half inch from the top of the page and start the first line slightly to the left of the center of the page— far enough to the left to avoid crowding the right margin.

2. A heading ordinarily has three lines: (1) the street address (or route or box number); (2) the city and state and ZIP code number; and (3) the date.

3. Do not abbreviate the name of the month. It is permissible to abbreviate the name of the state, using the capitalized two-letter abbreviation preferred by the Postal Service. Do not put a period after this kind of abbreviation.

4. Use two commas: one to separate the town or city from the state and one to separate the day from the year.

Salutation. The salutation is a greeting like "Good morning."

Begin the salutation at the margin, put a comma after it, and capitalize the first word and all nouns. Some correct salutations are

Dear Uncle Jeremy,	*Dear Mr. Matthews,*
Dear Rusty,	*Dear Miss Romaine,*
Dear Ms. Lombardo,	*Kitty dear,* (more intimate)
Dear Grandmother,	*My dear Mrs. Jenkins,* (more formal)

Body of the Letter. The letter substitutes for you in person.

Write the message or body of the letter in paragraphs. Indent each paragraph a half inch or more. Begin a new paragraph for each change of thought. Fairly short paragraphs are easier to read than long ones.

Closing. The closing says good-bye to the reader.

Begin the closing about halfway across the page. Capitalize only the first word and put a comma at the end. Do not begin the closing with *I am, I remain,* or *Hoping.* Some correct closings are

Affectionately yours,	*Love,*
As ever,	*Sincerely yours,*

Signature. The signature identifies the writer of the letter.

1. Write your name plainly without punctuation. Never type your signature. When using the indented style, start the signature a little farther to the right than the first letter of the closing; when using the block style, start under the first letter of the closing.

2. Sign your full name if you don't know your correspondent very well or if there is danger of confusion. For friends and relatives use your first name or the nickname you go by.

Envelope. The envelope makes the first impression.

1. Use an envelope that matches your stationery.

2. For the envelope and return address, use the same style that you used in the heading of the letter—indented or block.

3. Center your correspondent's name slightly below the middle of the envelope. Always use a title—*Mr., Mrs., Ms., Miss, Dr.*

4. Place the ZIP code number after the name of the state. Use no punctuation.

5. Place your name and address in the upper left corner. Write the state and ZIP code number on the same line with the city.

```
James Ebert
   791 South Olympia Avenue
    Tulsa, Oklahoma 74106



            Dr. Mary Preston
             511 Mounts Avenue
              Denton, Texas 76201
```

ACTIVITY 3   Writing a Friendly Letter   **W**

A. Write the letter you planned for Activity 2. Address an envelope for it. In class you will exchange letters with a classmate. Use this checklist to rate your classmate's letter.

1. Is the letter pleasing to the eye and easy to read?
2. Are the heading, salutation, and closing correctly arranged? Correctly capitalized? Correctly punctuated?
3. Does the beginning make you want to read on?
4. Is there a paragraph for each topic?
5. Are there enough details to make each topic interesting?
6. Is the letter conversational in tone?
7. Is the ending lively and likely to lead to an answer?
8. Are the grammar and spelling correct?
9. Are the two addresses on the envelope complete, accurate, and easy to read?

B. When your classmate returns your letter, rewrite it if any corrections are needed. Then hand it and the envelope in.

FRIENDLY NOTES

An invitation to an informal party may be issued by telephone. To invite a friend from out of town for a weekend, however, you will need to write a note.

INVITATIONS AND REPLIES

An invitation should be complete, clear, and friendly. A good note of invitation (1) gives exact information about the occasion, date, time, place, (2) makes the person feel that she's really wanted, and (3) gives ample notice—ten days to two weeks for a weekend or a party.

An invitation should be answered the same day if possible—certainly not later than the following day. You should definitely accept the invitation or express regret at having to refuse it. "I'll come if I don't have anything else to do" is never a polite reply.

A note accepting an invitation should (1) express pleasure at the invitation and (2) repeat the date, time, and place to prevent misunderstanding.

A note of regret should (1) give a definite and real reason for refusal, (2) repeat the date, (3) show regret at being unable to accept, and (4) express gratitude for the invitation.

For this assignment your teacher will divide the class into pairs.

1. Invite your partner to a beach party, barbecue, overnight visit, school play, or other imaginary event. Make the occasion sound so enjoyable that your partner will want to accept. Include any necessary directions—how to get there, what to bring, what to wear.
2. Accept or refuse your partner's invitation. Remember that if you refuse, you must give a definite reason for not coming.

THANK-YOU LETTERS

Certain courtesy letters must be written and written promptly.

Bread-and-Butter Letters

A special kind of thank-you letter is the bread-and-butter letter written after an overnight or a weekend visit.

1. Write your letter the day you return home or the next day.
2. Usually address it to your friend's mother. (She provided your food and did most of the work of entertaining you.)
3. Mention something you particularly enjoyed about the visit.

Thank-You Notes for Gifts

Write a note of thanks for every book, dollar bill, or anything else your friends and relatives (your aunts and uncles, or your grandparents) send you to mark a birthday or other special day.

1. Be prompt. Promptness shows appreciation and also lets the sender know that the gift arrived.

2. Be sincere. If you are especially pleased with a gift, say so, but don't exaggerate or pretend. Even if you don't like or need the gift, you can always thank the giver for his thoughtfulness.

3. Be specific. Tell how you will use the gift or quote a favorable comment someone has made about it. If you have received a gift of money, tell how you expect to spend it.

Write a thank-you letter for one of the following situations.

1. Someone has recently entertained you or done you a favor.
2. A friend or relative has given you a gift for your birthday.
3. You have received a gift you don't like or don't need. Remember that you can honestly praise the material, color, design, or attractiveness of the gift even though you have no immediate use for the article.

BUSINESS LETTERS

Like your friendly letters, your business letters should be neat, attractive, and correct.   When you want to order a sweater, request information, or inquire about the price of a piece of sports equipment, you will write a business letter.   An important point to remember is that you will be writing to a stranger who will not excuse bad manners as quickly as your friends may.   A good business letter gets something done.   If your letter is clear, concise, correct, and courteous, it will be more likely to accomplish its purpose.

HOW SHOULD A BUSINESS LETTER LOOK?

How do the appearance and form of business and friendly letters differ?

```
              R. D. 1
              Winfield, Pennsylvania 17889     Heading
              May 31, 19—

Sears, Roebuck and Co.                          Inside
4640 Roosevelt Boulevard                        Address
Philadelphia, Pennsylvania 19132

Gentlemen:                                      Salutation

      In the colored pages of the regular mail-
order catalog, you list a number of specialized
booklets which you invite your customers to order.   Body
May I request the Boating and Fishing Catalog,
please?

I am looking forward to hearing from you.

              Very truly yours,                 Closing

              Alan Burton                       Signature
```

Paper and Margins

Use unruled white paper 8½ by 11 inches and matching envelope. Center your letter on the paper.   The left and right margins should be at least one inch.

Writing

Type or write in ink.   Always use blue or black ink.   Write legibly.

Heading

Write the heading in indented or block style as you do for a friendly letter. Some people prefer the indented style for pen-written letters. Both are correct.

Inside Address

This is one part a friendly letter does not have. It consists of the name and address of the person you're writing to.

1. Place the name and address of the person written to at the left margin. It should be a little lower on the page than the date.

2. Keep the same style—block or indented—in the heading, the inside address, and the envelope address.

3. Insert a period after each abbreviation and a comma between the city or town and the state.

Salutation

Begin the salutation at the margin under the inside address, place a colon after it, and capitalize the first word and all names. Correct business letter salutations are

VERY FORMAL	Sir:	My dear Sir:
	Madam:	My dear Madam:
FORMAL	Dear Sir:	Gentlemen:
	Dear Madam:	Mesdames: *or* Ladies:
MORE PERSONAL	Dear Dr. Haines:	Dear Mrs. Franklin:

Body

To do the job you want it to do, your letter should be

1. Clear. Leave no doubt in your reader's mind about what you want him to do. Say exactly what you mean.

VAGUE   I'd like some information. Our class is going on a field trip, and we want to charter a bus. I'm wondering if you can tell us how much it will cost.

CLEAR   Please tell me how much it would cost to charter a bus to take the twenty-five members of my civics class and three chaperones to Richmond for a day. We would like to schedule the trip on any Friday in April.

2. Concise. Don't waste your reader's time. Where possible, make one word do the work of two or more. Avoid old-fashioned phrases like "enclosed please find," "beg to advise," "permit me to say."

Enclosed ~~please find~~ **is** a money order for ~~eight dollars and ninety-five cents~~ (8.95).

~~This is to advise you that~~ **Y**our letter about student government at Staples gives us just the information we needed.

3. Correct. Check your letter carefully. Avoid errors in grammar, spelling, and punctuation. Write complete sentences. Avoid abbreviations, except *Mr., Mrs., Ms., Messrs., Dr., St.* (Saint), *D.C., a.m., p.m.,* and *No.* with Arabic numerals. It is better to write out the names of months, states, and countries; first names except when initials are used; *street, avenue, building,* and *company.* Avoid *etc.*

NOT THIS   Suggest you write Mr. A. Duncan, pres. of the Camera Club at Douglas Co. H. S. in Castle Rock, Colo., for information about their exhibit Nov. 6.

BUT THIS   I suggest you write Mr. Arthur Duncan, president of the Camera Club at Douglas County High School in Castle Rock, Colorado 80104, for information about their exhibit November 6.

4. Courteous. Write simply, naturally, politely. Do not blame or accuse your reader. A polite letter will help you to get what you want.

BLUNT   You must be blind or plain stupid to send me a football instead of a basketball.

COURTEOUS   On November 5, I ordered one basketball, catalog No. SX155. Today I received a football, which I am returning by parcel post.

Closing

Begin halfway across the page, capitalize the first word only, and place a comma after the last word. Courteous closings are

VERY FORMAL	Respectfully yours,	Yours respectfully,
FORMAL	Yours truly,	Very truly yours,
LESS FORMAL	Sincerely yours,	Yours sincerely,
PERSONAL	Cordially yours,	Cordially,

Signature

Always sign your full name to a business letter. Begin it under the first word of the closing or slightly to the right as you would for block or indented style friendly letters. Never place *Mr.* before your name or a punctuation mark after your name.

Because of the new convenient title *Ms.,* a woman has a choice in her signature.   She can suggest the title by which she wishes to be addressed—*Ms., Miss, Mrs.*—by the way she signs her letter.

MS.   *Nancy Romero*

MISS   *(Miss) Freda Lane*

By not indicating *Miss* or *Mrs.,* Nancy Romero shows she wishes to be addressed as *Ms.*   Freda Lane wishes to be addressed as *Miss.*

MRS.   *Elsie Stowe Martin*
              (Mrs. William H. Martin)

Elsie Stowe Martin is Mrs. Martin's signature; Mrs. William H. Martin is the name by which she wishes to be addressed.

Envelope

Study this example of an envelope addressed in block style. Then refer to page 160 for an example of indented style and suggestions for writing the envelope addresses.

```
Bruce Lamont
325 Studebaker Street
Mishawaka, Indiana 46544




                    Premier Books
                    Fawcett Publications, Inc.
                    Greenwich, Connecticut 06830
```

ACTIVITY 6   Using Correct Business Letter Form   **W**

Write the heading, inside address, salutation, closing, and signature of each letter.   Punctuate correctly.   Then draw rectangles $6\frac{1}{2}$ inches by $3\frac{5}{8}$ inches, and address the envelopes.

1. From your school address write to Films, Incorporated, 1150 Wilmette Avenue, Wilmette, Illinois 60091.   Use indented style.
2. From your home address write Mr. Maurice Weare, Manager, The Cliff House, Ogunquit, Maine 03907.   Use block style.

WRITING FOR INFORMATION

One of the most frequent uses of the business letter is to write for information.

1. Don't write busy people for information you can secure in the library. Don't ask questions calling for long answers.

2. Make your question clear and concise. Give all the necessary information.

NOT   What store handles the boots in your advertisement?
BUT   Will you please tell me what store in my area handles the Spinkaster Waders you advertised in the June *Field & Stream?*

3. Explain briefly why you want the information.

I am going to talk about flash photography at the February meeting of my school Camera Club and would like to use the booklet as a reference.

4. Enclose a stamped, self-addressed envelope unless you are likely to repay your informant with an order or in some other way.

5. Be courteous. Do not demand information "by return mail," "at once," or "as soon as possible." Most firms are prompt because promptness wins friends for a business.

ACTIVITY 7   Writing Business Letters   W

1. Write to U.S. Geological Survey, Washington, D.C. 20025, for the folder describing topographic maps and symbols. There is no charge for the folder.

2. In a letter to the Lost and Found Department of a bus or railroad company or an airline, describe accurately a package, bag, umbrella, raincoat, or other article you left on a bus, train, or plane. (Look in the phone book for the name and address of a company in your area.) Tell definitely where and when you left it. Ask whether it has been turned in to the Lost and Found office.

3. You wish to spend the summer on a dude ranch in the Rocky Mountain area. Write Camp Advisory Service, 500 Fifth Avenue, New York, New York 10036, for information. Include your age and the approximate amount you can spend.

4. One month before your aunt's birthday you ordered a lifetime address book #6914 from Damar's, 545 Bloomfield Avenue, Montclair, New Jersey 07042. It is now ten days before her birthday, and you have not received the book. Write a letter, requesting immediate shipment or cancellation of your order.

11 *Publishing a Class Newspaper*

"I guess I'll have to wait till I'm a senior to work on the *Hickory Log*," sighed Glen.

"Aren't you forgetting about the class reporters?" asked Don.

"But this year's have been chosen," protested Linda.

"Would you three really like to see your words in print?" asked Miss Walter, their English teacher.

"Would we!" they chorused.

"Maybe you can't join the staff of the school paper right now," continued Miss Walter, "but you can publish a class paper. I must warn you, though, that meeting deadlines is hard work. Do you think you can persuade English 9B to cooperate with you?"

"Why don't we make a class paper the topic for the next meeting of Symposium 9B?" asked Glen. (See pages 231–234.)

"That's a good idea," said Linda. "In the meantime we'd better think of some good reasons for publishing a class paper."

"We can also do some research on how to go about it," added Don.

PUBLISHING A CLASS PAPER

Every student can be an editor or a reporter and can experience the need for teamwork in the publication of a newspaper. When you write for publication, you will use many of the skills you should master during the year. A good reporter talks easily to people, listens carefully, observes sharply, remembers accurately, and writes briefly and clearly. By trying news stories, feature stories, columns, editorials, and letters to the editor, you can find your special talent and prepare for work on the school paper.

STAFF

Everyone should have a specific assignment and know his duties. To provide experience in the different jobs, your class may decide to change positions for each issue. A class paper requires the following staff:

1. *Editor in chief*   writes editorials; arranges the material on the pages; has general charge of paper

2. *Assistant editors*   help the editor in chief

3. *News editor*   makes assignments to reporters; sets deadline for completion of stories; helps gather news; selects the best stories for publication

4. *Copy editor*   reads and revises material submitted, correcting errors in grammar, spelling, punctuation, and word choice; writes headlines

5. *Business manager*	supervises "publication"
6. *Art editor*	prints headlines; draws illustrations
7. *Reporters*	write news stories
8. *Special contributors*	write copy for special departments

ACTIVITY 1 Choosing a Staff   **S**

After studying the duties of the staff members for a class paper, choose a staff for your paper.

A NOSE FOR NEWS

TIPS ON BEING A GOOD REPORTER

1. Sharpen your news sense. Keep your eyes and ears open for unusual features in the most ordinary events. (See pages 121–128.)
2. Accept assignments cheerfully.
3. Be prompt in meeting deadlines.
4. Learn to talk easily with all kinds of people.
5. Get facts from every possible source.
6. Listen carefully. Write important details in your notebook.
7. Write briefly, clearly, and correctly. Use active, vivid verbs (see pages 264–267) and specific nouns (see pages 126, 127).

NOT   A student was on a club program yesterday.

BUT   Peggy Shippen, a Warwick ninth-grader, spoke about her experiences in Puerto Rico to members of her Spanish club on March 2.

Cut out deadwood (see pages 457, 458) and vague words like *fine, nice, very, so, quite.* Don't choke your sentences with adjectives and adverbs.

NOT   Made of pottery and brown in color and decorated with an awfully nice design along the lines of a cameo, this teapot came to America on the *Mayflower.*

BUT   Made of brown pottery and decorated with a cameo design, this teapot came to America on the *Mayflower.*

8. Be accurate. Don't twist facts. Double-check dates, times, places, and spelling of names.

ACTIVITY 2 Testing News Sense   **OS**

Can you pick out the newsworthy element in each set of facts? What point should be emphasized in each?

1. The Cavaliers, your ninth-grade basketball team, played the Beach-combers, another ninth-grade team, on February 17. The score was 47 to 29 in favor of the Cavaliers. The Cavaliers made 17 field goals and 13 foul shots. This victory brings the Cavaliers' winning streak to ten consecutive games. High scorer for the Cavaliers was Mike Mooney with 14 points. You are reporting the game for your class paper.

2. The Panorama will be held Saturday, December 6, in the Quincy Senior High gymnasium. The concert is sponsored by the Adams County Music Educators Association. Quincy will be the only school in the county to participate. The Panorama will be directed for the first time by the music teachers themselves. You are a reporter for the Quincy school paper.

ACTIVITY 3 Spelling Names Correctly   S

A list of the names appearing most frequently in the news is helpful to the editorial staff. As the start of such a list for your class paper, prepare a list of the organizations in your school with the names of the officers and faculty sponsor. Is every name correct?

CONTENTS

A class paper often contains both newspaper and magazine material. Many classes have followed the plan of devoting half the paper to school and class news and the other half to special departments, such as stories, poetry, travel, unusual experiences, hobbies, pupil problems, book and movie reviews, radio and television news, science notes, humor, and letters to the editor.

THE NEWS STORY

The backbone of the newspaper is the news story.

What are good sources? Start in your own classroom. Observe in the library, the cafeteria, or the halls. Watch the bulletin boards and exhibits. Talk with administrative officials, teachers, club and class officers, and other students. What's going on that will inform and entertain your readers?

ACTIVITY 4 Finding Sources for News   S

You have just been appointed a reporter on your school newspaper. Make a list of the persons and places in your school building that will make good sources of news.

Add to your list of news sources any local adult organizations that might be interested in the welfare of your school: Parents' Association, local public library, Board of Education, for example.

How do you gather information? Your own observation will probably provide all the facts you need to report on the championship baseball game. If you want to give some biographical details about a famous graduate, however, you'll probably do some research in the library (see pages 247–256). For information about a club meeting you didn't attend, you can interview the president or the sponsor.

TIPS ON INTERVIEWING

1. Learn all you can about the person to be interviewed.
2. Think of several questions to ask during the interview.
3. Arrange an appointment as a representative of your paper.
4. Dress neatly.
5. Arrive on time, introduce yourself, and state your purpose.
6. Carry on the interview as a conversation.
7. Ask permission to take notes or to quote specific items.
8. Be courteous. Thank the person for giving you his time.

ACTIVITY 5   Getting the Facts by Interviewing   LO

Interview someone in your school to get the facts for a news story that you want to write. You might, for example, interview (1) the manager about new uniforms purchased for the band or football team, (2) the principal about new study hall regulations, (3) the sponsor about the purpose of a new club, or (4) the director about the next Thespian production. Jot down the facts while they are fresh in your mind, and save them for Activities 9 and 12.

How do you write a news story? To write a good news story you must learn a special technique. Keep your paragraphs brief — fifty to one hundred words. Make each paragraph a complete unit in itself. Write your story in the inverted pyramid form ($\triangledown$). Tell the whole story briefly in the first paragraph, called the "lead" (pronounced *leed*). In the remaining paragraphs, give details about the facts of the lead in order of decreasing importance and timeliness.

The inverted pyramid form helps both the reader and the editor. The busy reader can quickly get the facts by reading just the lead. If late news makes it necessary to shorten a story, the editor can cut off the last paragraphs without leaving out any important facts. Apply the cut-off test to every news story you write.

ACTIVITY 6   Applying the Cut-off Test   RS

Examine the following news story about a field trip. Place a piece of paper over the last paragraph. Has any important fact about the trip been omitted? Move your paper up to cut off the last two paragraphs. Is the story still complete? Are all the important facts included?

STUDENTS ATTEND SCIENCE OPEN HOUSE

Fifteen Morton students saw for themselves how a **Important**
science research and testing center operates when **facts**
they attended the fifth annual Science Open House on
November 14 at the University of Chicago.

Presiding over the activities was Professor John
A. Simpson, head of the University's Cosmic Radiation
Group. Professor Simpson warned the 1000 teen-age
students from Illinois, Indiana, Michigan, and Wisconsin not ·to become overspecialized in their education. "You should have as part of your background
a knowledge of social studies and humanities," he
advised.

Professor Herbert L. Anderson, Director of the **Facts of**
University of Chicago Enrico Fermi Institute for **less**
Nuclear Studies; Marcel Schein, cosmic ray physicist; **importance**
and Richard H. Dalitz, elementary particle physicist
who toured Soviet laboratories last summer, gave
reports on the United States and Russian progress in
physics.

Students from East who attended the open house **Details of**
are James Dvorak, Robert Jablonski, John MacConnell, **least**
Simon Pilkis, Jeff Polz, Richard Toleikis, and Keith **importance**
Weir. These students were mainly interested in the
discussion of newer scientific developments through
research and in seeing the facilities at the University.

TIPS ON WRITING A LEAD

1. Tell the important facts — *what* happened, *who* did it, *where*, *when*, and sometimes *why* and *how* — in the lead.

   EXAMPLE One hundred fifty gold Christmas corsages (what) were made of beads, seedpods, leaves, and ribbons (how) by commercial art students of Mrs. Lillian Sinnott (who) for the Christmas party (why) at the Spencer State Hospital (where), December 22 (when).

2. Start with the most important fact. *What* or *who* is generally the most newsworthy detail; *when* or *where* the least.

3. Don't crowd the first sentence of a lead. If the *what* and *who* take up a whole sentence, put the other three *W*'s and the *H* in another sentence or even into the second paragraph.

CROWDED "The Magic of Magic" is the theme of the variety show to be presented in the school auditorium on Friday and Saturday, December 4 and 5, for the benefit of the student exchange project, according to Kathy Ensz, student producer.

IMPROVED "The Magic of Magic" is the theme of the variety show to be presented for the benefit of the student exchange project, according to Kathy Ensz, student producer. The show will be held in the school auditorium on Friday and Saturday, December 4 and 5.

4. Consider using participles, adverb or noun clauses, or infinitives to make your leads more compact. (See Chapters **30 and 31.**)

PARTICIPLE Selected as Junior Citizen of the Month of November, SGHS senior Pamela Crane was honored at a luncheon meeting of the Alhambra Civitan Club recently.

INFINITIVE To climax homecoming activities, 632 couples danced to the music of Iver Buerk's orchestra in the gym.

ADVERB CLAUSE If you can play a harp, dance a jig, or yodel, you're wanted for the variety show scheduled for February 19.

NOUN CLAUSE That American teachers are friendly and helpful is the opinion of ninth-grader Tony Kelly, new arrival from Durham, England.

5. Choose the first five or six words carefully. Avoid colorless phrases like "there have been" and vague words like "strange sounds."

NOT "There is to be a social event for the Library Club on October 23," announces Jeannette Cooper, president.

BUT "A hayride on October 23 is the first social event of the Library Club," announces Jeannette Cooper, president.

ACTIVITY 7 Studying Leads S

1. Refer to the lead in the news story on page 173. Indicate which of the five *W*'s each part of the lead answers. Does it answer the *H*? Show how the lead does or does not meet the preceding suggestions for writing a lead.

2. Clip and bring to class three leads from a daily newspaper. Point out the *W*'s and the *H*. Do any open with an adverbial clause, a participle, or an infinitive?

ACTIVITY 8   Rewriting Leads   **W**

You are the copy editor on a newspaper. Write these two leads in a more interesting way without omitting any facts.

1. A home is needed for next year's foreign exchange student. Any student may apply to Room 12B. Forms are now available. The announcement was made in assembly Friday by Mr. Lloyd Stephens, principal.

2. The Homemaking Department's class in Child Development recently borrowed a real child, baby brother of one of the members of the class. The class taught by Mrs. Dale Ford observed the lively infant for physical, social, and emotional abilities. Every student enjoyed the lesson that day.

ACTIVITY 9   Writing Leads   **W**

1. Refer to the notes of your interview for Activity 5. What are the essential facts? What is the most newsworthy fact? Write the lead for your news story.

2. As a reporter for the school newspaper you have made notes of the following facts for a news story. Pick out the essential information and write a short, vivid lead.

The Atomic Energy Club met on December 7 in the physics lab.

Program: checking half-life of a drop of iodine

Definition: Half-life is the time it takes the radioactivity in the iodine to decrease one half.

Procedure: drop placed in small container; Geiger counter and electroscope used to measure decrease in radiation; graph made to record decrease over short periods of time

Previous programs: (1) visited Blessing Hospital to learn how X ray works, uses of X rays, and safety precautions and (2) figured operating voltage of Geiger tubes

EDITORIALIZING

Your business as a reporter is to tell what you know, not what you think. In your news story give only the facts. Avoid "editorializing" — using *I* and *we* and expressing your own opinion. Leave to the editorial columns your comments on the news.

NOT   Boys at West High are more intelligent than the girls.

BUT   Figures released this week for the third grading period show that 54 percent of the West students listed on the Honor Scrolls are boys. (The reporter gives a fact that the reader may check.)

ACTIVITY 10   Avoiding Editorializing   W

Rewrite the following news stories omitting all expressions of personal opinion.   Condense the stories until only facts are left.

1. Two hundred and ten lucky freshman and sophomore girls were initiated into popular Hi-Tri on September 11.

In the impressive ceremony the lofty aims of Hi-Tri were superbly depicted by the talented Hi-Tri Council.   The main theme was the inspiring Hi-Tri motto, "We build the ladder by which we rise."

2. Lovely Linda Prince, the pride of Sharon Junior High School, received a well-deserved first place in the girls' slalom contest at the county-wide ski tournament last Saturday afternoon at Blue Mountain.

Three other of popular Coach Bahnson's courageous Trojans captured third-place ribbons in the more important events.

ACTIVITY 11   Studying a News Story   R

Read again the news story on page 173.   Does the story contain adequate, specific information?   Prove.   Did the reporter express his opinion or use *I* or *we*?   How do you think the reporter got the facts for his story?   What questions might he have asked during an interview with a member of the group?

ACTIVITY 12   Writing a News Story   W

1. In Activity 5 you collected facts for a news story and in Activity 9 you wrote the lead.   Complete the story.   Be sure you arrange the details in order of decreasing importance.   Check your story for accuracy and editorializing.   Apply the cut-off test. Perhaps your teacher will submit the best stories to the school paper.

2. Read the dramatization of the meeting of Symposium 9B. (See pages 231–234.)   Then write a news story about the meeting. Make sure that your lead gives the important facts in an interesting way.   Limit your story to about 100 words.

3. Using the notes about the Atomic Energy Club in Activity 9 and the lead you wrote, complete the story.   Find in the notes the important facts and put first things first.

HEADLINE WRITING

A good headline brightens the news page, accurately summarizes the lead, and encourages readers to read the story.   The copy editor, who reads and sometimes rewrites the reporter's copy, is responsible for writing headlines.   The size of the headline depends on the importance of the story.   The headline must fit its space.   Because print cannot be stretched, headline writers learn to compress a great deal of information into a brief space.

TEN TIPS FOR HEADLINE WRITERS

1. Use a subject and a verb. If the meaning is clear, omit forms of the verb *to be.*

Homemaking   Pagan Festival
Pupils View   Now Modern Holiday
Fashion Show   (*Is* has been omitted.)

2. Use the present tense for past or present events. Use the infinitive for future events.

PAST EVENT	FUTURE EVENT
Football Coach	Football Coach
Awards Letters	To Award Letters

3. Be specific. Use specific words, proper names, and numbers wherever possible.

POOR	GOOD
Department Wins Awards	Ag Department Wins
(What department? How many	15 Awards at Fair
awards?)	

4. Use lively verbs. Choose verbs that express action.

POOR   Globe-Trotter Is on Faculty
BETTER   Globe-Trotter Joins Faculty

5. Use active rather than passive verbs whenever possible. Avoid negative statements.

POOR   Laboratories Are Toured by Natural Science Club
BETTER   Natural Science Club Tours Laboratories

6. Make a clean break at the end of each line. Never divide a word. Do not separate a first name from a last name, a preposition from its object, or an adjective from the noun it modifies.

7. Do not clutter a line with *a, an, the,* or *there were.* Avoid helping verbs like *may.*

8. Capitalize the first and the last word of each line and all other words except prepositions and conjunctions.

9. Avoid abbreviations. Abbreviations like PTA, YMCA, and the initials standing for the name of your school are permissible, but never abbreviate a common word because of lack of space.

10. Write headlines that require little, if any, punctuation. Never use a period. A vivid headline will not need an exclamation point.

ACTIVITY 13   Improving Headlines   W

Using the preceding ten tips as guides, improve the following headlines. Supply any details you need to make a headline better. Keep the number of letters in each line approximately equal.

1. $150 Is Won by
   Jan Tate with Pie!
2. Group Has Plans
   for Spring; Visi-
   tors Are to Be Greeted
3. Letters Are Awarded
   To Many Players

4. M. Neuman Is Capt.
   of QJHS Patrol
5. Hornets Are the Victors
   over the Eaglets by a
   Large Margin
6. Generous Sum Is to Be Spent
   by Dads for School Projects

ACTIVITY 14   Writing Headlines   W

1. Write the headlines for the news stories you wrote for Activity 12.

2. Write headlines for the leads you rewrote for Activity 8 and for the news stories you rewrote for Activity 10.

THE EDITORIAL

When you write an editorial, remember that you speak for your paper and that your paper speaks for your school. In an editorial you may comment on news, interpret it, or express an opinion about it. The opinion may be your own. You may also present reasons for adopting a certain policy or suggest ways for reaching a desired goal.

To attract readers and stimulate them to thinking about a problem, base your editorials on school happenings. Keep your editorials brief — from 200 to 300 words. Don't command or scold; avoid a string of *don't*'s. Use a positive approach. State the problem clearly and suggest a remedy. Illustrate with a specific example, perhaps a hypothetical one. If you can, add a bit of humor.

ACTIVITY 15   Studying an Editorial   R

Read the following editorial. Does the title arouse your curiosity and make you want to read it? What is the school problem on which the editorial is based? Does the writer use a positive approach? Prove. What does the writer want the reader to do?

SAFETY FIRST

Almost daily, news stories tell of young would-be scientists who have injured themselves with homemade rockets.

Nothing beats the scientific method when it comes to learning facts. What would we do without the scientific spirit of research and determination and dedication? Most of the devices that make our day-to-day lives comfortable came into being through experimentation.

But there are times when experimentation should be confined to the laboratory. Experiments that could be dangerous in any way are properly carried on under controlled conditions, with adequate supervision, and with proper precautions against damage to person or property.

The *Journal* agrees that there is need for scientific study and research. But the *Journal* does not want to publish the story of a tragedy resulting from a student's backyard experiments with dangerous materials. The *Journal* will be happy, however, to publish reports of scientific experiments performed under controlled laboratory conditions. The *Journal* therefore urges all would-be scientists at Warwick to join the new science club.

ACTIVITY 16 Writing an Editorial   **TW**

In a vigorous editorial express a definite opinion on one of the following topics (or another topic) as it concerns your school. Choose a title that will attract readers.

1. Borrowers. 2. A new debt to Lincoln (or some other great American). 3. Library manners. 4. A cafeteria regulation. 5. Traffic in the halls. 6. Assembly manners. 7. The flag. 8. Making vacations safe. 9. Treatment of new students. 10. The meaning of Thanksgiving (or another holiday). 11. Gossip. 12. Litterbugs. 13. A tribute to a teacher. 14. Preparing for college. 15. Halloween pranksters. 16. Joining a school club. 17. Dance attendance. 18. United Fund, Junior Red Cross, or March of Dimes campaign. 19. The dictionary. 20. Learning to study. 21. Care of public property. 22. The school magazine. 23. Service to the school. 24. Examinations. 25. Fair play — on and off the field.

LETTERS TO THE EDITOR

Do you think some condition around school needs improvement? Do you disagree with the opinion expressed in an editorial? Do you think some person or group should be praised publicly? Write a letter to the editor of your paper. Be brief, factual, and courteous. Use as a salutation: *To the Editor of* (give the name of your paper). Omit the letter closing but sign your name.

A visit to the Lincoln Memorial, ideal subject for a feature story

Write a letter to the editor of your school paper about some condition in your school that needs improvement. If you wish, use a topic suggested in Activity 16.

FEATURES

Besides news stories and editorials, papers have feature stories, cartoons, and columns. Such features brighten the paper and increase the reader's understanding and enjoyment of his surroundings.

For a column for your class or school paper you may write brief items, jokes, or comment on such topics as sports, hobbies, books, and fashion. Avoid canned jokes. Look for humorous happenings around school. Don't gossip or include anything that may hurt anybody's feelings.

In a feature story you do not have to follow the inverted pyramid form. After catching the reader's attention in the first sentence, arrange the details of the story as you choose. You may leave the point of the story, or the punch line, until the last sentence.

Feature stories, like new stories, are based on facts, but they often enlarge upon the news in a free and often entertaining way. What's the news behind the front-page story about the student-council election results? You might write a feature about counting and tallying the ballots. Look for something funny, sad, or unusual about persons, places, or things. How did your classmates spend their vacations? What are their hobbies? Are there any twins in your school? Why were all the clocks stopped at 9:30? What does the foreign exchange student think of American football?

Winning A By-Line

A columnist or an outstanding writer is frequently awarded a *by-line*, the line that indicates authorship of a special article. In the following brightly written observation of the new band member's first day on the parade ground, Pat Bowen has won his by-line.

Left, Right, Wrong

by Pat Bowen

School has been in session about one week when the new students in the band have a startling revelation — this band marches and plays at the same time! On the first rainy day the band slogs out to the field.

"Ten hut! For'd march! 1! 2!"

Before all of these commands have passed in one of our beginner's ears and out the other, he is standing all alone,

watching the band march down the field. He starts to catch
up, and whoops! He falls headlong in the mud, a tangle of
arms and legs. But no time to bemoan the mess of his new
shirt; the band is already advancing toward him like a giant
lawn mower and he envisions an army of shoe soles trampling
him.

Finally, after an arduous struggle, he gets into line, but
that doesn't help a bit. He's still lost. Never before has
he had to know which is his left foot and which is his right.

Even worse, he's supposed to know the proper marching
form. First Mr. Hilgendorf demonstrates how to march with
your knees hitting your chin each time you take a step and
how only lazy characters march with their heels dragging
along the cement. Our beginner experiments, gets his chin
black and blue, and then goes back to dragging his heels.

Ah, now he's got it. They're playing follow the leader.
It's a cinch! He just follows that tough-looking upper-
classman ahead of him.

But it isn't long before he is confused again. The rest
of the band has turned around, and he's standing face-to-face
with that tough-looking upper classman.

ACTIVITY 18 Writing a Feature   W

Write a feature story on a topic that would interest the readers
of your school newspaper. Or write a sports, book, fashion, or
humor column. Be original.

THE SCHOOL MAGAZINE

To the magazine section of your class paper or to the school
magazine you may contribute short stories (see Chapter 6), poems
(see Chapter 14), articles (see Chapter 9), essays, humor, accounts
of travel, biographies, autobiographies, or art work. You can use
your imagination and restore *I* and *we* to your writing. Readers of
a school magazine want to know how you feel and what you think.

ACTIVITY 19 Sharing Experiences   W

You like to hear your classmates' experiences — where they have
traveled, what unusual sights they have seen, what adventures they
have had, and what they do in their spare time. Share one of your
experiences with your classmates by writing about it for your class
paper. The following suggestions may help you to choose a topic.

1. I win a blue ribbon. 2. A science club experiment. 3. I earn my first dollar. 4. My first night in the woods. 5. When I sat down to play. 6. I can laugh about it now. 7. I "shoot" my first deer. 8. I try acting. 9. The broken window. 10. Fun on skates. 11. I drive the tractor. 12. Dogs are people. 13. I paint my room. 14. My first roller coaster ride. 15. Building a model car (or airplane). 16. The day I took the vacuum cleaner (or something else) apart.

FORMAT

How will you present your news stories, features, editorials, short stories, poems, and magazine articles to readers? Because of the expense involved, a class paper can rarely be printed. Try one of these methods instead.

1. Write your contribution carefully on a strip of paper about 4 inches wide. A sheet of heavy wrapping paper 24″ × 40″ folded makes four pages 20″ × 24″ on which to paste the strips like columns of a newspaper. Assign your art editor the job of printing the name of the paper and the headlines.
2. Have articles typed on strips of paper about $2\frac{1}{2}$ inches wide — adding-machine paper, for example. Letter headlines by hand, arrange the articles for a page like the page of a newspaper, and then paste them on a folded sheet of 22″ × 30″ Bristol board.
3. After all contributions have been received and the editor in chief has planned the arrangement of the articles, have the paper stenciled page by page. When the stencils are run off on the mimeograph, each pupil will have his own copy of the class paper.

ACTIVITY 20 Studying Words in Action   VW

The following words were used in this chapter. The page number is after each word. What does each word mean in the context in which it appears? Use each word in a sentence of your own. Check your spelling.

cameo 170	sponsor 172	factual 179
consecutive 171	humanities 173	envisions 182
biographical 172	hypothetical 178	arduous 182

Unit Three — *Reading*

12   *Building Reading Skills*

Pete skimmed the front page of the newspaper. "A million dollars!" He whistled and began to read carefully.

U.S. HONORS A DEBT TO ROCKET'S PIONEER

By JOHN W. FINNEY

Special to The New York Times.

WASHINGTON, Aug. 4—The Government has agreed to pay $1,000,000 for infringing upon the patented rocket inventions of the late Dr. Robert H. Goddard, one of the early pioneers in development of today's space-age missiles.

The settlement marks the first sizable monetary recognition for the oft-scorned work that Dr. Goddard did three and four decades ago. At that time he developed rocket principles now incorporated into ballistic missiles that can span oceans and rockets that can hurl payloads deep into space.

The payment was also further but posthumous vindication for Dr. Goddard. During his lifetime he was often derided as "moon-mad Goddard." As early as 1919, he suggested in a scientific paper that it would be possible to build a rocket capable of going to the moon.

One group that did not deride his work was composed of the German rocket experts who incorporated many of his ideas into their V–2 rocket in World War II.

Dr. Goddard died in August, 1945, at the age of 62. At that time the military was just beginning to consider, and not too enthusiastically, the development of long-range ballistic missiles. His death came almost exactly fourteen years before the first rocket landed on the moon.[1]

"Moon-mad!" Pete exclaimed as his thoughts wandered for a moment to the far horizons beyond the earth.

The beginning of the news story from the *New York Times* gives a hint of the information you will find in most newspapers. Pete has learned that a newspaper helps him to be better informed and to have more fun. Do you, like Pete, read a newspaper regularly? And have you discovered how much profit and pleasure you can get from reading magazines and books too?

ACTIVITY 1 *Making an Inventory of Your Reading*   OS

For a week keep a list of at least ten items you read in newspapers, magazines, or books, other than your regular textbooks. Include the headline or title of an article or story. Prepare to discuss your inventory in class and suggest how to vary your reading program.

EXAMPLE

Week of —   My Reading Inventory
Wednesday: "G.I. Won't Walk If Army Has Way" *New York Times*
           "Estrada, Orioles, Blanks Tigers, 3–0"   "   "   "
           Television Program   "   "   "
           "The Wild, Wild West"   *American Heritage*
           Chapters 1 and 2   *No Room in the Ark*

[1] Reprinted by permission of the *New York Times*.

YOUR DAILY NEWSPAPER

A good newspaper avoids sensationalism. It reports news completely, accurately, and fairly. It keeps the reader informed about things that will affect him, his family, his town, and his country. It provides entertainment features like pictures, columns, and cartoons. It keeps a sense of proportion, recognizing that an announcement by the President is more important than a society divorce.

What kind of paper do you read?

ACTIVITY 2   Studying Newspapers   S

A. Study your newspaper, and prepare to answer the following questions. Be ready to prove your statements with examples.

1. How much space is devoted to local, state, national, and foreign news?
2. Is the news in the paper up to the minute? Does it use one or more of the news-gathering services like Associated Press (AP) or United Press International (UPI)?
3. How much space is given to divorces, murders, and scandals?
4. Are the headlines accurate, informative, in good taste?
5. Are the editorials based on important current events? Do the editors support their statements with facts?
6. Do the letters to the editor express intelligent opinions, or do the writers engage in name calling? Are there letters on both sides of a question?
7. Does your newspaper contain a helpful index to the news? Where is the index located?
8. Does your newspaper provide entertaining and worthwhile news about inventions and scientific discoveries? Art? Books? Business? Education? Movies? Music? Radio and television? The theater? Weather?
9. Is sport news reported colorfully, accurately, fairly?
10. How much of the paper is advertising? Are the advertisements attractive? Are they of interest or value to the reader? Do they avoid making extravagant claims?

B. Using the above questions as a guide, compare your newspaper with one from another city.

READING A NEWS STORY

You won't have time to read your paper from beginning to end. Learn to select. News stories are written and arranged for busy people. If you examine a typical news story, you will discover that the headline gives the most important facts. The first paragraph, or lead, tells the story briefly. The other paragraphs give details. By reading headlines, a number of first paragraphs, and a few complete stories of special interest, you can get a good idea of the day's happenings.

ACTIVITY 3   Studying a News Story   R

Reread the news story on page 185 and then answer these questions.

1. What fact is told in the headline?
2. What additional information is supplied in the first paragraph?
3. What information is provided in paragraphs two and three?
4. What details do the fourth and fifth paragraphs supply?
5. Of all the information given what are you most likely to remember? Why?

ACTIVITY 4   Following a News Story   R

In your daily newspaper follow an important news story for three or more days. On what page did the story first appear? Did it appear on another page the second or third day? Did the later reports change your opinion about the event? How?

READING AN EDITORIAL

An editorial comments on news, interprets it, expresses an opinion about news, presents reasons for adopting a certain policy, or suggests ways for reaching a desired goal. When you read an editorial, ask: "What was the editor's purpose in writing this editorial?" "What does she want me to do?" "How is the editorial related to the news?" (An editorial may appear a day or two after the news story.) "Does the writer present sound reasons for his opinions?"

ACTIVITY 5   Studying an Editorial   R

Read on page 188 the editorial that appeared in the *New York Times* the day following the news story about Dr. Goddard, the rocket pioneer.

1. What is the purpose of the editorial?
2. Which sentence sums up the purpose?
3. What does the editor want you to do?
4. What do *perspective* and *speculation* mean as used in this editorial? What common root do they have?

AMERICA'S ROCKET PIONEER

From the present perspective it seems incredible that only a few decades ago many of his neighbors scoffed at Dr. Robert H. Goddard and considered him "moon-mad." The passage of time has silenced the scoffers and today we know that this modest scientist from Worcester, Mass., was one of the founders of the age of space, one of the great pioneers of the modern science of rocketry with all its promise and all its dangers. The United States Government's decision this week to pay $1,000,000 for the infringements upon the basic Goddard patents simply represents a belated financial and legal recognition of his great contributions.

The case of Dr. Goddard reminds us once again of the importance of maintaining a climate of freedom of research and of willingness to aid the lone-wolf scientist who is looking beyond the immediate horizon of his field. Dr. Goddard died fifteen years ago. His entire life was lived, therefore, in a period when public opinion assumed that space travel was a matter of the very distant future, the proper field of speculation only for writers of science fiction.

Fortunately, there were those in this country who had a wider view. It was a historic service first of the Smithsonian Institution and then of the Daniel and Florence Guggenheim Foundation that they financed Dr. Goddard's research at a time when most people thought his goals were fantastic. This week's news should not only remind us of Goddard's greatness but increase our determination that similar pioneers struggling today receive the help they need, rather than be overlooked because of foreshortened vision or because of the notion that only highly organized scientific teams can come up with important fresh discoveries.[1]

ACTIVITY 6   **Reporting on a Special Feature**   **OR**

Prepare to tell the class about a special feature you enjoy — for example, a book review, a movie review, a teen-age column. Bring the newspaper to class and show where this feature usually appears.

WHAT MAGAZINES DO YOU READ?

Most of us know only a handful of magazines by name; yet the total number of magazines published in the United States is close to six thousand. Some appeal to certain groups — photographers, stamp collectors, sailing enthusiasts, boys and girls. Some magazines have stories, articles, cartoons, and advertisements that appeal to the entire family. Some report and analyze the news. With a little exploration you can find a magazine tailored to your interests.

ACTIVITY 7   **Taking a Magazine Poll**   **S**

Take a poll of the magazines read by your class. Which magazines are most popular? Why?

Bring copies of your favorite magazine to class. Your teacher may appoint one committee to classify the magazines according to type and another to arrange a display of the most popular magazines.

[1] Reprinted by permission of the *New York Times*.

ACTIVITY 8   Preparing a Magazine List   S

As a class project prepare a magazine list. Each student should examine a different magazine and jot down on a library card a brief description of its contents.

EXAMPLE *Popular Science Monthly* — magazine of science telling of events and discoveries — departments on hobbies and projects

ACTIVITY 9   Judging a Magazine   OS

Magazines vary in quality as well as content. Prepare to tell your classmates about the magazine you examined in Activity 8. Bring a copy to class and illustrate your points. Base your evaluation of the magazine on the following.

1. Purpose. What kind of magazine is it? How does it differ from others of similar type?

2. Appeal. What readers will enjoy the magazine most — older people, teen-agers, men, women, whole family, those with a special interest? What are its features? How does it differ from other magazines of the same type?

3. Contents. Are its articles timely, informative, varied, interestingly written? Are the stories worth reading? Does it try to give more than one side of a controversial issue?

4. Appearance. Is the magazine good-looking? Is the paper of good quality? Is the print easy to read? Are the photographs clear? Do the illustrations catch your eye?

5. Cost. How much does the magazine cost?' Is it worth the price?

6. Advertising. Is the advertising in good taste?

ACTIVITY 10   Reporting on a Topic of Current Interest   OR

Broaden your information on a topic of current interest by reading articles about it in two different magazines. Use these questions as a guide for a report to your classmates.

1. In what magazines did you find the two articles? What are the titles of the articles?
2. Who wrote each article? Is the author qualified to write on the subject? How did he get his information?
3. What was the main idea of each article? What points did each author use to develop his theme?
4. Is the information sound? Are there any errors in thinking in either article? Give specific examples to illustrate your answer. (See Chapter 17.)

5. What is your personal predisposition on the subject? Did you carefully weigh each idea before accepting or rejecting it? Why do you agree or disagree with each article?
6. What did you know about the subject before you read the articles? Did you learn anything new? How can you use what you have learned?

GETTING MORE FROM YOUR READING

If you don't enjoy reading, you probably haven't learned to read efficiently. To get more pleasure and profit from reading, know what kind of material you are reading and why you are reading it.

Adjust Your Speed to the Material and Your Purpose

The fable of the tortoise and the hare just doesn't work with reading. If you laboriously concentrate on every word, you may miss the point of the sentence or the paragraph. Read words in groups. The rapid reader usually understands best and remembers longest. Learn to vary your silent reading rate according to your purpose and the nature of the material.

CHART OF READING RATES

RATE	MATERIAL	POSSIBLE PURPOSE
Slow, thorough reading, with some rereading	Textbooks	To understand thoroughly
	Technical articles	To review for a test
	Editorials	To get another point of view
	Key news reports	To keep facts straight
	Directions	To make or do something
	Drama ⎱ Poetry ⎰	To prepare for reading aloud and to appreciate author's style
Average	Easy textbooks ⎱ Newspapers ⎰	To get the main idea and important details
	Magazines ⎱ Fiction ⎰	To spend pleasant, relaxing time
Skimming	Dictionary	To locate a specific answer
	Telephone directory	To find a telephone number
	Easy material	To find the main idea
	Newspapers ⎱ Magazines ⎰	To look for a particular item of interest
	Stories	To learn what happens next
	Study material	To get an overall picture

Which reading rate would be appropriate for the various activities listed below: (a) slow and thorough reading, with some rereading; (b) average speed; (c) rapid skimming for specific point?

EXAMPLE

Looking up a telephone number
Looking up a telephone number usually calls for skimming (c).

1. Doing a science experiment
2. Looking through a newspaper to see what movie is playing at the neighborhood theater
3. Reading a human interest story in a newspaper
4. Memorizing a poem
5. Reading an article about astronauts in the *Reader's Digest*
6. Building a hi-fi set from directions in a do-it-yourself kit
7. Reading an article on satellites in a scientific journal
8. Finding the pronunciation of *choleric* in the dictionary
9. Checking a timetable to see what time the next bus leaves for Fargo
10. Looking at the schedule board at the air terminal to see what time Flight 452 will arrive from San Francisco

Look for the Main Idea

Every book, story, or article is composed of paragraphs. A well-written paragraph develops one main idea, usually expressed in a topic sentence (see pages 55–57). Although it is often first, the topic sentence may come anywhere in the paragraph. The good reader looks for the main idea in each paragraph and mentally files it.

What is the main idea of the following paragraph? Where is the topic sentence? Read the entire paragraph.

A pair of elephants were grazing near the camp when we arrived, and we stopped the car about twenty yards away. As elephants go there was, I suppose, nothing very remarkable about this couple: they were medium-sized beasts with rather short tusks, and they were feeding on a clump of bushes with that quiet aldermanic dignity that one usually associates with the species. But this hardly describes the sensations that are almost bound to overtake anyone on first seeing elephants from close at hand in their natural surroundings. One has a moment of panic, of course, but it soon passes, and presently you find yourself absorbed in the simple act of watching. Elephants, when they are not hunted or disturbed, create a curious area of calm in the bush.   A kind of hush surrounds them, and this seems to have a reassuring effect not only on you, the observer, but upon all the other animals — the waterbuck, the wildebeest and even the warthogs — that may happen to be grazing in the same valley.   It is not the dull calm of the herds of munching buffaloes.   There is here a certain fastidiousness, a sense of great power used very gently and deliberately.   All this no doubt can be noticed in any circus or menagerie, but nothing can quite describe the delicacy with which the wild elephant selects and breaks off the exact bunch of leaves he wants, and then stows it neatly into his tricorne mouth with a rhythmical pendulum motion of his trunk.   When he has had enough of one tree and moves on to the next his footfalls never make a sound.[1] — ALAN MOOREHEAD, *No Room in the Ark*

Spot Important Details

Eyewitnesses at an accident often disagree because many people are poor observers.   Readers sometimes disagree because some people fail to note and remember important details.

ACTIVITY 13   Noting Details in Reading   R

Without looking back at the paragraph on elephants, see how many of the following questions you can answer.   Then reread the paragraph and try answering the questions again.   Keep rereading the paragraph until you are able to answer all of the questions correctly.

1. How many elephants did the author watch?
2. How far from them was he?
3. What animals may graze with elephants?
4. How does the elephant convey food to his mouth?
5. What does the wild elephant eat?
6. What was the author's first reaction on seeing the elephants?
7. With what other animal is the grazing elephant compared?
8. How does the elephant move from tree to tree?

Build Your Vocabulary

Learn how to guess at word meanings through context (pages 17, 18).   Use the dictionary (pages 20, 21).   Look up interesting new words and puzzling references.   Recognize that words do not always mean literally what they say; see the pictures in figurative language (pages 211–213).

[1] Reprinted by permission of Harper & Brothers.

1. In the reading selection in Activity 12, what do these words mean: *aldermanic, panic, reassuring, fastidiousness, tricorne?*

2. What comparison is being made in these words: *rhythmical pendulum motion of his trunk?*

Draw Conclusions from What You Read

Enthusiastic applause and shouts of "Bravo!" brought the cast of *Oklahoma!* back for curtain call after curtain call.

Although the sentence doesn't say so, you may reasonably conclude that *Oklahoma!* is some sort of theatrical production that has been well performed.

Every experience you have increases your understanding. If you have read about *Oklahoma!* or have seen it, you know it is a musical. You may conclude that the performers sang and danced. You may conclude that this was a stage production, not a movie, because of the applause, cheers, and numerous curtain calls. For the same reasons, you may conclude that the audience enjoyed the performance.

Do more; read more; widen your experience. Your reading will improve. When you read a selection, ask yourself, "How does this information tie in with what I already know?" Read with understanding. Ask yourself, "What conclusions can I draw here?"

After reading the following paragraph, answer the questions at the end.

People, with their Biblical three score years and ten, are outlived by many birds, mammals, fish, and of course trees. The crow and the eagle may live to be a hundred, as may the elephant. If they are fortunate, pike and carp may live 150 years. One of the oldest living things, however, is the General Sherman tree in California; its age is estimated at four thousand years.

I. Which of the following conclusions might you draw from the paragraph? Base your answers on the facts given in the paragraph and on what you already know.

   a. Pike and carp may outlive elephants.

   b. In California plants and animals live longer than they do in any other part of the world.

   c. Most pike and carp live 150 years.

II. In which sentence is the main idea of the paragraph expressed?

Read the selections and answer the questions.

A

Had it not been for Matthew Henson, Robert E. Peary might not have reached the North Pole. Henson, a black man, was the only person to accompany Peary on all of the explorer's Polar expeditions. At first Peary doubted that Henson could endure the arctic climate. During the eighteen years these two attempted to reach the Pole, Henson's unfailing good humor, courage, and skill proved invaluable. On the first expedition the Innuit Eskimos of Smith Sound greeted Henson as a brother, welcomed him into their stone igloos, and taught him their difficult language. Soon Henson became the most proficient of Peary's men, not only in speaking Innuit but also in handling a dog team. On later expeditions it was he who taught greenhorns how to drive a dog team and how to survive in the sub-zero climate. Beloved by the Eskimos, who called him "Miy Paluk," he persuaded them to accompany Peary into the uncharted regions where they believed evil spirits dwelled. On a nearly disastrous excursion across the ice cap in 1895, Henson twice saved Peary's life. Again and again Henson proved that he was capable of endurance and achievement, the final test coming in 1909 when he accompanied Peary and four Eskimos on the last lap of the successful dash to the Pole.

1. The best title for this selection is (1) Matthew Henson Proves Himself (2) A Polar Explorer (3) Robert E. Peary (4) Discovery of the North Pole.
2. In describing Henson's achievements the author does NOT mention (1) speaking Innuit (2) handling sled dogs (3) rescuing Peary (4) converting the Eskimos.
3. From this selection we may conclude that Peary's first Polar expedition was in (1) 1909 (2) 1895 (3) 1891 (4) 1893.
4. *Greenhorns* were (1) musk-oxen (2) inexperienced explorers (3) native guides (4) untrained dog teams.

B

Davy Crockett, Wyatt Earp, and other heroes of the Old West would hardly recognize the range over which they once rambled. Today the buffalos live in zoos or parks. You can hardly find a longhorn in the whole state of Texas. And the cowpoke may ride to the roundup in a jeep or a pickup truck.

The cowboy of gunsmoke days would be amazed to see his modern counterpart whirring along in a helicopter over miles of barbed wire fence. Spotting a "break," today's fence rider — or flier — can pick up his two-way radio, call the ranchhouse and ask the boss to send out a truck equipped with reels of wire, extra fence posts, and a complete set of tools.

Some resourceful ranchers even handle roundups from the air, using air-to-ground radios to direct horsemen to cattle that have strayed from the herd.

Guns aren't used much on the range these days — except in the movies.

"About the only thing we need pistols for now is shooting rattlesnakes," admitted one cattleman, with a trace of nostalgia in his voice.

Another casualty of the times is the range war, hackneyed topic of a thousand celluloid horse operas. Today understanding rather than bad blood prevails where feuding buckaroos once unlimbered their trusty Colts and Winchesters in gun battles.[1] — K. C. WINCHESTER

1. The best title for this selection is (1) Heroes of the Old Frontier (2) Fall of the Buffalo (3) The Range Today (4) Air Roundups.
2. In his modern helps for ranchers the author mentions all the following EXCEPT (1) radio (2) radar (3) helicopter (4) jeep.
3. From this selection we can assume that the longhorn (1) was once a familiar sight in Texas (2) is increasing in popularity (3) is now extinct (4) was once herded by Davy Crockett and Wyatt Earp.
4. A "celluloid horse opera" is (1) a cowboy movie (2) a light opera (3) a cavalry display (4) a roundup.
5. As used in the selection *hackneyed* means (1) exciting (2) cheerful (3) outworn (4) brutal.
6. The "break" referred to is (1) a sharp ridge (2) a dry creek bed (3) a breakdown in mechanical equipment (4) an opening in the fence.

Learn to Outline and Take Notes

You'll get more from your reading if you note the author's plan of organizing his material. Concentrate on the ideas presented and make an outline of the main points and the supporting details.

ACTIVITY 17 Making a Simple Outline   S

Read the following paragraph and complete the outline at the end, using your own words where possible.

A good reader does more than send her eye over lines of print. She is able to find the main idea in a selection. She can point out or recall the important details that support the main idea. A thinking reader draws conclusions from her reading and relates new information to her background of experience. She constantly enlarges her vocabulary with the new words she meets in print. The good reader uses her reading to enrich her life.

The skilled reader can do these things:

1.	4.
2.	5.
3.	6.

[1] Reprinted by permission of *Home & Highway*.

HINTS FOR TAKING NOTES ON WHAT YOU READ

1. Read the lesson through without writing a word. Watch for signals of important ideas — *italics*, **boldface,** numbered points, and topic sentences.
2. Think over what you have read; or, better yet, close your book and say it aloud.
3. As you read the lesson again, write down the main points briefly in your own words.
4. Group the notes under headings. Under the main topics list the details used to illustrate or prove the point. Do not try to write down everything. Your notes should be complete but brief.
5. Use freely abbreviations, contractions, &, +, −, and other symbols which you will understand when you read the notes. *Do not use these shortcuts in letters or compositions.* Omit *a, an, the,* and other unnecessary words.

TYPICAL NOTES

Names
n. & pr.
Modifiers
Adj. mod. n. & pr.
Adv. mod. v., adj., adv.

ACTIVITY 18 Taking Notes   S

1. Take notes this evening as you study one subject. Bring your notes to class to copy on the chalkboard. Be ready to explain the lesson from your notes.

2. Take notes on a magazine article and summarize it accurately and entertainingly in class. Your notes should be briefer than your summary.

3. Take notes on directions one of your teachers gives you. Prepare to tell clearly, accurately, completely what you are to do.

Summarize the Author's Ideas

To prepare for a class discussion, a report, or an essay-type examination, you must be able to summarize what you have read or heard. Writing a summary, or précis (pronounced "pray-see"), is good practice in getting the idea from your reading and listening. Furthermore, you'll remember better if you concisely express the thought of the material in your own words.

GUIDES FOR WRITING A SUMMARY

1. Find the central idea. Glance through the paragraph or poem to be summarized to get a bird's-eye view of it. Say to yourself, "This is about insects that help the gardener." or "This story is about a boy's efforts to make friends in a new neighborhood."
2. Find the supporting ideas. Read the paragraph or poem sentence by sentence. In your own words jot down each new thought but not the minor details. Use your dictionary for hard words.
3. Arrange the main points in the order of the original.
4. Check to see that you have eliminated quotations, illustrations, minor details, and all unnecessary words. Be sure you have avoided copying sentences of the original. Do not include your own opinion of the selection or a criticism of the ideas.
5. Write out the important ideas. Use your own words. Make nouns and verbs do most of the work. Cut out unnecessary adjectives and adverbs. Make one word do the job of three or four. Use a word instead of a phrase, a phrase instead of a sentence. Avoid expressions like "The author says" or "In this selection the main idea is."

   NOT THIS Saying something I couldn't understand, Buff went out of the room without lifting his feet.
   BUT THIS Mumbling, Buff shuffled out of the room.

6. Use about one third or one fourth as many words as there are in the original.
7. Revise your work, comparing it with the original to make sure you have stated all the main points accurately, and then copy it neatly and legibly. Have you boiled down the author's thoughts without including your own ideas on the subject?

ACTIVITY 19 Studying a Summary   RS

1. In the following selection key words are in boldface type. Study how the précis notes depend upon key words and ideas.

ORIGINAL (148 words)	PRÉCIS NOTES (34 words)
Ants have a **tenacity** that makes a bulldog seem mild by comparison. Once the **jaws** of an ant have closed on an object, it holds on no matter what happens. This **grip** often **does not weaken** even though the ant's	An ant's jaws are very strong. They hold onto an object even if the ant's head is cut off.

head is cut off, and after a battle between different kinds of ants, the victors often stalk about with the severed heads of their victims clinging to their legs.

In **India, Africa, South America,** and perhaps other parts of the world, **practical advantage** is taken of this characteristic. The ants are used for **suturing wounds.** The edges of a wound are held together, and the wide open jaws of **large ants** are **applied** to the **two edges.** When the irate **ants clamp** their **jaws** together, one jaw catches on each side of the wound. The **bodies** of the ants are then **cut off,** and the **wound is sealed.**[1]

In some countries large ants are used to hold the edges of a wound together.

— OSMOND P. BRELAND, in *Animal Friends and Foes*

An ant's jaws are so strong that they hold onto an object even if the ant's head is cut off. For this reason, in some countries large ants are used to hold the edges of a wound together.

2. How many words are there in the final summary?

3. What do the added words do?

ACTIVITY 20 Writing Summaries   VW

Make a careful summary of the following selection by boiling down the essential ideas of the original passage. Follow the steps on pages 197, 198. Write concise, complete sentences. Define each italicized word or give a synonym.

LIFE ON THE DESERT

The desert is a strange and wonderful laboratory for the study of animal life. Here, if one is properly endowed with patience and the power of observation, one finds the unusual and *unique*. Life isn't easy in an area where it does not rain for months at a time; yet living creatures are to be found there in *abundance*. Bird, insect, snake, lizard, mammal — all have adapted themselves to their environment and, strange as it may seem, not only survive but *flourish*, and they have developed many *ingenious* ways of doing so. When you live in a place where the harsh sun

---

[1] Reprinted by permission of Harper & Brothers.

can be your *mortal* enemy, the smart thing to do is to stay out of the sun; so most of the desert creatures are *nocturnal* in their habits and it is at night that the desert comes so wonderfully and vigorously to life. Nor is the lack of water a problem for these desert creatures. Moisture can be obtained from plants or from other living things preyed upon; so life goes on in a *placid* rhythm.[1] (178 words)

ACTIVITY 21   Writing Summaries   W

Write summaries of the selections on pages 134, 138, 151–153, and 191–196.

ACTIVITY 22   Outlining the Main Points   RS

This chapter discusses seven suggestions for getting more out of your reading. Outline them in your English notebook as a supplement to these additional hints.

[1] Reprinted by permission from *Arizona Highways*.

MORE HINTS ON IMPROVING YOUR READING

1. Determine to become a rapid reader. Find books and maga- zines that you like and read them. The best way to learn to read is by reading.
2. Have adequate light and a comfortable chair.
3. Read with a purpose and know what your purpose is.
4. Read silently; don't say words to yourself. Keep your tongue and lips still.
5. Train your eyes to move smoothly and quickly from left to right across the page. Don't let them jump back over words.
6. Take in a big eyeful at a glance. Read by phrases, not word by word. Don't use your finger to keep the place.
7. Pay special attention to nouns, pronouns, and verbs; they usually convey the main ideas.
8. Note chapter heads and subheads. Notice emphasis clues like **boldface,** *italics.*
9. Read summaries, study charts, and graphs.
10. Practice reading under a time limit. Force yourself to read faster than is comfortable, but don't sacrifice understanding to speed.
11. Try to read more than you read at present.
12. Concentrate.

ACTIVITY 23 Word Study   VW

The following words were used in this chapter. The page number is after each word. What does each word mean in the sentence in which it appears? Use each word in a sentence of your own. Check your spelling.

infringing	185	derided	185	fable	190
monetary	185	horizons	185	laboriously	190
recognition	185	sensationalism	186	skimming	191
posthumous	185	interprets	187	précis	197
vindication	185	policy	187	concisely	197

13 *Reading for Enjoyment*

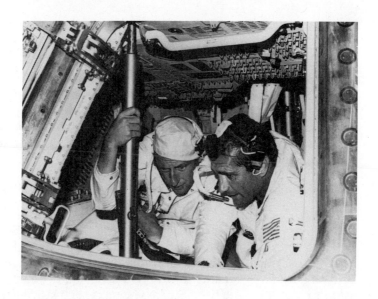

Would you like to sail to the South Seas on a raft? Stow away on a rocket to the moon? Learn how a teen-ager solved his problems? Understand grown-ups better? Dance before a king? Explore under the surface of the sea? Be a soldier in Napoleon's army? If you will read as little as fifteen minutes every day, you can share the experiences of many people in many lands in many ages. Books can open doors to the past, the present, and the future.

HINTS FOR SELECTING A BOOK

1. Browse. In libraries and bookstores look leisurely through currently popular books and those which reflect your particular interests. Don't overlook the many excellent paperbacks on sale everywhere.
2. To build a reading list, jot down titles of books recommended by your friends, teachers, or parents.
3. Read book reviews in newspapers and magazines. Glance at lists of best sellers.
4. Consult book lists on library bulletin boards, *Books for You*, and other reliable lists.
5. Use your library. Look through the card catalog under the names of authors you enjoy reading and under the headings of subjects that interest you. (See pages 247–256 on library techniques.)

Using at least two of the methods suggested above for selecting books, list the titles and authors of (1) three books on some subject you are especially interested in — for example, sailing, dog training, space travel, or nursing — or (2) three books about a person you have always wanted to know more about. Be prepared to tell how you found your books.

ACTIVITY 2 Planning a Personal Reading Program   **RW**

A. Plan a reading program for the year and budget at least fifteen minutes each day for reading. Choose four or five books you expect to read. Reserve one page of your English notebook for each book, listing the title and author at the top of the page. After you have read a book, think about it. Did it open any doors for you? In your notebook write two or three sentences summarizing the main theme and telling why you particularly liked or disliked it.

EXAMPLE

Rawlings, Marjorie K.
The Yearling

Twelve-year-old Jody Baxter lives with his mother and father in the lonely Florida scrub. In his search for companionship Jody takes an orphan fawn as a pet. Jody grows up when he has to face the death of his beloved pet.

I particularly liked Jody's father, Penny, who loved and understood Jody during a very difficult year.

B. If you prefer, contribute to a class catalog as well, using the notes you have prepared for A. Every time you read a book, record on a library card the author and the title. Transfer your notes (A) to the card and hand the card to your teacher or to a pupil who is keeping the catalog. Before deciding on your next book, look in the file to see what the pupils who have read the book say about it. The cards will be filed alphabetically according to the last names of the authors. The catalog is a handy reference file and a means of sharing book information.

SHARING READING EXPERIENCES

You enjoyed a book so much you want to tell your friends about it. Can you arouse their curiosity enough so that they will want to read the book too? Take a hint from the previews of coming attractions at the movies; don't retell the whole story.

FOUR WAYS TO TELL ABOUT A BOOK

1. Give a brief account of the most interesting or exciting incident.
2. Describe the most important or unusual character.
3. Dramatize a short scene.
4. Tell why you do or do not recommend the book.

ACTIVITY 3 Studying a Book Review   **OS**

Study the following book review. What method did the writer use to sell you on reading *New Worlds to Conquer?*

NEW WORLDS TO CONQUER
by Richard Halliburton

As the traveler looked down at the Aztec "Well of Death," he thought about the cruel history of the place. Here in the legendary home of the Aztec god of water, human sacrifice was once offered. Each year the loveliest maiden and the bravest youth were sacrificed to the god. The maiden believed she was about to become goddess of the water, but the youth knew they would both be killed. As the visitor looked down into the water, he had an overpowering impulse. Without thinking of the consequences he jumped — down, down into the darkness of the water. As he came up gasping for breath, he saw with horror that the rock walls rose abruptly on all sides of him. How could he possibly get out?

This question and many others are answered in *New Worlds to Conquer* by Richard Halliburton. It is the exciting story of Halliburton's travels along the routes taken by Cortez and Balboa. The romantic adventurer masqueraded as an organ grinder, climbed Mt. Popocatepetl, swam the Panama Canal, lived on Devil's Island, and even became another Robinson Crusoe.

The reader has come to expect danger, excitement, intrigue, comedy, and daring feats of courage in a Halliburton book. *New Worlds to Conquer* will meet that expectation. — STUDENT WRITER

ACTIVITY 4 Selling a Book   **LO**

Prepare a two-minute talk on a book you recently read. Choose one of the four methods described above to sell your classmates on reading it. Speak clearly and enthusiastically. Pronounce the name of the author and the title distinctly and write them on the board.

In a special section of their English notebooks labeled "Books to Read," students at their seats will jot down the titles and authors of the books they would like to read. Each speaker will judge her success by the number of students she has interested in her book.

Following the form of the news story on page 173 or the suggestions in Chapter 11, write an imaginary news story based upon a book or a short story you are reading. Select an important, dramatic incident and retell it in newspaper style. Choose a headline that will attract attention.

EXAMPLES

> Merchant Lyte Accuses Boston Boy of Theft (*Johnny Tremain*, by Esther Forbes)
>
> Heiress Dies under Mysterious Circumstances ("The Adventure of the Speckled Band" by A. Conan Doyle)

THE SPECIAL PLEASURES OF NONFICTION

"Dit-darr-darr, darr-dit-dit-darr, darr-dit-dit-dit." "WXB - - - WXB - - - WXB - - - de (from) - - - KHCAL." The blurred buzz of my own radio-sending rang in my ears. Through the cockpit cover I could see fog on the water ahead, motionless piles of light gray cotton wool with dark gray patches here and there. Out to sea the white wall of fog stood impassable and still as the ice packs from which it rose. Inland under floating islands of fog stretched the barren Arctic land. We were turning toward it as our only chance of reaching Point Barrow, the bleak northern tip of Alaska. Could we get through that night? If the weather ahead was not worse. I must get my message to the Barrow operator. "WXB - - - WXB - - - WXB," I called to him.[1]

Do the travelers reach their destination? If you're curious about what an airplane trip to the Arctic was like before the days of radar, read *North to the Orient* by Anne Morrow Lindbergh. As you read this and other nonfiction books, you will find new meaning in the familiar saying "Truth is stranger than fiction."

JUDGING A NONFICTION BOOK

When you read an exciting novel, you usually do not care whether the events described really took place. In reading nonfiction, however, you seek not only interest and excitement but accuracy. A science or history book is useless if it does not present a true picture. Therefore, in judging a nonfiction book, ask such questions as these:

1. Does the author seem to know his subject? An author must be qualified by training, experience, and research to handle his material adequately.

---

[1] Reprinted by permission of the publishers, Harcourt Brace Jovanovich, Inc.

2. Is the author careful to avoid letting personal feelings distort the truth? Is the author of a biography, for instance, relatively free from hero worship or dislike? Does she present her subject as a real person with true-to-life faults and virtues, successes and failures? Is the author of a travel book free from prejudice about the manners and customs of foreign peoples? Does she try to present a fair picture of the country she is describing?

3. Does the author have a reputation for reliability? Your teachers, the library, the encyclopedia, and book reviews by specialists in the author's field can help you answer this question.

4. Does the author stick to the facts? Most biographers, for example, use their imaginations to supply colorful details — to reconstruct scenes and conversations they could not possibly have witnessed or heard. Such material, however, must have a solid basis in fact — letters, diaries, or other records. If the author lets his imagination run riot, he is writing fiction.

GUIDES FOR WRITING A NONFICTION REVIEW

1. Tell what kind of book you're reviewing. Is the book biographical, descriptive, technical, historical? ·
2. Identify the subject. What does the author tell us about his topic? Does he present a well-rounded picture?
3. Indicate the author's purpose. Does the book aim primarily to entertain, inform, instruct, argue a special point of view?
4. Discuss the style. Is the book difficult to read? Is it exciting? Is it beautifully written?
5. Compare it with another book of the same type. If it is a biography, for example, compare it with other biographies of the person.
6. Describe an interesting episode or quote a significant passage.
7. State your reasons for recommending or not recommending the book.
8. Tell what you learned from reading the book.

ACTIVITY 6 Writing a Nonfiction Book Review   **RW**

Select a nonfiction book that your teacher approves. Write a review, following as many of the preceding guides as you think necessary. Prove your statements by illustrations from the book.

14 *Reading Poetry*

In his science class one morning Fred learned about the moon — its diameter, its surface characteristics, its distance from the earth, and many other facts. Fred thought he knew all about the moon. But in his English class a few days later Fred read a poem that described the moon as "a ghostly galleon tossed upon cloudy seas." Reading further, Fred came across an even more famous line which said the moon was like "a silver bow new-bent in heaven."

Fred realized that science had not told him everything about the moon. In his science class Fred had learned what the moon *is;* through poetry he had learned what the moon *can mean* to sensitive and imaginative people. Science, he realized, expressed one kind of truth; poetry revealed another.

WHAT IS POETRY?

A great poet once remarked, "If I read a book and it makes my whole body so cold no fire can ever warm it, I know that it is poetry." Have you ever recognized poetry this way?

In many ways poetry is similar to music. It appeals to the ear. It arouses our feelings. It has rhythm.

A poem, like a picture, can make us see ordinary things in an extraordinary way.

Poetry is also like painting. It can make us see ordinary things in an extraordinary way. Someone once called painting "silent poetry," and poetry "speaking painting."

Most poetry says a great deal in a very few lines. Since the language of poetry is often highly compressed, don't be surprised if you can't skim a poem the way you skim a newspaper column. Poetry may at times be difficult to understand, but it is usually pointed and forceful. Compare the following passages. Which is more forceful? Why?

PROSE Spring brought the beginnings of new leaves, summer the full green leaf, and autumn leaves of red. Now winter is here, the tree branches are bare, and the sky has lost its color.

POETRY The half leaf — the green leaf — the red leaf — is gone;
I see black branches
On a pale sky.[1] — STUDENT WRITER

ACTIVITY 1 Comparing Poetry with Prose　　　　　　　　**W**

Select a poem you admire and describe its content in a prose summary. Compare your summary with the poem itself. Which do you think more effective? Why?

[1] Reprinted from *Saplings*, copyright 1929 by Scholastic Magazines, Inc.

PAINTING WORD PICTURES

Perhaps you have never seen a storm at sea, but you begin to see it in imagination when the poet compares the sea to a boiling caldron and the wind to a spear of darkness. Poetry is full of such images — vivid descriptions that make you see what the poet wants you to see. To paint these word pictures, the poet often uses comparisons. When the comparison is expressed with *like* or *as*, it is called a simile.

Life goes on forever like the gnawing of a mouse. — EDNA ST. VINCENT MILLAY

But my heart is all a-flutter like the washing on the line. — NATHALIA CRANE

Like a small grey coffee-pot sits the squirrel. — HUMBERT WOLFE

When the comparison is implied — without *like* or *as* — it is called a metaphor.

Frost, invisibly thorough,
Spreads its thickening
Stiffening lacquer. — MELVILLE CANE

Friendship is a sheltering tree. — SAMUEL TAYLOR COLERIDGE

The yellow fog that rubs its back upon the window-panes,
The yellow smoke that rubs its muzzle on the window-panes.
— T. S. ELIOT

In each of the following what two things are compared? Is the comparison a simile or a metaphor? Follow the form in the example below. Which comparisons do you like best?

EXAMPLE   A heavy snowfall blanketed the city.
What are being compared — A snowfall and a blanket   Metaphor

1. The searchlight thrust long, probing fingers into the sky.
2. The fire snapped and crackled like a whip.
3. March is a tomboy with tousled hair and mud on her shoes.
4. My thoughts this morning are
   As tangled as my hair. — LADY HORIKAWA
5. There is no frigate like a book
   To take us lands away. — EMILY DICKINSON
6. The road was a ribbon of moonlight. — ALFRED NOYES

SIMILES AND METAPHORS IN EVERYDAY LANGUAGE

Perhaps you think similes and metaphors are found mainly in poetry. Actually they are a very important part of everyday speech. There is a kind of poetry in such names as *black-eyed Susan, weeping willow,* and *Storm King Highway* and in such phrases as *horns of a dilemma, skeleton in the closet, bull in a china shop.*

However, beware of phrases so worn with use they no longer make us see the pictures they suggest — *white as snow, heart of gold, red as a beet, cool as a cucumber.* Avoid also farfetched, ridiculous metaphors and similes ("Her hair was like a field of daisies in which he longed to run barefoot") and mixed metaphors ("The odor of lilacs shouted a welcome").

From books, magazines, newspapers, or radio and television programs collect three similes and three metaphors. Be prepared to tell what are being compared in each case and why you find the comparisons effective.

Complete three of the following sentences by creating vivid pictures. Try to make your comparisons as fresh and vivid as possible. Avoid farfetched or mixed metaphors.

1. The hail fell on the roof like ＿＿＿.
2. The skyscraper loomed like ＿＿＿.
3. The windows of the dilapidated house were ＿＿＿.

4. The hungry cats howled like ____.
5. Gentle and low, her voice was ____.
6. To the frightened child the dark shadows in the corners were ____.
7. For her, home was a ____.
8. The shield blazed like ____.
9. He bounded into the room like ____.
10. The slow-moving river was ____.

RHYTHM

"Emotion," says Nellie B. Sergent, author of *Younger Poets*, "tends to express itself in rhythm of some kind — in dancing, in music, in verse. Any speech charged with emotion tends to be rhythmical; the curses of a truck driver are in rhythms, and lovers are always poets." Rhythm is everywhere — in our heartbeats, in our breathing, in our walking, in the waves of the sea, in the sweep of the earth around the sun, in the waving corn, and in the steps of marching soldiers.

Matching Rhythm and Feeling

The rhythm of a poem must suit the mood the poem expresses. A poem about sorrow written in a quick, bouncy rhythm would be as absurd as graduates marching to "Turkey in the Straw." In these passages see how the poet matches rhythm and feeling.

Solemn, Serious Mood — Slow Rhythm

Sunset and evening star,
    And one clear call for me!
And may there be no moaning of the bar,
    When I put out to sea. — ALFRED, LORD TENNYSON

Quiet, Dreamy Mood — Smooth, Even Rhythm

Slowly, silently, now the moon
Walks the night in her silver shoon;
This way, and that, she peers, and sees
Silver fruit upon silver trees.[1] — WALTER DE LA MARE

Defiant Mood — Strong, Martial Rhythm

Ay, tear her tattered ensign down!
    Long has it waved on high,
And many an eye has danced to see
    That banner in the sky. — OLIVER WENDELL HOLMES

[1] From *Collected Poems* by Walter de la Mare. Copyright, 1920, by Henry Holt and Company. Copyright, 1948, by Walter de la Mare. By permission of the publishers.

ACTIVITY 5 Feeling the Mood   **OS**

Read the following aloud. What is the mood of each? How would you describe the rhythm of each? How do the rhythm and the sounds of the words help create the mood?

1. Alone, alone, all all alone,
   Alone on a wide, wide sea! — SAMUEL TAYLOR COLERIDGE

2. Sweet and low, sweet and low,
   Wind of the western sea,
   Low, low, breathe and blow,
   Wind of the western sea! — ALFRED, LORD TENNYSON

3. Strong gongs groaning as the guns boom far,
   Don John of Austria is going to the war. — G. K. CHESTERTON

Meter

When rhythm follows a definite, planned pattern, we say the line has *meter*. Each metrical line, or verse, is made up of a number of feet. A foot is a group of syllables consisting of one accented syllable with one or two unaccented syllables. There are four principal kinds of feet.

FOOT	MEANING	SOUND	WORD OR PHRASE
iamb	2 syllables accented on second	ta túm	alóne
trochee	2 syllables accented on first	túm ta	whísper
anapest	3 syllables accented on last	ta ta túm	with a leáp
dactyl	3 syllables accented on first	túm ta ta	gálloping

The example below has five iambic feet.

Trúe eáse | in wrít | ing cómes | from árt, | not chánce.
                                    — ALEXANDER POPE

However, variations in meter are often made to emphasize important words and to avoid monotony. Thus, in the following example, iambs and anapests both occur.

The flów | ers that bloóm | in the spríng, | tra lá. — W. S. GILBERT

Copy the following lines of poetry. Then put accent marks (ˊ) over the accented syllables and important one-syllable words and mark the unaccented syllables (˘). Then read each line aloud to decide whether it sounds like (1) tă túm, tă túm (iambic); (2) túm tă, túm tă (trochaic); (3) tă tă túm, tă tă túm (anapestic); or (4) túm tă tă, túm tă tă (dactylic). Mark off the feet and name the kind and number of feet in the line.

EXAMPLE The woods | are love | ly, dark | and deep — ROBERT FROST
  four iambic feet

1. When to the sessions of sweet silent thought — WILLIAM SHAKESPEARE
2. In Flanders fields the poppies blow — JOHN MCCRAE
3. As I came to the edge of the woods — ROBERT FROST
4. I cannot find my way: there is no star — EDWIN ARLINGTON ROBINSON
5. Prisoners now I declare you, for such is his Majesty's pleasure!
                                  — HENRY WADSWORTH LONGFELLOW
6. Two good friends had Hiawatha — HENRY WADSWORTH LONGFELLOW

RHYME

Although not all poetry rhymes, the use of rhyme frequently adds to the music of the verse and makes the poetry easier to remember.

Rhyme is a similarity of sound, usually at the ends of lines. Words which rhyme perfectly have (1) the accent on the rhyming syllables; (2) the same vowel sound in the accented syllable; (3) the same sounds after the vowel sound; (4) different consonant sounds before this vowel sound.

Rhyme is a matter of pronunciation or sound, not of spelling. *Sight, bite; bought, caught;* and *reign, plain* rhyme. *Rough, bough* and *weight, height* do not rhyme.

READING POETRY ALOUD

In preparing to read a poem aloud, study carefully the meaning, mood, rhythm, and music of the words. Then express your understanding of the poem through your voice and rate of reading. Speak whole thoughts, not words or lines. In reading these lines by Vachel Lindsay, for example, do not stop at *spring*, but swing around to *in the days of long ago.*

The flower-fed buffaloes of the spring
In the days of long ago. . . .

A. First read the following poem silently. What pictures do you see? What is the meter? Which lines rhyme? Then read the poem aloud to your class. Pronounce every word correctly and speak distinctly. (See pages 221–225.)

THE WIND

The wind went whining down the lane
　　And whistling through the sullen trees,
A lonely dog, which, crying low
　　One often hears, but never sees.

— STUDENT WRITER

B. Find a poem you like and prepare to read the poem, or part of it, to your class.

WRITING POETRY

Whenever you feel strongly about something, you have a subject for a poem. A sunset may awe you; a marching band may thrill you; a newspaper story may sadden or anger you. Anything that arouses your feelings may be expressed in verse. When you write your poem, tell exactly what you saw or felt. Or tell exactly what happened. Find a rhythm that fits your idea or mood. Make full use of word pictures, color, and fresh, original similes and metaphors.

Free Verse

In your first poems write in free verse — a style of poetry that has no rhyme and usually no regular pattern. End the lines where the reader would naturally pause for breath or where there is a break in the sense. For free verse at its best read Psalms and Proverbs in the Bible.

A student like you wrote the following poem. What pictures do you see as you read it? What similes or metaphors can you find? How does the division into lines follow the sense of the poem?

TALL TREES

The tallest trees
Are lacy-black scarves
That the white sky
Wraps about her shoulders
On cool nights.

— STUDENT WRITER

ACTIVITY 8 Writing Free Verse **W**

Select one of these or a topic of your own, and next to it jot down the pictures, sounds, smells, tastes, and feelings you associate with it. Then put these pictures, sense impressions, and feelings into sentences arranged as free verse. Or, if you prefer, tell the story of a fire, a hayride, or a trip to an airport, and arrange your sentences in free verse.

loneliness	the city	music	rain	night sky
an airport	autumn	sea gulls	sailing	dawn
a railroad station	crowds	hiking	a snowstorm	dancing
your cat	a carnival	mountains	wind	the woods
thunderclouds	a fire	frost	a wheat field	sorrow

Haiku

Try your poetic hand at the haiku, a three-line poem without rhyme or meter. The first and third lines should contain five syllables each; the second, seven. The haiku attempts to capture a single experience: a striking picture, a moment of insight, or a brief emotion. The haiku always reflect in some way a season of the year. The following haiku [1] were written by young people from Boulder, Colorado.

> The cabin is small   (five syllables)
> in the vast whiteness. Only   (seven)
> the smoke reveals it.   (five)

> As I wander in
> endless fields, golden grain bows
> at my feet, birds sing.

> On the mountaintop
> clouds turn pink, red, and orange.
> Soon it will be dark.

ACTIVITY 9 Writing Haiku **W**

Following the form described, write a haiku that will capture an experience, paint a picture, or reveal an emotion. You may use a suggestion from Activity 8 or one of your own.

[1] Reprinted by permission of *Woman's Day Magazine,* a Fawcett Publication.

The Ballad Stanza

If you'd like to tell a story in verse, consider the ballad stanza. This form was first used hundreds of years ago by unschooled people who wished to put into song an especially moving experience or tragic incident.

Ballads are easy to write. Each stanza has four lines with the second and fourth lines rhyming. Although the meter is usually iambic (tă túm), an anapest (tă tă túm) may be substituted for any iambic. Perhaps you know the old ballad "Get Up and Bar the Door." The author is anonymous.

> Ĭt fĕll | ă bóut | thĕ Már | tĭn măs tíme
> And ă gáy | tĭme ĭt | wăs thĕn.
> Whĕn óur | good wífe | gŏt púd | dĭngs tŏ máke,
> And shĕ's bóiled | thĕm ín | thĕ pán.

ACTIVITY 10   Writing a Class Ballad   W

Starting with a recent school happening, an event in United States history, or something original and purely imaginary, write the first stanza of a ballad. With your classmates choose the best ballad beginning, and with your teacher or a classmate at the chalkboard, continue the story by suggesting new lines and stanzas.

> Our Mr. Brown, who teaches art,
> Is always full of fun.
> No matter what the time or place —
> Beware his mighty pun!

> One day Noreen was deep in clay,
> Her fingers in a whirl;
> The teacher took one look and said,
> "A mighty putty girl!"

ACTIVITY 11 Writing a Poem   W

Write a poem on a topic in Activity 8 or on a topic of your own. Choose a verse form that fits the idea and the mood you wish to express. You may write free verse or ballad stanzas. Or you may make up your own pattern or follow the pattern of meter and rhyme you find in a poem you enjoy. Observe sharply and write vividly. Use fresh, original similes and metaphors.

ACTIVITY 12 Word Study   VW

The following words were used in this chapter. The page number is after each word. What does each word mean in the context in which it appears? Use each word in a sentence of your own. Check your spelling.

galleon	209	compressed	210	Psalms	216
sensitive	209	lacquer	211	Proverbs	216
extraordinary	210	martial	213	ballad	218

Unit Four — *Speaking*

15 *Basic Speaking Skills*

Winston Churchill — a famous orator who inspired millions of people and changed the course of history by his speeches

"**D**ick, I calleda finow wachadoin. Wouldja liketa gota demovies?"

This message started out as English. Can you translate it?

Good speech and a pleasing voice have a dollars-and-cents value. Poor speech is a handicap in school, in social life, and on the job.

ACTIVITY 1 Discussing Good Speech   o

1. In what occupations or professions is good speech essential? In what others is it a definite asset?

2. What do you think your future occupation or profession will be? How will effective speaking habits aid you on and off the job?

3. Why is good speech important to everyone in society?

GUIDES FOR SPEAKING TO A GROUP

1. Be careful of your posture. Good posture improves your voice and helps you breathe properly.

2. Stand erect, but not stiffly, with your head up and your weight slightly forward. Keep your stomach flat and your shoulders square.

3. Let your hands hang easily at your sides. Avoid unnecessary movements which may divert the listeners' attention from what you are saying to what you are doing. Don't finger your hair, rub your nose, pull your ear, twist a button, or play with a pen, pencil, or piece of jewelry.

4. Keep your eyes on your audience. Look from one group of people to another to make each person feel you are speaking to him. Don't talk to the floor, the ceiling, or a window. Don't recite to the teacher alone. When reading aloud, read to your audience, not to your book.

5. Relax; your tones will be smoother as you become less tense.

6. Occasionally vary your volume, your rate, and your pitch. If your voice is thin, squeaky, and sharp, lower your pitch. If you speak too low, raise your pitch.

7. Don't speak "Slurvian" like the boy quoted at the beginning of the chapter. Enunciate clearly. (Enunciation involves *clear* utterance of sounds in words.) Pronounce every word correctly. (Pronunciation involves *correct* sounds and the *right* accent.)

ACTIVITY 2   Hearing Yourself   OL

1. If equipment is available, make a record of your speaking voice. During the playback listen carefully for good qualities as well

as for bad. Perhaps your teacher will help you analyze your speech. After study and practice, make a second record to measure your progress.

2. Cup your hands behind your ears and listen to your voice as you talk. Experiment until your voice sounds more pleasing to you. Also ask your teacher, family, friends, and classmates to criticize your voice and suggest ways to improve it.

ACTIVITY 3 Pronunciation and Enunciation   O

Read the following sentences clearly and distinctly. Can you pronounce the italicized words correctly? If not, practice the sounds you have trouble with until you can say them without thinking.

1. After *walking up* the garden *paths leading to* the tennis courts, we came upon Mack and Stu *trying out* their rackets and *playing a* hard game of tennis.
2. After *swimming* the *length* of the pool *twice, Betty* had *little strength* left for a *second* try.
3. *Because moths* recognize the *better kinds* of wool, we *have to put* at *least thirty-five* moth balls in the *clothes* closet.
4. *Can't you give me* that *geography* text and *let me* go?

ACTIVITY 4 Practicing Clear Enunciation   OS

How might confusion result if the italicized words were not pronounced separately?

EXAMPLE   I enjoy *a nice* cold day in winter.
   If *a* and *nice* are not separated, listeners may think the speaker enjoys *an ice-cold day.*

1. *All eggs* were broken.
2. Don't swallow *your ice.*
3. He has earned *a niche* for himself.
4. We were amazed at *their rally.*
5. Sandy was terrified at the sight of a *small adder.*
6. They were annoyed at *my yawning.*

ACTIVITY 5 Practicing Difficult Combinations   O

Pronounce each of the following words.
A. There is no vowel sound between *l* and *m* or *s* and *m* in the following words.

elm	film	spasm	communism	overwhelm
helm	chasm	baptism	enthusiasm	realm

B. Make each sound clear in distinguishing the following words.

ax — acts	lass — last	with — width
ask — asked	pass — past	use — used
Bess — best	worse — worst	breath — breadth

C. Now try these familiar phrases and sentences. Don't slur any sound.

Give me that.	better than	It costs five cents.
Let me.	length and breadth	Could you?
What did you say?	don't know	Did you ever?
What are you doing?	Can't you go?	couple of fellows

D. Make every consonant sound clear in saying the following words.

attacked	first	library	pretexts	slept
attempt	guests	midst	rejects	strengths
defects	hundredth	mists	second	tempts
depths	intersects	nests	secretary	thousandths
fifths	kept	picture	sevenths	twelfths

ACTIVITY 6 Practicing Correct Sounds   O

Say each sentence aloud. Enunciate clearly.

1. What a pleasant surprise for my friends and me when my cousin brought out those sizzling steaks!
2. Because of our interest in the Middle East we boys asked Mr. Cousins to tell us all about his recent cruise and about his three years in Israel.
3. The hatter said it didn't matter that his clothing was in tatters.
4. Tell your daughter it will take a great deal of butter to make that batter better.
5. Carol courageously added the cabbages and pigeons to her baggage, paid the charges on all her luggage, and edged over to join her relatives.
6. Books that Tony has read for pleasure this month include *The Big Bridge*, *The Enchanted Village*, and *A Goodly Heritage.*
7. In the evening we lingered long near the hangar of a Long Island airport.
8. While trying out the bell, Ben kept swinging it and ringing it and singing, "Ring out, wild bells!"
9. They tried thirteen recipes before they thought of asking Grandmother the secret of her tasty Thanksgiving pie.
10. The thirty thirsty thieves gathered under the three trees.
11. Barbara rambled over rocks and hills in search of ripe red raspberries.
12. The ramblers rioted over the run-down trellis and drowned the air with rich perfume.

ACTIVITY 7   Pronunciation Practice   O

Check your pronunciation of these words with the pronunciations given in the dictionary.

accurate	chef	formerly	hundred	partner
across	children	friendly	ideal	perhaps
admirable	chimney	fusion	immediate	pests
alley	chocolate	gentleman	including	preferable
ally	chore	genuine	insects	quantity
aluminum	clanging	gesture	Italian	schedule
among us	clinging	gifts	least	sphere
appreciate	column	gist	let me	sprinkle
archbishop	coughing	going to	letter	statistics
arctic	decease	guarantee	licorice	terrible
architect	disaster	guests	long ago	theater
artists	disease	handkerchief	loose	try out
associate	detour	has to	lose	twenty
athlete	drowned	height	mileage	twice
auxiliary	edge	his	mingling	wanted
banquet	effects	holds	mischievous	widths
bringing	expressive	horizon	months	wrangle
cavalry	facts	hospitable	niche	writing
cello	February	human	ninety	yesterday
champion	film	humor	once	younger

ACTIVITY 8   Try Your Skill   VW

Select any twelve words from the list in Activity 7. Compose a topic sentence and write a meaningful paragraph using all twelve. Try following the suggestions on paragraphing, pages 49–79. Try some of the sentence patterns suggested on pages 462–468.

EXAMPLE

To my mischievous younger brother insects are not pests but friendly
guests who live happily in bottles and cages in niches throughout
his room.

ACTIVITY 9   Word Study   VW

The following words were used in this chapter. The page number is after each word. What does each word mean in the sentence in which it appears? Use each word in a sentence of your own. Check your spelling.

erect	221	volume	222	enunciation	222
divert	222	pitch	222	pronunciation	222

16 *Meeting and Discussing*

"**M**y parents just don't understand," sighed Kathy as Miss Walter entered the classroom. "Everybody else is allowed to stay out as late as they wish, but my parents won't let me."

"Everybody, Kathy?" asked Miss Walter. "Let's see what your classmates think. We're about to begin a unit on discussion. 'Should teenagers have to be home by a certain time?' will be our first discussion question. The topic should interest everyone, and there's plenty of opportunity for differences of opinion. Who knows what *discussion* really is?"

"Isn't it just pooling ideas and facts on a subject?" asked Vern. "If a discussion is any good, everyone learns something he didn't know before."

"Vern may be right," said Bonnie, "but I always thought discussion meant talking about a problem and finding a solution."

"Aren't Vern and Bonnie both right?" asked Earl. "Right now everybody should learn something about discussion from our pooling of information. If it were a question of organizing this class into a Friday discussion club, we'd be sharing our facts and ideas to decide whether or not to have the club."

"That's exactly it," said Miss Walter. "Some discussions are for learning more about a subject; others are for reaching a conclusion or a decision about a course of action. Joyce, did you want to add something?"

"I was just thinking, Miss Walter," said Joyce, "that we may not all agree at the end of a discussion but that we should have a better understanding of others' opinions. My parents don't approve of my staying out too late either. When we've discussed the question from all angles, maybe we'll understand our parents' viewpoint better."

"Yes," agreed Miss Walter, "some discussions do bring better understanding. Now let's see what we've learned about discussion."

ACTIVITY 1 Getting Facts from Your Reading   R

For help in answering the following questions, refer to the preceding discussion.

1. What is discussion?
2. What are the purposes of discussion?
3. What are the characteristics of a good discussion topic?

PREPARING FOR A DISCUSSION

You wouldn't think of giving a party without some preparation, would you? If you're going to contribute intelligently to discussion, you'll have to investigate the subject and weigh the information you gather.

Investigating the Subject. Find out ahead of time all you can about the subject. If your class chooses to discuss staying out late, for example, review your own experiences and those of your sisters, brothers, cousins, and friends. Talk to your parents and youth counselors. Consult the card catalog (see pages 251–254) and the *Readers' Guide* (page 144) for helpful books and articles on the subject. On index cards or small slips of paper make notes (see pages 196, 197) of important facts and figures and their sources. Identify your source carefully: you may need to verify your facts.

Distinguishing between Fact and Opinion. In your investigation distinguish between facts and opinion (see pages 241, 242). If you plan to tell the class that the majority of high school teenagers do not want to have to be home by a certain time, take a poll of the students in your class and report the results accurately.

TAKING PART IN A DISCUSSION

Your discussions will run more smoothly if everyone knows the rules of the game.

1. Save time by first agreeing on the meaning of important words in the question.
2. Contribute facts, examples, or statements of authority to back up your opinions.
3. Stick to the subject and keep your contributions brief.
4. Relate your contributions to what others have said. "Here's an experience I had that bears out Joan's statement."
5. Be courteous. Show that you believe everyone in the class is trying, as you are, to arrive at the truth.

NOT You're dead wrong.

BUT I agree with Ken that some parents are overly protective, but I've known a lot that weren't.

6. Speak clearly and forcefully.
7. Listen attentively and thoughtfully. Keep a mental summary of important points.
8. Be on the alert for flaws in reasoning. (See pages 237–245.) Help your class to draw those conclusions and only those conclusions that can be drawn from the facts presented.
9. Remember that a discussion is an exchange of ideas. Don't become angry if someone disagrees with yours.
10. Avoid making up your mind before you hear the different points of view on the subject. Accept with good nature a decision of the group.

LEADING A DISCUSSION

When it's your turn to be discussion leader, you will have a job that will keep you on your toes. Until then, appreciate what your leader is trying to do, and cooperate.

GUIDES FOR LEADING A DISCUSSION

1. State the topic to be discussed and help to get the discussion started.
2. Keep the discussion on the track.
3. See that all aspects of the topic are covered.
4. See that everyone has an equal chance to contribute.
5. Keep the discussion moving by summarizing the points already made and suggesting other points to consider.
6. Keep everyone in a friendly, cooperative spirit.
7. Remain neutral and speak little.
8. Summarize the main points that have been made.

ACTIVITY 2   Taking Part in a Discussion   OS

Prepare to contribute facts, ideas, and experiences in the discussion of one of the following topics or another topic approved by the class. The class may discuss as a group with the teacher as discussion leader, or it may be divided into groups of six students each with each group choosing its leader. If the class is divided into groups, the group leaders will report to the whole class the important facts presented in their discussions.

1. What are some alternative sources of energy to petroleum products? How can these sources be developed to fill our needs and at the same time be conserved as much as possible? 2. Should every student learn to speak a foreign language? 3. Are TV westerns true to life? 4. How much time should a teenager spend doing homework? 5. How late should a teenager stay out on weekends? 6. Should a teenager's allowance cover his clothing expenses? 7. Are extracurricular activities worthwhile? 8. Should teenagers hold afterschool jobs? 9. Should our class (or club) set up (or discontinue) a lunch counter at basketball games? 10. What are the recreational opportunities for teenagers in our community? 11. Which radio and television programs offer the best entertainment? 12. What's wrong with the comics? 13. What steps can be taken to preserve endangered species of animals? 14. Should public transportation be expanded? 15. Is interplanetary exploration a boon or a waste?

HOLDING A MEETING

No discussion can be successful if all the members try to speak at once. For fair play and orderly procedure, club and class meetings are conducted according to a set of rules called "parliamentary law." Parliamentary law is based on four principles: justice and courtesy, one thing at a time, rule of the majority, and rights of the minority.

Studying Parliamentary Law in Action

Last week Mr. Ramer's 9B English class voted to organize as a club. Today they're holding their second meeting. Let's listen in to see how parliamentary law works. Note particularly these points:

1. The call to order is given by the presiding officer.
2. The minutes include the name of the presiding officer, the date, time, and place of the meeting, and the action taken.
3. A committee report follows the reading of the minutes.
4. A member gets permission to speak, called "getting the floor," by rising and addressing the chair.
5. The chairperson recognizes the speaker, thus giving permission to speak by saying the speaker's name. Ordinarily the chair recognizes the first person to rise.
6. If a member wishes the group to take some definite action, he gets the floor and puts the suggestion in the form of a motion.
7. The seconder of the motion need not rise, address the chair, or be recognized.
8. The chair states the question after the motion has been made and seconded.
9. Discussion begins. Discussion cannot take place until a motion has been made and seconded and the chair has stated the question. The chair should give everyone a fair chance to speak and also get the business transacted without waste of time.
10. When the question has been fully discussed, the chairperson puts the question to vote by calling for a voice vote, a show of hands, or a ballot.
11. The president usually appoints committees, and the first person named becomes the chairperson. Committees are chiefly of two kinds: (1) standing committees provided for in the bylaws and appointed for the entire term; and (2) special committees appointed for a special purpose and ceasing to exist after the final report is filed with the secretary.
12. The chair can speed proceedings by assuming general consent to *routine* business. If there is any objection from the floor, of course a vote is taken.

ETHEL GORDON (*who was appointed temporary chairperson by Mr. Ramer, raps on the desk*). **[1]** The meeting will please come to order. The secretary will read the minutes of the last meeting.

ROBERT NICOLL (*rises and reads from his report*).

October 4, 19—

[2] A special meeting of Mr. Ramer's 9B English class was called to order by the temporary chairperson, Ethel Gordon, at 10:00 A.M. in Room 217. The chairperson appointed Robert Nicoll temporary secretary.

The chairperson then introduced Mr. Ramer, who explained the purpose of the meeting — the formation of a discussion club whose program would be planned entirely by the class. John Gantt moved that 9B English form such a club. The motion was seconded and was unanimously carried.

Joyce Collins moved that the chair appoint a committee of five students to prepare suitable bylaws for the club and present them at the next meeting. The motion was seconded and carried. **[11]** The chairperson appointed Victor King, Barry Denton, Estelle Mancini, Gladys Norton, and Dan Purdy.

Dave Sterns moved that the next meeting be held in Room 217 during the regular English period on the following Friday, October 11. The motion was seconded and carried.

The meeting adjourned on motion at 10:45 A.M.

Robert Nicoll
Temporary Secretary

CHAIRPERSON. You have heard the secretary's report. Are there any corrections or additions? (*She pauses.*) **[12]** If there are no corrections or additions, the minutes stand approved as read. The next business before the club is the report of the Committee on Bylaws.

VICTOR (*rising*). May I address the chair? **[3]** The committee appointed October 4, 19—, to prepare suitable bylaws for the club wishes to submit the following report. [*Reads the report.*]
Victor hands his report to the secretary.

CHAIRPERSON. What is your pleasure concerning the bylaws proposed by the Committee on Bylaws?

[4] PAT (*rising*). May I address the chair?

[5] CHAIRPERSON. Pat.

[6] PAT. I move that the proposed bylaws be adopted.

[7] DICK (*seated*). I second the motion.

[8] CHAIRPERSON. It has been moved and seconded that the proposed bylaws be adopted. The secretary will please read Article I. (*Secretary reads.*) Is there any discussion?

[4] LUCY (*rising*).   May I address the chair?

[5] CHAIRPERSON.   Lucy.

[9] LUCY.   Will someone on the committee please explain why Symposium 9B is proposed as the name of the club?   I think Fact-Finders would be a better name because it stresses one very important reason for discussing.

[4] BARRY (*rising*).   May I address the chair?

[5] CHAIRPERSON.   Barry.

[9] BARRY.   Many good names were suggested.   The committee discarded *Fact-Finders* because it emphasizes only one aspect of discussion. We propose *Symposium* because it suggests a friendly meeting for conversation and discussion.   That's what we want our club to be.   Also, we think the name will arouse the curiosity of the other English classes.

CHAIRPERSON.   Thank you, Barry.   If there is no further discussion of Article I, the secretary will read Article II.   (*The secretary reads each article, and the chairperson allows time for adequate discussion of each. The chairperson then rises.*)   [10] Are you ready for the question?   The vote is on the question that the bylaws proposed by the Committee on Bylaws be adopted.   Those in favor say "Aye."   (*Pupils vote.*)   Those opposed say "No."   (*Pupils vote.*)   The ayes have it; the motion is carried.   The new business before the club today is the election of officers. Nominations for president are in order.

[4] MARK (*rising*). May I address the chair?

[5] CHAIRPERSON. Mark.

MARK. I nominate David Sterns for president.

CHAIRPERSON. Dave Sterns has been nominated.

In the same manner Marcia nominates Carla Bower and Gladys nominates Barry Denton.

[4] DAN (*rising*). May I address the chair?

[5] CHAIRPERSON. Dan.

[6] DAN. I move that the nominations for president be closed.

[7] ESTELLE (*seated*). I second the motion.

[8] CHAIRPERSON. The motion has been made and seconded that the nominations for president be closed. [10] Those in favor of closing the nominations say "Aye." (*She pauses for the vote.*) Those opposed say "No." (*Another pause.*) The ayes have it; the motion is carried. There will be a brief recess for voting. Will Dick Martin and Sandra Shaw please act as tellers? (*Dick and Sandra distribute, collect, and tally the ballots.*)

CHAIRPERSON. The meeting will please come to order again. Are the tellers ready to report, Dick?

DICK. The tellers report that 31 votes were cast: 6 for Dave Sterns, 9 for Carla Bower, and 16 for Barry Denton. Barry has been elected president for this six-week term.

The Houses of Parliament, where parliamentary law originated

The temporary chairperson retires, and Barry takes the chair.

PRESIDENT.   Nominations for vice-president are in order.

Following the same procedure as for the election of the president, Symposium 9B elects a vice-president, a secretary, and a parliamentarian.

PRESIDENT.   [11] Article VI, Section 1, of our bylaws provides that the president shall appoint a Program Committee of three members.   I appoint Dave Sterns, Lucy Book, and Ruth Wilson.   Please write questions you would like Symposium 9B to discuss and hand them to the committee.   Will the committee please post on the class bulletin board no later than October 19 the question chosen for discussion at our next meeting, October 26.   We want to have time to prepare for the discussion.   Is there any further business?

[4] RUTH (*rising*).   May I address the chair?

[5] PRESIDENT.   Ruth.

[6] RUTH.   I move that we adjourn.

[7] CARL (*seated*).   I second the motion.

PRESIDENT.   [12] It has been moved and seconded that the meeting be adjourned.   If there is no objection from the floor, the meeting stands adjourned.

ACTIVITY 3   Discussing Parliamentary Procedure   OS

Prepare to discuss in class the topics listed below.   Refer to the report of the meeting of Symposium 9B and to one or more of the books on parliamentary procedure.

1. Organizing a club.   How does one go about organizing a club? How, for example, is the temporary chairperson selected?   What method besides the one used in Mr. Ramer's class might be used?   Who appoints the temporary secretary?   How long do the temporary officers serve? What business would probably be conducted at the organizational meeting?

2. Bylaws.   What are bylaws?   How do they differ from a constitution?   What is their purpose?   What do they ordinarily include?   How are they adopted?

3. Committees.   Why are committees set up?   What are the chief kinds?   What kinds of committees did Symposium 9B have?   Are committees always appointed by the president?   Who serves as chairperson of a committee?   What are the general duties of a committee?   What information is included in a committee report?

4. Officers.   How are officers elected?   What are the usual officers of a club?   What are their duties?   Does a nomination need to be seconded? What method besides nominating from the floor might be used?   When does the president take office?   Does he have to call for the negative vote?

5. Taking part in a meeting. What are the responsibilities of the member? How does he get permission to speak in a meeting? How does he get a group to take action? What can he do if the group tries to transact business without using correct parliamentary procedure?

ACTIVITY 4 Writing Minutes   RW

Read Robert's minutes on page 231 again. Then write the minutes for the Symposium 9B meeting reported on pages 231, 232. Report only what was done at the meeting. Use your imagination to report nominations and elections for vice-president, secretary, and parliamentarian. What date will you use to head your minutes?

ACTIVITY 5 Practicing Parliamentary Law   OS

A. Prepare to make or second one of the following motions or another motion and to discuss it. Make your remarks definite and pointed.

1. That the president appoint a TV committee to list on the board recommended programs each week.
2. That the president invite various people in the community to speak to the class on their vocations.
3. That the club visit a place of interest in the community — a historic spot, a museum, an industrial plant, a newspaper plant, a radio station.
4. That the president appoint a publicity representative to report the activities of the club to the school paper.
5. That the club hold a quiz program.
6. That the students select a magazine for class study.

B. With your teacher's permission, organize your English class as a club.

ACTIVITY 6 Word Study   VW

The following words or expressions were used in this chapter. The page number is after each. What does each word or expression mean in the sentence in which it appears? Check your spelling.

parliamentary	230	chair	230	aye	233
majority	230	routine	230	ayes	233
minority	230	minutes	231	carried	233
presiding officer	230	bylaws	231	nominate	233
recognizes	230	moved	231	closed	233
floor	230	ballots	233	tellers	233
motion	230	second	233	adjourn	234

Unit Five — *Resources*

17   *Clear Thinking*

How would you react to these comments?

1. "You don't believe an athlete once ran the mile in 3:48? Well, here's his picture."
2. "How can you agree with Charley Calvert's ideas for improving the Student Council? He's so terribly conceited!"
3. "For my last cold I drank a syrup composed of soda pop, lemon juice, and brown sugar. A week later my cold was gone. What a wonderful remedy this proved to be!"
4. "In 1957–59 there were 592 traffic deaths in Massachusetts and only 270 in Idaho. During that period Idaho's safety record was more than twice as good as that of Massachusetts."

ACTIVITY 1 Practicing Straight Thinking   T

What do you consider wrong with each of the preceding statements? Discuss your opinion in class and then consult page 238.

MAKING DECISIONS

How many decisions must you make each day? One? Several? A dozen? If you keep a decision diary for one day, you'll be surprised at the number of choices you must make: whether to have oatmeal or eggs for breakfast; whether to do your science homework before or after dinner; whether . . . whether . . . whether . . . !

Many of these minor decisions are made through habit, through emotion, or through chance. Some decisions, though, deserve more than a passing whim. Are you able to think through a more serious problem efficiently, or do you make your decision hastily and thoughtlessly? You will have to make many important decisions in the years ahead. How intelligently will you make them?

AVOIDING THE DANGERS

Thinking, like any other activity, requires both practice and a keen awareness of the pitfalls. Many activities in this book require practice in straight thinking. Discussion (pages 227–235), reporting (143–153), explaining (131–141), for example, all provide practice in organizing thoughts and thinking straight. If you can identify the obstacles to straight thinking, you can check your own arguments for loopholes and judge more critically the claims of others.

Pitfall 1 — Mistaking the Cause

"I forgot my lucky silver dollar today and failed a spelling test as a result."

"Ridiculous!" you comment. How often, though, do you assume that because something happened *after* something else it must have happened *because of* it? Through the years you have learned about cause and effect. When you hit your thumb with a hammer, you have every right to assume that the sudden painful swelling results from the blow. But if you credit the hammer blow with curing your sinus trouble, you are drawing a highly improbable conclusion.

Most events have many causes. Sometimes the causes are obscure and uncertain. It is dangerously tempting to oversimplify, to seize on the first cause you happen to think of. Sometimes there is really no connection between what seems like cause and effect. Sometimes what seems to be cause and effect is merely coincidence.

Superstition is based on a confusion of cause and effect. The superstitious person who fails a science test blames a black cat, a broken mirror, spilled salt, or Friday the thirteenth. He doesn't check his own study habits for the real reason. Self-deception is an obstacle to straight thinking.

ACTIVITY 2 Finding the Real Cause   T

The thinking in four of the following statements is muddled. Show in each of these four that there doubtless were other causes.

1. We just bought a beagle puppy. I have had the sniffles for a week. I must be allergic to the puppy's fur.
2. On a recent vocabulary test Maureen made a 98% and Polly only a 78%. Maureen is probably much brighter than Polly.
3. Colleges decide whom to admit on the basis of admission tests, high school marks, and participation in extracurricular activities. Although Carl Franklin had high marks and an excellent extracurricular record, Simpson College did not admit him, even though other students with slightly poorer records were admitted. Probably Cal did poorly on the admission tests.

(Answers to Activity 1, page 237)

1. The picture of the athlete does prove one thing: the athlete had his picture taken. There is no proof of his unbelievable running ability.
2. Consider a man's arguments on their merits, not on his personality.
3. There is no proof of cause and effect. The cold would probably have disappeared anyway.
4. The statistics disregard population and percentages. During the period mentioned the Idaho death rate was $2\frac{1}{2}$ times the Massachusetts rate.

4. For good luck Lew Arnold, our center fielder, always touches second base on his way to the dugout. Today he failed to touch second base once and as a result struck out.
5. Every time I try to budget my allowance something goes wrong — a broken bike chain or a stiff library fine. I get along better without a budget than with one.

Pitfall 2 — Rationalizing

"Instead of having the regular school lunch today, I'll have three desserts. Sugar provides a lot of energy, and I'll need energy for the baseball game this afternoon."

Self-deception takes many forms. The speaker is finding reasons for doing something he has already decided to do. His good judgment tells him that substituting sweets for nourishing food is unwise, but he wants the cherry pie, the ice cream, and the chocolate cake. He overpowers his good judgment by inventing a *reason* for doing what he wants to do. Providing self-deceptive or false reasons is called "rationalizing."

Be honest with yourself. Find the real reasons, and face them. Think straight.

ACTIVITY 3 Exposing Rationalization   T

Which of the following would you classify as clear thinking? Which sound like rationalizing? Can you add an example of rationalizing of which you have been guilty?

1. I'll let my science homework go till my study period tomorrow. After all, home is a place for relaxation, not work and strain.
2. Mr. Adams is setting up a special after-school study class in algebra. Since algebra is my weakest subject, I'm planning to join his group.
3. I think I'll watch *Guntwirlers* on TV now. I'll probably learn more history from this western than I can learn in my textbook chapters on western expansion.
4. I was supposed to water the lawn this afternoon, but what for? It's sure to rain tomorrow. I think I'll go swimming.
5. I won't bother Dad about my poor marks in math. He'll only worry.

Pitfall 3 — Hasty Generalizing

"Who says cats harm birds? Why, our Princess would let a canary sleep in her paws and never harm it!"

The implied generalization — that cats don't harm birds — is a hasty, ill-informed conclusion based on only one example.

Generalizations perform a useful purpose. We discover that poison ivy plants should be avoided, that compact cars tend to consume less gas than larger cars, and that roses do better in sun than in shade. Our minds are stocked with helpful generalizations based upon our experiences, but we must keep alert.

There are many dangers in generalizations. Here are five dangers to guard against:

1. Our generalizations may be based upon faulty thinking, like mistaking the cause.

2. Conditions change. Our generalizations may not have changed with them.

3. Nearly all generalizations have important exceptions.

4. Many generalizations are based upon too few samples or experiences, like the generalization about birds and cats.

5. The world is composed of *individual* persons and things. Generalizations are often merely a convenience of language. (See pages 39–42.) Absolute words like *all, every, always, never,* and *nobody* are often used loosely.

Keep an open mind. Remember that generalizations can be wrong. Remember, too, that even reliable generalizations have to be reexamined frequently.

Generalizations often do harm when they involve groups of people. Only the muddled thinker condemns a whole group because of an unpleasant experience with one, two, or half a dozen members of the group. Every group consists of individuals with differing characteristics, even though they are members of the same group.

ACTIVITY 4 Studying Faulty Generalizations   T

Why is each of the following generalizations likely to be unsound? Review the dangers listed above.

1. My friends Janet and Clara Peterson are blondes. Americans of Swedish descent are all blondes.
2. It's impossible to teach cats to do tricks. They're too stupid.
3. In a game with Fairbanks High School our star pitcher was spiked by the Fairbanks second baseman. Players from Fairbanks are poor sportsmen.
4. An unabridged dictionary is a complete listing of words in English. I'll be sure to find the new word I came across yesterday in this unabridged dictionary.
5. Children from Beeville did more poorly on the statewide tests than the children from Jaytown. The Jaytown children are undoubtedly smarter than the Beeville children.

Pitfall 4 — Misleading Comparisons

"Alice is allowed to go out on a Wednesday evening. Why can't I?"

How old is Alice? Was she allowed the same privilege at your age? Just how similar are your situations? Are there enough points of similarity to make the comparison fair?

Argument by comparison can be strong. Let's assume, for example, that your school is thinking of publishing a school paper. Let's assume, too, that some members of the faculty fear that the students will not support a paper. What arguments can you present that will convince the faculty members? You can point to a school in a nearby town with a successful paper. You can show that the school is similar to yours in every significant way. It has about the same number of students with much the same background and interests. Point by point you show similarity and argue that if a paper succeeds at that school, it will succeed in your own. The argument is convincing if there are enough points of similarity between the schools. If, however, the points of difference outweigh the similarities, then your argument will collapse.

ACTIVITY 5 Pointing Out Misleading Comparisons   T

Four of the following arguments by comparison are questionable. Show why the situations may not be similar.

1. Myrna Williams looks good in that new violet shade. I think I'll get a dress in the same shade.
2. Our science teacher said that four glasses of milk a day are better than just one. The doctor suggested I take a vitamin pill each day. I'll probably be better off if I take four.
3. Lime is an excellent plant supplement for lilacs. I think I'll put some lime around our azaleas and rhododendrons.
4. Alex Gifford says Arthur C. Clarke is an excellent writer of science-fiction tales. Since our tastes in reading are similar, I think I'll take a crack at one of Clarke's books.
5. Why do I have to take English? Jack London went to high school for only three months and certainly didn't study much English, but during his lifetime he wrote fifty-one successful books.

Pitfall 5 — Confusing Facts and Opinions

"The fact is that Carol Heiss is the greatest figure skater of all time."

"I believe that at the 1960 Olympics Carol Heiss won at least 1490 points for figure skating."

Which is a statement of fact and which of opinion? Though the first masquerades as a fact, it is really an opinion. Though the second seems to be an opinion, it is really a statement of fact. The second can be checked by reference to the *World Almanac*. The first cannot be checked at all.

Opinions are important. There is nothing wrong with stating an opinion that Carol Heiss is the greatest figure skater of all time. The danger is in accepting opinion as fact. Sometimes facts are quoted erroneously, but they can at least be checked.

Many facts cannot be established by firsthand observation or experience. The straight thinker who must rely on secondhand sources for her facts consults reference books and other reliable authorities. Before forming an opinion she examines the facts carefully. Then she arrives at a conclusion based on the facts.

ACTIVITY 6 Distinguishing between Fact and Opinion   T

Tell whether each of the following is a statement of fact or of opinion.

1. An American traveling in Europe needs a passport.
2. Traveling in Europe is an exciting experience.
3. Tin costs more per pound than zinc.
4. Tin is not a cheap metal.
5. The Washington cherry trees were planted during the Taft administration.
6. In spring the cherry trees along the Potomac are an unforgettable sight.

Pitfall 6 — Misusing and Misunderstanding Statistics

If the average height of boys on your baseball team is five feet six inches, a dozen baseball suits of that size would be of little help. Most boys deviate from the average.

Similarly, a brook with average depth of two feet will be a dangerous place for nonswimmers if the middle is six feet deep. *Average* is a tricky and confusing term.

As you go through high school, you will learn more and more about statistics, about how they are compiled and interpreted. Meanwhile learn to withhold judgment. Don't be bowled over by imposing statistics.

Pitfall 7 — Confusing Arguments and Personalities

If a person you dislike makes a statement, try to consider the statement on its merits. Similarly, when you attack a point of view, don't base your attack on your opponent's personality or on his mannerisms.

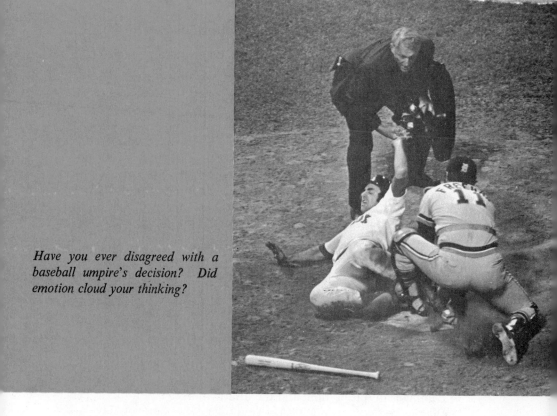

Have you ever disagreed with a baseball umpire's decision? Did emotion cloud your thinking?

Pitfall 8 — Letting Emotion Cloud Thinking

Emotion is a powerful force for good. It can force you to get out and act. But it can also get in the way of straight thinking. Use emotion as the gasoline in your thinking machine, but keep your mind on the wheel.

Pitfall 9 — Thinking in Circles

"It is a good idea to have an apple every day for lunch because everyone should have an apple in the middle of the day."

This statement, which has the form of an argument, is actually only an assertion. The opinion is followed, not by a supporting fact, but by the same opinion slightly disguised. "Eat an apple because you should eat an apple."

"Why do you think so?" you may ask your opponent in the middle of a discussion. If he answers, "Because I do," his arguments are going round in circles. This misuse of reason is sometimes called "begging the question."

ACTIVITY 7   Exposing Pitfalls in Thinking   T

In each of the following statements point out a possible error in thinking.

1. Gary's plan for improving the school newspaper is just nonsense. He's always so sure he's right.
2. That chow dog can't be gentle. Chows aren't gentle dogs.
3. I just don't feel happy at Central. I've had a disagreement with my best friend. I'm going to try to get a transfer.
4. At Remsen Industries we checked the salaries of six persons at random — three executives and three workmen — and found the average salary to be over $20,000 a year. Salaries there are extremely high.
5. I can't spell because nobody in my family is a good speller.

ACTIVITY 8   Studying Pitfalls in Thinking   T

Select any three pitfalls and construct an example demonstrating each pitfall. Test your classmates' ability to find the pitfall and check your understanding of it.

THINKING YOUR PROBLEM THROUGH

When you are faced with a decision, weigh the evidence. Be on guard against the pitfalls that lead your thinking astray. List the advantages in one column and the disadvantages in another. Determine the best course of action — and take it. When you have taken the step, forget about it and go on to the next problem.

ACTIVITY 9   Explaining How a Decision Was Reached   OT

Think of a recent decision you had to make. In two columns list the arguments for and against. Then explain clearly how you reached your decision. Perhaps these topics will help you to recall a problem you have thought out.

1. Should I try out for a school team? 2. Should I join the band, the orchestra, a particular club, or another school activity? 3. What course of study should I follow? 4. What is the best study schedule for me? 5. What vocation should I prepare for? 6. Should I study a foreign language? 7. How should I spend my allowance? 8. Should I buy this suit (or dress or hat) or that one?

ACTIVITY 10   Thinking Through a Problem   TW

Write about a problem that is worrying you. Put the title in the form of a question — for example, Should I be allowed to go out on weekday evenings? Should I have an increased allowance? What work should I be expected to do at home?

Before beginning to write, jot down the reasons you think support your point of view. Examine these reasons carefully and determine whether any of them stem from an error in thinking.

Then in one paragraph give your point of view and all the reasons to support it. In another give all the objections to your point of view. Your teacher will read the most interesting papers aloud and ask for suggestions. He will not announce the names of the writers.

ACTIVITY 11 Writing a Paragraph   SW

Review the points made in this chapter and write a paragraph with this topic sentence: *Self-deception is easy; facing reality is much more difficult.*

ACTIVITY 12 Word Study   VW

The following words were used in this chapter. The page number is after each word. What does each word mean in the sentence in which it appears? Use each word in a sentence of your own. Check your spelling.

react	237	rationalizing	239
whim	237	generalization	239
pitfall	237	masquerades	242
loopholes	237	erroneously	242
obscure	238	withhold	242
coincidence	238	mannerisms	242

18 Resources of the Library

"**W**here are you going, Chuck?" asked his friend Al. "Study hall's the other way."

"To the library," replied Chuck. "I need information for my report on helicopters."

In the library Chuck went quietly to the reference shelves where the encyclopedias were kept. He turned to the index in the H volume and was soon getting a bird's-eye view of his topic. Helicopters, he decided, was too broad a subject. He'd limit his report to the peace-time uses of helicopters.

After taking notes on the uses discussed in the encyclopedia article, he went to the card catalog to see what books his library had on the subject.

How about you? Can you find material in the library as quickly as Chuck did? With a little training in library skills you too can be at home in the library.

USING REFERENCE BOOKS

Reference books are usually kept on open shelves in the reference room or reference section of a library. Some you must ask for at the desk. An *R* above or before the call number of a book means "reference." A reference book may not be taken from the library.

Encyclopedias

Encyclopedias you will particularly enjoy using include the *World Book Encyclopedia* and *Compton's Pictured Encyclopedia*. These encyclopedias contain hundreds of illustrations as well as entertaining and informative articles. *The Golden Encyclopedia* is a simpler reference set. To use an encyclopedia efficiently, keep in mind the following points.

1. Arrangement of Topics. In an encyclopedia famous persons are listed alphabetically under their last names. To find other names, like *Sargasso Sea*, look for the first word. When you want information about practical nursing or the principles of the storage battery, look in the encyclopedia under the key word of your topic: *nursing* or *battery*.

2. Guide Letters. A letter or letters on the binding of a volume indicate the topics treated in that book. Information about nomads and Mary O'Hara can be found in a volume marked N–O.

3. Guide Words. In *Compton's* and the latest *World Book* guide words usually indicate the first and last topics treated on two facing pages.

4. Cross References. Cross references are directions for looking up information in other parts of the encyclopedia. The "See" reference after a title refers the reader to another subject for the information desired.

BRASS INSTRUMENT. See MUSIC (Musical Instruments.)

The "See also" reference in the body of the article or at the end directs the reader to articles with fuller information or articles on related subjects. In the *World Book Encyclopedia*, for example, after the article on POLAR BEAR is this entry:

See also ANIMAL; BEAR

5. Other References. After some articles an encyclopedia may list books that will give additional information on the topic. For an example of such a bibliography turn to the entry on birds in either *Compton's* or the *World Book*.

6. Index. In one edition of *Compton's* the main article on birds totals forty pages. Suppose you want to learn how birds are banded. Instead of hunting through all forty pages, turn to *Birds* in the index of the B volume and run down the column to *bird banding*. Here you will be referred to discussions of bird banding, volume B, pages 191–192; volume G, page 262; volume M, page 303; to a picture on page 192 of volume B and a color picture of a trap on page 192a of the same volume. If you read further under *Birds* in the index, you will find that intelligence of birds is discussed on pages 182d–183 of volume B.

The last volume of the *World Book* is a study guide. In addition, after many articles you will find outlines. After the article on birds in the B volume you will find an example of an outline.

ACTIVITY 1 **Examining Encyclopedias**   **S**

1. Which of the encyclopedias mentioned above does your school, community, or home library have? How many volumes are in the set? What is the copyright date? If the encyclopedia was copyrighted ten years or more ago, what caution will you have to exercise in using material?

2. Does your school, community, or home library have any of these encyclopedias: *Americana, Britannica, Collier's*, other? How many volumes are in the set? Is there an index? If so, where? Is an annual supplement issued? What is the purpose of an annual supplement? Do the volumes have guide letters, guide words, and cross references? Give examples of each.

ACTIVITY 2 Using Key Words   RS

Divide your paper into three columns. In the first column copy
the topics listed below. In the second column write the name of the
encyclopedia you are using. In the third column write the key word
of the topic — that is, the word under which the encyclopedia gives
information about the subject.

how a cameo is made	the World Calendar
how to plan a garden	leading sheep states
new ideas in education	standardizing measurement
camouflage at sea	Matthew Brady's photography

ACTIVITY 3 Finding Answers to Questions   RS

Using *Compton's* or the *World Book*, find an answer to five of
the questions in A and five in B. Then tell how you located the
information — whether you found it by using the regular alphabetical
arrangement or by using the index or cross references.

A.   1. When and where was the first tax-supported library in the United
States founded?
    2. Why do we know more about the contents of Babylonian and
Assyrian libraries than we do about the contents of the Egyptian
libraries?
    3. What was the most famous library in the ancient world?
    4. What contribution did the people of Pergamum make to libraries?
    5. Who founded the first subscription library in the United States?
    6. Whose library formed the nucleus of the Library of Congress when
it was rebuilt in 1815? Why was it rebuilt then?
    7. What was a scriptorium?
    8. What was Andrew Carnegie's contribution to libraries?
    9. For how long is a United States copyright good?
    10. For what achievement is the Newbery award given?

B.   1. How did Buffalo Bill get his nickname?
    2. What mistaken idea do many people have about porcupines?
    3. Is an iceberg made of fresh or salt water?
    4. For what is Sir Alexander Fleming famous?
    5. What causes a mirage?
    6. How does the sea horse hatch its eggs?
    7. What is the symbolism of the design of the state flag of Alaska?
    8. What historic event in railroading took place at Promontory,
Utah, in 1869?
    9. What is the largest member of the lizard family?
    10. What is the average weight of an elephant at birth?

S

Look up each of the following in an encyclopedia. To what topics are you referred for additional information? Check the index, if the encyclopedia has one, as well as the main entry.

compass	manganese	rope
insulin	phosphorus	Venice, Italy

ACTIVITY 5   Finding Out How to Make or Do Things   **OS**

In an encyclopedia find an explanation of one of the following. Be prepared to explain the procedure to the class. If you don't find a full explanation in one encyclopedia, try another.

1. How to make a kite. 2. How to keep score in bowling. 3. How to use a road map. 4. How to make introductions. 5. How to lay out an ice-hockey rink. 6. How to paddle a canoe. 7. How to mount insects and butterflies. 8. How to rid a lawn of dandelions. 9. How to can fruits. 10. How to make a simple telescope.

Books of Biography

Current Biography, a monthly magazine, has accounts of the outstanding people of the month. The twelve monthly issues are published also as a book.

Who's Who in America, published every other year, gives information about famous living Americans.

Twentieth Century Authors has pictures and short biographies.

Lippincott's Pronouncing Dictionary includes brief accounts of famous men and women of all countries of all time.

The *New Century Cyclopedia of Names*, published in three volumes, includes essential information about persons, living and dead, of importance in the English-speaking world.

Webster's Biographical Dictionary has short biographies of forty thousand noted men and women of all countries and all ages.

Brief biographical notes on famous persons are given in many dictionaries either in the regular alphabet or in the back.

ACTIVITY 6   Using Books of Biography   **S**

In any of the books just discussed find answers to these questions. If you don't find an answer in one book, try another.

1. What great discovery was made by Sir Alexander Fleming?
2. In what field did Charles Proteus Steinmetz achieve fame?
3. What was Mark Twain's real name?
4. What were the highlights of Thomas Jefferson's administration?

USING THE CARD CATALOG

What's in the Card Catalog?

Books and other material in the library are listed on cards which are filed alphabetically in drawers of a cabinet. Each drawer has a label showing how much of the alphabet is included in that drawer. Guide cards, standing higher than the others, mark the main subdivisions in each drawer.

The catalog will answer questions like these for you.

1. Does the library have any books by Sir Arthur Conan Doyle?
2. Are there any books on games?
3. Does the library have a copy of *Excuse It, Please?*

For most nonfiction books there are at least three cards in the card catalog.

1. Author card. The first line of this card has the author's last and first names, sometimes followed by the years of his birth and death.

2. Title card. The first line has the title of the book, disregarding *a, an,* or *the* as the first word.

3. Subject card. The first line has a topic, usually in red or black capitals. A book may have more than one subject card if it is about two or more subjects.

For a book of fiction, poetry, or drama there are at least two cards in the card catalog — an author card and a title card.

ACTIVITY 7 Learning to Use the Card Catalog

s

Here are ten labels copied from the drawers of a card catalog.

GAR–GRIL GRIM–HAR HAW–HIGH HIST–HY I–JAN
JAP–KY LA–LINC LIND–LY MA–MECH MED–MORT

In which drawer would you find a card for each of the following titles, authors, and subjects? Answer by naming the letters on the drawer. Except when used as a book title and alphabetized accordingly, a person's name appears under the first letter of the last name.

1. Modern Manners
2. Glass
3. Nathaniel Hawthorne
4. *Huckleberry Finn*
5. *Great Lady of the Theater*
6. *Johnny Tremain*
7. Horses
8. Walter Lord
9. *The Heavyweight Champions*
10. Medicine
11. Helen Keller
12. *Hot Rod*
13. *Men, Ants, and Elephants*
14. Guns
15. Magic
16. *Hospital Zone*

What's on the Cards?

Examine the labeled author card and discover how much it tells you.

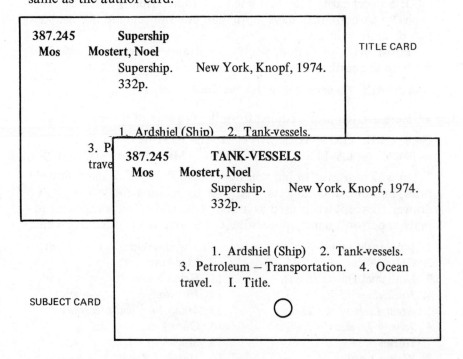

Except for the first line, the title card and the subject card are the same as the author card.

Some books may be indexed by more than one subject.

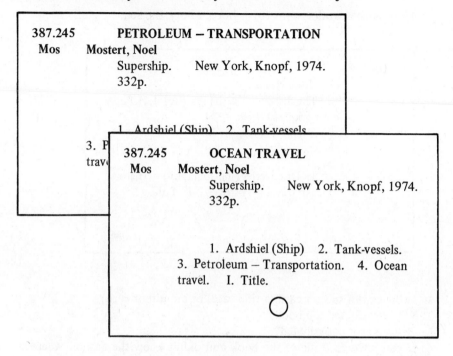

As in an encyclopedia, the card catalog may also have cross references. Suppose you want a book on space travel. You look for *space travel* in the card catalog and find this card.

> *See*
> *Card*   SPACE TRAVEL. see
>   SPACE FLIGHT.

On some subjects the catalog may have a *See also* card.

> *See*
> *also*   SPACE FLIGHT. see also
> *Card*   INTERPLANETARY VOYAGES.

Here is the catalog card for a book about the sea.

910.45
Par   Parry, John Horace
           The discovery of the sea [by] J. H. Parry.
     New York, Dial Press, 1974.
          302p.   illus.

          Bibliography.

          1. Discoveries (in geography) — History.
     2. Ocean travel — History.   I. Title.

---

1. Is the card a subject card, a title card, or an author card?
2. Who distributed the book?
3. When was it copyrighted?
4. If you knew the title of the book and didn't know the author, where would you look in the card catalog?
5. Under what subjects is the book indexed?

Using the card catalog in your school or town library, find the answers to the following questions and problems.

1. What books are there in your library by Thor Heyerdahl, Will James, Clarence Day, Howard Pease, Raymond Ditmars, and Mary O'Hara?
2. How many of the following books are in your library: *The Silent World; The Yearling; Penrod; The Wonder of Light; The Great Dissenters; Drag Strip; People and Places; Arctic Doctor; The Sea Wolf; Green Grass of Wyoming?* Copy each title with the author's full name.
3. Give the full title and name of the author of a book in your library on each of these subjects: atomic energy, cooking, democracy, sports, television.
4. What book have you especially enjoyed reading recently? What other books by the same author does your library have?

FINDING BOOKS

Books in most libraries are arranged according to their subjects. Novels are in one place, science books in another.

Novels and Biographies

The easiest books to find in a library are biographies and works of fiction. If you want to read *The Dark Adventure* by Howard Pease, go to the fiction section of your library. The section will be marked with a sign, or your librarian will point it out to you.

Works of fiction are arranged alphabetically by the author's last name. To find *The Dark Adventure*, go down the shelves alphabetically until you find *Pease*. Each author's books are arranged alphabetically by title, disregarding *a, an,* or *the:* Pease's *The Dark Adventure* will come before his *Heart of Danger*.

Biographies have their own section also but are arranged alphabetically by the last name of the person the book is about. A biography of Daniel Boone by James Daugherty will be under B. All biographies of one person are arranged alphabetically according to the biographers' last names: *Fighting Frontiersman* by J. E. Bakeless; *Daniel Boone* by J. H. Daugherty; *Daniel Boone* by Lillian Moore.

ACTIVITY 10   Finding Works of Fiction and Biographies   **S**

1. What name will you look for to find each of these works of fiction: *A Curtain of Green* by Eudora Welty; *Floorburns* by J. F. Carson; *Banner in the Sky* by James Ramsey Ullman; *The Scapegoat* by Daphne du Maurier; *The Call of the Wild* by Jack London?

EXAMPLE   *Swiftwater* by Paul Annixter   Annixter

2. What name will you look for to find each of these biographies: *Will Rogers* by Patrick Joseph O'Brien; *Jules Verne* by George H. Waltz; *Albert Schweitzer: Man of Mercy* by Jacquelyn Berrill; *He Heard America Sing: The Story of Stephen Foster* by Claire Lee Purdy; *Albert Einstein* by Elma Levinger; *Grenfell of Labrador* by George H. Pumphrey?

Nonfiction

Look at the catalog cards on page 252 again. Note that each card has a set of numbers in the upper left-hand corner. This set of numbers is the call number which tells the exact location of the book. The call number is also printed on the back of the book. When calling for a book, copy the call number along with the title of the book and the name of the author.

The top line of the call number is the Dewey Decimal System class number. In this famous system, devised by Melvil Dewey, there are ten large divisions. Books with call numbers between 000 and 099 are general works like encyclopedias and newspapers. In the 100–199 group are books on philosophy and psychology. Other major groups in this system are religion, social science, language, pure science, applied science, arts and recreation, literature, and history. These larger divisions are broken down into subdivisions like biology, animals, insects — under science.

On the shelves of the library the books are arranged clockwise around the room. Books in the 200's are to your right as you look at the 100 books.

The bottom line of the call number is the author number. The author number begins with the first letter or first two letters of the author's name.

Suppose you are looking for a book with the call number $\frac{621.38}{B458e}$.

Your first problem is to find the 600 shelf. Then look for 21 under 600; then .38 under 621; then B under 621.38; and finally 458e under $\frac{621.38}{B}$. Don't overlook a decimal point. Number 622 is larger than 621.38. On the library shelf 621.38 comes after 621.3 and before 621.4.

ACTIVITY 11   Investigating Your Library System   s

1. Does your school library use the Dewey Decimal System of classification? If not, ask your librarian to explain the system used.

2. What system of classification does your public library use?

3. Under what number or letter should you look for the kind of books you most like to read? In what part of the library would you find them?

4. What is the procedure for borrowing books from your school or public library?

5. Which books may you take out of the library?

6. How long may you keep books?

7. Where are newspapers and magazines kept in your library?

8. Does your public library have recordings? Pictures or paintings? May you borrow them?

HANDBOOK OF GRAMMAR, USAGE, AND STYLE

Diagnostic and Mastery Tests

19 *Sentence Structure: Subjects and Verbs*

You have a fairly competent understanding of English grammar. Does this statement surprise you? Ever since infancy you have been using the English language with considerable skill. You have been able to make yourself understood. Why, then, bother with more grammar? If you are like most people, your writing and speaking can be improved. In writing, particularly, you sometimes find that you cannot get across just what you are trying to express. To help you improve, your teacher will have to use basic terms like *subject* and *verb*. This chapter will help you to review some of the basic terms and to use them in building complete sentences.

A.1 **SENTENCE** A sentence expresses a complete thought. It contains a subject and a verb (or predicate), either expressed or understood.

SV

You can keep insects under control without a spray. Attract birds to your garden.

Conversation is filled with clipped sentences (see page 450). Unless you are reproducing conversation or including a properly identified fragment for style (page 451), however, be sure that every sentence you write has a subject and a verb.

DIAGNOSTIC TEST 2A Subject and Verb

Copy each subject and each verb. Draw one line under the subject and two lines under the verb (main verb plus any helpers).

1. The girls finished their science project and prepared it for display.
2. In the last of the ninth with two out and a runner on second, the hitter smashed the ball toward center field.

3. At three in the morning Josh and I were up and on our way to the trout stream.
4. A light on the rocket's control panel was blinking rapidly.
5. What prescription did the doctor give you for your sore throat?
6. What kind of work does your mother do?
7. There came a loud round of applause from the packed stands.
8. Do you like muffins, donuts, or sweet rolls?
9. For the first two months of school I did not attend the movies.

RECOGNIZING AND USING VERBS

A jack rabbit _____ through the scrubby undergrowth.
A rattlesnake _____ into a pile of rocks.
A hummingbird _____ from blossom to blossom.

How would you fill the blanks from these words: *flitted, hopped, slithered?* What a difference the choice of word makes! The missing words, which add color and vigor to the sentences, are verbs.

PRACTICE 1 Choosing Verbs   V

Fill each blank with a well-chosen word of your own. The words you choose will be verbs.

EXAMPLE
      soared
The rocket _____ into the sky.

1. The puppy _____ for its mother.
2. The car _____ down the mountain road.
3. The rain _____ all day.
4. The runner _____ across the finish line.
5. A flash of lightning _____ across the purple sky.

PRACTICE 2 Writing Sentences   VW

Write a vivid, colorful sentence using each of the following verbs. If you are not sure of the meaning of a word, look it up in a dictionary.

EXAMPLE
    clattered   The horses' hoofs clattered over the cobblestones.

1. shattered	4. kindled	7. whistled	10. spun
2. thrust	5. filtered	8. blazed	11. toppled
3. sank	6. scowled	9. hissed	12. sprang

In the examples and activities thus far the verbs have made statements. *Slithered*, for example, makes a statement about *rattlesnake*. Verbs may also help ask questions or give commands.

Are the Cardinals in town tonight? (*Are* helps ask a question about the *Cardinals*.)

For contrast, compare the pocket-sized chihuahua with the pony-sized St. Bernard. (*Compare* helps give a command.)

A.2 *VERB* **Verbs make statements, ask questions, or give commands.**

Although most verbs express action (*laugh, shout, cheer, sing*), some express being: *am, is, are, was, were, shall be, will be, has been, have been, had been,* and other verbs ending with *be* and *been.* Learn to recognize the being verbs. They are used frequently.

What action verbs are there in the following sentences? What being verbs?

STATEMENT   A cow gives less milk in hot weather.

Texas longhorns are now nearly extinct.

QUESTION   Is the raccoon a relative of the kangaroo?

Who kicked that extra point?

COMMAND   Announce the winner of the third race.

Be gentle but firm with a young puppy.

Are, is, and *be* are the being verbs. *Gives, kicked,* and *announce* are the action verbs.

STRUCTURE CLUES — VERBS

If you can find the verb, you can tell how the sentence is put together. Three excellent clues are (1) word endings, (2) location in the sentence, and (3) signal words.

ENDINGS

Sometimes the ending of a word is a clue to part of speech. Some common endings for verbs are *ing, ed, d,* and *t: walk, walked, walking; live, lived, living; sleep, slept, sleeping.*

SENTENCE PATTERN

The verb occupies a key position in the structure of a sentence. What you already know about English sentence structure will help you identify verbs.

Locusts _____ in great swarms.

Any word you supply is a verb: *travel, fly.* (Note that in Practice 1 the verbs occupied familiar positions.) Of course many words

that can be used as verbs are also used as other parts of speech —
for example, *try* hard (verb), a good *try* (noun).   Examine the entire
sentence before trying to decide part of speech.

SIGNAL WORDS

Read the word aloud, placing *he, it,* or *they* before it.   If the
phrase makes sense, the word can be used as a verb.

VERB	NOT A VERB
he wins — they win	he ats — they at
he falls — they fall	he talls — they tall
it blossoms — they blossom	it rugs — they rug

PRACTICE 3   Studying Possible Verbs   VW

Decide which of the following words can be used as verbs.   In
a picture-making sentence of your own, use as a verb each word that
can be used as a verb.

and	for	small	through	trip
believe	since	start	throw	whirl

PRACTICE 4   Finding Verbs

In each sentence find the verb.

THE FOUR CHAPLAINS

1. On a February night in 1943 the *Dorchester* steamed through the
Atlantic.   2. Suddenly a torpedo shattered the side of the troopship.
3. Panic gripped the majority of the 904 men on board.   4. Within twenty-
five minutes the *Dorchester* carried 638 men to icy graves.

5. Many survivors owed their escape to a Jewish rabbi, a Roman
Catholic priest, and two Protestant ministers.   6. With complete disregard
for their own lives, these four chaplains gave away their life jackets.
7. Calmly the four moved among the frightened men.   8. Here a chaplain
guided men over the rail into a lifeboat.   9. There a chaplain adjusted a
life jacket.   10. Then with prayers for the safety of the men on their lips,
the chaplains linked arms.   11. Their heroic sacrifice stirred the imagination of many people.   12. Today a chapel in Grace Baptist Temple in
Philadelphia commemorates the courageous chaplains.

A.3   *AUXILIARIES*   A verb may be preceded by one, two, or three
helping verbs, called "auxiliaries."

Look at the italicized verbs in each of the following sentences:

1. We *have spent* two summer vacations in Acadia.
2. Where *did* Chicago *get* its name?
3. Without Bud's help we *would* never *have found* the trail.
4. The names of the contest winners *should have been announced* last week.

The verbs *spent*, *get*, *found*, and *announced* have helping verbs. Sometimes, as in 2 and 3, there are words between the parts of the verbs. Auxiliaries are easy to remember in groups:

1. The *be* group: *be, am, is, are, was, were, been* (*am hoping, is lost, were challenged, are trying*)
2. The *have* group: *have, has, had* (*have contributed, has looked, had eaten*)
3. The *do* group: *do, does, did* (These are usually used for emphasis or to form questions: *Do* you *agree?* He *does enjoy* hard work. *Did* you *finish* your homework?)
4. Others: *may, might, can, could, must, shall, will, should, would*

A.4 AUXILIARIES AND MAIN VERBS The *be* verbs, the *have* verbs, and the *do* verbs can be main verbs or auxiliaries.

MAIN VERB	AUXILIARY VERB
Nancy *was* here.	Nancy *was elected.*
Jeremy *had* a soda.	Jeremy *had* already *eaten.*
Jim *does* research.	Jim *does go* to dances.

PRACTICE 5 **Using Helpers in Sentences** **W**

In interesting sentences of your own use each of the following verbs with one or more helping verbs. Underline the whole verb twice (main verb plus helpers).

EXAMPLE

I had always wished for a set of electric trains.

| climbed | fallen | hurried | sitting | volleyed |
| dropped | gasped | lying | tried | wished |

Fill the blank in each sentence with an appropriate verb. Be ready to identify the complete verb. (In sentence 2, for example, *did* is part of the complete verb.)

1. Lenny ____ into the room with his usual noisy clamor.
2. Did you ____ the car?
3. Alice, will you ____ me the scissors?
4. ____ the window. It ____ very stuffy here.
5. Larry ____ sometimes careless in his written work.
6. What have you ____ with the tickets?
7. From a gnarled branch on our old tree ____ two ripe apples.
8. There ____ thirty desks in our classroom.
9. Haven't you ____ your report?
10. Which students will ____ the staff of the school newspaper?

A.5   *IMPORTANCE OF THE VERB*   A vivid, colorful verb carries the sentence.

A well-chosen verb makes the difference between "The old house fell" and "The old house crumbled." Choose the right verb to convey your message.

In each sentence below choose the verb which makes the sentence more colorful or more accurate. Justify your choice.

1. The glass window (broke, fell, shattered) into a thousand tiny pieces.
2. Please don't (cover, litter, spread) the picnic area with discarded paper.
3. The light in the lonely house (gleamed, glittered, shone) in the distance.
4. The car (swerved, turned, twisted) to avoid hitting the stray dog.
5. The child (clutched, grabbed, held) the lollipop in one grubby hand.
6. The freckle-faced little boy (hopped, stood, teetered) for a moment on the thin rail fence and then jumped to the ground.

7. As Marie read the algebra problem, she scratched her head in bewilderment, and (frowned, laughed, whispered).
8. The miser (collected, gathered, hoarded) his wealth for many years before his lonely death.
9. The light rain (pattered, pounded, rippled) on the tent throughout the night.
10. "Watch out for that truck!" (screeched, called, yelled) the policeman.

PRACTICE 8 Supplying Colorful Verbs   V

For each sentence supply five different verbs. Be ready to tell how each suggests a different picture.

EXAMPLE The train _____ into the station.
roared, rumbled, crept, swept, glided

1. Outside the window the moth _____ against the glass.
2. The football team _____ down the field.
3. The clouds _____ across the prairie.
4. Tom _____, "I'm here."
5. The sudden noise _____ Jan.

RECOGNIZING AND USING NOUNS

The _____ was hidden behind the _____.
We saw a _____ and a _____ at the _____.

Complete the sentences. The missing words are all nouns.

A.6 NOUN A noun is a name.

A noun may consist of one, two, or more words: *ocean, house, home run, post office*. A book title (*The Return of the Native*) or a geographical name (*Bay of Biscay, Grand Canyon*) is one noun. If you are not sure whether an expression of more than one word is a noun or a noun with modifiers (page 355), look it up in a dictionary.
Nouns name:

Persons — girl, uncle, Nanette, sailor, Colonel Jones
Animals — elephant, coyote, fish, Spot, robin, black bear
Places — Italy, town, Brookfield Zoo, gymnasium
Things — ladder, ink, birdhouse, rain, tulip, hand, plum pudding
Collections or groups of persons or things — squad, crowd, committee
Qualities, conditions, actions, and ideas — heroism, inflation, kindness, capacity, treason, intention, ability

PRACTICE 9 Listing Additional Nouns   V

Write two more nouns for each of the six kinds listed above.

STRUCTURE CLUES — NOUNS

Three excellent clues to the identification of nouns are (1) word endings, (2) location in the sentence, and (3) signal words.

ENDINGS

Most nouns have a plural form, usually ending in *s* (page 306).

clock — clocks   aunt — aunts

SENTENCE PATTERN

Most nouns make a meaningful pattern with *is* or *are* at the beginning of a sentence.

clock is   aunts are

Nouns often precede verbs: *sparrows* chirp, *icicles* fall, *Larry* tries.

Of course many words that can be used as nouns are used also as other parts of speech — for example, legible *copy* (noun), *copy* the assignment (verb). A word is probably a noun if it completes a pattern like one of these:

The ____ saw the ____ near a ____.
The ____ was injured by the ____.

SIGNAL WORDS

Most nouns make sense when *a*, *an*, or *the* is put in front of them.

a clock   an aunt   the clock   the aunt

PRACTICE 10   Identifying Nouns

Find the nouns in Practice 4.

A.7   *SPECIFIC NOUN*   Use the specific noun to say what you mean.

Say *cello, violin, guitar,* or *harp,* not *stringed instrument.*

PRACTICE 11   Supplying Specific Nouns   **V**

Suggest more specific nouns for three of the following general nouns.

EXAMPLE
boat
rowboat, catboat, canoe, skiff, lifeboat, catamaran, dinghy, kayak

| 1. game | 3. automobile | 5. saw | 7. tree |
| 2. flower | 4. dessert | 6. insect | 8. clothing |

PRACTICE 12 Supplying Specific Nouns   **V**

Supply a specific noun or nouns for each of the italicized words or groups of words.

EXAMPLE

On a holiday my dad took *a relative, a friend,* and me on a visit to a *city.*

One Fourth of July my dad took my cousin Tom, Allan Kirby, and me on a visit to St. Louis.

1. As we drove along in our *car*, we saw some *animals* and a flock of *birds*. 2. When we arrived, we drove up *a street* to the zoo. 3. We liked best *an animal*. 4. Then we had lunch at *a restaurant*. 5. After this we went to *a place of interest* and then *another place of interest*. 6. We saw *many interesting things*. 7. After an exciting day, we left and drove home along *a river* and past *a lake*.

PRONOUN

George asked Tony, "Tony, could ~~Tony~~ give Hal and ~~George~~ a few
   (you)   (me)

pointers on batting? ~~Hal and George~~ are trying out for the freshman
   (We)

team. Please help ~~Hal and George~~."
   (us)

Notice how helpful the words *you, me, we,* and *us* are.

A.8   *PRONOUN*   A pronoun is a word used in place of a noun.

The prefix *pro* means *in place of.* A pronoun is a stand-in or substitute for a noun, as in the illustrations above.

Among the commonly used pronouns are these: *I, me, we, us, he, him, she, her, it, they, them, who, which, one, anyone* and *anybody, someone, no one, everyone, everybody.*[1]

PRACTICE 13 Studying Use of Pronouns   **W**

Write a brief paragraph describing a personal experience you had today. Using the George-and-Tony sentence above as your guide, use no pronouns. When you refer to yourself or another, use a

[1] The words *my, our, his, her* (before a noun), *its,* and *their,* which are forms of pronouns, usually act like adjectives and modify nouns. These are treated elsewhere: pages 388–401 and 407.

name. Double space the paragraph. When you have finished, lightly cross out some of the nouns and substitute pronouns. Be ready to tell what is gained in the revised paragraph.

SUBJECT

A.9 *SUBJECT* The subject answers the question "Who?" or "What?" before the verb. It is commonly a noun or a pronoun.

Platinum was first discovered in Colombia. (Who or what was discovered? *Platinum* was discovered. *Platinum* is the subject.)

Many North American birds spend the winter in South America. (Who or what spend? *Birds* spend. *Birds* is the subject.)

Some parts of Brazil have never been thoroughly explored. (Who or what have been explored? *Parts*, not *Brazil*, is the subject.)

Which one of the West Indian islands was the first to be discovered by Columbus? (Who or what was? *One*, not *islands*, was. *One* is the subject.)

Many members of the orchid family grow wild in woods and meadows. (Who or what grow? *Members*, not *family*, grow. *Members* is the subject.)

A.10 *SUBJECT NOT EXPRESSED* Frequently in commands and requests the subject is not expressed.

Leave your boots in the hall.
Don't miss the new movie at the Rialto.

You is understood to be the subject of both sentences.

PRACTICE 14 Finding Subjects

Find the subject of every sentence in Practice 4.

A.11 *BACKBONE OF A COMPLETE SENTENCE* The simple subject and the verb are the backbone of the sentence.

PRACTICE 15 Finding Subjects and Verbs

On your paper copy the subjects and the verbs of these sentences. Underline a subject once and a verb twice.

AMERICA'S VOLCANO

A. 1. Last July the five members of our family visited Lassen Volcanic National Park. 2. We entered the park territory from the south. 3. Our first stop inside the park was at Sulphur Works. 4. The overpowering smell of sulphur gave an eerie quality to the bubbling hot springs. 5. We drove along Lassen Peak Highway by snowdrifts ten feet high.   6. From the summit of the drive we had an excellent view of Mt. Lassen.

B. 1. Not many years ago the cone of Mt. Lassen sent forth smoke, lava, and volcanic ash.   2. The area of devastation is still visible farther north.   3. From the high point on the highway we drove down to Kings Creek Meadows.   4. Great patches of snow still lay throughout the camping area.   5. After a restful night in camp Dad took us on a hike to Kings Creek Falls.   6. All of us were enthusiastic about our stay in this northern California mountain park.

A.12   *INCORRECT DOUBLE SUBJECT*   When a noun and a pronoun mean the same person or thing, they should not both be the subject of the same verb.

Nancy ~~she~~ wants to be a secretary.
Captain Kidd and Blackbeard ~~they~~ were both pirates.
One of my brothers ~~he~~ played fullback on last year's team.

PRACTICE 16   Getting Rid of Incorrect Double Subjects

Correct the sentences.   What is the verb in each sentence?   What is the double subject?

1. The goalie he made a great play for the United States Olympic team.
2. The winners they complimented the losers on their strong comeback.
3. Diane Byrd she has an important role in *The King and I.*
4. After school my brother he delivers the *Sentinel.*
5. The student-body elections they were held during the week of November 4.
6. Calamine lotion it is sometimes used for poison ivy.
7. My cousin he can run the mile in four minutes thirty seconds.
8. The blizzard it marooned a herd of cattle in the north pasture.
9. *Seventeenth Summer* it tells the story of a summer romance.
10. The members of the track team they voted for Lanny Ellis as captain.

COMPLETE SUBJECT

A.13   *MODIFIER*   A modifier is a word or group of words that makes clearer or limits the meaning of another word.

Hats (can mean any hats)
Two hats (Answers the question "How many?")
Felt hats (Answers the question "Which?" or "What kind of?")
Hats *with red feathers* (Adds additional details)

Put the modifiers and the noun together and you know exactly which hats are meant: *Two felt hats with red feathers.* . (See pages 362–363 for more about prepositional phrases as modifiers.)[1]

A.14   *COMPLETE SUBJECT*   The complete subject is the simple subject with its modifiers.

> *The sting of a scorpion* is very painful but seldom fatal. (*The* and *of a scorpion* modify *sting*. *Of a scorpion* answers the question "Which?" or "What kind of?")

COMPLETE PREDICATE

A.15   *COMPLETE PREDICATE*   The complete predicate is the verb with all its modifiers and the words that complete its meaning.

Ordinarily every word in a simple sentence belongs either to the complete subject or the complete predicate.

> A few <u>herds</u> of wild horses │ still <u><u>roam</u></u> the Western plains. (*Roam* makes a statement and is the verb.   The complete predicate consists of the verb *roam* with its modifier *still* and its completer *the Western plains*.   A vertical line separates the complete subject from the complete predicate.   The simple subject is underlined; the verb has two lines under it.)
> North American <u>Indians</u> │ <u><u>made</u></u> their wampum beads from seashells.

To find the complete subject and the complete predicate of a simple sentence, follow these steps:

1. **Find the verb — the word that makes the statement, asks the question, or gives the command.** In the sentence above, the verb, *made*, makes the statement.
2. **Find the simple subject.** In this sentence ask, "Who or what made?" The answer, *Indians*, is the simple subject.
3. **Find all modifiers of the simple subject.** In this sentence the modifier is *North American*. The subject with its modifier, *North American Indians*, is the complete subject.
4. **Everything not included in number 2 and number 3 is the complete predicate.**

PRACTICE 17   Supplying Predicates   **W**

For each of these complete subjects supply an appropriate predicate of your own.   Strive for an effective, vivid picture.

---

[1] Some teachers prefer to introduce the term *headword* for the word modified. A noun headword with its modifiers is sometimes called a "noun cluster." A verb headword with its modifiers is sometimes called a "verb cluster."

EXAMPLE
The runt of our beagle's litter
The runt of our beagle's litter had the best disposition and friskiest manner of all of the pups.

1. A sudden gust of wind
2. A studious-looking freshman with a faraway stare
3. The white picket fence around the corner house
4. A perky robin on a fence post in the garden
5. The lonely, deserted house near the edge of town
6. Two members of the freshman wrestling squad

PRACTICE 18   Building Complete Subjects and Predicates   **W**

By adding modifiers and other words, build up each of the following into complete sentences. Do not add verbs.

EXAMPLE
road wound
The rutted mountain road wound along the shoulder of a ridge near Snow Peak.

1. ice glistened	7. horse galloped
2. water oozed	8. car ran
3. sand blew	9. tree fell
4. stew simmered	10. school opened
5. smoke curled	11. children shouted
6. boys rambled	12. swimmer dived

PRACTICE 19   Matching Complete Subjects and Predicates

Match a complete subject with a complete predicate to make a meaningful sentence. Use each item only once. For each sentence underline the simple subject once and the verb twice.

COMPLETE SUBJECT	COMPLETE PREDICATE
1. The rickety table	glistened in the sun's rays.
2. The tawny lion	still stood on the old house site.
3. The mica in the rock	is a patchwork of color in early spring.
4. A lonely chimney	lifted its two red blossoms above the leaves.
5. Our stereo	had gold drapes and brown wallpaper.
6. The reporter	suddenly collapsed to the floor with a bang.
7. The geranium	paced back and forth in the cage.
8. Dad's vegetable garden	questioned eyewitnesses at the fire.
9. The whale	needs a set of new tubes.
10. Carla's room	may reach a length of a hundred feet.

INVERTED ORDER

A.16 *INVERTED ORDER*   A sentence in which the verb or any part of it comes before the subject is said to be in inverted order. Most sentences are in natural order.

INVERTED ORDER   At the bottom of the Caribbean Sea lie many sunken Spanish galleons.

NATURAL ORDER   Many sunken Spanish galleons | lie at the bottom of the Caribbean Sea.

A.17 *THERE*   *There* at the beginning of an inverted sentence is an introductory word, *not the subject.*

There is a good western at the Community Theater this week.
A good western | is at the Community Theater this week. (*There* is omitted in the natural order.)

A.18 *QUESTION*   A question may be in the natural order or in the inverted order.

NATURAL ORDER   Which planet | is closest to the earth?
INVERTED ORDER   How far away from us is the North Star? (The North Star | is how far away from us?)
INVERTED ORDER   When was the last eclipse of the moon? (The last eclipse of the moon | was when?)

Often the subject is between the main verb and its helper.

Do frogs hibernate?
How far north do palm trees grow?
Not until the present century were many rare animals protected by conservation laws.
Only rarely do whooping cranes breed in captivity.

A.19   *OTHER WORDS BEFORE SUBJECT*   Frequently a portion of the complete predicate precedes the subject.

OTHER WORDS BEFORE SUBJECT   In an old trunk Betsy discovered her grandmother's faded wedding dress.

REARRANGED   <u>Betsy</u> | <u><u>discovered</u></u> her grandmother's faded wedding dress in an old trunk.

Putting part of the predicate before the subject is a good way to gain smoothness or to draw attention to something in your sentence (pages 455, 456). To find the complete subject and the complete predicate, however, you will have to rearrange the sentence.

PRACTICE 20   Finding Subjects and Verbs

Copy the following sentences, arranging inverted sentences in the natural order. Rearrange those sentences that have something before the subject. Then draw one line under the simple subject and two lines under the verb. Draw a vertical line between the complete subject and the complete predicate.

EXAMPLES

In the Pacific Northwest region lies some of the most picturesque country in America.

<u>Some</u> of the most picturesque country in America | <u><u>lies</u></u> in the Pacific Northwest region.

In this colorful land there is one natural wonder above all others.

One natural <u>wonder</u> above all others | <u><u>is</u></u> in this colorful land.

MT. RAINIER NATIONAL PARK

A. 1. Near the busy cities of Tacoma and Seattle towers Mt. Rainier. 2. From both cities there is a good view of the mountain. 3. The mountain was climbed for the first time in 1870. 4. Mt. Rainier National Park was established in 1899. 5. Mt. Rainier is a part of the beautiful Cascade Range.

6. The entire Cascade Range is a series of dormant volcanoes. 7. The cone of Mt. Rainier was built by successive volcanic eruptions. 8. On the higher slopes are many glaciers. 9. Forests of hemlock and other evergreens clothe the lower slopes.

10. Mt. Rainier National Park is a popular recreation center. B. 1. To the snowcapped peaks of the Cascade Range come thousands of skiers. 2. Throughout an average winter fifty feet of snow falls in Paradise Valley. 3. In summer, visitors come for the magnificent mountain scenery 4. In the appropriately named Paradise Valley are vast fields of wild flowers.

5. The name of the mountain has an interesting history. 6. Mt. Rainier was named for a friend by Captain George Vancouver of the British Navy. 7. Many natives of Washington preferred the name *Tacoma.* 8. This name was an old Indian one. 9. After several editorial battles and court decisions the name remained *Mt. Rainier.* 10. To residents of Tacoma and Seattle, Mt. Rainier is simply "the mountain."

COMPOUND SUBJECT OR COMPOUND PREDICATE

A.20   *COMPOUND SUBJECT OR PREDICATE*   The subject, the predicate, or both may be compound.

ONE SUBJECT AND ONE PREDICATE   Young hens lay very small eggs at first.

COMPOUND SUBJECT   Asters and chrysanthemums bloom in the fall.

Jane, Jean, and Joan are three forms of the same ancient name.

COMPOUND PREDICATE   Dandelion leaves can be eaten raw like lettuce or can be cooked like spinach.

Tadpoles develop hind legs first, then grow front legs, and finally lose their tails.

COMPOUND SUBJECT AND COMPOUND PREDICATE   Both honeybees and bumblebees gather pollen and live in colonies.

The potato and the sweet potato look somewhat alike and cook alike but are not close relatives.

A.21   *SIMPLE SENTENCE*   A simple sentence has one subject and one predicate, either or both of which may be compound.

CONJUNCTION

Have you noticed that in each compound subject and compound predicate *and*, *but*, or *or* is used as a connecting word?   Such connecting words are conjunctions.   Conjunctions, like pronouns (page 267), help us express ourselves compactly and economically.

Algae have no roots.   Fungi have no roots.   They do not have seeds. They do not have flowers.   They do not have fruits.

Algae *and* fungi have no roots, seeds, flowers, *or* fruits.   (The conjunctions *and* and *or* help us to join ideas.)

A.22   *CONJUNCTION*   A conjunction connects words or groups of words.

Swing music *and* boogie-woogie grew out of jazz.
Aluminum weighs little *but* is very strong.

A.23   *PAIRED CONJUNCTIONS*   Paired conjunctions like *either . . . or* and *neither . . . nor* are sometimes called *correlative conjunctions*.

Either E. B. White writes about Maine *or* T. H. White does.
Neither Mercury *nor* Venus has a natural satellite.

In the following sentences either the subject or the verb is compound, or both are compound. On your paper copy the subjects, verbs, and conjunctions. Underline a subject once and a verb twice. Write the abbreviation **conj.** over a conjunction. Do not write in this book.

EXAMPLE

Under authority of the Constitution our government coins money and regulates its value.

conj.

government coins and regulates

COINS OF THE UNITED STATES

A. 1. A collection of coins shows famous Americans and gives a thumbnail sketch of American history. 2. Before the adoption of the Constitution there was no central system or plan for uniform coinage. 3. The states and even private individuals coined money. 4. Foreign money circulated throughout the country and was accepted in payment of debts. 5. Indeed, because of the shortage of coins the Mexican peso and certain other foreign coins were legal tender until 1857.

6. In 1792 the United States Mint began the issuance of coins and stabilized the currency. 7. Because of public distrust of paper money, the Mint issued no paper money for seventy years but concentrated on coins. 8. Gold and silver were the most popular metals for coins. B. 1. The gold coins were used for higher amounts and were issued regularly until 1933. 2. In the United States nickel, copper, tin, zinc, and even steel have been used in coins.

3. Throughout the years certain coins were tried but were finally dropped. 4. A half-cent piece and a twenty-cent piece were once minted but are no longer in circulation..

5. The famous Indian head penny lasted from 1859 to 1909 and was uniformly popular. 6. It circulated for many years after 1909 but eventually became a collector's item. 7. The Liberty head nickel, the "Mercury" dime, and the Liberty quarter once circulated along with more recent coins. 8. All these have disappeared from general circulation and have found their way into coin collections.

By using either a compound subject or a compound predicate, change each group into one good sentence. Underline a subject once and a verb twice. Write **conj.** over a conjunction. Do not write in this book.

EXAMPLE

From 1703 to 1909 our common coins did not show any man's portrait. They pictured instead Liberty and the American eagle.

From 1703 to 1909 our common <u>coins</u> <u>did</u> not <u>show</u> any man's por-

       conj.   **conj.**

trait but <u>pictured</u> instead Liberty and the American eagle.

1. The Lincoln penny broke with tradition. It became the forerunner of other coins honoring famous men.
2. Since that time Jefferson has been honored on a coin. Roosevelt has been similarly honored. So have Washington and Franklin.
3. The buffalo nickel honors the American Indian. The Indian head penny also honors the American Indian.
4. The model for the penny was thought to be a real Indian in war bonnet. It was actually the twelve-year-old daughter of the Mint's chief engraver.
5. A great many coins are minted each year. They are put into circulation.
6. From time to time certain coins are needed in a hurry. They are provided by emergency schedules.
7. A new sales tax may create a sudden demand for a particular coin. So may a change in subway fares.
8. During one period in 1955 a shortage of pennies temporarily ended production of all other coins. It forced the Mint to make nothing but pennies.
9. Pennies are always in great demand. So are nickels and dimes.
10. Quarters represent a relatively small percentage of total production. So do half-dollars.

Have you mastered subject and predicate? What was your mark on the diagnostic test? How much higher will your mark on the mastery test be?

MASTERY TEST 2B Subject and Verb

Copy each subject and each verb. Draw one line under the <u>subject</u> and two lines under the <u>verb</u> (main verb plus any helpers).

1. The report of an approaching tornado blurted from the radio and hurried us to the cellar.
2. Then Ruth and Joan jumped into the water.
3. On the walls hung cheap copies of famous works of art.
4. What do you remember about the book?

5. There were seventeen crew members on the sinking ship.
6. From the questions, one can judge the difficulty of a test.
7. Which job should we give to Susan?
8. Yesterday the scouts prepared their equipment for today's hike.
9. Have you ever seen large flights of ducks in the fall?

SENTENCE AND SENTENCE FRAGMENT

A.24 *SENTENCE FRAGMENT* A sentence has a subject and a verb. If one or the other is missing, the group of words is called a "sentence fragment." (See pages 446–450.)

Which of these word groups are sentence fragments? Why?

1. The Wright brothers' first airplane flight on December 17, 1903.
2. The Wright brothers' first airplane flight took place on December 17, 1903.
3. Got your postcard yesterday and showed it to Timmy and Marvin.
4. I got your postcard yesterday and showed it to Timmy and Marvin.

PRACTICE 23 Completing Sentence Fragments

Six of the following are sentences, and six are sentence fragments. Change the sentence fragments to complete sentences. Underline each subject and put two lines under each verb.

1. Linda Clark has been chosen as the cover girl for the April issue of *Practical English.*
2. A display from the arts and crafts department in the lobby of the auditorium.
3. Joe Bowman in sixth place in the nationwide archery tournament.
4. A special ceremony and election of officers will follow the program.
5. Most of the June graduates are attending colleges in the Midwest.
6. A lonely freshman in the bleachers after the seventh inning.
7. The Devils Tower is a striking rock formation in northeastern Wyoming.
8. Gave the distinguished foreign visitor the keys to the city and made a speech of welcome.
9. Leverock's Town in the Dutch West Indies is located inside an extinct volcano.
10. The children around the large Christmas tree with their eyes aglow.
11. Rattlesnakes and all other poisonous snakes periodically shed their fangs.
12. Took the ball from the quarterback and raced seventy yards through the Jefferson line for a touchdown.

20 *Capitalization*

1. Which sentence would arouse worldwide interest?

   a. The president has suddenly resigned.
   b. The President has suddenly resigned.

2. Which deals with astronomy?

   a. Class disappointed as mercury disappears.
   b. Class disappointed as Mercury disappears.

3. How do you explain this sentence?

   Mel Baxter is both a democrat and a Republican.

4. Which doesn't make sense?

   a. The little building is one of the largest in Boston.
   b. The Little Building is one of the largest in Boston.

Capitalization makes writing easier to read and provides important clues to meaning. This chapter will help you to use capitals correctly.

DIAGNOSTIC TEST 3A Capitalization

In each sentence copy and capitalize the words that need capitals. If you omit a needed capital letter or insert a capital that is not needed, the sentence is wrong. The figure in parentheses at the end of each sentence shows how many capital letters are missing in the sentence.

1. We flew to denver on trans world airlines. (4)
2. In the middle of april my aunt marilyn and uncle john invited us to dinner at christy's on fort dodge avenue. (9)
3. In my junior year at john f. kennedy high school, I studied advanced algebra, spanish, english, and drama. (7)
4. The partridge hotel in dallas is one of the most comfortable in the entire southwest. (4).

5. Next saturday my uncle will take sally and me to the zoo in forest park. (4)
6. Last thanksgiving day michigan state university defeated nebraska in the closing minutes of the final period. (6)
7. The islands of guernsey and jersey are located in the english channel and have been a part of great britain for a long time. (6)
8. In 1609 henry hudson, an englishman sailing for the dutch east india company, discovered the hudson river and thought he had found the long-sought shortcut to india. (10)
9. In his novels *the pearl* and *the grapes of wrath* john steinbeck tells of the problems faced by poor people in central america and oklahoma. (10)
10. Sally fraggos said that a friend of hers graduated from high school last year and won appointments to both annapolis and the united states military academy at west point. (8)

WHAT WORDS TO CAPITALIZE

B.1 *FIRST WORDS* Capitalize the first word of (1) a complete sentence (2) a quoted sentence, (3) the remark of each new speaker in conversation, (4) a line of poetry or verse, and (5) each topic of an outline. (See pages 147–148.)

SENTENCE Two groups of Americans climbed Mount Everest simultaneously.

QUOTED SENTENCE Can you remember who said, "We have met the enemy, and they are ours"?

CONVERSATION "Where was she when the fire broke out?"
"In bed asleep."

LINES OF VERSE And what is so rare as a day in June?
Then, if ever, come perfect days.
— JAMES RUSSELL LOWELL

B.2 *LETTERS* In the salutation of a letter capitalize the first word and all nouns; in the closing capitalize only the first word.

Dear Mr. Oliver: Yours as ever,
My dear Ms. Thompson: Sincerely yours,

B.3 *I, O* Capitalize the pronoun *I*, both alone and in contractions (*I'll, I've*), and the exclamation O.

The answer I've written is the line, "Build thee more
stately mansions, O my soul!"

B.4 *PROPER NOUNS* Capitalize proper nouns and their abbreviations. (See specific rules under B.5.)

A proper noun is the name of a particular person, place, or thing: *Helen Grasso, Dodge, Los Angeles Coliseum.*   A common noun refers to any one of a class of persons, places, or things and is not capitalized: *a girl, an automobile, a sports stadium.*

B.5   RULES FOR CAPITALIZING PROPER NOUNS

1. Capitalize names of particular persons.

PROPER	COMMON
Jack Lemmon	an actor
Mrs. Alice Anderson	a woman
Dr. James E. Foster	a doctor

2. Capitalize titles of organizations, institutions, and buildings.

PROPER	COMMON
Union Machinery Company	a company
St. Patrick's Cathedral	a church
Oak Park High School	a high school
Rotary Club	a club
Metropolitan Life Building	a building

3. Capitalize geographical names.

Europe, Scandinavia, Rocky Mountains, Pike County, Yosemite National Park, Sheridan Road, Missouri River

4. Capitalize words like *South, East,* and *Northwest* when they name particular parts of the country.   When these words refer to directions, they are not capitalized.

PART OF COUNTRY   Cactus gardens are as common in the Southwest as rose gardens are in the East.

DIRECTION   When the wind shifts suddenly from the southwest to the east, look out for a storm.

5. Capitalize names of political parties and their members, and names of peoples, their languages, and their religions.

Republican (party), Democrat, Greek, Methodist, Jew, Catholic

6. Capitalize names of historical events, periods, and documents.

World War I, Yalta Conference, Renaissance, Treaty of Versailles, Declaration of Independence

7. Capitalize names of governmental bodies and departments.

Congress, State Department, Interstate Commerce Commission, Federal Reserve Board, Bureau of Labor Statistics

8. Capitalize titles showing office, rank, profession, or family relationship when used with the name of a person.

Governor Hadley, Major Tenney, Judge Isaacs, Professor R. G. Davis

A title denoting high rank may be capitalized when used alone to refer to a specific person. When *President* refers directly to the President of the United States, it is usually capitalized.

The President is expected to appoint a new crime commission.

Most titles without names are not capitalized.

A mayor, a governor, and two congressmen were on hand for the launching of the new submarine.

Words of family relationship (like *father*, *uncle*, *grandfather*) are preferably capitalized when used instead of a person's name. They are always capitalized when used with a person's name.

PREFERRED   Last weekend Mother and Dad drove three hundred miles to surprise Grandmother on her birthday.

ALSO RIGHT   Last weekend mother and dad drove three hundred miles to surprise grandmother on her birthday.

Words of family relationship when preceded by a possessive noun or pronoun are not capitalized unless used with a person's name.

My uncle knew Jim's father and mother when they were all in high school together.

My Uncle Pete knew Jim's Aunt Gertrude many years ago.

9. Capitalize a descriptive name, title, or nickname used as a proper name or part of it.

William the Conqueror, the Black Prince, the Hoosier State, Big Ben, the White House, the Great Divide, the Great White Way

10. Capitalize the names of stars, planets, satellites, and constellations. *Sun, earth,* and *moon* are not usually capitalized.

the Dog Star, Mars, the Southern Cross, Mercury, the Milky Way

11. Capitalize the specific part of the trade name of a product.

Lux soap, Borden's milk, Red Heart dog food, Ivory Snow

12. Capitalize names of days of the week, months of the year, holidays, and holy days (but not seasons).

Tuesday, June, Fourth of July, Holy Thursday, Labor Day
But: summer, winter, autumn, fall, spring

13. Capitalize titles of books, plays, articles, poems, and newspapers. In titles the first and the last word and other words except articles (*a, an, the*), prepositions (like *through, into, for*), and conjunctions are capitalized.

The Lady or the Tiger

BOOKS *The Old Curiosity Shop, Life with Father, North of Boston*
SHORT STORY, ARTICLE, POEM "The Lady or the Tiger?" "Do It Today," "The Bell of Atri"

Except in bibliographies do not capitalize *the* as the first word of the name of a newspaper or of a magazine.

the *Chicago Sun-Times*, the *Christian Science Monitor*, the *Reader's Digest*

14. Capitalize names referring to the Deity, the Bible, and divisions of the Bible.

the Old Testament, Jehovah, the Lord, Exodus, the Scriptures

15. Capitalize the names of school subjects that are languages or numbered courses.

History 1A, Art 2, English, Spanish, French, German, Latin
But: history, biology, math, art, mechanical drawing

PRACTICE 1 Writing Sentences with Proper Nouns   W

Write sentences using any five of the words below as common nouns and as proper nouns (a total of ten words). For an extra challenge write a meaningful paragraph using all ten.

EXAMPLE school
   After graduating from Chamberlain High School, I hope to attend a
      technical school in Georgia.

airport	city	company	father	northwest
aunt	captain	cousin	hospital	railroad
bank	church	doctor	mountains	street

B.6 *PROPER ADJECTIVES* Capitalize proper adjectives.

talian literature
rench-fried potatoes

Proper adjectives are derived from proper nouns.

France — French door   Italy — Italian literature
Queen Victoria — Victorian period   Rome — Roman numeral

Some frequently used adjectives derived from proper nouns are not capitalized.

diesel engine, dotted-swiss blouse, japanned tray, herculean task, holland cloth, china cups, epicurean tastes

PRACTICE 2 Capitalizing Words and Expressions

Capitalize the following words and expressions as you would if you were using them within sentences. Prepare to give a reason for each capital.

A. 1. statler hotel
    2. typing, english, and civics
    3. grover cleveland high school
    4. summer and fall
    5. jack london's *call of the wild*
    6. lake michigan
    7. monday
    8. general motors corporation
    9. rock island railroad
   10. eloise j. mcgraw's *sawdust in his shoes*
   11. north of salt lake city
   12. halloween
   13. missouri river
   14. national security council
   15. a chinese restaurant
   16. a british naval officer
   17. a high school in sacramento
   18. the library of congress
   19. history, spanish, math, and english
   20. jupiter and saturn

B. 1. the standard oil company
    2. cologne cathedral
    3. the twenty-third psalm
    4. rip van winkle bridge
    5. a trip to death valley
    6. clarence day's *life with mother*
    7. sequoia national park
    8. pure food and drug act
    9. the city of seattle
   10. peter pan peanut butter
   11. the pacific northwest
   12. my uncle from tallahassee
   13. robert frost's poem "mending wall"
   14. revere copper and brass incorporated
   15. a teacher in nursery school
   16. pan american world airways
   17. a former french colony
   18. the french and indian war
   19. michigan boulevard
   20. national geographic society

Write six sentences telling facts that you learned in citizen education, science, health education, art, or some other subject. Work in at least one proper noun or proper adjective in each sentence.

EXAMPLE   The Congress of the United States is composed of two houses: the Senate and the House of Representatives.

PRACTICE 4   Capitalizing Sentences

In each sentence copy and capitalize the words that need capitals. Prepare to give the reason for each capital inserted.

OUR TRIP TO THE ROCKIES

A. 1. Last thanksgiving my mother and father took me to visit grandmother barker in denver, colorado. 2. After a smooth flight in a united air lines jet, we arrived at the airport at noon. 3. Though a snowstorm had hit the denver area a week before, the day we arrived was like a summer's day. 4. As we rode toward grape street, where my grandmother lives, we could see the towering peaks of the rocky mountains directly ahead of us. 5. Though denver is one of the largest cities between the mississippi river and the pacific coast, it is only a few miles from some of the most beautiful wilderness areas in america.

B. 1. Proudly showing us the beauties of her city and state, grandmother barker took us to the university of denver and the many state and federal buildings, including the united states mint. 2. The next morning we took a trip southward to colorado springs, where we visited the garden of the gods, a magnificent clump of unusual rock formations. 3. We passed the united states air force academy and looked beyond it to the towering mass of pikes peak. 4. On saturday we visited the city of boulder, where the university of colorado is located, and took a breathtaking ride through boulder canyon. 5. On november 29 we said goodbye to my grandmother and arrived home in chicago in time for a leisurely sunday dinner.

PRACTICE 5   Writing a Paragraph with Proper Capitalization   **W**

In a paragraph of six or more sentences describe a trip you took. Mention at least five places of interest. Capitalize each properly.

MASTERY TEST 3B   Capitalization

Copy and capitalize the words that need capitals. Omitting a needed capital or inserting an unnecessary one makes a sentence wrong. The figure in parentheses shows how many capitals are missing.

1. My uncle paul joined the united states army when he was eighteen years old. (5)
2. Our governor, one of our state senators, and mayor hatcher met at city hall on march 14. (5)
3. On the fourth of july, my family always has a picnic at heatherton state forest. (5)
4. Both my aunt claudette and mr. hudson graduated from the university of missouri. (6)
5. Many states in the south, georgia especially, have experienced tremendous growth during the last half of the present century. (2)
6. Mr. sturgis, our guidance counselor, advised me to take math, english, french, typing, and history in my junior year. (3)
7. During the thanksgiving vacation I read walter lord's *a night to remember,* a book about the sinking of the *titanic.* (7)
8. At our principal's invitation, lieutenant maguire of the tacoma police department spoke to the seniors about careers in law enforcement. (5)
9. The principality of andorra, the republic of san marino, and the state of vatican city are among the smallest countries in the world. (8)
10. On saturday, july 14, we made reservations for our trip to yellowstone national park. (5)

21 *Punctuating Simple Sentences and Quotations*

Watch your punctuation a handy device for helping the reader can you punctuate this introduction for clearness conciseness and readability

Effective punctuation makes sentences easier to read. Notice how punctuation marks affect the meaning of the following pairs of sentences.

1. a. Jimmy said his brother made the all-city basketball team.
   b. "Jimmy," said his brother, "made the all-city basketball team."
2. a. Three people knew the secret. All told.
   b. Three people knew the secret, all told.
3. a. When are you feeding the sharks Mr. Durant?
   b. When are you feeding the sharks, Mr. Durant?
4. a. Training a dog to be honest with you requires patience.
   b. Training a dog, to be honest with you, requires patience.

Punctuation may sometimes seem a baffling subject, but application of a fairly small number of rules will solve all your punctuation problems. Before reviewing punctuation, take the following diagnostic test to find out how well you punctuate.

DIAGNOSTIC TEST 4A Punctuation

Copy the following sentences and supply the needed punctuation. If you either omit a necessary punctuation mark or insert a useless mark, the sentence is wrong. The number in parentheses tells how many marks are needed. A pair of quotation marks is counted as one mark.

1. I don't believe remarked my uncle that we are on the right road (5)
2. New Bedford Massachusetts a seaport on Buzzards Bay was at one time an important whaling town (4)
3. I said *tomorrow* not *today* (2)
4. Well I think Carla now lives at 78 Trenton Street Louisville (3)
5. The only things we found in the closet were three empty cans a spool of thread and an old newspaper (3 or 2)

6. After we arrived in Chicago we looked for a hotel (2)
7. Gerry do you have to see Ms Ames after school (3)
8. Like Guernsey and Sark Jersey is also an island in the English Channel (2)
9. Antarctica a large mass of land wasn't really explored until the twentieth century (3)
10. Jim does not however play baseball tennis or hockey (5 or 4)

QUESTION MARK, EXCLAMATION POINT, PERIOD

End-of-Sentence Marks

C.1 *QUESTION MARK* Use a question mark after a question.

Have you become interested in the Puerto Rico story?
Do you plan to visit the island some day?

C.2 *EXCLAMATION POINT* Use an exclamation point to express strong or sudden feeling.

Use this mark sparingly.

How enticing those travel folders are!
What a magnificent view of San Juan!

C.3 *PERIOD* Use a period after a statement or a command.

STATEMENT "Operation Bootstrap" is Puerto Rico's name for its program of industrial development.
COMMAND Read this article about the new frozen-food plants on the island.

C.4 *POLITE REQUEST* A period is usually used after a polite request in the form of a question.

Will you return the magazine to me as soon as you can.

PRACTICE 1 Writing Commands and Requests   **W**

Write and correctly punctuate three commands or requests that you have heard recently.

EXAMPLE

Mow the lawn.   Rake up the grass clippings.

PRACTICE 2   Inserting End Punctuation

Place the correct punctuation mark at the end of each sentence. Do not write in this book.

1. Look at this picture of Morro Castle
2. Doesn't it remind you of our trip to Puerto Rico last year
3. What a wonderful time we had
4. We left Idlewild Airport on a Pan American clipper
5. How chilly the airport was
6. We arrived at the San Juan airport in the late afternoon
7. Have you ever left winter and found summer a few hours later
8. The tropical air felt moist and warm
9. What a colorful display the flowers provided
10. Visit this Caribbean jewel yourself

PRACTICE 3   Writing Varied Sentences   **W**

Choose four of the following topics or four other topics that interest you.   About each of them write four sentences — a statement, a command, a question, and an exclamation.   Label each sentence **S** (statement), **C** (command), **Q** (question), or **E** (exclamation).

EXAMPLE

A FAIR

S   The town fair is always held the last week in August.
C   Go straight out Maple Street to the fairgrounds.
Q   Did you see the puppet show at the last fair?
E   What a crowd there was around the cake-selling booth!

1. A carnival or circus.   2. My brother (sister, cousin, or friend). 3. An exciting movie or TV show.   4. A local park or place of interest. 5. My favorite class.   6. The school cafeteria.   7. Trees.   8. The trip I'll never forget.

Other Uses of the Period

C.5   *ABBREVIATIONS, INITIALS*   Use a period after initials and most abbreviations.

Mr. R. F. Finley   A.D.   p.m.   R.S.V.P.
Alexander the Great died in 323 B.C.   (Notice that there is only one mark at the end of the sentence.)

Did Alexander the Great die in 323 B.C.? (Both the period and the question mark are needed.)

Do not use a period after *percent* or after a Roman numeral within a sentence.

Sterling silver is 92.5 percent pure silver and 7.5 percent alloy.
Richard I of England is usually known as "Richard the Lion-Hearted."

In the abbreviations of many well-known organizations, periods are not required: YMCA, GOP, USO, A & P, TWA. Nor are periods needed in such familiar abbreviations as DDT, SOS, OK, TV, FM, and GI.

PRACTICE 4 Inserting Periods

As you copy these sentences, place periods where necessary after abbreviations and initials and at the end of statements and commands.

1. At 8:15 p m Dr M C Cook will address a faculty meeting at South Country School
2. Mr Louis J Simms is vice-president of A A Thompson, Inc, in Washington, D C
3. Common abbreviations in writing term papers include *ed* (edited by), *ibid* (in the same place), and *vol* (volume)

THE COMMA

Though there seem to be many uses of the comma, there are basically only two: the *single comma* to separate and *double commas* to set off. The second use causes the most difficulty for beginning writers.

Double Commas to Set Off

Double commas are used to set off expressions that interrupt the normal order of the sentence or present material not closely linked grammatically with the rest of the sentence.

Guernsey, *a cattle-raising island in the English Channel,* gave its name to an important breed of dairy cattle. (The italicized expression interrupts the normal flow of the sentence and is not closely connected grammatically with the rest of the sentence.)
Lima beans, *like many kinds of peas,* have to be shelled before cooking.

Unless the interrupter comes at the beginning or the end of the sentence, do not leave out one of the two commas.

One important breed of dairy cattle got its name from Guernsey, *a cattle-raising island in the English Channel.* (The period after *Channel* takes the place of the comma.)

Like peas, lima beans have to be shelled before cooking. (The beginning of the sentence clearly sets off *like peas.* A comma before *like* is unnecessary.)

Notice how the various kinds of interrupting expressions below (C.6 to C.15) are set off by commas.

C.6 *PARENTHETIC EXPRESSIONS* Use commas to set off parenthetic expressions. These give additional information or comment but are loosely connected with the structure of the sentence.

The yak, like the buffalo, is just a kind of ox.
Mules, according to my uncle, are not stupid at all.
Any cut or scratch, however small, can become infected.
Cream cheese, however, contains little calcium.
Over seven hundred feet high, Boulder Dam is the largest dam in the world. (Why is there only one comma?)

Ordinarily, insert a comma where a person speaking the sentence would pause. Usually *however, on the other hand, by the way, for example, for instance, after all, at any rate, in the first place,* and *to tell the truth* are set off.

Gravy stains, however, should be sponged with cold or lukewarm water. (Two pauses. The parenthetic expression is *however.*)
The Mexican burro can be trusted on any mountain trail, however steep or slippery. (No pause after *however.* The parenthetic expression includes all four words: *however steep or slippery.*)

C.7 *CONTRASTING EXPRESSIONS* Use commas to set off contrasting expressions. They may be introduced by *not, but not, though not,* and similar expressions.

Nashville, not Knoxville, is the capital of Tennessee.
Mount Whitney, though not the highest mountain in North America, is still an impressive sight with its snowy mantle.
East St. Louis is in Illinois, not Missouri. (Why is there only one comma?)

C.8 *YES, NO* Use commas to set off (1) *yes* or *no;* (2) the conversational *well, why,* or *now;* (3) *etc.;* and (4) *oh* unless an exclamation point is needed.

Oh, yes, I can read a fever thermometer.

Well, you should have told me before. (Why is there only one comma?)

The numbers *1, 3, 5, 7, 9,* etc., are odd numbers. (The abbreviation *etc.* is rarely used in good writing.)

Oh, I wonder what he meant.

But: Oh! Smoke is coming out of the garage!

C.9 *PERSON ADDRESSED* Use commas to set off the name of the person addressed.

Bring your bathing suit, Anne, and don't forget your cap.

Miss Rann, is Dr. Saltus in his office? (Why is there only one comma?)

You're wanted on the phone, Mother. (Why is there only one comma?)

PRACTICE 5 Punctuating Sentences with Interrupters

As you copy the following sentences, punctuate them. If you omit a needed punctuation mark or insert a mark that is not needed, the sentence is wrong. Prepare to give a reason for each mark used.

A. 1. No Sally our pup isn't pedigreed
   2. Ostriches for instance have wings but cannot fly
   3. Well Bud we can always put off the picnic till next weekend
   4. Redwood like cypress is used in greenhouses because of its resistance to water
   5. The burro despite its small size can carry unbelievably heavy loads
   6. Banana oil is derived from fermented potatoes or beets not from bananas
   7. The pumpkin like other squashes was unknown in Europe before the discovery of America
   8. However warm the days are on the desert the nights are usually chilly

B. 1. Edgar Rice Burroughs not John Burroughs created Tarzan of the Apes
   2. Why George left the field at least an hour ago
   3. Yes I can see Ted and Louella standing on the main deck of the Mayflower II
   4. Death Valley unlike most other national monuments attracts nearly all its visitors during the winter season
   5. Jefferson was the third President of the United States not the second
   6. Susan like her two sisters is especially good in science
   7. Skimming along the water on a pair of water skis is in my opinion the most thrilling of sports
   8. No intruder however cautious can slip past a watchful German police dog

C.10 *APPOSITIVE* Use commas to set off most appositives.

An appositive explains the noun or pronoun it follows and names the same person or thing. When you set off an appositive, include with it all words that modify it.

> The cardinal, a brilliantly plumaged songbird, adds welcome color to a winter landscape. (Cardinal = songbird)
> Bering Strait, a strip of water about fifty-six miles wide, separates Alaska from Siberia. (Bering Strait = strip)
> I have just finished reading *Roughing It,* Mark Twain's vivid account of life along the Western frontier. (Why is there only one comma?)

C.11 *APPOSITIVE WITH OR* Use commas to set off appositives preceded by *or.*

> The avocado, or alligator pear, is a fairly recent addition ·to the American diet.

C.12 *EMPHASIS OR IDENTIFICATION BY APPOSITIVE* Omit the commas if the appositive is used for emphasis or identifies the person or thing by telling which one of two or more.

> The captain *himself* congratulated Frank on his quick thinking. (Emphasis)
> William the *Conqueror* landed in England in the year *1066.* (*Conqueror* tells which William and *1066* tells which year.)
> A year is only eighty-eight days long on the planet *Mercury.* (Which planet?)
> In the preceding sentence do not place a comma after the word *planet.* (Which word?)

C.13 *TITLES AND DEGREES* Use commas to set off titles or degrees after a name.

> I proudly pointed out that Robert C. Mandel, D.D.S., is my brother. Did Harry Carey, Jr., carry on his father's work? *Or* Did Harry Carey Jr. carry on his father's work?

PRACTICE 6 Punctuating Appositives

As you copy the following sentences, underline each appositive and draw an arrow to the noun or pronoun it goes with. Punctuate the sentences correctly.

EXAMPLE

We left San Juan the capital of Puerto Rico and headed southwest

We left San Juan, the capital of Puerto Rico, and headed southwest.

PHOSPHORESCENT BAY, PUERTO RICO

A. 1. We arrived at Parguera a sleepy fishing village on the south coast 2. Bobby my oldest brother was eager for some skin diving in the quiet waters of the Caribbean 3. Bobby promptly unpacked his two most precious possessions a diving mask and a snorkel and headed for the beach 4. We rented the only available craft a glass-bottomed boat 5. On his second dive Bobby stepped on a sea urchin the prickly porcupine of the Caribbean 6. Black dots the embedded quills of this tiny animal covered the sole of his right foot

B. 1. That evening we took another boat to Phosphorescent Bay an outstanding attraction near Parguera 2. The moving boat disturbed the plankton the tiny organisms in the water 3. The bay came alive with a silver glow the cold light produced by the plankton 4. The captain's assistant a young lad from Parguera poured the silvery water from a bucket 5. How beautiful were the streaks of light caused by moving fish the startled inhabitants of the bay 6. Try to visit Phosphorescent Bay on a moonless night the most fitting time for the brilliant display and enjoy the fireworks

PRACTICE 7   Putting Appositives to Use   W

In sentences of your own, use five of the following word groups as appositives. In each sentence underline the appositive and draw an arrow to the noun or pronoun it goes with. Punctuate the sentences correctly.

EXAMPLE

a common wild flower

The black-eyed Susan, a common wild flower, is the state flower of Maryland.

the tallest building in town	my home town
my favorite magazine	a delicious dessert
a popular singer	a recent movie
our next-door neighbors	my favorite author
a new hit tune	a beautiful tree

C.14 *APPOSITIVE ADJECTIVES* Ordinarily use commas to set off adjectives in the appositive position. (See page 353.)

The old house, gaunt and deserted, was a challenge to the imagination of the passerby.

PRACTICE 8   Punctuating Appositive Adjectives   W

Use three of the following in vivid, lively sentences of your own. Punctuate each sentence correctly.

EXAMPLE   muddy and wet
> The lost hikers, muddy and wet, straggled into camp just before sundown.

clear and sparkling	dull and lifeless	clever but saucy
red and gold	cold and rainy	small but energetic

C.15 DATES AND ADDRESSES In an address or a date use commas to set off every item after the first.

The name of the month and the number of the day are considered one item (April 4), as are the name of the state and the ZIP code number (Utah 84636). Do not place a comma between the name of the state and the ZIP code number.

> On December 16, 1773, American colonists boarded English ships and destroyed a cargo of tea.
> The village of Lombard, Illinois, is widely known for its lilacs.
> My sister ordered three tubes of oil paints from Bocour Artist Colors, 500 West 52nd Street, New York, New York 10019.
> President Polk's message to Congress in December, 1848, announced the discovery of gold in California. *Or* President Polk's message to Congress in December 1848 announced the discovery of gold in California.

Omission of the comma after the year (as in *1773* above) is becoming increasingly common in modern writing. The commas may also be omitted when just the month and the year are given (as in *December 1848*).

PRACTICE 9 Punctuating Sentences with Addresses and Dates

As you copy the following sentences, punctuate them. Prepare to tell why each comma is needed.

1. The most disastrous earthquake in American history struck San Francisco California on April 18 1906
2. The club secretary has ordered a year's supply of stationery from Goldsmith Brothers 77 Nassau Street New York New York 10008
3. Abraham Lincoln was born on February 12 1809 in a log cabin in Kentucky
4. On April 6 1917 the United States entered the First World War
5. Sandra moved from 89 Southard Avenue Rockville Center New York 11570 to 47 Main Street Clearwater Florida 33515
6. On July 4 1826 both John Adams and Thomas Jefferson died
7. Ann ordered a world map from Pioneer Publications 1790 Broadway New York New York 10019
8. Paul bought some of his power tools from Roberts Electric Company 894 West Grand Avenue Chicago Illinois 60622

9. William Henry Harrison died on April 4 1841 after being President of the United States for only one month
10. Most of the representatives signed the Declaration of Independence on August 2 1776 not July 4 the date of adoption

PRACTICE 10 Punctuating Correctly

The following sentences were written by students. Two are correctly punctuated. Each of the other ten contains an unnecessary mark or a wrong mark, or requires punctuation. On your paper write C after the numbers of the correct sentences and punctuate the wrong sentences correctly. Prepare to give a reason for every change you make.

A. 1. I read *The Story of My Life* a book by a blind and deaf woman.
2. Fanny Brice one of the greatest comediennes of the Twenties, died on May 29 1951.
3. In our family there are four children, two girls and two boys.
4. Yes the divers finally raised the sunken submarine the *Squalus.*
5. Book reports, like other compositions should be well organized.
6. Come to Old Orchard, Maine for a restful vacation.
B. 1. Mike I am writing to tell you about a funny experience.
2. Ronnie our center fouled the tall guard on the opposing team.
3. Mark Twain's mother jokingly turned the tables on Mark.
4. The first reading of articles for the *Star* is done by the staff not by the faculty adviser.
5. The assistant minister a young man from Princeton Seminary, preached his first sermon on Sunday.
6. Many people, you will find do not enjoy quiz shows on television.

PRACTICE 11 Writing Sentences with Addresses and Dates   W

Write three sentences with real dates and three sentences with real addresses. Make your sentences interesting and informational. Punctuate them correctly.

EXAMPLE
On January 31**,** 1958**,** my brother Tim was born in Davenport, Iowa.

One Comma to Separate

The single comma is used to prevent confusion, to keep items from running into each other. There is a great difference between *more useful suggestions* and *more, useful suggestions.*

C.16   *SERIES*   Use the comma to separate items in a series.

A *tired, dirty, bedraggled* group of boys huddled around the campfire. (The italicized words are a series of modifiers. Commas separate them.)

Betty sings, dances, and plays the piano. (*Sings, dances,* and *plays* are separated by commas because they are a series of verbs.)

Blackberries, raspberries, and strawberries are all members of the rose family.

Edgar Allan Poe wrote poetry, edited a literary magazine, and created the modern detective story.

When a conjunction is used between the last two items in a series, it is usually correct either to place a comma before the conjunction or to omit the comma.

RIGHT   greyhounds, collies, and wolfhounds
ALSO RIGHT   greyhounds, collies and wolfhounds

Sometimes the comma prevents misreading; in such cases include the comma.

NOT CLEAR   This year the Hobby Club will present special programs on photography, horses, nature lore, music and dancing. (Four or five special programs?)

CLEAR   This year the Hobby Club will present special programs on photography, horses, nature lore, music, and dancing. (Five special programs)

NOT CLEAR   For lunch I had a frankfurter, a bacon sandwich and a hamburger with onions. (Do the onions belong with the bacon sandwich?)

CLEAR   For lunch I had a frankfurter, a bacon sandwich, and a hamburger with onions.

When conjunctions are used throughout a series, no commas are needed unless they make the sentence clearer.

The tables for the spring banquet will be decorated with daffodils and hyacinths and yellow tulips.

We pushed and shoved and fought our way out of the toy department.

Two tests will help you to punctuate modifiers before a noun.

Test 1.   If inserting *and* between the modifiers does not change the meaning, the comma is needed.

SERIES	NOT SERIES
a damp, dismal day	a damp spring day
(a damp *and* dismal day)	(NOT a damp and spring day)
a frisky, playful Scotty	a little black Scotty
(a frisky *and* playful Scotty)	(NOT a little and black Scotty)

Test 2. If switching the modifiers does not change or spoil the sense, the comma is needed.

SERIES	NOT SERIES
a noisy**,** bustling street	a small brown box
(a bustling, noisy street)	(NOT a brown small box)

PRACTICE 12 Punctuating Sentences Correctly

As you write the following sentences, punctuate them. Prepare to give a reason for each mark inserted.

A. 1. Two Adamses two Harrisons and two Roosevelts have been President of the United States
   2. Their half-grown German shepherd puppy is already the biggest strongest toughest dog on the block
   3. In the bottom drawer of my desk were five pencils a dozen Christmas seals one gym shoe three snail shells an overdue library book and several other unusual collector's items
   4. In science class we tested the hardness of quartz feldspar copper and gypsum
   5. A minuet is a slow stately dignified dance
   6. Four common flowering trees are the cherry the dogwood the peach and the hawthorn
B. 1. Four kinds of apples available during the winter are the Winesap the McIntosh the Rome Beauty and the Delicious
   2. The combine a large harvesting machine reaps the grain threshes it and cleans it
   3. W H Hudson the author of *Green Mansions* was born of American parents grew up in Argentina and spent most of his adult life in England
   4. The lazy days were spent in swimming fishing hiking and loafing
   5. Bill Denig the best player on our team can hit well run fast and field like a professional
   6. Last winter the ice bent to the ground the oldest tallest most beautiful white birch in our garden

PRACTICE 13 Punctuating Words in Series

Copy the following sentences, filling each blank with a series of three or more appropriate items. Punctuate the sentences correctly.

EXAMPLE   On his hamburger Jerry put __onions, ketchup, and relish__.

   1. This year in school I am taking _____.
   2. When I was a child, I enjoyed playing _____.

3. _____ are three cities I'd like to visit.
4. My favorite ice cream flavors are _____.
5. _____ are three magazines I enjoy reading.
6. Before leaving on the picnic, we _____.
7. Last year we elected _____ as class officers.
8. A _____ pine tree stood on the edge of the cliff.
9. _____ are some of the students in my English class.
10. During the summer I hope to _____.

C.17 *MISUNDERSTANDING*   Use a comma to prevent misreading or confusion.

Before shooting, Dick took careful aim.
In filling out Form 2112, 107 students failed to sign their full names.
Next to Timmy, Lewis looks gigantic.
Inside, the room was hot and stuffy.

PRACTICE 14   Punctuating Sentences Correctly

As you write the following sentences, punctuate them.   Prepare to give a reason for each mark inserted.

1. Before eating the raccoon washes its food
2. The warbler darted fluttered and swooped through the branches of the plum tree in search of aphids and other insects
3. Above a glider soared gracefully along
4. Near Celia Allen and Paul were having an argument.
5. In 1776 54 delegates signed the Declaration of Independence,

QUOTATION MARKS

C.18 *DIRECT QUOTATION*   1. Use quotation marks to enclose a direct quotation.   Quotation marks go in pairs.   Do not leave out one of a pair of marks.
2. Use a comma to set off a direct quotation from the rest of the sentence.

"It is better to have a hen tomorrow than an egg today," said Thomas Fuller.   (A comma follows the quoted sentence.)
Thomas Fuller said, "It is better to have a hen tomorrow than an egg today."   (The quoted sentence is preceded by a comma and followed by a period.   *It* begins with a capital letter.)

C.19 *QUESTION AND EXCLAMATION*   When the quotation is a question or an exclamation, use a question mark or an exclamation point at the end of the quoted sentence. Do not add a comma or a period.

"How did jazz start?" asked Ed. (A question mark follows the quoted sentence.)

C.20 *INSIDE OR OUTSIDE* Place a period or a comma inside quotation marks. Place a question mark or an exclamation point inside when it is part of the quotation — otherwise outside.

Ed asked, "How did jazz start?" (A question mark follows the quoted sentence. *How* begins with a capital letter.)

Did Mary say, "The party's off"? (The question mark is outside the quotation marks because the entire sentence, not the quotation, is a question.)

"Watch that end!" shouted the middle guard. (An exclamation point follows the quoted exclamation.)

The middle guard shouted, "Watch that end!" (An exclamation point follows the quoted exclamation. *Watch* is capitalized.)

C.21 *BROKEN QUOTATION* When a quoted sentence is broken in the middle by an expression like *he said,* use two pairs of quotation marks.

"Cauliflower," said Mark Twain, "is nothing but cabbage with a college education." (A comma ends the first part of the quoted sentence. *Is* begins with a small letter.)

The broken quotation could also have been written in the unbroken style explained above.

Mark Twain said, "Cauliflower is nothing but cabbage with a college education."

"Cauliflower is nothing but cabbage with a college education," said Mark Twain.

What happens when a word like *said* or *asked* is inserted between two sentences?

Have you ever done any canoeing? We'd like to get up a group for a canoe trip early this summer.

"Have you ever done any canoeing?" asked Lawrence. "We'd like to get up a group for a canoe trip early this summer." (A period follows *Lawrence,* and *We'd* begins with a capital.)

"I'd like a canoe trip a lot," Alvin replied. "Could you help me brush up on my paddling first?"

What Alvin said was two sentences: 1. I'd like a canoe trip a lot. 2. Could you help me brush up on my paddling first?

C.22 *NO MARKS* Do not use quotation marks unless a definite speaker and a verb of saying are included.

Speak up! (No quotation marks are used.)
I need your help. (No quotation marks are used.)
Do you know Sally Edmonds? (No quotation marks are used.)

Exceptions to this rule occur in the conversation of stories.

C.23 *INDIRECT QUOTATION* Do not set off an indirect quotation from the rest of the sentence.

INDIRECT   Mr. Batten asked whether I was going out for baseball.
DIRECT   Mr. Batten asked, "Are you going out for baseball?"
INDIRECT   Jimmy asked Mr. Potter, the oldest inhabitant, what kind of people had first settled in Carson City.
DIRECT   Jimmy asked Mr. Potter, the oldest inhabitant, "What kind of people first settled in Carson City?"

The direct quotation is often more colorful and more exact than the indirect quotation.

PRACTICE 15 Punctuating and Capitalizing Direct Quotations

As you copy the following sentences, punctuate and capitalize them correctly. Prepare to give a reason for each punctuation mark or capital inserted.

A. 1. Who discovered Australia Jeremy asked
    2. Report to the locker room half an hour before the game ordered the coach
    3. From the dock we called do you have room for three more in your boat
    4. Look out for the bus yelled Jules
    5. Our luxuries joked Ambrose Bierce are always masquerading as necessities
    6. I have had many troubles in my life said James Garfield but the worst of them never came
    7. From one of the rooms in the deserted house a voice cried out who's there
    8. Use a direct quotation in that sentence suggested the teacher
    9. Elbert Hubbard once wrote don't make excuses — make good
  10. Basketball explained our coach is a matter of good sense and team-work
B. 1. Did you know there is a volcano in California asked my father it last erupted less than fifty years ago
    2. Human history H G Wells remarked becomes more and more a race between education and catastrophe

3. Have you seen the new boy asked Leslie have you found out his name
4. Silver coins explained Uncle Will were once 90 percent pure silver
5. An angry man opens his mouth and shuts his eyes said Cato
6. The mango George explained is a tropical fruit
7. One should eat to live wrote Benjamin Franklin not live to eat
8. Have you tried Mother's new grape jam asked Harriet the grapes were from our own arbor
9. It is easy said Aesop to be brave from a safe distance
10. A pedestrian the comedian said is a car owner with a wife and two teen-age children

USING QUOTATION MARKS AND UNDERLINING

C.24   *TITLES*   1. Use quotation marks around the title of a literary work that is not a whole book — chapter, article, essay, lecture, composition, song, short poem, short story, short play.

Do not put quotation marks around the title at the beginning of your composition.

"Richard Cory" and "Bewick Finzer" are character studies in verse.

2. Underline the titles of books, magazines, newspapers, full-length plays, and motion pictures.

In print these are usually *italicized*.

I gave a report on an article in the Reader's Digest last week and am now writing a book report on Johnny Tremain.

C.25   *LETTER, WORD, PHRASE*   Ordinarily underline a letter spoken of as a letter, a word as a word, or a phrase as a phrase.

How many c's are there in recommend?
The expression going full blast originated in steel mills.

In print these are usually *italicized*.

PRACTICE 16 Punctuating Correctly

Punctuate and capitalize the following sentences.

A. 1. Well Gwen how did the story turn out
2. A whale ship was my Yale College and my Harvard declared Herman Melville
3. In the woods behind our house are rabbits squirrels mice frogs and a thousand and one kinds of insects

4. After defrosting frozen foods should be used immediately
5. Carmel one of the oldest towns in California was founded as a Spanish mission
6. I sent an order for a pocketknife to Land and Company 37 Buckley Street Port Jervis New York 12771
7. On the dusty shelf lay an old baseball mitt a pair of battered sneakers a worn copy of Penrod and a football with broken laces
8. What we obtain too cheaply declared Thomas Paine we esteem too lightly
9. My favorite short stories are The Purloined Letter The Man Who Would Be King and The Waxwork
10. Are there two m's in committee

B. 1. May we use the auditorium Mr Johnson Jean asked
2. Selfishness is the greatest curse of the human race Gladstone said
3. Three good books about horses are Black Beauty My Friend Flicka and Smoky
4. The tiny Yorkshire terrier was sleeping between the paws of the friendly protective Great Dane
5. That chicken salad complained Arnie was all salad and no chicken
6. Danny did you write that thank-you letter to Uncle Ralph asked Mother
7. I have never been hurt by anything I didn't say observed Calvin Coolidge
8. Mac McCown won a letter in soccer basketball football and track
9. Francisco Coronado early Spanish explorer brought the first horse to America in 1540
10. No Janie I haven't yet read Men of Iron

COLON

C.26 *COLON* Use a colon before a list of appositives or before a list of items, especially when the list of items comes after expressions like *as follows.*

The Halloween Committee will award prizes in these categories: funniest costume, most beautiful costume, most original costume, most hideous costume, and best homemade costume.

In Switzerland official announcements have to be printed in four languages: French, German, Italian, and Romansch.

Do not, as a rule, use the colon after a form of the verb *be.*

My favorite sports are basketball, volleyball, swimming, and tennis.

But: These are my favorite sports: basketball, volleyball, swimming, and tennis.

1. Using a colon correctly, write a sentence listing five movie stars or sports figures you admire.

2. In a sentence tell some of the things you have learned in gym classes (or in another subject) this year.   Use words or phrases in series.

3. Using an appositive, write a sentence about a pet you or a friend has owned.

4. Write a conversation of about six sentences between a camp counselor (gym teacher, YMCA instructor, parent, or another adult) and a teen-ager.   Use direct quotations and introductory words. Include two words in direct address and one date (month, day, and year).

MASTERY TEST 4B   Punctuating Simple Sentences and Quotations

Copy the following sentences and supply the punctuation that is needed.   Underline the title of a book.   If you either omit a necessary punctuation mark or insert a useless mark, the sentence is wrong.   The number in parentheses tells how many marks are needed in the sentence.   A pair of quotation marks is counted as one mark.

1. Yes we all stared at the test amazed and confused (3)
2. Rita how does your mother feel (2)
3. At Fort Dix New Jersey on January 16 1972 my brother entered the army (5)
4. One of the most striking differences wrote Mark Twain between a cat and a lie is that the cat has only nine lives (5)
5. It is usually human carelessness not a faulty car that causes accidents (3)
6. A whale for example lives in the sea but needs air to live (3)
7. The Cop and the Anthem one of my favorite short stories has a very amusing ending (4)
8. Instead of watching the large crowd ignored the safety demonstration (2)
9. The local fishermen catch flounder cod mackerel sea bass and blue fish (5 or 4)
10. My aunt bought an old scratched broken table and restored it perfectly (3)

22 *Plurals and Possessives of Nouns*

Forming plurals boils down to a few manageable rules and some memorization. In half an hour of study, you can learn enough about plurals to handle most writing situations. Here's a handy scheme for mastering the plurals of nouns.

HOW TO FORM AND USE THE PLURAL

D.1 **S, ES** To form the plural of most nouns, add *s* or *es* to the singular. (See the chart on pages 306, 307.)

This rule takes care of all but a small percentage of nouns.

D.2 **'S** Add *'s* to form the plurals of letters, figures, signs, and words discussed as words.

Putting two *c*'s in *recommend* is a common error.
Miss McIlhenny deducted five percent for the two *&*'s I had used in my composition.
In your composition change some of those *and*'s and *but*'s to *although, when, because,* and *since.*

D.3 **IRREGULAR PLURALS** A few common nouns form their plurals in some other way than by adding *s* or *es.*

These are such common words you probably use the correct form automatically.

child, children	louse, lice	ox, oxen
foot, feet	man, men	tooth, teeth
goose, geese	mouse, mice	woman, women

D.4 **NO CHANGE** A few nouns have the same form in the singular and the plural.

MOOSE   MOOSE

Animals   cod, deer, fowl, moose, salmon, sheep, trout   (In hunting terminology common nouns for animals and birds may not add *s* for the plural: hunting for *possum*, *bear*, or *duck*.)
Others   headquarters, series, means

D.5   *PLURAL MEANING*   Some nouns are used only in the plural or have special meanings in the plural.

ashes, barracks, billiards, clothes, fireworks, goods, (golf) links, morals, oats, odds, pincers, pliers, proceeds, riches, scissors, shears, slacks, suds, spectacles, thanks, tongs, trousers

D.6   *SINGULAR MEANING*   A few nouns ending in *s* are singular in meaning.

civics, economics, mathematics, the United States

D.7   *FOREIGN PLURALS*   Some nouns borrowed from foreign languages keep their foreign plurals.   Some have a plural in *s* as well.

A foreign word that is commonly used tends to adopt an English plural in time.   Thus *concerti*, the foreign plural of *concerto*, has given way to *concertos*.   *Antenna* has two plurals: *antennae* (biology) and *antennas* (radio).   When foreign plurals have been retained, they are formed in a variety of ways.

a to **ae**	**us** to **i**	
alumna (feminine), alumnae (nē)	alumnus (masculine), alumni (nī)	
larva, larvae	syllabus, syllabi or syllabuses	

um to **a**	**is** to **es**	
bacterium, bacteria	analysis, analyses	diagnosis, diagnoses
medium, media	oasis, oases	synopsis, synopses

D.8 *DICTIONARY CHECK*   When in doubt about a plural, consult the dictionary.   If the dictionary does not give a plural form, the plural ends in *s*.

ADD *S*

1

Most nouns, including proper nouns, form the plural by adding *s* to the singular.

baboon, baboons	Fletcher, Fletchers	mountain, mountains
cage, cages	floor, floors	pie, pies
Drew, Drews	hour, hours	unit, units

2

Words ending in *y* preceded by a vowel add *s*.

alley, alleys	donkey, donkeys	play, plays	ray, rays
boy, boys	journey, journeys	pulley, pulleys	toy, toys
day, days	joy, joys	Ranney, Ranneys	valley, valleys

3

Most common *o* words form the plural by adding *s* to the singular.

alto, altos	Eskimo, Eskimos	poncho, ponchos
curio, curios	Filipino, Filipinos	rodeo, rodeos
dynamo, dynamos	piano, pianos	soprano, sopranos

4

Some nouns ending in *f* or *fe* add *s*. (Nouns ending in *ff* always add *s*.)

belief, beliefs	grief, griefs	proof, proofs	cliff, cliffs
chief, chiefs	gulf, gulfs	roof, roofs	puff, puffs
dwarf, dwarfs	handkerchief, handkerchiefs	safe, safes	whiff, whiffs

---

5

Most compound nouns add *s*.

aftereffect, aftereffects	mouthful, mouthfuls
classroom, classrooms	post office, post offices
leftover, leftovers	spoonful, spoonfuls

(Note: In a few compound nouns the first part of the compound is the main word and is made plural: *editors in chief; hangers-on; passersby; sisters-in-law*.)

ADD *ES*

1

Nouns ending in *s*, *x*, *z*, *ch*, *sh*, add *es* to form the plural.

Burns, Burnses	annex, annexes	punch, punches
cross, crosses	tax, taxes	marsh, marshes
gas, gases	waltz, waltzes	sash, sashes
Jones, Joneses	bench, benches	wish, wishes

If you try to pronounce a word like *waltzes*, you'll see why the extra syllable with *es* is needed.

2

Words ending in *y* preceded by a consonant change the *y* to *i* and add *es*.

ally, allies	copy, copies	cry, cries	lady, ladies
berry, berries	country, countries	fly, flies	tally, tallies

EXCEPTIONS: proper names (*Murphys*), and the word *standbys*.

3

A few common *o* words form their plurals by adding *es*. (Memorize this list.)

echo, echoes	innuendo, innuendoes	tomato, tomatoes
embargo, embargoes	no, noes	torpedo, torpedoes
hero, heroes	potato, potatoes	veto, vetoes

4

Some nouns ending in *f* or *fe* change the *f* to *v* and add *es*.

calf, calves	leaf, leaves	shelf, shelves
half, halves	life, lives	thief, thieves
knife, knives	self, selves	wife, wives

A few nouns ending in *f* form the plural either way: *scarf, scarfs* or *scarves*; *wharf, wharfs* or *wharves*.

PRACTICE 1 Writing Plurals

Applying the *s-es* rules, write the plural of these words:

arch	crash	gas	hostess	peach	shoe
blush	dress	glass	moss	prince	splash
branch	fox	host	niece	Russell	wax

Write the plural of these *o* words:

alto	echo	piano	radio	soprano
auto	Filipino	poncho	rodeo	tomato
dynamo	hero	potato	solo	veto

Applying the rules for *y* after consonants and after vowels, write the plural of these words:

alley	butterfly	cry	monkey	turkey
ally	city	ferry	relay	victory
bay	comedy	lady	story	volley

Write the plural of these compound nouns:

aircraft carrier	cupful	forget-me-not	merry-go-round
baby-sitter	daughter-in-law	high school	passerby
cave-in	field goal	lean-to	playroom

PRACTICE 2 Writing Plurals

Write the plural of the following. Refer to the preceding rules .and examples. If you are not sure of the plural form, find it in your dictionary.

alumnus	Chinese	formula	parenthesis	tooth
analysis	clutch	handful	proof	torpedo
bacterium	county	leaf	pueblo	treaty
basis	crisis	life	reef	waitress
belief	cure-all	Lucy	rodeo	wolf
bush	deer	monkey	species	10
but	focus	mystery	spy	?

PRACTICE 3 Writing Sentences with Plurals

Prepare to write from dictation these eight sentences:

1. Among the kings of England there have been four *Williams,* eight *Henrys,* two *Charleses,* and two *Jameses.*
2. The *sopranos* and *altos* sing the *verses,* and the *tenors* and *basses* sing the *choruses.*

3. For the past two *Saturdays* we *children* have helped Dad plant *tomatoes, potatoes, radishes,* and other *vegetables.*
4. One of my *hobbies* is collecting *photos* of *animals* such as *wolves, rhinos,* and *monkeys.*
5. Totem *poles* often symbolized *victories,* family *histories,* or the downfall of *enemies.*
6. Gerrie likes *stories* about *elves, fairies, princesses,* and *witches.*
7. On exhibit at the fair were *sheep, oxen, calves, turkeys,* and *geese.*
8. The two *policemen* risked their *lives* as they chased the armed *thieves* across the *roofs* of the tenement *houses.*

D.9 COLLECTIVE NOUNS Many nouns that are singular in form may have a plural meaning. These nouns name groups of persons or things and are called collective nouns: *audience, board, council, crowd, gang, group, jury, team, troop.*

Collective nouns, like other nouns, have plural forms: *boards, crowds, juries, teams.*

D.10 CORRECT PLURALS In your speech and writing use these correct plurals:

George Pellman, who plays center on our basketball team, is only six
  feet tall.
On the mountain road we could go only fifteen *miles* an hour.
Dad ordered two *tons* of coal.

PRACTICE 4 Writing Plurals

As you copy the following sentences, write the plural of every italicized word.

FORESIGHT

1. The *Koehler* and the *Ross* were very pleased that their *child* were to be married on November 3. 2. The *guest* had been invited, and everyone was busy with the *preparation.* 3. The *family* appreciatively looked over the wedding *gift,* which included two *radio,* several serving *dish,* a dozen steak *knife,* two dozen *glass,* four *ashtray,* and three spice *shelf.*

4. For the reception the *host* and *hostess* had planned to order two *turkey,* two *basket* of *tomato,* two *kind* of smoked *salmon,* two *loaf* of bread, and four *pound* of roast beef for *sandwich.*

5. One evening two *week* before the wedding, the bride said, "We'll have to postpone the date at least fourteen *day.*"

6. "Good *heaven!*" cried the *woman* of the two *household.* "Why?"

7. "Well," said Barbara Ross, "I just remembered that *election* are always held the first part of November, and you know I want to go into politics. 8. I don't want to spend our *anniversary* at election headquarters."

PRACTICE 5   Writing a Paragraph with Plurals   **W**

Here's a test of your skill and ingenuity. Select any ten plurals
from Practice 2 on page 308 and weave them into an original paragraph on a subject of your choosing. Your paragraph may tell an
anecdote, describe a scene, retell an incident, explain a process, or
urge a point of view. Refer to pages 49–79 for help in constructing
your paragraph.

HOW TO FORM AND USE THE POSSESSIVE

DIAGNOSTIC TEST 5A   Possessive

Number your paper from 1 to 10. Next to each number write
the correct possessive form of the word in parentheses.

1. In last (month) election, (Nancy James) mother was chosen for
   the town council.
2. Western (Airline) flight to Los Angeles took off after a half (hour)
   delay.
3. The (girl) athletic field at King High School is the same size as the
   (boy).
4. The (woman) Olympic events were as well attended as the (man).
5. Paula (Ramirez) brother chews a (year) worth of bubble gum in a
   single day.
6. Paul amazed the audience with his ability to play one of (Chopin)
   pieces and a sonata of (Beethoven).
7. My (cousin) home is just a (day) journey from Grand Canyon.
8. The (circus) arrival in town is a (child) dream come true.
9. A lot of (child) books appeal to adults rather than to kids.
10. We followed the (policeman) directions and found (Juanita) house
    without any trouble.

D.11   *USING THE POSSESSIVE* The possessive denotes ownership,
possession, or connection. Use the possessive form when an of
phrase can be substituted for the noun.

> Dick's saxophone = saxophone of Dick
> an hour's drive = drive of an hour
> the boys' lockers = lockers of the boys

In a few expressions both the *of* phrase and the possessive sign
are used.

that dress of Molly's   friends of David's   a song of Irving Berlin's

D.12   *APOSTROPHE WITH POSSESSIVE* Use the apostrophe to
show the possessive form of all nouns.

D.13 *POSSESSIVE SINGULAR* To form the possessive of any singular noun, add 's.

Do not add or omit a letter. Just write the word and put 's at the end.

> baby + 's = baby's   editor in chief + 's = editor in chief's
> fox + 's = fox's   mother-in-law + 's = mother-in-law's

Though proper nouns ending in *s* may take the apostrophe only, you will be right if you add 's (*Iris'* or *Iris's*).

D.14 *JOINT OWNERSHIP* To show joint ownership, use the apostrophe with the last noun only.

> Nan and Joanne's records

D.15 *SEPARATE OWNERSHIP* To show separate ownership, add an apostrophe to each noun.

> Nan's and Joanne's records

PRACTICE 6 Writing Sentences with Possessives

Prepare to write from dictation these eight sentences.

1. Our grandfather's dairy farm is an hour's drive from my uncle's house.
2. The coach's picture is in this morning's *Herald*.
3. Miss Winslow's drama class is doing scenes from *Our Town*.
4. Gregory's house is just around the corner from Jean's.
5. Is that striped tie your father's or your brother's?
6. That rabbit's foot is Mike's good-luck charm.
7. Was that the first baseman's error or the shortstop's?
8. Governor Allen's speech is analyzed in this week's *U. S. News and World Report*.

D.16 *POSSESSIVE PLURAL* To form the possessive of a plural noun, first write that plural. Then if the plural ends in *s*, add an apostrophe. If the plural does not end in *s*, add 's.

If, for example, you are planning to write *men's suits*, remember that the plural is *men*, not *mens*.

In the list below, the plurals that end in *s* are checked.

SINGULAR	PLURAL	POSSESSIVE PLURAL
baby	babies ✓	babies'
deer	deer	deer's
fox	foxes ✓	foxes'

SINGULAR	PLURAL	POSSESSIVE PLURAL
Lutz	Lutzes ✓	Lutzes'
policeman	policemen	policemen's
sister-in-law	sisters-in-law	sisters-in-law's
wife	wives ✓	wives'

PRACTICE 7   Writing Possessives

Write in four columns the singular, the possessive singular, the plural, and the possessive plural of the following words:

Barry	city	hero	month	toy
boss	fisherman	hour	mouse	Wallace
box	fly	lady	party	week
calf	foot	man	thrush	woman
child	girl	minute	tooth	year

PRACTICE 8   Distinguishing between Plurals and Possessives

As you copy the following expressions, insert an apostrophe wherever it is needed. Use the possessive form when an *of* phrase can be substituted for the noun. You will notice that two phrases do not need apostrophes.

1. a sailors uniform
2. an hours ride
3. two of Buds friends
4. the wolves tracks
5. Mr. Ryans keys
6. a vacation of three weeks
7. childrens books
8. Crosse and Blackwells soups
9. ladies pocketbooks
10. Mrs. Alcotts tomatoes
11. three weeks delay in shipment
12. a mothers helper
13. a secretarys duties
14. the girls gymnasium
15. a dollars worth
16. Barbaras and Coras books
17. a coyotes howl
18. three days later
19. a months vacation
20. the mens department

PRACTICE 9   Writing Sentences with Possessives and Plurals

Prepare to write these sentences from dictation:

1. After the day's ride the horses were turned loose to graze.
2. The men's and boys' departments at Marshall Field's are located in a separate building.
3. My uncle's store is only a few minutes' walk from our house.
4. A secretary's hours are much shorter than a housewife's.
5. Eli Whitney's cotton gin and Robert Fulton's steamboat were two early American inventions.
6. The mud in beavers' dams is held together by leaves, roots, and tough grasses.

7. An account of my sister's wedding was on page one of yesterday's *News*.

8. Thompson has advertised a three days' sale of boys' and girls' shoes.

PRACTICE 10   Using Plurals and Possessives   **W**

Write sentences about clubs, school, animals, hobbies, or other topics and include at least five plurals, eight possessive singulars, and four possessive plurals. You may use some of the words from Practice 7. Draw one line under a possessive singular and two lines under a possessive plural. Check the other plurals.

EXAMPLE   The Career Club's officers have chosen the speakers for the next two months' meetings.

PRACTICE 11   Spelling Plurals and Possessives Correctly

As you copy the following sentences, correct all mistakes in forming plurals and possessives. Where a singular is used for a plural, supply a correct plural. For the correct sentence in each part write **C**. Prepare to explain how you recognized each possessive.

A. 1. Harriets' sisters got jobs as counselors at a childrens day camp.
   2. To make the clam chowder for the party, Mother used three dozen clams, two quarts of milk, and two pound of potatoes.
   3. Most of the boys in the class have already read Will James *The Lone Cowboy*.
   4. Uncle Jacks hunting dogs' are Labrador retrievers.
   5. That picture book of Billys is about Eskimoes.
   6. One of the performers in Buffalo Bills Wild West Show was Annie Oakley.
   7. The thieves stole twenty jars of instant coffee from Darby's Delicatessen.
   8. *Robinson Crusoe* is one of the worlds great adventure storys.
   9. The ashes from Mr. Maxwells cigar dribbled all over Aunt Ellens wing chair.
   10. Robin Hoods lieutenant was called "Little John"; yet he was seven foot tall and four foot wide.
B. 1. Dons and Neils fathers umpired last summer's Little League games.
   2. In most tennis tournaments the women's play-offs are held before the mens.
   3. The MacGregor's poodle and the Joneses collie are both pedigreed dogs.
   4. Every year the girls in the Dramatic Club put on a hilarious skit in which all the boys' parts are played by girls.

5. Betty Anns favorite stories are about princes and princess.
6. Our towns welcoming committee gives newcomers baskets filled with home preserves, loafs of bread, cookys, fresh eggs, and poultry.
7. In recent years mens' and boys' clothing has not changed so much as womens and girls.
8. Over the weekend two pair of sneakers were found in the girls locker room.
9. Brunos and Mike's suggestions for the spring carnival were accepted unanimously by the clubs thirty members.
10. Bob Kohls prize-winning safety poster is on the bulletin board in the students lounge.

PRACTICE 12   Using Plurals and Possessives   VW

Use each of the following words correctly in a sentence. You may use two or more of the words in one sentence.

cowboys, cowboys'	horse's, horses	sailor's, sailors
day's, days'	hours, hours'	teachers, teachers'
fireman's, firemen's	minute's, minutes	week's, weeks
girls, girls'	months, months'	year's, years

Your score on the mastery test will show whether you now understand the possessive and how much you have learned about it this year. Enter your test mark on your achievement graph.

MASTERY TEST 5B   Possessive

Number your paper from 1 to 10. After each number write the correct possessive form of the word in parentheses.

1. The (doctor) advice was that my father take a (week) vacation.
2. The (newspaper) report of the accident was very different from the (television) version.
3. Abigail Adams was John (Adams) wife and John Quincy (Adams) mother.
4. It is (Fred) turn to do the dishes, not (Janice).
5. After a (moment) pause, we resumed our climb up the (cliff) steep side.
6. That (boy) personality has improved enough to gain (everyone) respect.
7. A (day) trip to Cape Cod was our (family) only vacation last summer.
8. My (aunt) promotion was announced in (yesterday) *Los Angeles Times*.

9. The (mirror) surface was marked by a (child) fingerprints.
10. The (man) dressing room was on the (gym) lower level.

PRACTICE 13   Time Out for Review

As you copy the following sentences, capitalize and punctuate them correctly. Correct the double subjects and the errors in the use of plurals and possessives.

AMERICA'S NATIONAL PARKS

A. 1. Every year millions of tourists visit americas national parks to see wild animals glaciers geysers and other wonders
    2. The national park service a bureau of the department of the interior was established on august 25 1916 for the maintenance of our national parks
    3. An expedition in 1870 under henry d washburn and nathaniel p langford led to the creation of yellowstone national park the first national park anywhere in the world
    4. In yellowstone there are deer moose bears buffalos geysers hot springs gorges and waterfalls
    5. Old faithful the best-known geyser shoots about ten thousand gallons of water 120 to 170 feet into the air about every sixty-five minutes
    6. Mount rainier national park is dominated by mount rainier a snow-capped inactive volcano 14,408 foot high
    7. In oregons dark blue crater lake wizard island an extinct crater rises 776 feet above the water
    8. Sequoia national park is the home of the general sherman tree one of the largest and oldest living things on the earths surface
    9. Cliff house the largest ancient cliff dwelling in colorados mesa verde national park has two hundred rooms
   10. In utahs bryce canyon national park rain and desert winds have worn the rocks into odd shapes in varying shades of red pink copper and cream
   11. Yosemite national park in central california has beautiful domes pinnacles lakes rivers and waterfalls
   12. In colorados rocky mountain national park one of the highest regions in the united states tourists can go on guided field trips nature-study walks game-stalking outings and campfire hikes
   13. During a three weeks vacation last summer betsy holloways two brothers they rode muleback down bright angel trail in the grand canyon one of the worlds greatest wonders

14. This summer betsys brothers plan to spend their months vacation in glacier national park on the canadian border
15. In glacier national park once a part of the blackfoot indian reservation there are glaciers icebergs mountains canyons and hundreds of lakes and streams
16. For christmas betsy gave her brothers *exploring our national parks and monuments* a publication of the national parks association
17. In grand teton national park a favorite of experienced mountain climbers the best climbing season is july august and early september
18. It is estimated that five million bats live in one section of carlsbad caverns national park a chain of huge underground caves in southeastern new mexico

B. 1. Big bend national park one of the newest comprises mountains and deserts along the shores of the rio grande
2. This park though not the most famous is my uncles favorite
3. He enjoys its wild scenery its lonely grandeur its feeling of isolation
4. In contrast to the deserts of big bend national park a tangled rain forest greets visitors to olympic national park in washington
5. Rich soil mild winters and abundant rainfall create an almost tropical forest at the latitude of quebec and montreal
6. A recently active volcano is the attraction in lassen volcanic national park a spectacular treat for anyone interested in geology
7. On may 19 1915 red-hot lava rose in the crater overflowed the rim and poured down the slope for a thousand foot
8. The lava destroyed vegetation melted the snow and sent torrents of water down the mountainside
9. A hot blast leveled trees on mount raker three mile away
10. National parks have been established in alaska and hawaii not merely in the continental united states
11. Mount mckinley the highest mountain in north america lies within the boundarys of alaskas mount mckinley national park
12. Hawaii national park like lassen park has rugged volcanic scenery
13. The west has a majority of our national parks though not all
14. Isle royale in michigan and wind cave national park in south dakota draw an increasing number of visitors each year
15. In the east the great smoky mountains offer mile-high mountains rich vegetation and pioneer settlements
16. Floridas everglades national park is a subtropical wilderness with cypress swamps orchids and rare birds
17. Kentuckys mammoth cave one of the largest known caves has blind fish beetles and crickets
18. Write to the national park service washington d c for circulars about our national parks

23 *Agreement of Verbs with Their Subjects*

"Ernie don't need much help with verbs," said Arnold admiringly.

Perhaps not, but Arnold certainly does! Are *you* verb sure? This chapter will help you to use the right verb every time.

E.1 NUMBER Make the verb agree with its subject in number (singular or plural).

An *s* added to a verb makes it singular; an *s* added to a noun makes it plural.

SINGULAR	PLURAL	SINGULAR	PLURAL
a girl dances	girls dance	a shrub grows	shrubs grow

To make the verb agree with its subject, ask yourself two questions: (1) What is the subject? (2) Is it singular or plural? Then choose the correct verb form.

E.2 DON'T, DOESN'T Avoid the error "he don't."

Don't = *do not* (third person plural); *doesn't* = *does not* (third person singular).

(Doesn't, Don't) your brother have his driver's license now?
(*Does*, ending in *s*, is singular to agree with its singular subject, *brother*. *Doesn't* is right.)
Carl (doesn't, don't) remember the address. (The subject, *Carl*, is singular; *does remember*, the singular verb, is right.)

PRACTICE 1 Using *Doesn't* and *Don't* Correctly

Copy each of the following sentences on a sheet of paper, substituting the correct verb, *doesn't* or *don't*, for the blank. Draw an

317

arrow from the verb to the subject. Be sure the verb agrees with the subject. After you have checked your answer for correctness, say each sentence aloud until it sounds right to you.

1. ____ this story appeal to you? 2. Victor ____ object when his father offers to take him for a driving lesson. 3. It ____ take long to reach the rolling hills of the neighboring countryside. 4. His father ____ say anything as his son rolls past a railroad crossing without coming to a full stop.

5. "Pop," says Victor, "____ this trip to the country make you glad you're still alive?"

"Glad!" replies his father. "I'm amazed."

E.3   *YOU WERE*   Always use a plural verb with the subject *you.* "You was" is wrong.

Were you at the class party last weekend?
You *were* in the skit, *weren't* you?

PRACTICE 2   Agreement with *You*

In each sentence choose the correct verb. Read the correct sentences aloud to form the habit of saying *you were* and *you weren't.*

1. You (wasn't, weren't) at the class picnic on Saturday, (was, were) you? 2. You (was, were) really missed. 3. Miss Arkwright hoped you (wasn't, weren't) sick. 4. We all wondered where you (was, were). 5. We knew that if you (wasn't, weren't) there by three, you probably (was, were) not coming.

E.4   *INVERTED SENTENCE*   When the subject comes after the main verb or one of its helpers, find the subject and make the verb agree with it. (See page 272.)

There is often used to begin an inverted sentence, but it is an introductory word, never the subject.

What is the subject in each sentence? Which verb is correct?

(Do, Does) the glee club members get free tickets to Monday's concert? (The subject, *members*, is plural; *do get*, the plural verb, is right.)

There (are, is) two boys here to see you. (The subject, *boys*, is plural; the plural verb, *are*, is right.)

At the very bottom of the trunk (was, were) the missing stamp albums. (The subject, *albums*, is plural; the plural verb, *were*, is right.)

Where (are, is) the pickles for the minced-ham sandwiches? (The subject, *pickles*, is plural; the plural verb, *are*, is right.)

PRACTICE 3   Using Correct Verbs in Inverted Sentences

Copy each of the following sentences on a sheet of paper, choosing the correct verb. Draw an arrow from the verb to the subject. Be sure the verb agrees with the subject. After you have checked your answer for correctness, say each sentence aloud until it sounds right to you.

EXAMPLE

There (are, is) two fullbacks on a soccer team.

There are two fullbacks on a soccer team.

1. In the knapsacks (was, were) enough food for a week's trip.
2. In the mountains of Vermont there (are, is) several famous ski resorts.
3. On the cover of the magazine (are, is) pictures of the President's family.
4. Here (are, is) the photos of the class party.
5. At the head of the parade (was, were) two brass bands.
6. There (are, is) no more tickets left for Saturday's game.
7. At the foot of the dock (was, were) two old rowboats.
8. (Are, Is) there any good remedies for poison ivy?
9. Where (are, is) the letters for mailing?
10. On Dale's workbench (are, is) several unfinished boat models.
11. Here (are, is) the two library books you wanted.
12. In the basket (was, were) six kittens with their eyes still closed.
13. There (are, is) only a few swimmers entered in the hundred-yard race.
14. In the last column of the paper (was, were) two advertisements for collie pups.
15. (Are, Is) there any museums in Cooperstown, New York?
16. In *Seventeen* there (are, is) many excellent articles for girls.
17. (Are, Is) there more telephones in America than in any other country?
18. In tropical countries there (are, is) usually several rainy months.
19. There (go, goes) two high-flying jet planes.
20. Where (are, is) the maps for today's trip?

E.5   *MODIFIER AFTER SUBJECT*   Don't be deceived by a modifier after the subject. Search out the subject and make the verb agree with it.

Words introduced by *with, together with, as well as, including,* or similar expressions are not part of the simple subject and do not influence the number of the verb.

The purpose of the exhibition games is to raise money for new uniforms. (*Of the exhibition games* is a modifier of the subject.)

The engine together with the first three cars was derailed. (*Together with the first three cars* is a modifier.)

The principal as well as the teachers has approved the new plans for the Spring Festival. (*As well as the teachers* is a modifier.)

PRACTICE 4 Making Verbs Agree with Their Subjects

In each sentence what is the simple subject? Is it singular or plural? Choose the correct form of the verb. Say each sentence aloud until it sounds right to you.

A. 1. Bill (doesn't, don't) like detective stories.
2. The members of the Frosh-Soph Glee Club (has, have) been invited to the Springfield Music Festival.
3. A home chemistry set with a dozen extra test tubes (was, were) on sale at $9.98.
4. There (are, is) three helicopters at the Meadowbrook Airport.
5. Here (come, comes) the Plainfield High cheerleaders.
6. The channel between the two islands (are, is) marked by buoys.
7. One of Tim's brothers (are, is) at Lafayette College.
8. (Are, Is) the Cokes all gone?
9. Carmel, as well as other towns on the Monterey Peninsula, (was, were) founded by the Spanish.
10. The seeds of the dill plant (are, is) the special flavoring ingredient in dill pickles.
11. (Are, Is) the umpires at a major-league baseball game dressed in black?
12. The election of Student Council officers (are, is) supervised by the Election Committee.
13. Where (are, is) the Kodachromes from our trip?
14. The outcome of the class elections (are, is) being announced in assembly today.
15. There (are, is) two Holstein cows in Jim Hooper's herd.
16. (Doesn't, Don't) Kay like chocolate-cream pie?
17. One of our oak trees (was, were) struck by lightning.
18. The craters of the moon (are, is) visible in a low-power telescope.
19. Five members of our class (are, is) representing us at the election assembly on Wednesday.
20. The twins, as well as Al, (are, is) invited to the Leap Year Dance.

21. (Doesn't, Don't) Terry plan to run for class scribe?
22. There (are, is) several cold, snowy mountain peaks located right on the equator.
23. There (are, is) two slices of watermelon on ice.
24. Mary Lou (doesn't, don't) know whether or not to wear her folk-dance costume to the party.
25. Two students from our school (was, were) sent to Washington to a press conference.

B. 1. The service academy for Coast Guard officers (are, is) located at Kings Point, New York.
2. The paintings in the Metropolitan Museum of Art (are, is) insured for millions of dollars.
3. The boys on Pinetree Street (has, have) organized a baseball team.
4. The brakes on my bike (wasn't, weren't) working.
5. There (are, is) still dozens of farms and small ranches within the city limits of Los Angeles.
6. The soil of the American prairies (are, is) especially suitable for wheat growing.
7. Several medieval castles on the Rhine in Germany (has, have) been restored and opened to the public.
8. "An athlete must eat and sleep well in order to play well," (say, says) high school coaches.
9. A big lunch including milk and hot rolls (was, were) a bargain at Harry's Hangout.
10. Shape, as well as size, (help, helps) determine the value of a pearl.
11. The students in our class (are, is) planning a fashion show.
12. Which one of the planets (has, have) a ring around it?
13. There (was, were) three lonely bathers in the cold waters of Casco Bay.
14. Ammonia, as well as many other household cleaners, (are, is) dangerously poisonous.
15. In the hayloft of the barn (was, were) two secret meeting rooms for the boys in our club.
16. Dad, with my two uncles from Madison, (are, is) planning a hunting trip into northern Michigan.
17. It (doesn't, don't) seem like Christmas without snow on the ground.
18. Three boys on the baseball team (are, is) participating in the sports assembly.
19. Molly, as well as Dee, (are, is) coming to the freshman picnic.
20. (Doesn't, Don't) Robert expect to take typing next year?
21. There (are, is) six bright-eyed puppies in Princess's litter.
22. (Was, Were) you able to find *Paintbox Summer* at the library?

23. Three members of our class (are, is) interested in the cooperative work project.
24. (Are, Is) foreign words included in your dictionary?
25. Where (are, is) the new thirty-two-inch bats?

PRACTICE 5 Constructing Sentences W

Using the examples in E.4 and E.5 as a guide, construct five original sentences with the verb *is*, *are*, *was*, or *were*. Be sure to use the correct form, singular or plural.

EXAMPLE

The suggestion of the boys was to plan a school sing for the spring semester.

E.6 *SUBJECT WITH* AND As a rule, use a plural verb with a compound subject connected by *and*.

Betsy's desk and chair *are* painted yellow.

Which verb is correct?

A hot sun and a cool lake (are, is) all I need for a happy summer vacation. (*Sun* and *lake* are two things; therefore the plural verb *are* is right.)

PRACTICE 6 Subject with *And* W

Using the examples above as a guide, construct original sentences with a correct form of the verb *is*, *are*, *was*, or *were*. Use any five of the subjects suggested.

EXAMPLE

the Cutlass and the Pacer
The Cutlass and the Pacer are popular cars.

1. the oak and the elm
2. Mother and Dad
3. a freshman and a sophomore
4. a dog and a cat
5. the rose and the lilac
6. a lake and a swimming pool
7. Sally and Paul
8. a lawn and a garden
9. football and basketball
10. Saturday and Sunday

E.7 *COMPOUND SUBJECT, BUT ONE IDEA* Use a singular verb with a compound subject that names one person, thing, or idea.

(See also rule D.6 on page 306.)

Bread and butter is served free with every meal. (One dish)
The co-captain and left halfback of the team is Bert Peterson. (One person)

E.8 *OR, NOR* When two subjects are connected by *or* or *nor*, make the verb agree with the nearer subject.

If you are in doubt, mentally block out the other subject and say what you would say for the nearer subject alone.

Marie or Jeanne (are, is) going to bring toasting forks to the picnic. (Block out *Marie*. Jeanne *is* going. *Is* is correct.)

Neither the *Times* nor the *Daily News* (has, have) the scores of last night's games. (The *Daily News has; has* is correct.)

Either my brother or my parents (are, is) going to take me to the rodeo. (My parents *are; are* is correct.)

Some writers prefer to rephrase the sentence if the two subjects normally take a different form of the verb.

RIGHT   Either Cynthia or the twins have taken the house keys.
ALSO RIGHT   Either Cynthia has taken the house keys or the twins have.
RIGHT   Either Jeff or I am bringing the fishing bait.
ALSO RIGHT   Either Jeff is bringing the fishing bait or I am.

PRACTICE 7 Agreement with Compound Subject

What is the subject in each of the following sentences? Is it singular or plural? Choose the correct verb. After you have checked your answer, say each sentence aloud until it sounds right to you.

A. 1. Neither Madison nor the neighboring towns (was, were) touched by last night's severe thunderstorm.
2. (Are, Is) milk or ground meat a better food for a month-old puppy?
3. Careful pruning and frequent spraying greatly (increase, increases) the yield of an apple orchard.
4. Either black or brown (are, is) a good basic color for a wardrobe.
5. The quarterback and the left halfback (has, have) worked for weeks on that tricky option play.
6. A hamburger and bun (are, is) my favorite sandwich.
7. *Going on Sixteen* and *Spring Comes Riding* (was, were) written by Betty Cavanna.
8. The president and the vice-president of the Stamp Club (was, were) reelected.
9. Neither the President nor his aides (was, were) prepared for such a warm welcome in Bogotá.
10. (Do, Does) a very warm day and a cool evening bring fog?
B. 1. Neither Philadelphia nor New York now (has, have) a championship National League baseball team.
2. A compass and a pocketknife (was, were) the downed aviator's only equipment for survival.

3. A few pine boughs, some straw, and a piece of heavy canvas (make, makes) a good bed on a camping trip.
4. Eddie Byrd or Lynn Smith (are, is) giving the first oral report today.
5. Neither Mother nor Ben (know, knows) how to replace a fuse.
6. Either rain or snow (are, is) predicted for tomorrow.
7. A cheerful disposition and a ready smile (are, is) characteristic of Ronnie.
8. Wind or a rising temperature (dispel, dispels) fog.
9. The captain and first baseman this year (are, is) Jud Belfield.
10. How (do, does) Lois and Madge like their roles in *The Egg and I?*

E.9 *PLURAL IN FORM BUT SINGULAR IN IDEA* Use a singular verb with a subject that is plural in form but names one object or idea.

Mathematics is closely linked to art as well as science. (*Mathematics* is one area of human thought; *is* is right.)

Which verb is correct?

Nine tenths of Katie's spare time (are, is) spent talking on the phone. (Nine tenths is one part of Katie's spare time; *is* is right.)
Six dollars (was, were) all Joey could spend on Christmas presents. (Six dollars is one sum of money; *was* is correct.)

E.10 *COLLECTIVE NOUN* Use a singular verb with a collective noun when the group is thought of and a plural verb when the individuals are thought of.

How do these sentences differ in meaning?

The Arrangements Committee is planning to hire a band for the winter dance. (*Committee* means the group as a unit; therefore the verb is singular.)
The committee are unable to agree which band to hire. (*Committee* here means the individuals in the group; therefore the verb is plural.)

E.11 *A NUMBER OF, THE NUMBER OF* Use a singular verb with *the number* of and a plural verb with *a number of*.

The number of baseball candidates *is* higher this year than last.
A number of boys *are* trying out for infield positions.

E.12 *EACH, EVERY, AND SIMILAR WORDS* Ordinarily use a singular verb with *each, every, either, neither, many a* (an), *a person,* and compounds with *body* and *one* (*everybody, someone,* etc.).

Everybody in the Dramatics Club (are, is) trying out for a part in *You Can't Take It with You.* (*Everybody* means "every member." *Is* is correct.)

Neither of the loudspeakers (was, were) working. (The subject *neither* means "neither one." *Was* is correct.)

The rule holds even with a compound subject.

Each boy and girl *is* allowed to bring one outside guest to the class picnic.

PRACTICE 8   Making Verbs Agree with Their Subjects

What is the subject in each of the following sentences? Is it singular or plural? Choose the correct verb. After you have checked your answer, say each sentence aloud until it sounds right to you.

A. 1. Either the battery or the bulb in my flashlight (has, have) just failed.
   2. There (are, is) five or six different kinds of herons on the Atlantic coast.
   3. The number of toll roads in the country (has, have) increased greatly over the past fifteen years.
   4. The United States (has, have) owned Saint Croix in the Virgin Islands since 1917
   5. (Has, Have) everyone in the class signed up for the free movie tomorrow afternoon?
   6. Every boy in the advanced swimming groups (are, is) invited to the swimming-team tryouts.
   7. The date of the spring picnic and the place (has, have) not been announced yet.
   8. (Was, Were) *The Three Musketeers* ever made into a movie?
   9. Ten tons (are, is) the weight limit for trucks on the old Channel Street Bridge.
  10. Fifty years ago, three hundred dollars (was, were) a reasonable price for a new car.
  11. One of today's algebra problems (was, were) too hard for me.
  12. Three fourths of the wheat crop (was, were) damaged by heavy rains.
  13. Twenty dollars (has, have) been collected by the English class for the library's Buy-a-Book fund.
  14. Neither of the record players (has, have) a really faithful tone.
  15. Nearly three fourths of the earth's surface (are, is) covered by salt water.
  16. Not one of the boys (was, were) able to reach the summit of Mt. Adams.

17. Bread and peanut butter (are, is) a good pick-me-up.
18. Either Raleigh or Durham (are, is) easily reached from the airport situated between the two cities.
19. The sports editor and the copy editor (was, were) reappointed for another year.
20. Two members of our golf team (was, were) able to go around the course in five over par.
21. There (was, were) many Los Angeles rooters in the San Francisco grandstand.
22. Each of us (has, have) pledged to collect a boxful of old clothes for the Red Cross drive.
23. Every bicycle in the Fourth of July parade (was, were) decked out in streamers and ribbons.
24. Neither the instructor nor the student (was, were) harmed in the crash.
25. (Was, Were) you ever in Glacier National Park?

B. 1. Speed and accuracy (are, is) stressed from the very first day of the typing course.
2. A wreath of shiny green holly leaves (are, is) hanging on the door.
3. No one in the neighboring classrooms (was, were) aware of the fire in the science lab.
4. Nobody in the entire cast (has, have) missed a single rehearsal.
5. My height and weight (are, is) average for my age.
6. Three dollars (are, is) a fair price for that book.
7. (Wasn't, Weren't) you marching with your scout troop in the Founders' Day parade?
8. Both steamboats had rounded the bend and (was, were) out of sight.
9. Rodgers and Hammerstein (was, were) awarded a special Pulitzer Prize for their musical comedy *Oklahoma!*
10. Many an important discovery (has, have) been made by accident.
11. A nurse or a nurse's aide (are, is) always on duty at the school health office.
12. Off the coast of Maine there (are, is) many small, rocky islands.
13. (Doesn't, Don't) that deserted house look ghostly with the moonlight on the broken windowpanes?
14. The team (was, were) fighting among themselves over the choice of captain.
15. Every student and teacher (was, were) present at the ceremonies dedicating the new athletic field.
16. There (wasn't, weren't) many correct answers for the third problem today.

17. Neither Fran nor her sisters (are, is) fond of shrimp salad.
18. (Are, Is) the number of television sets in large cities greater than the number of telephones?
19. Every boy and girl (has, have) promised to learn the cheers.
20. On the hillside near Keene, New Hampshire, there (was, were) two sugar maples, golden in the October sun.
21. Neither Mars nor Jupiter (are, is) ever as bright as Venus.
22. Patience and skill (are, is) needed to build a boat inside a bottle.
23. In the picnic basket there (was, were) two sandwiches for each boy.
24. Moisture and warm air (are, is) needed in raising orchids.
25. Neither the dugouts nor the grandstand (was, were) damaged.

PRACTICE 9   Rapid Drill on Agreement of Subject and Verb

Read aloud the following, and quickly supply *is* or *are* after each. Then repeat the exercise, using *isn't* or *aren't*, *was* or *were*, *wasn't* or *weren't*, *doesn't* or *don't*, *has* or *have*.

1. it
2. she
3. you
4. we
5. they
6. the kitten
7. one of the teams
8. Mr. and Mrs. Cotter
9. either Howie or Dana
10. the box of walnuts
11. ten dollars
12. their old Ford
13. every boy and girl
14. a number of swimmers
15. the list of members
16. many a listener
17. the number of points
18. the girls in the class
19. *Field and Stream*
20. Ginny with her two friends
21. either the duck or the chickens
22. Mr. Lund as well as the boys
23. every cow in the herd
24. Jay and his brothers

PRACTICE 10   Writing a Paragraph   W

Do you enjoy a challenge? Choose any five items from 6–24 of the previous practice. Write an original, meaningful paragraph including the five. Be sure your verbs agree with their subjects. Begin your paragraph with one of the items in a topic sentence.

EXAMPLE OF A BEGINNING

Ten dollars was a lot of money to pay for a part-Siamese kitten. The kitten wasn't anything special.

PRACTICE 11   Noting Verb Errors   LO

Jot down errors you hear in the use of verbs, and bring them to class. Be ready to correct the sentences and to explain each correction.

In each sentence which verb is correct? On your paper write your choice after the number of the sentence.

1. Both Paul Bunyan and Pecos Bill (are, is) legendary heroes in American folklore.
2. *Handbook of the Stars,* a collection of articles for amateur astronomers, (are, is) in our town library.
3. Mark Twain's desire to become a river pilot and his experiences in that occupation (are, is) described in *Life on the Mississippi.*
4. (Doesn't, Don't) the new girl in our class want to play softball?
5. The church group (is, are) planning a picnic in Evergreen State Forest.
6. Rarely (has, have) there been so many students interested in the school newspaper.
7. The articles about the early years of the Virginia colony (was, were) especially interesting.
8. Here (come, comes) the marching band.
9. The Recreation Commission (has, have) already turned in their annual reports.
10. Neither the principal nor the assistant principals (has, have) given us permission for the dance.
11. The feeding time of pheasants (differs, differ) according to the season of the year.
12. The chirping of crickets (lull, lulls) me to sleep on summer evenings.
13. The cabin's pleasant atmosphere and convenient location (make, makes) it our family's favorite vacation spot.
14. Last month almost eight hundred dollars (was, were) collected for our scout troop.
15. Protection against fire and other hazards (is, are) necessary for every homeowner.
16. My father (don't, doesn't) like smudgy fingerprints on his clean car windows.
17. (Aren't, Isn't) there enough gasoline left to get us to Topeka?
18. Each of our representatives (has, have) announced support of the bill to increase the income tax.
19. Two very popular winter sports (are, is) skiing and sledding.
20. Yesterday everyone in our math class (was, were) given a final grade for the semester.

In each sentence which verb is correct? On your paper write your choice after the number of the sentence.

1. Our algebra teacher (doesn't, don't) mind if we ask questions.
2. Four-fifths of most people's income (are, is) set aside for necessities.
3. One of the streets (was, were) closed due to the flooding of the Aspen River.
4. Tickets for the last game of the season (are, is) all sold.
5. One of Gerald Durrell's books (are, is) about his collecting animals in Argentina.
6. Fifteen dollars (are, is) too much for a year's subscription.
7. Neither the vacationers nor the permanent residents (realize, realizes) the seriousness of the approaching hurricane.
8. My father and I (was, were) in the finals of the three-legged race.
9. Every one of the soldiers (was, were) trained and retrained in crowd control.
10. The food, tents, and cooking equipment (are, is) on the truck already.
11. The committee (have, has) already decided on its meeting dates for next year.
12. The clothes on the line (was, were) blowing in the breeze.
13. Each of you (are, is) asked to bring something to the party.
14. There (are, is) thousands of bathers on the beach on a hot summer day.
15. The recent series of sporting events in the city's parks (was, were) organized by the Future Olympians Club.
16. (Was, Were) you planning to help us with the paper drive next Saturday?
17. That (doesn't, don't) sound like a normal jet plane.
18. My stamp collection and my sister's coin collection (was, were) built up over a number of years.
19. In the evening there (are, is) always a few deer drinking from the lake.
20. The new arrangement of flowers in Amman Park (was, were) planted by local volunteers.

24 *Using Verbs*

Ted had a fishing pole for three years.
Dick has had a fishing pole for three years.

If you wanted to borrow a fishing pole, would you ask Ted or Dick? If you know your verbs, you realize Ted no longer owns a pole.

Distinctions like these make verbs the most useful, most informative, and most difficult words in our language! Form the habit of using correct verbs, and you will cut your grammar mistakes in half.

TENSE

Choose the right tense of the verb to express your meaning.

F.1 **TENSE Tense has to do with time. The present tense is used for present time; the past tense, for past time; and the future tense, for future time.**

Is present, past, or future time expressed by the verb in each of the following sentences?

1. The telegraph *replaced* the pony express in 1861.
2. Alaskan pilots *land* on skis in the winter.
3. Moving sidewalks soon *will be* a feature of most large airline terminals and railroad stations.

The first sentence expresses past time; the verb is in the past tense. The second sentence expresses present time; the verb is in the present tense. The third sentence expresses future time, and the verb is in the future tense.

PRESENT TENSE	PAST TENSE	FUTURE TENSE
Now he has	Yesterday he had	Tomorrow he will have
Now he listens	Yesterday he listened	Tomorrow he will listen

The present tense nearly always indicates customary action or general truth.

Iron is hard.

F.2 *TENSE SHIFT* In telling a story choose either the past or the present tense and stick to it.

Most writers use the past tense.

Lawrence spent all day on the beach and *came* home with a bad sunburn. (NOT *comes*)

The Eagle halfback loses his balance for a moment but *hangs* on to the ball. (NOT *hung*)

PRACTICE 1 Avoiding Careless Tense Shift

In the following sentences the present tense and the past tense are mixed. One sentence is correct. Change one or more of the verbs in each of the other seven sentences to make the tenses consistent.

1. The kitten stalked into the center of the room and then makes a sudden dash for a rubber mouse.
2. Washington's army crossed the Delaware and marched eight miles to Trenton.
3. The sight-seeing boat left at noon, completely circled the island of Manhattan, and comes back to the dock at three.
4. Thunderhead ran away and Ken searches for him everywhere.
5. The huge Douglas jet passes over the city and then headed southeast toward San Juan.
6. The beagle caught sight of the aristocratic Siamese cat and takes off after it with a yelp.
7. Jack London joined the Klondike gold rush in 1897, and a year or two later he writes his first stories about the Far North.
8. Jean walked bravely to the front of the room and faces her classmates.

F.3 *ED, D* Don't drop the *ed* or *d* of a verb in writing: *asked, called, used, walked.*

Dad and I *hoped* to go fishing last weekend. (NOT *hope*)

There *used* to be hundreds of trout in Bowline Creek. (NOT *use*)

Bert *said* he wanted to see the Maple Leafs play. (The past tense of *say* is *said.*)

PRACTICE 2 Using Past Tense Correctly

In the following anecdote add *d* or *ed* to verbs as needed.

WASTE NOT, WANT NOT

President Calvin Coolidge had a reputation for thrift. One day a visitor ask Mr. Coolidge for a cigar.

"This is not for me," the visitor declare. "I have a friend who is collecting cigar bands from famous smokers all over the world."

Mr. Coolidge thought for a moment. Then he reach over for a cigar. Carefully slipping the band from the cigar, he hand the band over to the visitor and replace the cigar in the box.

The Past and the Present Perfect Tenses

How do these sentences differ in meaning?

PAST TENSE   Bud *played* the drums for a year.
PRESENT PERFECT TENSE   Bud *has played* the drums for a year.

Which sentence means that Bud no longer plays the drums? Which sentence means that Bud played the drums in the past and still plays them?

F.4   *PRESENT PERFECT TENSE* (*has* or *have* + verb form) The present perfect tense represents a present situation resulting from action which began or occurred at some time in the past.

Indefinite past time

Naomi *has read* all the novels of Thomas Hardy. (The reading took place over a lengthy, indefinite time in the past.)

Nancy Robertson *has moved* to St. Petersburg. (The speaker doesn't say exactly when Nancy moved.)

BUT   Nancy Robertson *moved* to St. Petersburg in July. (Use the past tense for past action at a definite time.)

Past action continuing in the present

Joan *has been* here all day. (Still here)

The Eiffel Tower *has dominated* the Paris skyline for over half a century. (Still dominates it)

   have been
I   ~~am~~   in Springfield High six months. (Do not carelessly use the present tense for the present perfect. Note that omission of the time words, *six months*, would make the present tense right.)

PRACTICE 3   Studying Tenses

A. Explain the difference in meaning between the two sentences at the beginning of this chapter.

B. Explain the difference in meaning between the two verbs in each of the following sentences.

1. The train (arrived, arrives) in San Diego at 5:32.
2. I (have taken, took) swimming lessons for several months.
3. Dad (had, has had) trouble with the car recently.
4. Butch (put, puts) his skis in the basement for the summer.
5. Archer (entered, has entered) the candid-camera contest.
6. Betty Anne (has lived, lived) in Omaha three years.
7. I (did, do) my homework right after school.
8. Merry's brother (flew, flies) a helicopter.

PRACTICE 4 Using Past and Present Perfect Tenses Correctly

In each sentence select the correct or never-questioned form of the verb. Give a reason for your choice. Read each correct sentence aloud until it sounds right.

1. In assembly Monday, Red Saunders (announced, has announced) the names of the new class officers.
2. Betsy (hasn't been, wasn't) at rehearsal since Tuesday.
3. At camp last summer Tim and his brother (have learned, learned) water skiing.
4. For the past four days the girls' chorus (has practiced, practiced) every afternoon.
5. We (have known, know) Jaimie and his brother for two years.
6. On Christmas Eve the church carolers (have sung, sang) several beautiful but unfamiliar Christmas carols.
7. From fall until now, Madge (had, has had) perfect attendance.
8. Fred (began, has begun) playing the cornet in July.
9. Since 1900 the earth's climate (has warmed, warmed) up considerably.
10. By 1935, subtropical birds (have been, were) found in Iceland.

The Past and the Past Perfect Tenses

F.5 **PAST PERFECT TENSE** (had + verb form) Use the past perfect tense for the earlier of two past actions. The past perfect tense is the "before-past" tense.

When Alex (had raked, raked) the leaves, he went for a ride with the Gormans. (The raking came before the going for a ride. *Had raked*, the past perfect, is correct.)

The past tense may be used for before-past time if it is not important to show that one action preceded another.

When the rain stopped, the picnickers came hesitantly from the cars and began to spread the wet tables.

PRACTICE 5 Using Past and Past Perfect Tenses Correctly

In each sentence select the correct or never-questioned form of the verb. Give a reason for your choice.

1. Lanny was sure he (had seen, saw) Sarah Jane somewhere before.
2. We got to the theater three minutes late and found that the play (already started, had already started).
3. Not until the next morning did I realize that I (had worn, wore) somebody else's coat home from the party.
4. After two hours of hiking, the patrol leader began to wonder whether he (had taken, took) the wrong trail.
5. Nan said that she (had mailed, mailed) only half the invitations.
6. Laura discovered that she (forgot, had forgotten) the picnic basket.
7. At the dinner sponsored by the Quarterback Club, the players learned that their coach (had won, won) the sportsman-of-the-year award.
8. The speaker announced that Sid Young (had run, ran) the hundred-yard dash in ten seconds.
9. Deborah realized that she (had left, left) her locker key in her other handbag.
10. Jim Hawkins discovered that John Silver (betrayed, had betrayed) the faithful party.

The Future Perfect Tense

F.6 *FUTURE PERFECT TENSE* (*shall have* or *will have* + verb form) Use the future perfect tense to express action that will be completed before some future time.

This tense is seldom used.

By the time this letter reaches you, Louise *will have graduated.*

PROGRESSIVE AND EMPHATIC FORMS

F.7 *PROGRESSIVE FORM* If you add a form of the verb *be* to an *ing* form of a verb, you have the progressive form of the verb.

How do these sentences differ in meaning?

1. When Sherlock Holmes entered the room, Dr. Watson *stood* up.
2. When Sherlock Holmes entered the room, Dr. Watson *was standing* up.

In sentence 1 the standing was a single completed action. In sentence 2 Watson had been standing before Holmes entered, and he continued to stand. The verb *was standing* is in the progressive (in progress, continuing) form of the past tense.

PRESENT   he is standing
PAST   he was standing
FUTURE   he will be standing
PRESENT PERFECT   he has been standing
PAST PERFECT   he had been standing
FUTURE PERFECT   he will have been standing

F.8   USE OF PROGRESSIVE FORMS Progressive forms are frequently used as regular tense forms.

I *have been reading* Franklin's *Autobiography* for two months.
What *is* Rita *playing?*

F.9   PRESENT PROGRESSIVE FOR FUTURE TENSE The present progressive form is frequently used in place of the regular future tense.

I *am going* to Big Bend National Park next Easter. (Instead of *will go*)
I *am trying* out for freshman baseball in the spring. (Instead of *will try*)

F.10   EMPHATIC FORM If you add the present or past of *do* to the present tense of a main verb, you have the *emphatic* form of the verb.

PRESENT   I do ride   PAST   I did ride

These forms are often used in questions and with *not*.

Did you *get* a new mystery story? No, I *did*n't *go* to the library.

F.11   OVERUSE Don't overwork the emphatic forms. When overused, they make writing dull.

PRINCIPAL PARTS

The present tense *see*, the past tense *saw*, and the past participle *seen* are the three principal parts of the verb *see*. Sometimes the present participle, *seeing*, is given as another principal part. From the three chief parts, all the tenses are formed. (In the Appendix, study the formation of tenses.)

F.12   REGULAR VERBS Regular verbs form the past tense and the past participle by adding *ed* or *d* to the present.

PRESENT TENSE	Today I	paint	hike	wish
PAST TENSE	Yesterday I	painted	hiked	wished
PAST PARTICIPLE	I have	painted	hiked	wished

F.13   *IRREGULAR VERBS*   Verbs that do not form the past tense and past participle by adding *ed* or *d* are irregular.

The dictionary lists the principal parts of irregular verbs.

Irregular verbs, sometimes called "strong verbs," are some of the oldest and most common words in our language. You will find that you already know the principal parts of most of these verbs. Now is the time to learn the principal parts you don't know and to practice using the right forms.

The arrangement in groups 1–4 shows how the principal parts are used to form tenses of the verb. In groups 5 and 6 on page 339, the principal parts only are given.

PRINCIPAL PARTS

PRESENT TENSE	PAST TENSE	PRESENT PERFECT TENSE (*Past participle in italics*)
		1
I begin	I began	I have *begun*
I drink	I drank	I have *drunk*
I ring	I rang	I have *rung*
I run	I ran	I have *run*
I shrink	I shrank	I have *shrunk*
I sing	I sang	I have *sung*
I sink	I sank	I have *sunk*
I spring	I sprang	I have *sprung*
I swim	I swam	I have *swum*

Rung, shrunk, sung, sunk, and *sprung* are permissible in the past tense but are seldom used.

		2
I break	I broke	I have *broken*
I choose	I chose	I have *chosen*
I freeze	I froze	I have *frozen*
I speak	I spoke	I have *spoken*
I steal	I stole	I have *stolen*
I swear	I swore	I have *sworn*
I tear	I tore	I have *torn*
I wear	I wore	I have *worn*
I weave	I wove	I have *woven*

Weaved is also permissible for *woven*.

3

I blow	I blew	I have *blown*
I fly	I flew	I have *flown*
I grow	I grew	I have *grown*
I know	I knew	I have *known*
I throw	I threw	I have *thrown*

4

I arise	I arose	I have *arisen*
I drive	I drove	I have *driven*
I ride	I rode	I have *ridden*
I rise	I rose	I have *risen*
I stride	I strode	I have *stridden*
I strive	I strove	I have *striven*
I write	I wrote	I have *written*

PRACTICE 6 **Using Principal Parts**

Complete each sentence with the right form of the verb. Do not use the present tense. Do not write in this book. Say aloud the correct sentences until they sound right.

A. 1. We have (ring) every doorbell in the neighborhood during the current Old Clothes Drive.
 2. Rehearsals for *The Princess and the Goblin* have not (begin) yet.
 3. I have (write) to Doc about a job as junior counselor.
 4. In half an hour Jimmy and his friends have (drink) all the Cokes in the house and most of the milk besides.
 5. My brother has (drive) to Kankakee to see his college roommates.
 6. With his dying breath Roland (blow) a last long note on the horn.
 7. The leading man in *Life with Father* has (grow) his own mustache for the part.
 8. Several supposedly "unsinkable" ships besides the *Titanic* have (sink).
 9. Matt and Lenny (swim) ashore from their overturned canoe.
 10. At the end of his daily stint, a pony express rider had (ride) about thirty miles at full gallop and had changed horses three times.
 11. Every licensed airline pilot has (fly) at least a thousand hours.
 12. Tom Sawyer had (know) about Miss Watson's will all along.
 13. Lee Grosscup (throw) the pass fifty yards down the field.
 14. We arrived in Glasgow at seven-thirty in the morning on Christmas Day, but the sun had not yet (rise).
 15. England had (fly) commercial jet airplanes before the United States began to use jets for nonmilitary purposes.
 16. Have you ever (ride) in a Corvair, a Falcon, or a Valiant?

17. Lenore (know) that Jack would come to the party dressed as a pirate.
18. Until Monday's assembly I had never (speak) to a large group.
19. Have you ever (drive) an outboard motorboat?
20. When the hailstorm caught us unprepared near the summit of Mt. Jefferson, we were nearly (freeze) in our light summer clothing.
21. Tom and Huck had (swear) undying loyalty to each other.
22. "What book have you (choose) for your report on adventure?" Allan asked Dud.
23. Without warning, the leopard (spring).
24. The second baseman (throw) the ball over the shortstop's head.
25. Athletes have (break) every supposedly unbreakable record.

B. 1. Our new dog has just (tear) the entire Sunday paper to shreds.
    2. The judges of the class-song contest haven't (choose) a winning entry.
    3. Until 1875 no one had ever successfully (swim) the English Channel.
    4. The temperature has (rise) twenty-one degrees since six a.m.
    5. Mother has (freeze) quarts and quarts of blueberries for the winter.
    6. My new watch strap has (break) after just four days.
    7. Mattie Vernon has (steal) more bases than any other player.
    8. Several English sovereigns have never actually (wear) the crown of England.
    9. According to the latest election returns, Mayor Smith's lead over his opponent has (shrink) to only a few hundred votes.
   10. Tenors have almost always (sing) the heroes' roles in opera.
   11. The Tigers have (swear) revenge against the Spartans in their return match.
   12. Davy Crockett (begin) his political career at the age of thirty.
   13. The coach has (speak) to our parents and obtained their permission for our overnight stay in Westfield.
   14. Mel has (throw) the shot more than forty feet.
   15. Oh, I've (tear) my new skirt on that nail!
   16. Caroline is the most unselfish person I have ever (know).
   17. At the warning bell all the students (begin) to pick up paper scraps.
   18. Has an American ever (run) the mile in less than four minutes?
   19. When the bell had (ring) three times, we knew we were to be dismissed from school.
   20. Our puppy has (grow) eight inches in the last two months.
   21. Have you (write) the sense-impression composition for English?
   22. The oriole has (steal) some string from the garden for its nest.
   23. I don't think the wind has ever (blow) harder than it did during last August's hurricane.
   24. Have you ever (wear) wool next to your skin?
   25. Many cities have (arise) on the ruins of Homer's Troy.

PRINCIPAL PARTS OF OTHER IRREGULAR VERBS

PRESENT TENSE	PAST TENSE	PAST PARTICIPLE
	5	
bind	bound	bound
bring	brought	brought
buy	bought	bought
catch	caught	caught
find	found	found
fling	flung	flung
hold	held	held
lay (*place*)	laid	laid
lead	led	led
leave	left	left
pay	paid	paid
say	said	said
show	showed	showed, shown
sit	sat	sat
spin	spun	spun
stand	stood	stood
stick	stuck	stuck
swing	swung	swung
teach	taught	taught
win	won	won
wind	wound	wound
wring	wrung	wrung
	6	
bid (*offer*)	bid	bid
burst	burst	burst
cost	cost	cost
hurt	hurt	hurt
let	let	let
put	put	put
set	set	set

PRACTICE 7 Using Principal Parts

Complete each sentence with the correct form of the verb named. Do not use the present tense. Do not write in this book. Read each correct sentence aloud until it sounds right to you.

1. I (show) my student's card at the museum ticket office and was admitted free.
2. As Marjorie hurried to the bus, her bulging suitcase (burst) open.

3. After we had (sit) quietly for a half hour, we became restless.
4. My brother has (teach) Sunday school for five years.
5. Have you (pay) for the ties you ordered from Filene's?
6. Perry Mason's client had been (lead) to expect a quick solution.
7. Mighty Casey (swing) at the third strike and missed.
8. Libby and Merle (bring) two jugs of lemonade to the picnic.
9. After we had (wring) out our bathing suits, we hung them to dry.
10. The trapeze artist (swing) gracefully from one platform to another.
11. When I was ill, my brother (bring) me breakfast in bed.
12. The balloon floated against a sharp twig and (burst).

PRINCIPAL PARTS OF OTHER VERBS

Which of these verbs are regular?

PRESENT TENSE	PAST TENSE	PAST PARTICIPLE
am	was	been
attack	attacked	attacked
bear (*carry*)	bore	borne
beat	beat	beaten, beat
become	became	become
bite	bit	bitten, bit
climb	climbed	climbed
come	came	come
do	did	done
drag	dragged	dragged
draw	drew	drawn
drown	drowned	drowned
eat	ate	eaten
fall	fell	fallen
forget	forgot	forgotten, forgot
get	got	got, gotten
give	gave	given
go	went	gone
lie (*recline* or *rest*)	lay	lain
see	saw	seen
shake	shook	shaken
slay	slew	slain
take	took	taken

PRACTICE 8   Using Principal Parts

Complete each sentence with the correct form of the verb named. Do not use the present tense. Do not write in this book. Read each correct sentence aloud until it sounds right to you.

A. 1. For the past three summers Stretch Waller has (take) the Explorer scouts on a canoe trip.
   2. I (see) two Broadway plays on our trip to New York.
   3. Bob (do) a wonderful takeoff on popular singers at the last class party.
   4. Caesar's Roman troops first (come) to Britain in 55 B.C.
   5. Before World War II the United States had (give) the Philippines a guarantee of independence.
   6. Achilles (drag) the body of Hector around the walls of Troy.
   7. Preston (see) a skeleton of a brontosaurus in the Dinosaur Hall of the American Museum of Natural History.
   8. The forces of Antony (attack) the armies of Brutus and Cassius on the plains of Philippi.
   9. Little Les has (fall) from a tree several times, but he still likes to climb.
   10. In four years of rivalry we have not yet (beat) Pitman in baseball.
B. 1. Everyone in town thought that Tom Sawyer and his friends had (drown).
   2. By 1776 some Loyalist families had already (go) back to England.
   3. In art appreciation we (see) slides of American landscapes.
   4. Yes, Mrs. Wright, Denny has (go) home.
   5. Last fall we (climb) the steep face of Mt. Tom with real mountaineering equipment.
   6. Cocker spaniels have (fall) from first place as America's favorite breed.
   7. Three boys who tried to cross the thin ice of Lake Mohawk were nearly (drown).
   8. Within the past few years pizza has (become) a popular snack.
   9. Have you ever (eat) real Hungarian goulash?
   10. The Barn Dance Club (see) a movie on folk singing.

PRACTICE 9 Using Correct Verb Forms

In each sentence select the correct form of the verb. Read each correct sentence aloud until it sounds right to you.

A. 1. Paul Bunyan (swang, swung) his ax and toppled the oak with one blow.
   2. Hamlin Garland's stories (showed, shown) the disagreeable side of pioneer life.
   3. Marie and Bob (brang, brought) two spaniel puppies to the dog show.
   4. The soap bubble soared nearly out of sight and then (burst, busted).
   5. Who (did, done) the screenplay for the movie *Gone with the Wind?*

6. Sir Lancelot had (drank, drunk) the magic potion unsuspectingly.
7. Before the formation of the Republican Party, Lincoln had (ran, run) for office as a Whig.
8. The McAllisters have always (gave, given) their dog a present on his birthday.
9. Has anyone ever (catched, caught) the measles more than once?
10. Before the outbreak of the Revolution, several members of the English Parliament had publicly (taken, took) the side of the American colonists.
11. Jane Addams, the founder of Hull House, (did, done) most of her settlement work in Chicago.
12. Priam realized with a heavy heart that Achilles had (slain, slew) his beloved Hector.
13. Our coach, Mr. Pardoen, has always (bore, borne) our team's defeats with cheerful resignation.
14. By the time the anchor men started on the final lap of the relay, Ben had (drawn, drew) twenty steps ahead of the others.

B. 1. George has (ridden, rode) every horse at the Elmtree Stables.
2. By 1778 Ticonderoga had (fallen, fell) to the British.
3. Astronomers have (gave, given) numbers instead of names to many recently discovered stars.
4. The first missionaries (came, come) to California about 1769.
5. Lake Erie has never (froze, frozen) over completely.
6. Until about 1500 no one in Europe had ever (ate, eaten) chocolate.
7. Woodrow Wilson (taught, teached) at Princeton University for twelve years.
8. Teams of mules (dragged, drug) the flat-bottomed boats up the Erie Canal.
9. Lisa and I (saw, seen) the figure-skating championships last year.
10. If we had not (taken, took) the wrong turn at Middle Island, we'd have arrived on time.
11. By nightfall Aunt Polly had (became, become) very much upset at Tom's disappearance.
12. By the time we gathered the children together, three chicks had already (broke, broken) out of their shells.
13. My sister has (sang, sung) twice on a television program.
14. Mickey Mantle (threw, throwed) the ball on a line from center field to nab the runner at the plate.

PRACTICE 10   Correcting Verb Errors

There are ten verb errors in the following anecdote. Recopy the anecdote, making all necessary corrections in verb forms. Do not change a correct form.

HIGHER MATHEMATICS

Little Lonnie walked into a drugstore and clumb onto a stool at the soda fountain. "A large piece of apple pie, please," he says politely to the counterman.

The counterman brung him the pie. Then Lonnie announced, "I just come to a new decision. I want a chocolate soda instead of that pie."

Lonnie finished the soda and begun to leave, but the counterman called after him, "You have went away without paying for your soda."

"Don't you remember?" Lonnie asked. "I give you back the piece of pie in exchange for it."

"But you hadn't payed for the pie either," protested the counterman.

"Of course not," Lonnie answers. "I hadn't ate a bite of that pie."

PRACTICE 11   Using Irregular Verbs in Sentences   **W**

In sentences of your own use the following verbs correctly. You may use two or three of them in one sentence.

arose	climbed	has become	has gone	have chosen
ate	drowned	has burst	had grown	have flown
became	fell	had driven	had run	have given
began	swam	had drunk	has seen	have risen
broke	swung	has eaten	has shaken	have sung
brought	wrote	has fallen	had torn	have torn

LIE, LAY, SIT, SET

The principal parts of four troublesome verbs are:

PRESENT TENSE	PRESENT PARTICIPLE	PAST TENSE	PAST PARTICIPLE
lie (*recline* or *rest*)	lying	lay	lain
lay (*put down* or *place*)	laying	laid	laid
sit (*occupy a seat*)	sitting	sat	sat
set (*place*)	setting	set	set

F.14   **LIE *AND* SIT**   Ordinarily use *lie* and *sit* to show position. They do not take objects.   (See pages 366–369.)

We *lie* in a hammock or *sit* in a chair.

Jimmy *lies* on the floor to read the paper. Jimmy *is lying* on the floor. Jimmy *lay* on the floor watching TV. Jimmy *has lain* on the floor doing a puzzle since dinner.

F.15 LAY *AND* SET Ordinarily use *lay* and *set* to show a person at work. Both verbs usually take objects.

Lay your books on the kitchen table. Jimmy *is laying* his books down. Jimmy *laid* his books on the table. Jimmy *has laid* his books down and is getting a sandwich.

Notice that the past tense of *lie* is the same as the present of *lay*.

My parents get upset if I *lay* wet scarves and gloves on their new table.

I turned off the light and *lay* down.

Which is correct?

1. The delivery boy (laid, lay) the package on the porch swing. (The past tense of *lay*, the verb meaning *put down*, is needed. *Laid* is correct.)
2. Nan (laid, lay) on the lawn, chewing a blade of grass. (The past tense of *lie*, the verb meaning *recline* or *rest*, is needed. *Lay* is correct.)
3. Greg's letter (has laid, has lain) on my desk for three days. (The present perfect of *lie*, the verb meaning *recline* or *rest*, is needed. *Has lain* is correct.)

PRACTICE 12   Using *Lie* and *Lay* Correctly

Complete each sentence with the correct form of *lie* or *lay*.

WILLIE MAYS BECOMES A GIANT

1. On May 25, 1951, gloom —— over the Giants' dressing room.
2. An eleven-game losing streak —— behind the fifth-place team.
3. "What kind of season —— ahead of us?" wondered the players.
   4. A youth with a battered suitcase entered, —— down a golf bag containing three bats, grinned, and said, "Say-hey! My name is Willie Mays. Is Mr. Leo Durocher here?"
   5. Players who were —— down sat up to inspect the newcomer.
6. Walking over to him and —— a hand on the golf bag, Al Dark asked, "What do you go around in, Willie?"
   7. Willie's reply, "Oh, I never played golf. That's a rich man's game," brought chuckles that dispersed the gloom —— over the dressing room.
8. —— down their gear, his new teammates crowded around. 9. While they were looking at the bag that —— on the bench and listening to Willie's explanation that it was a gift from Minneapolis admirers, Leo Durocher walked in. 10. Warmly greeting Willie, Durocher —— out a uniform and told him to get ready for batting practice. 11. Stepping onto

the field, Willie selected one of the bats that had —— in the golf bag.
12. He —— the bat down, rubbed his hands with dirt, and then faced
the pitcher. Crack went the bat. The rest is baseball history!

PRACTICE 13 Using *Sit* and *Set* Correctly

Complete each sentence with the correct form of *sit* or *set*.

MEMORY COURSE

1. The audience —— patiently waiting for the guest speaker to arrive.
2. The train was late, and the audience had —— quietly for nearly half
an hour. 3. The chairman, who had been —— with his head in his hands,
looked up expectantly as the door opened. 4. The lecturer strode confidently in, —— a large package down on the table, and began to speak.
5. After speaking nearly an hour on "Training Your Memory," he ——
down, picked up a glass of water, and quietly awaited the question period.
6. A man —— in the first row asked whether a good memory is inborn.
7. The lecturer —— down the glass of water he had been sipping and
replied, "No, a good memory can be acquired through training."

At the end of the question period, the lecturer stood up, bowed, and
walked with dignity off the stage, forgetting his package.

PRACTICE 14 Using Troublesome Verbs Correctly   **W**

In sentences of your own, use correctly the four forms of *lie*
(*lie, lying, lay, lain*), the three forms of *lay* (*lay, laying, laid*), the three
forms of *sit* (*sit, sitting, sat*), and the two forms of *set* (*set, setting*).
You may use two or three forms in one sentence.

ACTIVE VOICE AND PASSIVE VOICE

F.16   *ACTIVE VOICE*   A verb that has a direct object is in the
active voice. (See pages 366–368.)

> Buses have replaced streetcars in most large cities. (*Streetcars* is the
> direct object.)
> Who wrote the music for *Camelot?* (*Music* is the direct object.)

F.17   *PASSIVE VOICE*   A verb in the passive voice consists of some
form of *be* with a past participle: *is written, will be seen, had been
frozen, has been brought.*

> Streetcars *have been replaced* by buses in most large cities. (*Have
> been* + past participle *replaced* = passive)
> The first skyscrapers *were built* in Chicago. (*Were* + past participle
> *built* = passive)

If an active verb is changed to the passive, the direct object of the active verb becomes the subject of the passive verb.

Ocean currents often carry *bottles* thousands of miles.   (*Bottles* is the direct object of *carry*.)

Bottles are often carried thousands of miles by ocean currents.   (*Bottles* is the subject of *are carried*.   This sentence gives greater prominence to *bottles*.)

PRACTICE 15   **Recognizing Active and Passive Voice**

Which of the following verbs are active?   Which are passive? In each case tell how you know.

A. 1. The ruins of ancient Carthage have been uncovered by archaeologists.
   2. The White House now has more than 100 rooms.
   3. Several London department stores are guarded at night by watchdogs.
   4. The *Information Please Almanac* contains a wealth of information on many different subjects.
   5. The moons of Jupiter can be seen with good binoculars.
   6. Walter Farley wrote the "Black Stallion" books.
B. 1. The White House was rebuilt from 1948 to 1952.
   2. Do not use steel wool on wooden spoons and bowls.
   3. Tonight we'll study the constellations around the Little Dipper.
   4. Use a glass-bottomed box for underwater observation.
   5. The Gulf Stream warms the west coast of Europe.
   6. A diamond can be shattered by a sharp blow.

Using the Active and the Passive Voice

F.18   *USING THE ACTIVE*   Use the active voice for vigor and directness.

PASSIVE   Millions of dollars for public libraries were contributed by Andrew Carnegie.

ACTIVE   Andrew Carnegie contributed millions of dollars for public libraries.

F.19 *USING THE PASSIVE* Use the passive voice when the doer of the action is unknown or unimportant, when it is tactful not to name the doer, or when you wish to emphasize the receiver.

Collies *are* still *used* as sheep dogs in Scotland.
The lamp *was broken* during Mother's absence.
Our first batter *was hit* by a pitched ball.

PRACTICE 16 **Using the Active Voice for Vigor** **W**

Rewrite the following sentences, changing the passive verb to the active, except where the passive is more appropriate. There are three such sentences. Write **C** after the numbers of these sentences. Prepare to explain why the passive is necessary in each.

1. Rare orchids are grown as a hobby by our science teacher.
2. Herds of wild horses are still found in some parts of the Southwest.
3. His swim in the old quarry after dark will never be forgotten by Mitch Anderson.
4. More than a hundred different types of dogs are bred in American kennels.
5. A diary was kept by Admiral Byrd during his expedition to the South Pole.
6. American white oaks have never been successfully transplanted to Europe.
7. Huge copper weather vanes were made by early American metal-workers.
8. During the past few years great interest in Antarctica has been shown by many nations.
9. A film about space platforms will be shown by the Science Club.
10. Religious freedom was promised to settlers by William Penn.

F.20 *TRANSITIVE* A verb is transitive if it has an object or if it contains a form of *to be* plus a past participle. Thus a verb in the active or passive voice is transitive.

F.21 *INTRANSITIVE* A verb which does not have an object or is not made up of a form of *to be* plus a past participle is voiceless and hence is intransitive. Thus a verb which is in neither the active nor the passive voice is intransitive.

TRANSITIVE (ACTIVE) The boys' chorus *sang* three songs by Richard Rodgers. (*Sang* is a transitive verb because it has a direct object, *songs.*)

TRANSITIVE (PASSIVE) Three songs by Richard Rodgers *were sung* at Thursday's assembly. (*Were sung* is a transitive verb because it is composed of *were* plus a past participle.)

INTRANSITIVE   The boys' chorus *sang* at Thursday's assembly.   (*Sang* is intransitive because it has no object and because it is not composed of some form of *be* with a past participle.)

Note that *sang*, like many verbs, may be transitive in one sentence and intransitive in another.

PRACTICE 17   Labeling Verbs Transitive and Intransitive

Tell which verb in each pair of sentences is used transitively.   Tell which is used intransitively.   How do you know?

1. a. Has the bell *sounded?*
   b. *Sound* your horn.
2. a. In our production of *Iolanthe*, Cheryl *sang* a duet with Dan.
   b. The chorus *sang* last.
3. a. Don't you *see?*
   b. Don't you *see* that hawk high above the Neversink Valley?
4. a. *Try* this ravioli.
   b. Lynn doesn't really *try* hard enough.

PRACTICE 18   Looking Up Transitive and Intransitive   V

Look up each of the following words in a good dictionary.   Tell whether the word is generally used transitively, intransitively, or both ways. What differences in meaning arise from differences in use?   Use each word in sentences of your own which reveal these differences. (In most dictionaries transitive verbs are listed after *v.t.;* intransitive verbs after *v.i.*)

appear	discover	dismiss	nudge	seem
be	dismay	furnish	occur	solve

PRACTICE 19   Studying Transitive and Intransitive Verbs   V

The transitive and intransitive meanings of the following verbs have interesting differences.   With the help of your dictionary give a common meaning for each use.

become	board	cleave	flourish	grow

CONJUGATION

Conjugating a verb means giving all its forms in order.
Study the conjugation of *to choose* in the Appendix.

PRACTICE 20   Conjugating Verbs

Conjugate these verbs: *break, know, steal, teach, wear*.   Perhaps your teacher will divide the class into five groups for this activity.

AIN'T AND OTHER VERB USAGES

I am not = I'm not   is + not = isn't   are + not = aren't

F.22   *AIN'T* Avoid *ain't*. Get into the habit of saying *I'm not, it isn't, they aren't, I haven't, he hasn't.*

F.23   *OF FOR HAVE* Do not use the spelling of for *have.*

May have been, must have been, could have been, and *would have been* are correct. "Had of" is never correct in formal writing.

The Grand Canyon must ~~of~~ **have** been a big surprise to the first explorers in the Southwest.

F.24   *OUGHT* Don't use "hadn't ought." Say either *ought not* or *shouldn't.*

The Widow Douglas told Huck he ~~hadn't ought to~~ **ought not to (*or* shouldn't)** smoke.

PRACTICE 21   Improving Sentences

Change the sentences in accordance with the previous suggestions. Give your reason for each change. One sentence need not be changed.

1. The Dodgers ain't even started spring training yet.
C 2. During a trial, members of the jury ought not to discuss the case with outsiders.
3. Leather gloves hadn't ought to be put on a radiator to dry.
4. According to the coach, Ollie may of broken the City League record for the high jump.
5. I ain't been able to solve the fourth algebra problem.
6. Early American silversmiths must of developed their skill and patience to a remarkable degree.
7. The new supermarket on North Road ain't got enough parking space for all the cars.
8. The Burlington baseball team hadn't ought to start the game without batting practice.
9. Ain't you getting ready for the picnic?
10. There should of been a *Wet Paint* sign on the park railings.

MASTERY TEST 7A   Verbs

In each of the following which word or expression in parentheses is the correct or never-questioned one? On your paper write your choice after the number of the sentence.

1. The patrol reported that the enemy had (broke, broken) through the city defenses.
2. The trawler (dragged, drug) its nets right through the school of mackerel.
3. The sleeping bear was (laying, lying) in his warm cave.
4. Paul saw a half dollar (laying, lying) at the bottom of a puddle.
5. Four large cows were (sitting, setting) on the scarecrow's shoulders.
6. We (ain't, haven't) decided whether to go this weekend or the next.
7. The ship's captain (laid, lay) in his bunk, fighting a terrible cold.
8. A circus troupe has finally (come, came) to town.
9. We (saw, seen) two heron at the lake this morning.
10. The heavy winds have (tore, torn) some limbs from our trees.
11. The boy (set, sat) on the bench, waiting for a chance to play.
12. One October morning I noticed that the pond had (froze, frozen).
13. After weeks of thought the team had finally (chose, chosen) a mascot.
14. The contractor had (laid, lain) the foundation before the cold weather set in.
15. As a summer job I (ran, run) one of the rides at an amusement park.
16. That dog has (laid, lain) in the shade for three hours in a row.
17. That team has (stole, stolen) more bases than any other in both leagues.
18. Our family has (gone, went) to Whisper Lake for eight straight summers.
19. For the past half hour, that robin has been (setting, sitting) motionless on the fence.
20. The visiting head of state had (spoke, spoken) to a joint session of Congress in the morning.
21. The climber should (of, have) reached the highest peak by now.
22. Bill aimed at the clay pipes and (missed, misses).
23. You (hadn't ought, ought not) to plant the squash so close together.
24. Thirty minutes after the first downpour, another thunder storm (come, came) along.
25. He passed the summer (laying, lying) in a hammock, sipping lemonade.

If you did not do well on Mastery Test 7A, review pages 330–349 before taking Mastery Test 7B.

MASTERY TEST 7B Verbs

In each of the following which word or expression in parentheses is the correct or never-questioned one? On your paper write your choice after the number of the sentence.

1. The missing sailboat was found (laying, lying) on its side on a beach four miles from the inlet.
2. No matter what anyone says, (I ain't, I'm not) walking five miles in this heat.
3. The girl always (sits, sets) in the hall and waits for her mother to come home from work.
4. That telephone hasn't (rang, rung) for three hours.
5. For seven innings the team had been (gave, given) many opportunities to score some runs.
6. You certainly should have (gone, went) to the Friday evening dance.
7. People (ought not, hadn't ought) to venture into the woods without proper equipment.
8. The birds have (ate, eaten) the five pounds of grass seed we had spread last week.
9. My father's favorite lamp was (broke, broken) because of my carelessness.
10. The sprinter had (ran, run) the 500-yard dash in record time.
11. That group hasn't (sang, sung) together in more than three years.
12. That old trunk has been (laying, lying) in our attic for as long as I can remember.
13. Once I had climbed to the roof of the house, I knew I should (have, of) stayed on the ground.
14. A lot of people in this country have never (saw, seen) the inside of an airplane.
15. Until about an hour ago my allowance was (laying, lying) on the table in the kitchen.
16. By the time he was twenty, Mozart had already (wrote, written) some of the world's most memorable music.
17. As soon as we turned the corner, we (saw, seen) the moving van in front of Molly's house.
18. Although the engineers had (did, done) the best they could, the flood carried the old bridge away.
19. Before the linemen could figure out the play, the quarterback had (gone, went) for ten yards.
20. The giant elm had (fell, fallen) across the road.
21. When our coach shouted, the entire gymnasium (shakes, shook).
22. The curtain came down as soon as the actress had (spoke, spoken) the play's final line.
23. We had (went, gone) to Colorado many times before.
24. After the principal had (gave, given) the signal, a hush fell over the auditorium.
25. An obstacle (lies, lays) in our way.

25 *Three Kinds of Modifiers*

"Review rule."

Although this is a complete sentence, with a subject understood, you cannot follow the suggestion. Why not? You have every right to ask, "Which rule?"

"Review the third rule in the preceding chapter."

Now the suggestion is meaningful. It identifies *rule* by using modifiers: *the, third,* and *in the preceding chapter.* (See page 269). Modifiers add vigor, color, and exactness to your sentences.

G.1 **MODIFIER** A modifier is a word or group of words that limits or makes clear the meaning of another word.[1]

In this chapter you will learn about three kinds of modifiers: adjectives, adverbs, and prepositional phrases.

RECOGNIZING AND USING ADJECTIVES

G.2 **ADJECTIVE** An adjective is a word that modifies a noun or a pronoun.

Deerhounds have *shaggy, gray* hair and *long* tails.

An adjective usually answers one of these questions: "What kind of?" "Which?" "How many?" "How much?"

Mexican foods are often flavored with *red* pepper. (What kind of foods? What kind of pepper?)
These cactuses can go for *six* months with *no* water. (Which cactuses? How many months? How much water?)

A, an, and *the,* the most common adjectives, are also called "articles."

---

[1] Teachers may wish to introduce the term *headword* for the word modified. See also page 270.

PRACTICE 1 Using Adjectives to Identify Objects

Select an object in the classroom. Write a sentence that will identify the object so positively that a classmate will be able to point to it. If possible, choose an object of which there are two or more in the room. Begin your sentence with "I am pointing out . . ."

EXAMPLE   I am pointing out a tiny broken piece of red chalk on the front chalkboard tray.

STRUCTURE CLUES — ADJECTIVES

Two additional helpful clues to the identification of adjectives are (1) endings and (2) location in the sentence.

ENDINGS Certain suffixes, or word endings, are frequently used for adjectives.

–al	–ary	–ful	–less
–an	–ed	–ic	–ose
–able (–ible)	–en	–ile	–ous
–ac	–ern	–ish	–some
–ant (–ent)	–esque	–ive	–y

These aids should always be used in connection with other clues to identification. The final test of part of speech is use in a sentence.

SENTENCE PATTERNS Most adjectives readily fit into three common patterns in the sentence.

NORMAL POSITION   In *many Japanese* homes *this* kind of *miniature* tree is grown indoors in *shallow* bowls. (The italicized adjectives precede the nouns they modify.)

PREDICATE POSITION   The Japanese gardener is *patient*. (The italicized adjective follows the linking verb. See page 370.)

APPOSITIVE POSITION   The opera fan, *jubilant* and *triumphant*, bought the last tickets *available* for the Tebaldi concert. (The italicized adjectives immediately follow the nouns they modify. See page 293.)

ADJECTIVES AS NOUN MARKERS Words like *the, some, each,* and *an* frequently signal that a noun follows.[1]

Each boy took *some* ice cream from *the* refrigerator.

---

[1] Some teachers prefer to use the term *determiner* for this special type of signal word. These words occur as adjectives only in the normal position — before nouns.

List at least three words for ten of the adjective suffixes listed in Structure Clues above. Be ready to define each word you list and to use each in a meaningful sentence as an adjective.

EXAMPLE   –ful   helpful, careful, useful

For each of the following write a pair of colorful, interesting sentences. In the first sentence use the adjectives in the predicate position. In the second use the adjectives in the appositive position.

EXAMPLE   gold and purple sunset
The sunset after the thunderstorm was gold and purple.
The sunset, gold and purple, threw a brilliant glow over the green meadow. (Notice the use of the comma pair. See page 289.)

clumsy but crafty bear   sudden and violent storm
windswept and leafless tree   generous but thoughtless friend

DIAGRAMING

Diagraming shows the relationship of parts of a sentence.

Diagraming Sentences with Adjectives

1. The big gray horse bucked.

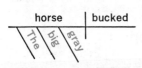

In the diagram the subject and the predicate are on a straight line and are separated by a short vertical line. The modifiers are placed on slant lines below the word they modify and are joined to it.

2. That old-fashioned building was remodeled.

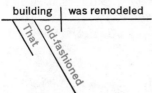

The compound adjective *old-fashioned* is diagramed like any other adjective. A compound adjective is made up of two or more words joined by one or more hyphens.

3. The young fisherman, tired but happy, entered.

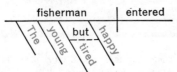

The conjunction *but* joins the two adjectives *tired* and *happy*.

If, in your diagraming, you find two or more words used as a single unit, check the dictionary to see if the group is given as a separate entry. If so, diagram the group as though it were one word. Examples of such groups are *Bill of Rights*, *Labrador dog*, *blue ribbon*.

PRACTICE 4 Recognizing Subjects, Verbs, and Adjectives   **D**

In the way shown diagram the following sentences.
OR   Copy the following sentences, skipping a line after each line you write. Underline the simple subject once and the verb twice. Write **adj.** over every adjective.

A. 1. Those little red ants bite.
    2. The damaged brick wall collapsed.
    3. A large silver trophy has disappeared.
    4. The bedraggled, wet puppy shivered.
    5. The shy, red-faced boy gulped.
    6. The expensive antique desk was sold.
B. 1. The colorful new uniforms have arrived.
    2. A cold, monotonous rain fell.
    3. The two championship teams will meet.
    4. That jet airplane will crash!
    5. Some lively jazz numbers were played.
    6. A red-and-white bicycle was stolen.

G.3   *USING ADJECTIVES* Don't pile adjective on adjective. If you are in doubt about an adjective you use, ask yourself, "Does it add vigor, color, picturesque detail, exactness?" If the answer is *no*, leave it out.

POOR   The *two* twins sloshed along the *wet*, muddy, *soggy* road. (Why are the italicized adjectives unnecessary?)
GOOD   *Small blue-and-white* flowers bloomed only a *few* inches from the *icy* border of the glacier. (The italicized adjectives add vivid detail.)

PRACTICE 5 Getting Rid of Unnecessary Adjectives   **W**

Rewrite the following paragraphs, leaving out all useless adjectives. Keep the adjectives that make the sentences vivid and exact.

OUR PICNIC ON THE LAKE

For a picnic, yesterday was a beautiful, brilliant, crisp, perfect day with a refreshing, bracing breeze and fleecy, soft-and-white clouds. Mother packed a mouth-watering, delicious lunch in a big, enormous picnic basket. Mother, Dad, my brother Bill, and I piled into our faithful, trusty Ford and rolled over crooked, winding, zig-zagging roads to a green, grassy spot on a calm, placid lake.

Bill soon went to look for wild woodland flowers. Mother sat reading an interesting, entertaining story. Dad lay on the soft, comfortable grass with his hat over his face; and I — bold, daring, energetic, and vigorous — climbed into the sturdy, thick branches of a stately, giant oak.

PRACTICE 6   Using Appropriate Adjectives   W

A. Read the following episode and then think up a suitable adjective for each blank. Rewrite the episode, adding appropriate modifiers. You may choose to treat it as part of a ghost story or part of a fairy tale, or you may make it humorous, matter-of-fact, or exciting.

Finally the ____ boys came to a ____ cabin. They opened the ____ door and found themselves in a ____ room. In the room they found a ____ table and ____ chairs. Then they heard a ____ noise. One ____ boy went ahead to investigate. He came back and reported, "There's a ____ man in the next room. He told me in a ____ voice that this was a ____ cabin. I think we'd better leave."

B. List five adjectives that describe five of the following. Then write a sentence in which you use one of the five adjectives exactly.

EXAMPLE

beach —— rocky   sunny   shell-strewn   moonlit   windswept
A dark figure walked slowly along the moonlit beach.

| 1. A sailboat. | 3. A horse. | 5. An airplane. | 7. A flower. |
| 2. An athlete. | 4. A fire engine. | 6. A storm. | 8. A house. |

PRACTICE 7   Using Adjectives in Description   W

A. In a sentence for each, describe a friend's home, a main street in your town, a teacher you had in elementary school, a nearby lake (hill, woods, etc.), an unusual tree, plant, animal you have seen. Use vivid, exact adjectives. Underline each adjective you use.

B. In a brief paragraph describe the picture on page 210. Underline the adjectives.

A. Complete the skeleton paragraph below by selecting appropriate adjectives that suggest a cheerful, happy room. Use an adjective only once.

B. Then complete the same paragraph by selecting other adjectives that suggest a gloomy, dismal room. Use an adjective only once. You may supply words other than those listed.

I opened the door and stepped into the ____ room. The ____ light from the ____ windows revealed a(n) ____ desk. Throughout the room was a(n) ____ smell. The ____ ____ color of the ____ wallpaper confirmed the original ____ impression.

airy	crisp	gloomy	musty	sunny
bright	dark	gray	peeling	tiny
cheerful	dreary	inadequate	rickety	unpleasant
clean	gay	large	sturdy	yellow

RECOGNIZING AND USING ADVERBS

Adverbs tell us whether Jack swims *poorly* or *well*, whether Mother spoke *sharply*, *wearily*, *suddenly*, *rapidly*, *thoughtfully*, or *cheerfully*. Like adjectives, adverbs permit us to add vividness, color, and exactness to our expression.

G.4 *ADVERB* An adverb is a word that modifies a verb, an adjective, or an adverb.

MODIFYING A VERB The Giants played the Dodgers *today*. (*Today* modifies *played* by telling when.)

MODIFYING AN ADJECTIVE An *extremely* promising rookie pitched for the Giants. (*Extremely* modifies *promising* by telling how promising.)

MODIFYING AN ADVERB Credit for the Giant victory went *almost* entirely to the young pitcher. (*Almost* modifies *entirely*.)

Adverbs answer the questions "When?" "Where?" "How?" "Why?" "How much?" and "How often?" and help to ask questions.

	yesterday, then, today.	(When?)
	here, there, nearby, everywhere.	(Where?)
Allan played	*expertly, clumsily, quietly, angrily.*	(How?)
	never, frequently, rarely, seldom.	(How often?)
	too carelessly, *very* sadly.	(How much? To what degree?)

ASKING A QUESTION *Why* did Allan play so carelessly?

STRUCTURE CLUES — ADVERBS

Two additional helpful clues to the identification of adverbs are (1) endings and (2) location in the sentence.

ENDINGS   Many adverbs are formed by adding *ly* to an adjective: *sweet, sweetly; honest, honestly; healthy, healthily.*

Ly, however, is not a sure sign, for many adjectives are formed by adding *ly* to a noun: *coward, cowardly; friend, friendly; neighbor, neighborly.* The final test of part of speech is use in a sentence.

SENTENCE PATTERNS   Most adverbs fit into a variety of places in the sentence. Emphasis frequently determines placement.

Suddenly a rabbit darted past the startled dog.
A rabbit *suddenly* darted past the startled dog.
A rabbit darted past the startled dog *suddenly.*

ADVERBS AS SIGNAL WORDS   Words like *rather, very, somewhat,* and *unusually* frequently signal that an adjective or an adverb follows.[1]

very cloudy,   *somewhat* doubtful,   *unusually* bright,   *quite* happy, *really* difficult,   *rather* foolishly

---

PRACTICE 9   Adjective or Adverb?

Which of the italicized words ending in *ly* are adverbs? Which are adjectives? All the words followed by nouns are adjectives. The rest of the *ly* words are adverbs.

1. *early* riser	5. *daily* classes	9. *friendly* pup
2. *quickly* done	6. *curly* hair	10. *poorly* written
3. *lonely* mood	7. *certainly* right	11. *silly* excuse
4. *easily* imitated	8. *slovenly* appearance	12. *happily* married

[1] Some teachers prefer to use the word *intensifier* for this special type of signal word. These words, unlike other adverbs, do not move about freely in the sentence pattern. They are placed in front of words they modify.

G.5 *ADVERBS NOT ENDING IN LY* Many words used as adverbs do not end in *ly* — for example, *almost, always, here, never, not, now, sometimes, soon, there, too, very.*

Some words are used as adjectives and also as adverbs.

bright	close	fast	high	loud	slow
cheap	dark	full	light	pretty	well
clear	fair	hard	long	quick	wrong

ADJECTIVE *hard* day, *quick* start   ADVERB play *hard*, go *quick*

Some of these adverbs have also a form with *ly.*

Drive *slow.*

When his turn came to speak, Slim gulped and then walked *slowly* to the front of the room. (The rhythm of the sentence suggests the *ly* form here.)

Diagraming Sentences with Adverbs

1. The canoe tipped over instantly.

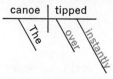

The adverbs *over* and *instantly* modify the verb *tipped.*

2. The suddenly alert watchdog prowled very quietly back and forth.

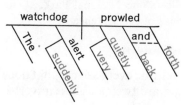

The adverb *suddenly* modifies the adjective *alert.* The adverbs *quietly, back,* and *forth* modify the verb *prowled.* The adverb *very* modifies the adverb *quietly.* *And* is placed on a broken line between the words it connects.

PRACTICE 10 Recognizing Subjects, Verbs, and Modifiers   **D**

Diagram the following sentences.

OR   Copy the following sentences, skipping a line after each line you write. Underline the simple subject once and the verb twice. Write **adj.** over every adjective and **adv.** over every adverb.

A. 1. The monkeys chattered noisily overhead.
   2. Little Billy talks surprisingly clearly.
   3. The reply came almost immediately.
   4. Genevieve always drives very carefully.
   5. The violets have bloomed unusually early.
   6. The injured halfback limped up and down.

B. 1. Then Carolyn apologized good-naturedly.
    2. Al spoke briefly and convincingly.
    3. Four perfectly matched white horses pranced ahead.
    4. Why did you leave so early? (It will help if you arrange the sentence in natural order.)
    5. A meteor usually burns up completely.
    6. Don't come too early. (Diagram the subject, *you* understood, by placing *x* in the subject position. Divide *don't* into *do* and *n't* — the adverb *not*.

G.6 *USING ADVERBS* Be sure every adverb you use has a job to do. Cut out every useless adverb.

POOR Janie sped *quickly* to the grocery. (How else could she speed? *Quickly* is a useless adverb.)
GOOD It *sometimes* snows in July in Yellowstone National Park. (The adverb *sometimes* is essential to the sense of the sentence.)

PRACTICE 11   Getting Rid of Useless Adverbs

Rewrite the following paragraphs, omitting every adverb that does not help express a clear meaning. There are twelve useless adverbs.

IN THE GRAVEYARD

Tom crept carefully and quietly along the woodshed roof. Then he leaped quickly to the ground. From the darkness Huck hissed sharply, and both boys disappeared into the night. In a half hour they were hurrying swiftly through the tall grass of the graveyard.

As three figures approached nearer through the gloom, Tom quickly seized Huck's arm, clutched it tightly, and croaked hoarsely, "What's that?"

"They're human," Huck whispered quietly. "That's Muff Potter talking, and that's Injun Joe and Doc Robinson with him."

As Tom and Huck watched attentively, the three men began to argue heatedly. Suddenly Injun Joe knifed Doc, and two terribly terrified boys fled swiftly into the dark.

G.7 *VERB AND ADVERB* Where possible, substitute a *colorful verb* for a *colorless verb with an adverb.*

For *speak loudly*, try *bellow*, *shout*, *clamor*, *screech*, *shriek*, *squawk*, *yell*, *whoop*, *roar*, or *yammer*. (Review verbs on pages 264, 265.)

PRACTICE 12 Supplying Colorful Verbs V

Supply at least three colorful verbs to replace each of the following expressions.

talk carelessly	run rapidly	drop noisily
walk slowly	speak quietly	write illegibly

PRACTICE 13 Putting Adverbs to Work VW

A. Select four colorful adverbs to modify each of the following verbs. Don't use an adverb twice. Choose adverbs that do a job.

EXAMPLE
    call — insistently, urgently, frantically, feebly

1. climb   2. cook   3. reply   4. watch   5. sleep   6. look
7. study   8. fly   9. drive   10. sing   11. dance   12. chew

B. Select one colorful adverb for each of the verbs in A and write a vivid sentence with the verb and its adverb.

PRACTICE 14 Demonstrating Adverbs by Actions

Picture an adverb by dramatizing one of the following actions before the class. Then ask someone to tell what adverb you acted out.

EXAMPLE
    enter the room — You may enter the room *shyly, pompously, inconspicuously,* or *excitedly.*

1. applaud 2. read 3. shake hands 4. wave 5. raise your hand
6. nod 7. write on the board 8. turn around

PRACTICE 15 Using Adverbs Effectively V

To fill each blank in the following paragraph, substitute a colorful, effective adverb. Compare your choices with those of your classmates.

Terry and his sister had _____ strayed from their mother and were enjoying themselves _____ riding on the elevators. After Sally had _____ bought ice cream cones for her and her brother, they _____ entered a crowded elevator. On this trip a(n) _____ well-dressed woman in an expensive fur coat was wedged _____ against the little boy.

_____, Sally called out to her brother, "Watch _____, Terry! You're getting fur all over your cone!"

RECOGNIZING AND USING PREPOSITIONS AND PREPOSITIONAL PHRASES

Modern parkways go *around* large cities, not *through* them.

What a difference to drivers the italicized prepositions make!

G.8 *PREPOSITION* A preposition shows the relation of the noun or pronoun following it to some other word in the sentence.

It combines with a noun or pronoun to form a phrase and act as a modifier.

After school I usually have a Pepsi *at* Green's drugstore *with* the rest *of* the crowd.

G.9 *OBJECT OF PREPOSITION* The noun or pronoun after a preposition is the object of the preposition.

Crocodiles and alligators lay their eggs on dry *land*.
Aluminum is known for its *lightness* and *durability*.

G.10 *PHRASE* A phrase is a group of connected words not containing a subject and a predicate.

Phrases may be used as adjectives, adverbs, or nouns.

G.11 *PREPOSITIONAL PHRASE* A prepositional phrase is a preposition and its object with or without modifiers. It is ordinarily used as either an adjective or an adverb.

ADJECTIVE The little *two-masted* boat is a yawl.
PREPOSITIONAL PHRASE USED AS ADJECTIVE That little boat *with two oak masts* is a yawl. (The phrase *with two oak masts* tells what kind of boat.)
ADVERB The scouting party listened *silently* to the captain's instructions.
PREPOSITIONAL PHRASE USED AS ADVERB The scouting party listened *in intent silence* to the captain's instructions. (The phrase *in intent silence* tells how the party listened.)

G.12 *CONCISENESS* Always use the simple word unless the phrase provides additional information.

corner
The ∧ house ~~on the corner~~ was sold.

SOME FREQUENTLY USED PREPOSITIONS

about	below	except	on	till
above	beneath	for	onto	to
across	beside	from	opposite	toward
after	besides	in	out	under
against	between	inside	outside	underneath
along	beyond	into	over	until
among	but (*except*)	like	past	up
around	by	minus	round	upon
at	despite	near	since	with
before	down	of	through	within
behind	during	off	throughout	without

G.13 *COMPOUND PREPOSITIONS* Compound prepositions act like single prepositions. Some of the most common are *because of, by means of, east of, in spite of, instead of,* and *on account of.*

Diagraming Sentences with Prepositional Phrases

1. The statues in ancient Greek temples were originally painted in bright colors.

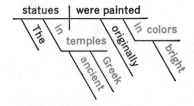

The preposition is placed on a slant line; its object, on a horizontal line joined to the slant line. The complete phrase is placed below the word or words it modifies.

2. The Indians of the Western plains depended on the buffalo for food and clothing.

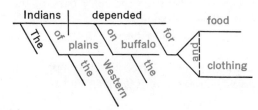

Note the position of *food* and *clothing*, compound object of the preposition *for.* *And* connects *food* and *clothing.*

3. In 1783 two Frenchmen flew to a height of five hundred feet in a hot-air balloon.

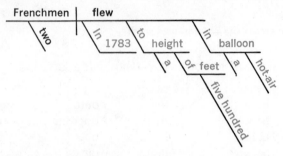

PRACTICE 16 **Recognizing the Parts of the Sentence** **D**

Diagram these sentences.

OR Copy the following sentences, skipping a line after each line you write. Underline the simple subject once and the verb twice. Write **adj.** over every adjective and **adv.** over every adverb. Enclose each prepositional phrase in a pair of parentheses.

        adj.   adj.   adv.   adj.
EXAMPLE A flock (of bewildered pigeons) circled overhead (during the

   adj.   adj. adj.
opening bars) (of the band concert) (in Grant Park).

A. 1. The unwilling baby seal was pushed into the pool by the mother for an unexpected swimming lesson.
  2. The water opossum of South America lives almost entirely on fish. (Water opossum is a name.)
  3. After many fatiguing hours of flight Lindbergh landed in Paris.
  4. Grain crops like wheat are grown widely in the Middle West.
  5. English is used by a quarter of the people of the world.
  6. A pale, cobwebby moon shone through the trees.
B. 1. The tiny mountainous country of Andorra lies on the border between France and Spain.
  2. The arena of the Colosseum in Rome could be flooded with water.
  3. The first championship water-polo match was held in England in 1888.
  4. The flavor of root beer comes partly from the spicy bark of the root of the sassafras. (*Root beer* is a name.)
  5. The frightened squirrel leaped through a narrow opening in the hedge.
  6. After the steep climb the hungry and thirsty hikers stopped at a roadside stand for hot dogs and soda pop. (*Hot dogs* and *soda pop* are names.)

WHAT PUTS THE JUMP IN THE JUMPING BEAN?

C. 1. Mexican jumping beans are sold in novelty shops and other stores. (*Mexican jumping beans* is a name.) 2. Here is the story behind these curiosities. 3. The eggs of a moth of the apple-worm family are deposited in some of the seedpods of the arrow plant. (*Apple-worm* modifies *family. Arrow plant* is a name.) 4. These eggs hatch into small caterpillars. 5. In late summer most of the seedpods snap open. 6. The pods with the caterpillars inside them do not burst. 7. The seeds have been eaten by the caterpillars. 8. These pods drop off the plant onto the ground. 9. During rising temperatures the caterpillar pushes against the walls of the pod with its legs. (*Its* is diagramed as an adjective.) 10. With each jerk of the caterpillar's body the pod hops. (*Caterpillar's* is diagramed as an adjective.)

PRACTICE 17 Putting Phrases to Work   V

Complete each blank with an appropriate, effective word or a prepositional phrase. One phrase, italicized, has already been supplied. Compare your choices with those of your classmates.

SUNK

The teacher _____ spoke _____. "Tomorrow you will have a test _____. You will be tested _____ and _____. All _____ should study _____ five hours _____."

A student groaned _____. "Don't worry," the teacher added; "all _____ will be *in the same boat.*"

"Yes," agreed a student, "the *Titanic!*"

PRACTICE 18 Using Prepositional Phrases   W

In a letter to a friend whom you met at camp or on a trip last summer and who is coming to visit you, explain why you can't meet him at the station and tell him that your brother (or sister), whom he doesn't know, will meet him. Explain where your brother (or sister) will be waiting. Add a description so vivid that the friend will recognize your brother (or sister). Enclose all prepositional phrases in parentheses.

PRACTICE 19 Finding Examples of Effective Modifiers   R

In your reading during the next week look for examples of effective modifiers: adjectives, adverbs, or prepositional phrases. Cut these out (if they are from a newspaper) or write them down. Include the sentence in which the modifier appears.

26 *Complements*

The noisy fan shouted hoarse during the first half. In the third quarter he became and whispered to his neighbor, "I've lost my."

"Don't worry," replied the other fan. "You'll find in my left ear."

Now read the story with the missing words inserted.

The noisy fan shouted himself hoarse during the first half. In the third quarter he became quiet and whispered to his neighbor, "I've lost my voice."

"Don't worry," replied the other fan. "You'll find it in my left ear."

The missing words — *himself, quiet, voice,* and *it* — are completers, or complements, of the verbs.

DIRECT OBJECTS

H.1 *DIRECT OBJECT* The direct object answers the question "What?" or "Whom?" after an action verb.

SVO

I visited _____ and saw _____.

Whatever you insert in the blanks will be direct objects.

	TEST QUESTION	DIRECT OBJECT
No one knows the origin of the grapefruit.	Knows what?	origin
Mr. Ellis told the story of this popular fruit.	Told what?	story
West Indians have been eating grapefruit for centuries.	Have been eating what?	grapefruit
An established tree will bear 1500 pounds of fruit each year.	Will bear what?	pounds

Verbs that show ownership take direct objects.

    v.   d.o.

Dad owns a Volkswagen.

    v.   d.o.

The car has a sliding top.

Diagraming Sentences with Direct Objects

1. The excessive heat and high humidity of that July day caused almost unbearable discomfort.

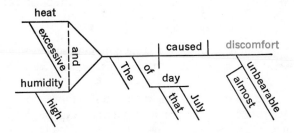

Discomfort, the direct object of the verb, is placed on the same line with the verb and is separated from it by a short vertical line.   *The* and *of that July day*, the modifiers of the compound subject, are joined to the single line representing the whole subject.

2. The satellite shot past the moon and sought a permanent solar orbit.

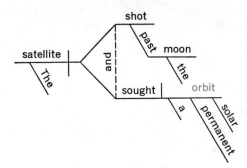

Shot past the moon and *sought a permanent solar orbit* are compound predicates.   *Orbit* is the object of the verb *sought*.

3. The furniture and the wooden parts of a house change their size and shape with changes in temperature and humidity.

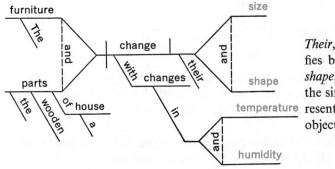

Their, which modifies both *size* and *shape*, is joined to the single line representing the whole object.

Diagram the following sentences.

OR   Copy the sentences.   Underline every <u>simple subject</u> once
and every <u>verb</u> twice.   Write **d.o.** above every direct object.

LOST OPPORTUNITY

1. Mark Twain had a fondness for money-making schemes.
2. After several bad experiences, he lost his patience with the so-called inventors.
3. A tall, lean man later visited him and requested money for an invention.
4. Mark Twain described his previous unhappy experiences and refused any money.
5. The man thanked Twain politely and turned to the door.
6. In desperation Alexander Graham Bell took his invention to another backer!

Combine each of the following pairs of sentences into a single
sentence by using compound direct objects.   Do not use a compound
verb.   Eliminate all useless words.

EXAMPLE   We found quartz crystals in the Ellenville mine.   We also discovered some galena there.

We found quartz crystals and some galena in the Ellenville mine.

ROCK HOUND

1. I enjoy rock-hunting.   I also like the challenges of geology.   2. My
Dad takes my brother on field trips.   He also takes me along.   3. For
mineral specimens we explore excavations.   We don't overlook road cuts.
4. We have examined stream beds.   We have also checked quarries.
5. We have found fossils in Watkins Glen.   We have discovered igneous
rock in Oregon.   6. Rock-hunting provides information about the structure of the earth.   It also provides the excitement of visiting far-off places.

INDIRECT OBJECTS

Mother broiled my *sister* a hamburger.

The sentence doesn't alarm us because we know *sister* is not a
direct object.   *Sister* tells for whom mother broiled the hamburger.
Sister is the indirect object of the verb *broiled.*

H.2   *INDIRECT OBJECT*   The indirect object answers the question
   "To whom?" or "For whom?" after an action verb.

The indirect object usually comes between the verb and the direct object.

	TEST QUESTION	INDIRECT OBJECT	TEST QUESTION	DIRECT OBJECT
Mr. Klempner read us the first chapter of *Kim*.	Read to whom?	us	Read what?	chapter
Alf lent Buddy and me his leather-craft set.	Lent to whom?	Buddy and me	Lent what?	set
Dad made Perky a Viking shield.	Made for whom?	Perky	Made what?	shield

As a rule, placing *to* or *for* before the indirect object does not change the meaning: *read to us, lent to Buddy and me, made for Perky.*

Diagraming Sentences with Indirect Objects

1. The treeless plains afforded the settlers no protection from sudden storms.

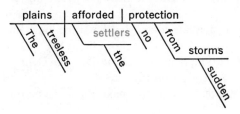

Settlers, the indirect object of *afforded*, is diagramed like the object of a preposition.

2. Teach Eddie and me a few basic rules about dry-fly fishing.

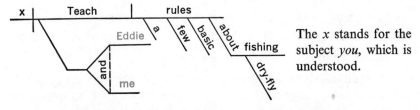

The *x* stands for the subject *you*, which is understood.

PRACTICE 3 Recognizing the Parts of the Sentence **D**

Diagram the following sentences. For sentence diagrams turn to Answer Book.
OR As you copy the following sentences, underline the simple subject once and the verb twice. Write **i.o.** above an indirect object and **d.o.** above a direct object.

COVER UP

1. Uncle Ted told me some of his experiences on army maneuvers. 2. Good camouflage provided his company excellent protection from aerial observation. 3. Once an officer gave my uncle and his buddies a sharp rebuke.

4. "Your shadows are furnishing those planes a blueprint to your position. 5. Do me a favor and eliminate those shadows."

6. One of the men gave the officer a quick nod and threw sand on the shadows.

PRACTICE 4 Using Direct and Indirect Objects Effectively   W

By using indirect objects and eliminating useless words, combine each pair of sentences into one good sentence. Label each direct and indirect object.

EXAMPLE   The Evanses were extremely generous. They offered the use of their cottage to us for two weeks in August.

i.o.   d.o.

The Evanses generously offered us their cottage for two weeks in August.

1. Uncle Mark gave the *Windjammer* recording to me. He gave it to me for my birthday.
2. The magazine offered many dressmaking hints. It offered the hints for the readers.
3. Mr. Alexander gave a combination ticket to Disneyland to Denny. He also gave a similar ticket to Denny's brother.
4. Will you make blueberry pancakes? Will you make them for us for breakfast?
5. Aunt Milly sent seed necklaces from Puerto Rico to Dotty. Aunt Milly also sent some to me.

PREDICATE NOUNS AND PREDICATE PRONOUNS (PREDICATE NOMINATIVES)

According to Edna Mitchell you are a _____.

How anxiously you await the completion of the sentence! *Genius* will cheer you; *fool* will depress you. The word that completes the word *are* is a predicate noun. It means the same as the subject.

Mary Ann was secretary of her class last year. (*Secretary* completes *was* and explains *Mary Ann*. Mary Ann = secretary)

H.3 *PREDICATE NOUN AND PREDICATE PRONOUN*
A predicate noun or predicate pronoun answers the question "Who?" or "What?" after a linking verb.

The predicate noun or predicate pronoun, except after a negative, means the same person, place, or thing as the subject. (Predicate nouns and predicate pronouns are also called "predicate nominatives.")

Amethyst is another *name* for purple quartz. (amethyst = name)
That's *it!* (That = it)

After *not* a predicate noun explains the subject by telling what. the subject is not.

Shellfish are not fish. (Shellfish *does not* = fish)

Diagraming Sentences with Predicate Nouns and Predicate Pronouns

1. The attractive girl with the blue dress and shoes is *she*.

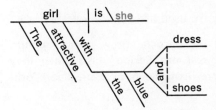

The predicate pronoun, *she*, answers the question "Who?" after the verb and means the same person as the subject. Therefore the line between the verb and the predicate slants toward the subject.

2. Two of the most famous natural bridges in the United States are Rainbow Bridge in Utah and Natural Bridge in Virginia.

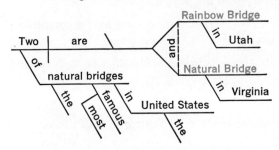

The two predicate nouns, *Rainbow Bridge* and *Natural Bridge*, are placed on horizontal lines. The conjunction *and* connects the two predicate nouns.

PRACTICE 5 Recognizing the Parts of the Sentence

Diagram the following sentences.

OR As you copy the following sentences, underline the simple subject once and the verb twice. Write **p.n.** over a predicate noun and **p.pr.** over a predicate pronoun.

1. The Grand Canyon is the largest gorge in the world.
2. Was the boy in the clown costume you?
3. The bullterrier was originally a cross between the bulldog and the fox terrier.
4. The red-haired girl at the piano is she.

5. The sea otter is a playful mammal with a flattish head and long whiskers. (*Sea otter* is one name.)
6. Los Alamos in New Mexico is the site of atomic research laboratories.

PREDICATE ADJECTIVES

Melanie is *cheerful, generous, thoughtful,* and *sincere.*

The adjectives complete the verb *is* and tell us something about Melanie. Since these adjectives occur in the predicate after a being verb, they are called "predicate adjectives." (Review pages 353–354 for three common adjective positions.)

H.4   PREDICATE ADJECTIVE A predicate adjective completes the verb and describes the subject.

Predicate adjectives are used after linking verbs.

H.5   LINKING VERBS The verbs *be, become, grow, seem, appear, taste, smell, sound, look,* and *feel* are linking verbs when they join a predicate adjective, a predicate noun, or a predicate pronoun to the subject.

The egg-salad sandwich with relish tasted *good.*

These verbs aren't always linking verbs.

How *did* your sandwich *taste?* (*Did taste* doesn't have a completer.) *Taste* the spaghetti sauce. (*Taste* has a direct object.)

Why is *aggressive* in the following sentence *not* a predicate adjective?

Sonny James is an aggressive ballplayer.

Aggressive modifies the predicate noun *ballplayer,* not the subject.

Diagraming Sentences with Predicate Adjectives

Diamonds are extremely hard but quite brittle.

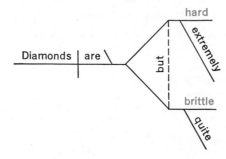

Since the predicate adjective completes the verb and modifies the subject, the line separating the predicate adjective from the verb slants toward the subject. Compound predicate adjectives are placed on horizontal lines.

H.6 *PASSIVE FORM* A predicate noun or a predicate pronoun usually follows a passive verb like *is called, was named, were named, has been considered,* or *have been elected.*

p.n.

My dad's boat is called the *Flora Dory*. (*Flora Dory* = boat)

PRACTICE 6 Recognizing the Parts of the Sentence

Diagram the following sentences.

OR As you copy the following sentences, underline the simple subject once and the verb twice, and draw an arrow from the predicate adjective or predicate noun to the subject.

EXAMPLE The blueberries will be ripe by mid-July.

1. At ninety, George Bernard Shaw was still hot-tempered and sharp-tongued.
2. Isn't Hank allergic to seafood?
3. The Indian costumes for the dance pageant look authentic.
4. By the end of his second term in office, Woodrow Wilson was seriously ill.
5. The milk in the refrigerator has turned sour.
6. Bonnie has been elected president of our class.

PRACTICE 7 Using Predicate Adjectives Effectively **W**

A. Complete each of the following sentences with vivid, exact adjectives.

     1. The night was unusually ＿＿＿.
     2. The untamed stallion looked ＿＿＿.
     3. The flowers in the florist shop smelled ＿＿＿.
     4. The storm became more and more ＿＿＿.
     5. The onion-smothered steak tasted ＿＿＿.
     6. The orchestra's last selection sounded ＿＿＿.

B. Write five sentences of your own using effective, specific predicate adjectives. Try to create a picture that your classmates will remember.

PRACTICE 8 Parts of the Simple Sentence

Copy the italicized words in a column and number them 1 to 25. Then, using the abbreviations listed below, indicate the use in the sentence of each word. Write the correct abbreviation to the right of each word.

s.s. — simple subject	**p.n.** — predicate noun
v. — verb	**p.a.** — predicate adjective
d.o. — direct object	**o.p.** — object of preposition
i.o. — indirect object	

EXAMPLE   *Asphalt is* a petroleum *product*.

Asphalt — **s.s.**   is — **v.**   product — **p.n.**

PITCH LAKE

1. *Mr. Kingsley showed* our science *class* a *film* about *asphalt*. 2. The *island* of Trinidad off the *coast* of South America is *famous* for its natural asphalt *lake*. 3. For four hundred *years men have taken asphalt* from Pitch Lake. (*Have taken* is one item.) 4. On a *voyage* in 1498 Christopher Columbus *discovered* the sticky *substance* and *used it* as waterproofing for his ships. 5. Sir Walter Raleigh *was* another early *explorer* of this island. 6. To *him* the *supply* of natural waterproofing material seemed *inexhaustible*. 7. Asphalt from Pitch Lake originally *paved Pennsylvania Avenue* in Washington. (*Pennsylvania Avenue* is one item.)

PRACTICE 9   Parts of the Simple Sentence

Follow the directions for Practice 8.

1. Trinidad's Pitch Lake *covers* one hundred *acres*. 2. At the *center it reaches* a *depth* of two hundred feet. 3. From this *center flows* a grayish-black *mass*. 4. Here the *asphalt* is *fresh* and *soft*. 5. Exposure to the *air hardens* the thick *liquid*. 6. The *surface* of the lake *is* a *series* of uneven *folds* and creases. 7. With a *pick* the pitch-cutters *dig* huge *chunks* of crude asphalt from the lake. 8. The refined *asphalt is dumped* into barrels or drums for *shipment* to Europe and the United States. (*Is dumped* is one item.)

PRACTICE 10   Writing Sentences with Completers   **W**

Write five sentences including some information you learned in school this week. Be sure each sentence has a completer. Label each completer **d.o.**, **i.o.**, **p.n.**, **p.pr.**, or **p.a.**

                             p.n.
EXAMPLE   A monadnock is an isolated hill in the middle of a plain.

H.7   *SUBJECTIVE COMPLEMENT* Subjective complement is a convenient term used to refer to any completer that renames or describes the subject.

Predicate nouns, predicate pronouns, and predicate adjectives are all subjective complements. A subjective complement answers the question "Who?" or "What?" after a linking verb.

27 *Using Adjectives, Adverbs, and Prepositions*

Greg took one look at this chapter heading and said, "Well, I don't need no help with this here chapter." Would you agree with him?

This chapter will help you to use adjectives, adverbs, and prepositions correctly.

DIAGNOSTIC TEST 8A   Adjectives and Adverbs

In each sentence which word or expression in parentheses is the correct or never-questioned one? On your paper write your choice after the number of the sentence.

1. Fifty cents is (a half, half) a dollar.
2. The decorations for this year's Halloween party look (beautiful, beautifully).
3. Marie thought (optimistic, optimistically) about finding a summer job as a lifeguard.
4. Who is the (taller, tallest), Vince or Tom?
5. Did you know that there aren't (any, no) snakes in Ireland?
6. (Them, Those) two houses are the oldest on the street.
7. Sandra painted the window frames very (careful, carefully).
8. (These, This) kind of crayon is easier to use than the others.
9. You should wear (that, those) kind of shoe for hiking.
10. The principal and (coach, the coach) of the tennis team went to college together.
11. I don't like shoveling snow (neither, either).
12. Even an expert (could, couldn't) hardly tell the difference between the real and the counterfeit bill.
13. After searching through the grass for (a half, half) an hour, Joan lost all hope of finding her ring.
14. (A, An) hour's sleep will be most welcome.

15. (This, This here) coin must belong to you.
16. I haven't seen a deer (anywhere, anywheres) near this forest.
17. The boys always played very (good, well) together throughout elementary school.
18. Tulips (have, haven't) never done well on that side of the yard.
19. We didn't do very (good, well) because we had no chance to practice.
20. Of the three buildings facing the square, the post office is the (larger, largest).

COMPARISON OF ADJECTIVES

"The green car is a *good* buy. The blue one is still *better*, but that two-tone gray one is the *best* of the three."

If you purchase a bicycle, a baseball mitt, or a pocketbook, you may do some comparison shopping to give you the best buy for your money. The change in adjectives is also called "comparison." Note how the following adjectives change.

POSITIVE   This test was *hard*.
COMPARATIVE   This test was *harder* than the last.
SUPERLATIVE   This test was the *hardest* of the term.

I.1   *COMPARISON* Many adjectives change form to show differences in degree. This change is called "comparison."

I.2   *ER, EST* Most adjectives of one syllable and some adjectives of two syllables are compared by adding *er* and *est* to the positive.

brave	braver	bravest
happy	happier	happiest

I.3   *MORE, MOST* If adding *er* or *est* to a two-syllable adjective makes a clumsy word, the comparative and the superlative are formed by putting *more* and *most* (or *less* and *least*) before the positive.

helpless	more helpless	most helpless
loyal	more loyal	most loyal

I.4   *THREE OR MORE SYLLABLES* Adjectives of three or more syllables are compared by putting *more* and *most* (or *less* and *least*) before the positive.

trivial	more trivial	most trivial
vigorous	less vigorous	least vigorous

1.5   *IRREGULAR COMPARISON* A few adjectives are compared irregularly.

bad, evil, ill	worse	worst
good	better	best
much, many	more	most
little	less	least

PRACTICE 1   Comparing Adjectives

Pair each modifier in columns 1 and 2 with an appropriate noun in columns 3 and 4, and give the comparative and superlative of the modifier with its noun.

EXAMPLE small kitten   smaller kitten   smallest kitten

abrupt	hard	answer	problem
crowded	high	assignment	room
difficult	violent	dog	sheep
friendly	woolly	mountain	storm

1.6   *COMPARING TWO* Use the comparative when comparing two people or things. To compare more than two persons or things, use the superlative.

        friendlier
Brucie is the ~~friendliest~~ of our two beagles.

        more
Sharon is the ~~most~~ considerate of the twins.

1.7   *ANY OTHER* When comparing one with others in its group, ordinarily use *any other*, not *any*.

        other
That television tower is larger than any ^ structure in our city. (Since the tower is a structure, it is included in "any structure in our city." How can the tower be larger than the tower? That's what the original sentence says.)

1.8   *DOUBLE COMPARISON* Do not use both *more* and *er* for the comparative or both *most* and *est* for the superlative.

"More kinder" and "most kindest" are incorrect.

I.9 *CLEAR COMPARISONS* Make clear what you are comparing.

NOT THIS The boys' gymnasium in our school is larger than the girls.
(Here *gymnasium* is being compared with *girls*.)
BUT THIS The boys' gymnasium in our school is larger than the girls'.

PRACTICE 2 Using Comparatives and Superlatives

Eight of the following sentences contain errors in comparison. As you copy the incorrect sentences, make the necessary corrections. Prepare to give a reason for each change you make.

1. On the tape recording Nan's voice sounded much higher than Loretta.
2. Norman Rockwell is our most best-known magazine illustrator.
3. Florida is more farther south than any other state except Hawaii.
4. Which will live longer, a turtle or a goldfish?
5. Jane is the youngest of the two Compton girls.
6. Is the salary of a secretary usually higher than an accountant?
7. Jane's house is larger than any house on her block.
8. That was the most happiest day of my life.
9. Midge's dog barks more often and more noisily than Betsy.
10. Of the two finalists Sally Ann has the better chance of winning.

USING ADJECTIVES CORRECTLY

I.10 *THIS, THAT, THESE, THOSE* *This* and *that* are singular and modify singular nouns; *these* and *those* are plural and modify plural nouns.

Form the habit of saying *this kind, that kind.* In *this kind of shoes*, *this* modifies *kind*, not *shoes*.

I'll never buy (that, those) kind of gloves again. (The singular, *that*, is correct. It modifies the singular noun, *kind*.)

I.11 *THIS HERE, THAT THERE* Do not use "this here" or "that there" to modify a noun.

Say *that chair*, not "that there chair," *this apple*, not "this here apple."

I.12 *THEM, THOSE* Never use *them* as subject of a verb. Never use *them* to modify a noun. (See also page 394.)

Those
~~Them~~ are fresh-picked tomatoes.
Those
~~Them~~ tomatoes have just been picked.

PRACTICE 3   Forming Good Habits

This rapid drill will help you form the habit of using correct adjectives. Read the following expressions aloud quickly, putting *this* or *these* before each. Repeat with *that* or *those*.

kind of shoes .	sort of gloves	kind of trousers
kind of TV shows	sort of mittens	kinds of bedroom slippers

PRACTICE 4   Using *This, That, These, Those*

Be ready to read each of the following sentences aloud, choosing the correct or never-questioned word or expression in parentheses. Prepare to explain your choices.

1. Aren't (them, those) horses from Creeley's stables?
2. Our science class raised (that, those) kind of rabbits last year.
3. (These, These here) plastic roller skates are for beginners.
4. Is there a flash attachment for (this, this here) camera?
5. The Coast Guard flies (them, those) flags as storm warnings.
6. (Them, Those) are unusual pearls.
7. David Livingstone wore (these, this) kind of boots when he traveled in the jungle.
8. (This, This here) knapsack has a tricky expansion pocket.
9. (Them, Those) large black grapes are juicy and sweet.
10. (That, That there) hockey equipment is pretty expensive.

I.13   **A, AN**   Use *a* before consonant sounds and *an* before vowel sounds.

Think of sounds, not letters. *An hour* is right because the *h* is silent.

I.14   **CLEARNESS OR EMPHASIS**   Repeat *a, an,* or *the* before each item in a series for clearness or emphasis.

CLEARNESS   The center and *the* captain of the team walked to the side of the court. (One player or two? Two is right.)

EMPHASIS   Timmy ate the three frankfurters, *the* three hamburgers, and *the* two bacon sandwiches.

I.15   **DIFFERENT OBJECTS**   When two or more adjectives modify a noun, repeat the article if different objects are meant.

The saddest and *the* happiest days of my life were two days in June last year. (Two days)

Jill fell in love with a tan and *a* black puppy and couldn't make up her mind which to take. (Two puppies)

I.16 *A HALF, HALF A (AN)* Say *a half* or *half a (an),* never "a half a."

Half a foot from the finish line, Red Peril led the other caterpillar by *a half inch.*

I.17 *NAMES OF COUNTRIES* Although *the* is not ordinarily used before the name of a country, it must be used with a few such names: *the United States, the Union of South Africa, the Soviet Union.*

New states in recent years include *the* Republic of Guinea and *the* Federation of Malaya.

PRACTICE 5 Using A, An, *The*

Choose the correct word or expression in parentheses, and give a reason for each choice.

A. 1. The final business meeting and (picnic, the picnic) will be held on Friday and Saturday respectively.
2. Hummingbird eggs are sometimes less than (a half, half) an inch long.
3. How many states are there in (United States, the United States)?
4. (A half a, Half a) mile down the trail Pinto lost a shoe.
5. Hovering low over the scene of the crash, (a, an) Air Force helicopter dropped food and supplies to the seven survivors.
B. 1. Can a jeweler tell the difference between a natural and (a synthetic, synthetic) ruby?
2. The producer and (director, the director) of a movie usually receive top billing.
3. The judges for the citizenship awards will be the civics teacher and (coach, the coach) of the football team.
4. Tuesday is certainly (a, an) unusual name for a dog.
5. After 1801 several attempts were made to relocate the capital of (the United States, United States); all failed.

USING ADVERBS CORRECTLY

I.18 *DOUBLE NEGATIVE* Avoid the double negative — the use of two negatives together.

Most negatives begin with *n* — *not, no, never, nothing, none, no-body.* *N't* is the contraction for *not.*

                  any
I hope we don't have ~~no~~ homework over the weekend.

WRONG   Don't never leave without a dime to call home in an emergency.
RIGHT   Never leave (*or* Don't ever leave) without a dime to call home in an emergency.

l.19   *OTHER NEGATIVES* Watch out for *hardly, scarcely, only,* and *but* (when *but* means "only"). These words are negative in meaning and should not be used with a second negative word.

There aren't hardly any campsites left at Lake George.
Nathan Hale regretted that he hadn't but one life to give for his country.

An intentional double negative is occasionally used to produce an affirmative statement. Common negative prefixes are *un* (*uncertain*), *non* (*nonconformist*), and *dis* (*disallow*). The prefix *in* (*incompetent*) meaning "not" sometimes appears in a variety of forms: *il* (*illogical*), *im* (*impossible*), and *ir* (*irregular*).

Do*n't* think me *un*fair if I disagree. (Think me fair.)

PRACTICE 6 **Avoiding the Double Negative**

Eight of these sentences are wrong. Correct them and give a reason for each change you make.

1. There isn't no more sherbet for the punch bowl.
2. I didn't go nowhere near the beach today.
3. Don't feed Bruno nothing before his dinner time.
4. We scarcely know the McAllisters.
5. Bud hasn't never seen *High Noon.*
6. Dad was so sleepy he couldn't hardly keep his eyes open.
7. Paula hasn't done nothing about the decorations for the party.
8. When we saw Alex in his scout uniform, we didn't hardly know him.
9. I'm not going to pick no more berries this summer.
10. Uncle Al can hardly wait to see the Colts play again.

l.20   *STANDARD USE* Do not add *s* to *anyway, anywhere, everywhere, somewhere, nowhere.*

NOT   anyways, anywheres, everywheres, somewheres, nowheres
BUT   anyway, anywhere, everywhere, somewhere, nowhere

l.21   *ADVERB USAGE* Use an adverb to modify a verb, an adjective, or another adverb.

Which is right?

Bunny speaks too (rapid, rapidly) to be easily understood. (*Rapidly*, the adverb, is right because it modifies the verb *speaks*.)

Some adverbs have two correct forms — one with and one without *ly*.

Talk slow *or* slowly. Walk quick *or* quickly. Shout loud *or* loudly.

I.22 PREDICATE ADJECTIVE After *be, become, grow, seem, appear, look, feel, taste, smell,* and *sound,* use a predicate adjective to describe the subject.

That turkey looks (= is) *tempting.*
The telephone bell sounds (= is) *softer* than before.

I.23 GOOD, WELL In formal English *good* is used as an adjective, not as an adverb.

Tom's stroke is *good.* He swims *well.*
The buns smell *good.* Janice cooks *well.*

When *well* means "in good health," "attractive," or "satisfactory," it is an adjective.

Susan looks *well* (or *good*) in tailored suits.
All is *well* (adjective) that ends *well* (adverb).

PRACTICE 7 Using Good and Well

Read each of the following sentences quickly, filling the blank with *good* or *well.*

1. Oaks grow ____ here.
2. My, the lilacs smell ____.
3. Mickey is batting ____.
4. That old Ford runs ____.
5. Ann doesn't sew very ____.
6. Carmen knows her Spanish ____.
7. Cheryl sings ____.
8. Beat the frosting ____.
9. The Tigers played ____.
10. A shower will feel ____.

PRACTICE 8 Using Correct Adjectives and Adverbs

Choose the modifier in parentheses in accordance with the preceding suggestions. Tell what the word or words modify.

A. 1. Holmes gazed (thoughtful, thoughtfully) at the hansom cab stopping in front of his Baker Street residence.
2. Dennis dives (good, well), but his brother Mike is even better.
3. The lost child (tearful, tearfully) accepted the lollipop from the policeman.
4. The cocoa needs more sugar; it still tastes (bitter, bitterly).

5. At the first rehearsal Keith was reading his lines much too (quiet, quietly).
6. When I woke up after the operation, I felt (miserable, miserably).
7. Ginny's suit fits very (good, well).
8. Everett looks (snappily, snappy) in his cap and gown.
9. Jo and Meg looked (beautiful, beautifully) in their white organdy dresses.
10. Tom plays the cornet very (good, well) after only ten lessons.

B. 1. The newborn walrus was fed (regular, regularly) every four hours, just like a human baby.
2. I'll tell you (definite, definitely) tomorrow whether I'll be able to go.
3. After a summer in Quebec, Jimmy speaks French (good, well) enough to impress his French teacher.
4. The instructor at the dog obedience school worked very (patient, patiently) with Prince.
5. Johnny Tremain had never gotten along (good, well) with Dove.
6. Dad looked the secondhand Buick over (good, well) before buying it.
7. Mrs. Carr always drives (careful, carefully), especially in heavy traffic.
8. Whatever Alan Martin does, he does (good, well).
9. The ball bounced (crazily, crazy) off the rim and then dropped through — Harrison 51, Tuxedo 50!
10. Grandmother's pecan buns smelled (delicious, deliciously) as we entered the old farm kitchen.

Your score on the mastery test will show you how much you have learned about adjectives and adverbs. After taking the test, enter your mark on your achievement graph.

MASTERY TEST 8B   Adjectives and Adverbs

In each sentence which word or expression in parentheses is the correct or never-questioned one? On your paper write your choice after the number of the sentence.

1. I prefer (that, those) kind of pants for working around the house.
2. I never do (good, well) whenever I have to pitch on a hot day.
3. Frances (can, can't) hardly wait to buy a stereo system with the money she has earned.
4. San Francisco is (farther, farthest) away from New York than Los Angeles.
5. Japanese beetles covered the leaves (everywhere, everywheres) we looked.

6. Dave wrote (frequent, frequently) to Aunt Carolyn while he was in the army.
7. Skeptical people claim that (a, an) honest person is very hard to find.
8. A catcher and (a centerfielder, centerfielder) have yet to be selected for the team.
9. Our car radio never works (good, well) during a thunderstorm.
10. Haven't the police found (a, no) suspect yet?
11. Does Donna prefer (that, those) kinds of flowers?
12. My father asked me to water the lawn (complete, completely).
13. We've seen (that, that there) car in many races this year.
14. For (a half, half) a dollar, we could use the tennis courts .
15. Some of the flowers in the garden did not seem (erect, erectly), but they were still pretty.
16. Squinting through the rain-splashed windshield, the taxi driver couldn't see (anything, nothing).
17. (Them, Those) young people with the red jackets are ushers.
18. The company (had, hadn't) but eight openings for the twenty-three applicants.
19. Do robins prefer (this, these) kinds of trees for nest-building?
20. My transistor radio always works (good, well) at the beach.

USING THE RIGHT PREPOSITION

l.24 *RIGHT PREPOSITION* Be sure to use the right preposition. Consult the following list.

at, by Use *by* when you mean "past," "by way of," or "by means of." Otherwise use *at*.

  We stopped *at* Duncan's house for the baseball equipment. We had to go *by* the firehouse. Ted went *by* bike.

at, in Use *in* to mean "within." Use *at* for a place thought of as a mere location on a map.

  We turned off the New Jersey Turnpike *at* Runnemede and arrived *at* Aunt Dot's in time for dinner. It was our first evening *in* New Jersey.

at, to Use *to* for motion, not *at*.

  We stayed *at* Aunt Dot's for two days and then went *to* Philadelphia.

different from *Different from* is always correct. *Different than*, however, is often used in informal speech and writing.

  PREFERRED Swimming in fresh water is quite different *from* swimming in the ocean.

To introduce a clause, *than* is a convenient and acceptable short-cut for *from*.

At the end of *Pygmalion*, Eliza speaks differently than she did at the beginning.

Or: At the end of *Pygmalion*, Eliza speaks differently from the way she did at the beginning.

from, off   Use *from* when speaking of persons: get the tickets *from* Fred, borrow a tie *from* Bud, buy a watermelon *from* the peddler. Most speakers and writers avoid "off of." When in doubt use *off* or *from*.

Ferd fell off ~~of~~ the float into the water.
> **from**
Borrow a cup of sugar ~~off of~~ Mrs. Thompson.

in, into   Use *into* ordinarily to express motion from one place to another. Use *in* when the meaning is "within."

Pat and Roy jumped from the second floor of the barn *into* the pile of hay on the floor. They rolled around *in* the hay for two or three minutes.

over, to   Don't use *over* for *to*.

Let's all go *to* (not *over*) my house and surprise Mother!

with, by   Don't use *by* for *with*.

Your plan for the picnic is all right *with* (not *by*) me.

PRACTICE 9   Using Correct Prepositions

Choose the word or expression in parentheses in accordance with the preceding suggestions.

A. 1. Didn't Mark Twain live (at, in) New York City for a number of years?
2. On Wednesday we were (at, to) the Museum of Science and Industry with the rest of the class.
3. Going to Glenn's house after the meeting is all right (by, with) us.
4. Clarice stopped (at, by) the Williams Inn overnight.
5. A swallow flew through the open window right (in, into) the Wentworths' living room.
6. In Indianapolis we stopped (at, by) the home of James Whitcomb Riley on Lockerbie Street.
7. Dad borrowed this quarter-inch drill (from, off, off of) Mr. Enlund.
8. Seven Presidents of the United States were born (at, in) Ohio.
9. Uncle Nate pushed the car from the driveway (in, into) the garage.

10. Tomorrow we're going (over, to) the Smoke Hole Caverns.
B. 1. The cat has scratched all the paint (off, off of) the legs of my desk.
    2. Is it all right (by, with) your mother if Howie goes to the farm with you?
    3. We bought a quart of maple syrup (from, off, off of) a Vermont farmer's wife.
    4. The whole fourth grade is coming (over, to) our house for my little brother's birthday party.
    5. A Canadian accent is quite different (from, than) an English accent.
    6. The All-American Turkey Show is different (from, than) the ordinary poultry exhibit.
    7. I'm going (over, to) Kenneth's house to help him with his new ramjet engine.
    8. While we were (at, to) the Cherokee Indian Fair, someone broke (in, into) our house.
    9. I borrowed *The Mystery Reader* (from, off, off of) Lloyd.
   10. We enjoyed every minute of our two weeks (at, in) the Great Smoky Mountains.

PRACTICE 10   Time Out for Review

As you copy the following sentences, capitalize and punctuate them. Correct the errors in spelling and in the use of adjectives, adverbs, and prepositions.

MT. RUSHMORE NATIONAL MEMORIAL

A. 1. "What did you most enjoy on your trip through united states? asked jean abbott.
    2. "I was impressed by the colors of bryce canyon the size of grand canyon, and the majesty of the rocky mountains," replied mr collins.
    3. "But there isn't scarcely a sight anywheres," he continued, that matches one view in south dakota."
    4. "What is that" jean asked?
    5. "From fifty mile away we could see the sculptured faces of four of our Presidents on mt rushmore," explained mr collins.
    6. "They looked beautifully in the morning sunlight," he added.
    7. Jean asked uncertain, "Where is those unusual statues"?
    8. "They are not too far from harney peak the highest peak east of the rockies," he declared.
    9. "Was you surprised?" she asked, "when you seen the size of the faces."
   10. "No a naturalist had wrote all about them in an interesting book, *your western parks*," replied mr collins.

11. "This here magazine article will tell you more than I can," he added.
12. Gutzon borglum the famous sculptor planned to carve from a cliffside the likenesses of four great men.
13. Borglum a man with gigantic dreams was born on march 25 1867.
14. He begun work on them profiles in 1927 and devoted fourteen years to this massive effort.
15. After his death in 1941 his close assistant, his son Lincoln put the finishing touches on the monuments.

B. 1. Everyone of the many tourists find it hard to grasp the size of these faces.
2. Each face it is sixty foot high, with facial dimensions to match.
3. Theodore Roosevelts mustache for example, is twenty foot wide.
4. A grown man can stand in Lincolns eye socket, which is more larger than many full-sized statues.
5. Egypts famous monument the sphinx has a head only half the size of rushmores washington.
6. The famous pyramids they were built in a hot barren dry climate.
7. Erosion don't present much of a problem in Egypt.
8. In south dakota rainfall as well as winter freezing present real hazards to the monuments.
9. After the winter has froze the water in many tiny cracks and has tore away tiny pieces, a "beauty squad" gives the monuments a facial. (The comma after *pieces* is correct.)
10. Every small crack in the features are repaired with a blend of dry white lead, linseed oil, and granite dust.
11. Them courageous face-lifters dangle perilously over the gigantic features of the four men.
12. Alfred Hitchcock the famous movie director must of always had an ambition to make a movie here.
13. He planned as the climax of one of his movies a chase over the gigantic features of mt rushmore.
14. In *north by northwest* he achieved his goal in a terrifying climax.
15. Within a relatively small area around rushmore you'll find the following attractions: badlands national monument, wind cave national park, custer state park, and jewel cave national monument.

28 *Using Pronouns*

The *girls* met the *boys*.   The *boys* met the *girls*.
We met *them*.   *They* met *us*.

The nouns in line 1 have the same form when they are used as subjects and when they are used as objects. But the pronouns in line 2 change their forms. Just a few pronouns in English cause a great deal of difficulty. Learn about these pronouns now and save yourself trouble later.

This chapter will help you to use correct pronouns. Take the diagnostic test to find out how much you know about pronouns.

DIAGNOSTIC TEST 9A Correct Pronouns

In each of the following which word or expression in parentheses is the correct or never-questioned one? On your paper write your choice after the number of the sentence.

1. (She and I, Her and me) have been collecting buttons for years.
2. One of the women from the mayor's office called you last week but didn't leave (her, their) name.
3. Sandra went to the movies with Dave and (I, me).
4. (We, Us) people need to take more interest in all levels of government.
5. Jim, let's you and (I, me)grab our rods and spend an afternoon at the trout stream.
6. Will someone be kind enough to lend me (her, their) pen?
7, 8. If the team had four or five players like (she, her) and (I, me), it would be in first place.
9. The girl on the white horse, in the center of the second line, is (she, her).
10. Interested and energetic people like Tony and (he, him) should join our track team.
11. Has either of the roads been resurfaced along (its, their) entire length?
12, 13. Juan sent (she, her) and (I, me) an invitation to his piano recital.
14, 15. Ms. Aronson asked (he, him) and (she, her) to work as reporters on the school newspaper.
16. Every group at the convention will get a chance to make (its, their) vote known.
17. Nancy, you and (I, me) have a bit of a misunderstanding.
18. Any individual who wants to submit (his, their) painting in the contest must do so by noon on Saturday.

19. Any boy scout still working on (his, their) life-saving merit badge will find summer camp to be a good place to complete it.
20. Every girl interested in figure skating should bring (her, their) skates to the rink next Friday evening.

PERSONAL PRONOUNS

The personal pronouns need watching.   There are several different forms for each person.   (See page 267.)

First person (the speaker) — *I, my, mine, me, we, our, ours, us*
Second person (the person spoken to) — *you, your, yours*
Third person (the person or thing spoken of) — *he, his, him, she, her, hers, it, its, they, their, theirs, them*

J.1   **PRONOUNS WITH AND**   If you have trouble with pronouns before and after *and,* say what you would say if the pronoun stood alone.

(He, Him) and Gil learned the swan dive.   (He learned.   Gil learned. He and Gil learned.)
Uncle Arch took Beverly and (I, me) to Freedomland.   (Took Beverly. Took me.   Took Beverly and me.)
Grandmother has planned a surprise for Stella and (he, him).   (For Stella.   For him.   For Stella and him.)
Last year Grandmother gave (her, she) and (I, me) a trip to Radio City.   (Gave her.   Gave me.   Gave her and me.)

PRACTICE 1   Using Correct Pronouns

Fill each blank with *I* or *me; he* or *him;* and *she* or *her*.   Supply three pronouns for each sentence.   Then say each sentence three times.   Do not write in this book.

1. Did you call Becky and ____?
2. Did Neil and ____ have tickets?
3. Mother and ____ waited at the airport.
4. Mr. Mott gave Pat and ____ a lift.
5. Is there room for Al and ____?
6. Charlie and ____ put on a skit.
7. Give Jeff and ____ the key.
8. Did you and ____ win?
9. Dan saw Meg and ____ downtown.
10. Did you and ____ go to the fair?
11. Will you talk to Ed and ____?
12. Show Jim and ____ the photos.
13. The class elected Joshua and ____.
14. Will you and ____ sing?

15. Send Guy and _____ postcards.
16. Ask Frank and _____.

PRACTICE 2   Using Correct Pronouns

Select the right pronoun of each pair in parentheses. Say what you would say if the pronoun stood alone.

A FISH STORY

Every Saturday last May, Dad and 1 (I, me) went fishing. A friend of Dad's had told 2 (he, him) and 3 (I, me) about a well-stocked trout stream in the Tuscarora Mountains near Blain. Dad set our alarm for five o'clock and packed a big lunch for 4 (he, him) and 5 (I, me) then 6 (we, us) both got an early start.

One Saturday Bud Askins joined Dad and 7 (I, me). The fellows in our gang call 8 (he, him), Dick Bryant, and 9 (I, me) the "fishing fools." Shortly before five-thirty Bud met Dad and 10 (I, me) at our house. We stowed our fishing tackle in the rear of the station wagon and climbed into the front seat. A shout from Mom stayed Dad's foot on the accelerator. 11 (Her, She) and Aunt Jane ran out with our fishing rods.

"Did I ever tell you about fishing in the Gulf of Mexico?" Bud asked Dad and 12 (I, me). "Last Christmas, Mother, Dad, and 13 (I, me) visited my grandparents in St. Petersburg. Dad and 14 (I, me) went fishing almost every day. One day Mother went with us. For a long time 15 (her, she) and 16 (I, me) didn't catch anything, and Dad began teasing 17 (her, she) and 18 (I, me). In a minute 19 (he, him) and 20 (I, me) saw Mother's rod bend. Both Dad and 21 (I, me) shouted instructions. Then we watched Mother wage a furious battle with a marlin and finally land it. I took a picture of the fish with 22 (her, she) and 23 (he, him) standing beside it."

"Show us the picture," chorused Dad and 24 (I, me).

"I can't," replied Bud. "That fish was so big the picture is too heavy to carry in my pocket."

Last Saturday, Dad, Bud, and 25 (I, me) didn't catch any fish as large as the marlin, but we had a lot of fun and had fresh trout for our Sunday dinner.

PRACTICE 3   Using Correct Pronouns

Make each italicized word in the following sentences a compound pronoun with *and*. Use the correct forms.

EXAMPLE   Mary waved to *us* in the supermarket.
          Mary waved to her and me in the supermarket.

1. Dad gave *us* good advice on trout fishing.
2. *We* enjoyed the band concert last evening.
3. The sophomore led *us* to the new music room.
4. Mr. Martinson gave *them* good advice.
5. *They* were proud of their marks on the algebra test.

Subjects and Predicate Pronouns

J.2 *SUBJECTS AND PREDICATE PRONOUNS* Use *I, we, he, she,* and *they* as subjects and as predicate pronouns. (See Appendix.)

He and Barnaby are the top spellers in Mr. Knowlton's room. (*He* is one subject of the verb *are.*)

We girls are planning an old-fashioned quilting bee. (If you say the sentence without *girls,* you see why *we* is correct.)

Hugh Custer is a better swimmer than *I.* (Finish the comparison: Hugh Custer is a better swimmer than *I* am.)

I am no longer as tall as *he.* (I am no longer as tall as *he* is tall.)

Where's Curly? That's *he* in the plaid shirt. (A predicate pronoun is needed. That = he.)

PRACTICE 4 Pronouns as Subjects and as Predicate Pronouns

Choose the correct pronoun in each sentence. Say the correct sentences aloud till they sound right to you.

A. 1. Jean, Diane, and (her, she) were lost in the Maze of Mirrors.
    2. (Us, We) three sailed the *Sea Daisy* to Fir Point and back.
    3. Leslie is three years older than (he, him).
    4. (Us, We) city boys were exhausted after one morning's work on the farm.
    5. (Us, We) band members are practicing for the Veterans Day parade.
    6. Was that (her, she) with Hazel and Marian?
    7. (Her, She) and Naomi Foster are hostesses for the Strawberry Festival at church.
    8. Jack is almost as tall as (her, she).
    9. Yes, Norma is a better diver than (I, me).
    10. Is that (he, him) or Tony at the popcorn concession?

B. 1. The other senator was much older than (he, him).
    2. The leaders of the French expedition were (he, him) and Louis Joliet.
    3. (Them, They) and the Wallaces have gone to the rodeo at Pendleton.
    4. (Us, We) judges had a hard time picking the best poster for the Spring Festival.

5. Do students in European schools really study harder than (us, we)?
6. Is that (he, him) on the palomino?
7. (Us, We) students made fifty sandwiches and three gallons of lemonade for the class picnic.
8. Which dancer is Cecelia Morris?   Is that (her, she) on the right end of the first row?
9. (Her, She) and (I, me) were eager to join the Camera Club.
10. (Us, We) boys are practicing every day to get ready for the swimming meets.

Objects

J.3   *OBJECTS*   Use *me, us, him, her,* and *them* as objects of verbs and of prepositions.   (See Case in the Appendix.)

Mr. Lynch congratulated *us* boys on our mimeographed newspaper. (Omit *boys* and say the sentence.   Mr. Lynch congratulated *us*.)

Let's you and *me* act as campaign managers for Toby Victor.   (Let's = let us.   *Us* means you and me.   *Us* and *me* are object forms.)

Girls like *her* should major in mathematics.   (An object of the preposition *like* is needed.)

This agreement is between you and *me* only.   (An object of the preposition *between* is needed.)

PRACTICE 5   Using Correct Pronouns

Choose the correct pronoun in each sentence.   Give your reason for each choice.   Repeating the right sentences will help you to get into the habit of using correct pronouns.

A.   1. In Provincetown, Dad's going to rent a tandem bicycle for you and (I, me).
2. Let's you and (I, me) practice underwater swimming this afternoon.
3. During the storm (he, him) and (I, me) were out in a rowboat on Barnegat Bay.
4. A package just came for Walter and (I, me) from New Orleans.
5. The figure in the World War I uniform, at the far right of the photograph, is (he, him).
6. Between you and (I, me), Mike will never make the track team.
7. After the meeting Mr. Reynolds praised (us, we) scouts.
8. Let's you and (I, me) paint the rowboat red and white.
9. Who is that blonde girl sitting between Larry and (he, him)?
10. Miss Troop warned (us, we) girls about the tide at Willets Cove.

B.   1. (Us, We) junior lifeguards are on duty at the pool every afternoon.
2. Gloria's parents invited (us, we) girls to their summer cottage for a weekend.

3. It was (he, him) who designed the Guggenheim Museum.
4. Miss Dumont is giving (us, we) dancers white-and-gold costumes for the Centennial Pageant.
5. Put the picnic basket between Sally and (I, me).
6. (Us, We) boys took a bus to the Franklin Park Zoo.
7. Landlubbers like you and (I, me) should stick to dry land.
8. (Us, We) boys ran for our lives when we saw the enormous bull.
9. Let's you and (I, me) start a Folk Dance Club.
10. Isn't Moira going with (us, we) girls to the hockey game?

PRACTICE 6 Using Pronouns in Sentences   **W**

In sentences of your own, use these expressions correctly and explain how each is used in its sentence.

1. us boys	6. she and I	11. you and me
2. Jill and I	7. Doc and he	12. you and I
3. him and me	8. He and Mr. Drew	13. we players
4. she and Jan	9. her and Val	14. Mother, Dad, and I
5. Alex and me	10. we girls	15. us members

Watch These Pronouns

J.4 *PRONOUN MANNERS* When you speak of another and yourself, mention the other person first as a matter of courtesy.

Les and I
~~I and Les~~ were chosen for the vocabulary quiz.
                    Carol and me
Mr. Young told ~~me and Carol~~ about his experiences in Kenya.

J.5 *PRONOUNS WITH SELF* *Self* (or *selves*) is sometimes added to a pronoun: *myself, ourselves, yourself, yourselves, himself, herself, itself,* and *themselves.* These words are called "compound personal pronouns." They are also called "reflexive" and "intensive pronouns".

Although compound personal pronouns usually do not cause trouble in speaking and writing, three of them need watching.

1. *Hisself* and *theirselves* are not good English.

With considerable annoyance Dad said he'd do the job ~~hisself~~. **himself**

Did the twins make ~~theirselves~~ breakfast? **themselves**

2. Ordinarily, do not use *myself* as a substitute for *I*.

My two brothers and ~~myself~~ went on a ski weekend to Mt. Mansfield. **I**

J.6 THEM *MISUSED* Do not misuse *them*, an object form, as a subject. (See also page 378.)

~~Them~~ are our finest roses. **They**

~~Them~~ are the oddest foreign cars I've ever seen. **Those**

PRACTICE 7 Using Correct Pronouns

Choose the correct word or words in parentheses in each sentence.

1. Carl, Vannie, and (I, myself) went bobsledding near Iron Mountain.
2. Alan is getting (himself, hisself) a Coke from the machine.
3. Tina and (I, myself) are to be co-hostesses at the Turnabout Hop.
4. Can you lend (me and Richie, Richie and me) two tennis rackets?
5. Sandy and Lisa Jones have bought (theirselves, themselves) matching raincoats.
6. (I and my sister, My sister and I) are making a ruffled skirt for our vanity table.
7. Jon cut (himself, hisself) with the carving knife.
8. (Them, Those) are the juiciest peaches we've had this summer.
9. Lefty and Roger ducked under an underpass to protect (theirselves, themselves) from the driving rain.
10. (Them, Those) are Rosemary's pearl earrings.

PRACTICE 8 Choosing Correct Pronouns

Number your paper 1 to 15. After each number write the sentence correctly. Then explain your choice. Read the correct sentences aloud until they sound right to you.

EXAMPLE Give the sandwiches to Bix and (I, me).
Give the sandwiches to Bix and me. object of preposition

1. Walk between Saul and (I, me).
2. Don't forget (us, we) boys.
3. (I and Peg, Peg and I) dug for clams.

4. The man now speaking is (he, him).
5. The prize money was divided among (us, we) three.
6. (Them, Those) are Irish wolfhounds.
7. That was (he, him) on the carnival float.
8. Let's you and (I, me) try the high dive.
9. Tell (us, we) boys a story.
10. Ben and (I, myself) cleaned up.
11. The governor (himself, hisself) spoke.
12. It's between Ida and (her, she).
13. (Helen and I, I and Helen) won.
14. (Us, We) boys just arrived.
15. The guests enjoyed (theirselves, themselves).

PRACTICE 9 Choosing Correct Pronouns

Read the following story. Choose the correct word in each pair of parentheses, and show that each pronoun you choose is right.

WHAT'S IN A NAME?

My troubles all began when Frank and Mike, the ten-year-old twins across the street, got a half-grown spaniel pup for their birthday. After the twins had showed him to my family and 1 (I, me), Frank said, "Ted, 2 (us, we) boys have decided to call the dog after you. Is it all right if Mike and 3 (I, me) name him 'Ted'?"

I was flattered, and the twins looked so pleased with 4 (theirselves, themselves) that I couldn't have refused anyway. When my parents and 5 (I, myself) were talking about it later, however, Dad told Mother and 6 (I, me) that he didn't think the idea was a very good one.

"Why?" Mother and 7 (I, me) asked, surprised.

Dad grinned at 8 (us, we) two and said, "You'll see why."

We saw why soon enough. The next afternoon I heard the twins calling my name loudly. Thinking one of them must have hurt 9 (himself, hisself), I yelled, "What's wrong?"

Frank shouted back, "Mike and 10 (I, me) aren't calling *you*, Ted. We're calling Ted, the *dog*."

Later on, at the dog's feeding time, guess who answered the dinner call! Right — the dog and 11 (I, me) both came on the run. The next day things were even worse. When my mother called me in to lunch, the dog showed up too. 12 (Us, We) two collided at my front door and went down in a heap. Mother laughed at 13 (he, him) and 14 (I, me) but said, "Just between you and 15 (I, me), I'm glad you're bigger than 16 (he, him). Otherwise you could have been hurt!"

After two more collisions between my namesake and 17 (I, me), I got smarter. I stopped answering to my own name. This solution worked until last Saturday, when Paul Bartlett and 18 (I, myself) had planned a breakfast cookout in the woods. My alarm clock didn't go off, however, and by the time I woke up 19 (he, him) and his father had driven away.

"Dad and 20 (I, me) called outside your window," Paul told me later. "21 (Us, We) two couldn't understand why you didn't answer."

"Oh, no!" I groaned. I had heard 22 (he, him) and his father but, half asleep, I'd thought it was the neighbors calling the other Ted.

So I had a long-overdue talk with the twins. 23 (Them, They) and 24 (I, me) agreed that something had to be done. "Frank and 25 (I, me) can't change Ted's name, though," Mike objected. "It might upset a young dog like 26 (he, him)."

I gave in. The dog's name is still Ted.

As for 27 (I, me) — well, from now on, just call me "Theodore."

AGREEMENT WITH ANTECEDENT

J.7 ANTECEDENT The word for which a pronoun stands is its antecedent.

Dogs perspire through *their* foot pads. (*Dogs* is the antecedent of *their*.)

Take out every St. Lawrence Seaway stamp in your possession and examine *it* for an inverted center.

J.8 NUMBER Make a pronoun agree with its antecedent in number.

After the rebuttal our leading debater had lost *his* confidence. (Singular antecedent; singular pronoun)

After the rebuttal our three debaters had lost *their* confidence. (Plural antecedent; plural pronoun)

J.9 OR, NOR Use singular pronouns to refer to two or more singular antecedents joined by *or* or *nor*.

Either Loretta or Katherine will have *her* report ready. (Either Loretta will have *her* report ready, or Katherine will have *her* report ready.)

Neither Keith nor William has sold *his* sports car.

J.10 EACH, EVERY In formal English always use singular pronouns to refer to *each, every, either, neither, many a, a person, one,* and compounds of *body* and *one.*

Every man must do *his* share of the work.

Every girl completed *her* dress in time for the Freshman Sing.

Many people criticize the English language because it usually uses the masculine pronoun *his* in sentences like "Everyone carried his own pack" even though *everyone* might include girls as well as boys, women as well as men. Consequently many feel that in a sentence like this *his or her* or *her* can be used just as well as *his*. Since usage seems to be changing on this point, you and your teacher may wish to decide which you prefer. Then you may wish to use whichever seems appropriate in the material you are writing.

In informal speaking and writing the plural pronoun is acceptable with a word like *everybody*, when the pronoun clearly refers to more than one and is at some distance from the antecedent. Since your reader may consider such a usage careless, however, it is usually better to rewrite such a sentence using an unquestionably plural antecedent.

ACCEPTABLE   Every boy on the soccer team brought *their* parents to the first game.

BETTER   All boys on the soccer team brought *their* parents to the first game.

ACCEPTABLE   Each one of the candidates promised *their* support to the membership drive.

BETTER   All the candidates promised *their* support to the membership drive.

PRACTICE 10   Making Pronouns Agree with Antecedents

Choose the correct or never-questioned word or expression in each sentence. What is the antecedent of each pronoun chosen?

A. 1. The Rose Bowl games, with the elaborate ceremonies surrounding (it, them), are always held on New Year's Day.
2. Motorists should buy tickets for their cars at the ferry entrance before driving (it, them) onto the boat.
3. Neither of the girls received (her, their) Senior Lifesaving certificate.
4. Has every puppy been given (its, their) meal?
5. Neither Kate nor Sue got (her, their) basketball letter this year.
6. If any boy on the track team needs a collapsible drinking cup, I can let (him, them) have one.

7. Either Lloyd or Morris will bring (his, their) guitar.

8. I prefer jobs like mowing lawns and shoveling snow because I get paid well for doing (it, them).

B. 1. Every girl in the Camera Club should choose five of (her, their) best pictures for the club exhibit.

2. Neither Stu nor Chick has (his, their) badminton racket here.

3. At the picnic every mosquito left (its, their) mark on my tender skin.

4. Ned took a lot of luggage to his summer quarters and had trouble getting (it, them) off the train.

5. The delivery boy brought the groceries to the front door and left (it, them) there on the stoop.

6. Not one of the kittens cleaned (its, their) dirty paws.

7. Will someone lend me (her, their) skirt?

8. Neither Dolores nor Virginia remembered to return (her, their) locker key.

VAGUE ANTECEDENT

J.11   NOUN NEEDED   Supply a noun if it is needed for clearness.

NOUN SUPPLIED   The next time the children come home with wet sweaters,
     the sweaters
.   please don't hang ~~them~~ up by the necks.

SENTENCE REWORDED   The next time the children come home soaking wet, please don't hang their sweaters up by the necks.

NOUN SUPPLIED   Although I make few spares and fewer strikes, I enjoy
bowling
~~it~~ just the same.

J.12   PRONOUN SHIFT   Do not use *you* or *your* when another pronoun is clearly needed.

Can you tell me whether I should apply for a summer job now, or
     I
whether ~~you~~ should wait till June.

PRACTICE 11   Making Sentences Clear

Revise each sentence to make its meaning clear. If a corrected sentence contains *he, him, she, her, it, they,* or *them,* draw an arrow from the pronoun to its antecedent. Do not write in this book.

EXAMPLE   When Achilles and Hector finally met on the battlefield, ~~he~~ **Achilles**

slew his enemy.

1. We tried to call Joanne five minutes ago, but it was busy.
2. The neighbors took their new stove out of the packing crate and gave it to my little sister to play house in.
3. The mule kicked Zeke on the leg as he unharnessed him.
4. Remove the old bandage from your arm and throw it into the fire.
5. When the teacher announces the word to be checked, open it at once to the proper page.
6. Anyone can learn to swim if you try hard enough.
7. I decided to become a chemist when I first studied it in high school.
8. Almost everyone likes to read if it is interesting.
9. A family of black ants attacked the cupcakes before we could taste them.
10. I like sailing because you get plenty of sun. Why do you like sailing?

PRACTICE 12   Using Correct Pronouns

Correct or improve the faulty sentences and give a reason for every change you make. Three of the sentences are correct.

1. Without you and he for callers the square dances wouldn't be nearly as much fun.
2. Mario told Judy and I amusing stories about his childhood in Rome.
3. Last summer we senior campers went on a four-day pack trip.
4. Me and you actually deserved better grades on that science test.
5. Four-year-old Dickie dresses hisself but can't tie his own shoelaces.
6. Dad and I repainted the garage last weekend.
7. Did every boy fill their canteen before leaving Buffalo Springs?
8. Nan's brother gave her and I his sight-seeing map of Chicago.
9. Mr. Dale blamed we boys for the broken hedges.
10. Ellen and myself are planning to spend next summer on a Wyoming ranch.
11. Last Wednesday me and him explored Robber Lewis's cave.
12. In a democracy everyone has a right to express their opinions.
13. Every scout in our troop did his best to win merit badges.

14. Divide the rest of the watermelon between you and he.
15. Let's you and I run the popcorn stand at the track meet.

MASTERY TEST 9B Correct Pronouns

In each of the following which word or expression in parentheses is the correct or never-questioned one?   On your paper write your choice after the number of the sentence.

1. Dad sent (he, him) and Paulo a set of rock-collecting equipment.
2. Neither Dolores nor Candy has had (her, their) turn at bat yet.
3. That is (he, him) leaning against the car.
4. The coach gave special help to Nancy and (I, me).
5. The policeman told Ted and (I, me) to report any suspicious people we might see.
6. Hard workers like you and (I, me) have to learn to relax more often.
7. The polar bear at the zoo took one look at (we, us) girls and yawned.
8. No one may walk across the gym floor with (her, their) shoes on.
9. How would you like to clean up the yard with Nancy and (I, me)?
10. The principal hired Fred and (I, me) to take tickets at the annual play.
11. Has every member paid (his, their) dues for the year?
12. Mrs. Freeman gave Tom and (I, me) a glass of iced tea.
13. Neither Bill nor Fred submitted (his, their) report on time.
14. Wanda and (I, me) decided to work together on the science project.
15. Later in the evening Bob and (I, me) had to look at the slides my mother and father had taken.
16. There were no finalists except Anne, Peter, and (I, me).
17. Susan Cortez and (I, myself) represented our class at last night's meeting of the hospital volunteers.
18. The coach insisted that each boy memorize (his, their) plays.
19. A beaver works feverishly to build (its, their) dam.
20. Neither Ms. Harnett nor (we, us) students understood the judge's decision.

PRACTICE 13 Time Out for Review

As you copy the following sentences, capitalize and punctuate them correctly and correct all the errors.

A LESSON IN HORSEMANSHIP

1. Last columbus day dad took bob johnson jerry block bud simpkins and I on a all-day visit to my uncles dairy farm near libertyville

2. Besides the dairy barn the other outstanding features of uncle jims farm is several acres of corn and wheat a huge garden a old-fashioned swimming hole and a barnyard with chickens pigs and horses

3. We arrived at 7:30 a m and was met by uncle Jim aunt betty my cousins judy and nora and mr hopkins uncle jims assistant manager

4. After a big farm breakfast of hot biscuits and ham and eggs the other boys and me was took on a tour by mr hopkins

5. Judy and nora they come along on the tour with us boys

6. At the dairy barn bud simpkins the show-off in our group remarked these here hereford cattle look like good milkers

7. My cousins giggled to theirselves at buds statement

8. Mr Hopkins replied them are jersey cows not herefords

9. The vegetable garden and aunt bettys flower garden was next

10. There wasn't no vegetables left except potatos pumpkins and a half a dozen overripe tomatos

11. Bud the know-it-all he seen the tomatos and says I and my father growed much better-looking tomatos than them last summer

12. Them tomatoes of yours probably don't look so wonderfully in october though objected judy

13. Don't mind him I whispered to she and nora

14, 15. Alone with we boys he acts all right I explained he's only showing off for you girls

16. Well me and nora aren't impressed judy answered

17. The shed for the horses and pigpen are next mr hopkins announced

18. He led us in the horse shed and showed us the two horses

19. Bud to judy and noras disgust begun talking like a champion rider

20, 21. May we ride them two horses asked bud a good rider like I should have the fastest one

22. Prince the black one is more faster judy said very sweet

23. Why don't you ride him she continued and try jumping the stream

24. In a half a minute bud had sprang on the horse and had rode off

25. Him and the horse was headed at a fast trot toward the pasture stream

26. At the streams brink however prince stopped sudden set down and shook bud into the water

27, 28. Oh I should of told you one other fact judy laughed that there horse has already throwed five people into that stream

29. Bud went back to the house with she and nora and borrowed some dry clothes off of uncle jim

30. After that him and the girls declared a truce and got along good together the rest of the day

29 *Parts of Speech*

What part of speech is *slow?* Before you answer, look at these sentences.

1. Buddy took a *slow* train from Boston. (Adjective — modifies the noun *train*)
2. To run a good cross-country race, *slow* your pace a bit. (Verb— gives a command)
3. Go *slow* in the school zone. (Adverb—modifies the verb *go*)

USE IN THE SENTENCE

To determine part of speech, see how the word acts in a sentence. A word becomes a "part of speech" only when it is used in a sentence.

K.1 *PART OF SPEECH* To find what part of speech a word is in a sentence, ask, "What does the word do in this sentence?"

PARTS OF SPEECH	USES OF WORDS
verb	maker of statement, question, command
noun, pronoun	name and substitute for name
adjective, adverb	modifier
preposition, conjunction	connective
interjection	strong feeling

OTHER CLUES

"The snark was a boojum."

In this famous line from Lewis Carroll's "The Hunting of the Snark," we decide that *snark* is a noun used as subject of *was.* We decide that *boojum* is a noun used as predicate nominative. We can determine part of speech even though we are not sure just what a snark or a boojum is. We realize that there are clues other than meaning.

STRUCTURE CLUES — PARTS OF SPEECH

Three excellent clues to part of speech are (1) word endings, (2) location in the sentence, and (3) signal words.

ENDINGS

Nouns, verbs, adjectives, and adverbs have suffixes that provide helpful clues to part of speech. Common noun suffixes are *ance*, *hood*, *ity*, *ment*, *ness*, and *tion* (*defiance*, *statehood*, *superiority*, *filament*, *goodness*, *constitution*). Common verb suffixes are *en*, *fy*, *ate*, *ize* (*soften*, *magnify*, *regulate*, *criticize*). Adjective and adverb suffixes are shown on pages 353, 358.

SENTENCE PATTERN

Note that in each of the following sentences the missing part of speech is clear from the sentence pattern.

1. The ____ opened the ____ and discovered a ____ on the ____. (Nouns needed)
2. A ____ lion bore down upon the ____ antelope. (Adjectives needed)
3. Larry waited ____ for the first pitch and swung ____. (Adverbs needed)
4. The snow ____ the ground and ____ transportation difficult. (Verbs needed)
5. Alice ____ Pudge played a set of tennis ____ went swimming. (Conjunctions needed)
6. Go ____ the store and buy a loaf ____ wheat bread. (Prepositions needed)

SIGNAL WORDS

Certain words signal that certain parts of speech will follow. *A*, *an*, *the* tell us a noun will follow. Auxiliaries like *may*, *will*, *should* signal verbs. Prepositions like *to*, *for*, or *by* signal nouns or pronouns.

The __1__ will __2__ for __3__. (1—noun, 2—verb, 3—noun or pronoun needed)

All these aids should help determine part of speech. The final test of part of speech is use in a sentence.

PRACTICE 1 Supplying Parallel Parts of Speech

Complete the empty boxes with the correct words.

EXAMPLE

NOUN	VERB	ADJECTIVE	ADVERB
softness	soften	soft	softly

	NOUN	VERB	ADJECTIVE	ADVERB
1.	fright			frightfully
2.				continually
3.		beautify		
4.			enjoyable	
5.				brightly

PRACTICE 2 Identifying Part of Speech by Sentence Placement V

Try your skill. What part of speech will complete each blank in the following sentences? Complete each sentence with meaningful words.

1. ____ to the ____.
2. The ____ sailboat glided ____ along the ____.
3. The ____ was ____ unhappy at the ____ news.
4. The rocket ____ from the launching pad ____ sped into the sky.
5. The majority ____ the winners ____ the spelling bee are excellent English students.

SAME FORM

Although suffixes are clues to part of speech, some words are used as different parts of speech without any change in form. The word *quiet*, for example, may be a verb (*quiet* the puppy), a noun (the *quiet* of the forest), or an adjective (a *quiet* hour).

NOUNS AND ADJECTIVES

Some words that are usually nouns may be used as adjectives.

NOUN Collins found a magnificent quartz *crystal* in the old Ellenville lead mine. (*Crystal* is the object of the verb *found*.)

ADJECTIVE The water in Emerald Pool had a *crystal* clearness. (*Crystal* modifies the noun *clearness*.)

PRACTICE 3 Recognizing Nouns and Adjectives V

Tell the part of speech of each italicized word and explain why it is a noun or an adjective.

1, 2. *Glass* brick is often used in construction.   Many kinds of *glass* are popular building materials.
3, 4. Do you call a *radio* engineer when your *radio* fails?
5, 6. The mason patched the *cement* wall with mortar *cement*.
7, 8. *Steel* output depends upon the demand for *steel*.
9, 10. A *secret* grows with additional *secret* information.

PRONOUNS AND ADJECTIVES

Some words, like *this, that, these, those, each, some, many, what, any, both,* and *either,* are used both as adjectives and as pronouns.

ADJECTIVE   *Many* candidates filed petitions.   (*Many* modifies *candidates.*)
PRONOUN   *Many* were disappointed.   (*Many* is a substitute for a name.)

PRACTICE 4   Recognizing Pronouns and Adjectives

Tell the part of speech of each italicized word and explain why it is a pronoun or an adjective.

1, 2. *Those* boys took *some* apples.
3, 4. *Those* took *some.*

5, 6. *What* breed is *that* roan pony?
7, 8. *What* is *that?*

ADVERBS AND PREPOSITIONS

What part of speech is *below* in sentence 1?   In sentence 2?

1. Go *below* before the storm.   (Adverb — has no object and modifies the verb *go.*)
2. Go *below* decks quickly!   (Preposition — joins its object *decks* to the verb *go.*)

K.2   *PREPOSITION AND ADVERB*   A preposition always has an object.   An adverb never has an object.

PRACTICE 5   Recognizing Prepositions and Adverbs

Is the italicized word in each sentence an adverb or a preposition? How do you know?

1. We walked *along* swiftly.
2. We walked *along* the lake.
3. A plane flew *over*.
4. A plane flew *over* our house.

5. George slept *near* the fire.
6. The wolves drew *near*.
7. Linda picked Rex *up*.
8. Linda shooed Rex *up* the steps.

NOUNS AND VERBS

What part of speech is *mint* in sentence 1? In sentence 2?

1. We visited the Denver *mint*. (*Mint* is the object of the verb *visited*. It is a noun.)
2. Did the government *mint* enough pennies this month? (*Mint* with its helper *did* helps to ask a question. It is a verb.)

PRACTICE 6 Recognizing Nouns and Verbs

Explain why each italicized word is a noun or a verb.

1. We visited the *exchange*.
2. *Exchange* your dictionary for a college edition.
3. That was a good *try*.
4. *Try* again.

5. Cactus plants store *water*.
6. *Water* cactus plants weekly.
7. I'll *race* you to the tree.
8. Who won that *race?*

PRACTICE 7 Recognizing Parts of Speech

Using the preceding sentences as examples, tell the part of speech of each italicized word in the following sentences and explain what the word does in the sentence.

1, 2. *Turn left*.
3, 4. A *left turn* will bring you there.
5, 6. *Both* would like *some*.

7, 8. *Both* girls would like *some* pie.
9, 10. Susan cut *off* the *rose*.
11, 12. Susan cut the *rose* blossom *off* the bush.

PRACTICE 8 Using a Word as Different Parts of Speech   WV

As what parts of speech can each of the following words be used? Refer to a good dictionary. Then for each word write original sentences to illustrate all its uses.

EXAMPLE

mind — noun, verb
The human *mind* is an incredibly complicated instrument.
Angie, *mind* Cassie for me a moment.

beneath	fast	home	level	over
cry	foster	inside	major	well

WORDS AT WORK

K.3 *PRONUNCIATION* Some words are pronounced differently when they are used as different parts of speech: reCORD (verb) and RECord (noun).

K.4 *WORDS WITH DOUBLE ROLES* Some words perform two jobs at the same time.

Once a week I pick up a pile of papers and handle my older *brother's* paper route.

Brother's plays a double role. It modifies *route* like an adjective. It is modified by *older* like a noun. It performs both jobs at the same time. There are six common groups of words that play double roles.

1. The *possessive noun* acts like a noun and an adjective. It is diagramed like an adjective.

A domestic *cat's* eyes are usually green. (*Domestic* modifies *cat's; cat's* modifies *eyes.*)

2. The *possessive pronoun* acts like a pronoun and an adjective. It is diagramed like an adjective. (See page 354.)

Nell did *her* homework. (*Her* modifies *homework* like an adjective. It also has an antecedent, *Nell*, like a pronoun.)

3. The *adverbial noun* acts like a noun and an adverb. It is diagramed like a prepositional phrase. (See Appendix.)

Max threw the shot forty *feet.* (*Feet* modifies *threw* like an adverb. It has an adjective modifier *forty*, like a noun.)

4. The *participle* acts like a verb and an adjective. (See pages 410–418.)

5. The *gerund* acts like a verb and a noun.   (See pages 410–418.)

6. The *infinitive* acts like a verb and a noun, a verb and an adjective, or a verb and an adverb.   (See pages 410–418.)

PRACTICE 9   Studying Words Playing Double Roles

Which words in the following sentences play a double role?

1. I visited my new friend's house.
2. He lives two miles from town.
3. On Saturday afternoon he introduced me to his father and his older sister's friend.
4. We talked about the town's athletic program.
5. The new boy's father will manage one of the Little League teams next season.

PRACTICE 10   Recognizing Parts of Speech

Copy the following sentences, skipping a line after each line you write.   Then, using the following abbreviations, tell what part of speech each word is.   (A compound like *St. Lawrence Seaway* is one noun.)   Write the abbreviation above the word.

n. — noun	**v.** — verb	**prep.** — preposition
pr. — pronoun	**adv.** — adverb	**conj.** — conjunction
adj. — adjective		

THE ST. LAWRENCE SEAWAY

1. Shippers in the Midwest have always looked longingly toward the Atlantic Ocean.   2. The Great Lakes have always had a large amount of traffic.   3. Large steamers sailed fairly easily from Duluth to Detroit.   4. A major problem has been the linkage of this traffic on the lakes with the ports of the East Coast and of Europe.   5. The rapids of the St. Lawrence River prevented effective passage between the inland ports and the mouth of the St. Lawrence.   6. The completion of the St. Lawrence Seaway connected Chicago with the sea and opened the Midwest directly to oceangoing ships.

7. A ship can now sail from the western end of Lake Superior to any port in the world.   8. Most oceangoing vessels can sail successfully through the Seaway.   9. The most important part of the Seaway is a stretch from Montreal to Lake Ontario.   10. Here a series of locks raises and lowers the huge ships like toys.   11. Because of tremendous demand the Seaway will enlarge all facilities in the future.   (*Because of* is one part of speech.)   12. This avenue of water has become an artery to the heart of America.

MASTERY TEST 10A   Parts of Speech

Copy the following sentences, skipping every other line.   Then, using the following abbreviations, tell what part of speech each word is.   Write the abbreviation above the word.   There are fifty words.

n.—noun   **v.**—verb   **prep.**—preposition
pr.—pronoun   **adv.**—adverb   **conj.**—conjunction
adj.—adjective

EXAMPLE

   n.   **v. adv. adj. conj. v.**   **adv.**   **v.**   **prep. adj.**   **n.**
Snakes are not slimy but are actually covered with dry scales.

1. People depended upon the ferry for transportation across the river.
2. Branches of the tree shaded the house and the garden.
3. My grandfather had never left the farm before last year.
4. The airplane delivers food but does not transport heavy items.
5. During the first inning the pitcher had a little trouble.

MASTERY TEST 10B   Parts of Speech

Copy the following sentences, skipping every other line.   Then, using the following abbreviations, tell what part of speech each word is.   Write the abbreviation above the word.   There are fifty words.

n.—noun   **v.**—verb   **prep.**—preposition
pr.—pronoun   **adv.**—adverb   **conj.**—conjunction
adj.—adjective

1. The weather was poor during the first week of August.
2. The explorers struggled exhaustedly toward the Pole against icy winds.
3. Lois easily opened the bottle of pickles and served them.
4. The herd of shaggy buffaloes thundered across the grassy plain.
5. The mountain defeated the young climbers on their first attempt.

30 *Verbals: Participles, Gerunds, and Infinitives*

Chapter 29 described six groups of words that perform different jobs at the same time (pages 407–408). In this chapter we study three of those groups more closely: participles, gerunds, and infinitives. These three are called "verbals."

In grammar *verbal* means "like a verb." Verbals add conciseness and maturity to expression. Though verbals cannot make sentences by themselves, they can take objects and adverbial modifiers like verbs. They also act like adjectives, adverbs, and nouns.

PARTICIPLES: VERBALS USED AS ADJECTIVES

L.1 *PARTICIPLE* A participle is a form of the verb that is used as an adjective. A participle is *part* adjective and *part* verb.

Many participles end in *ing* or *ed*. The participles of the regular verb *to call* are: *calling, called, having called, being called, having been called*. The participles of the irregular verb *to speak* are: *speaking, spoken, having spoken, being spoken,* and *having been spoken*. (See Appendix.)

L.2 *TEST FOR PARTICIPLE* To find what word a participle modifies, ask the question "Who?" or "What?" about the participle.

We could hear the planes *circling* overhead, *waiting* to land. (What circling? Planes. What waiting? Planes. *Circling* and *waiting* are participles modifying *planes*.)

A cup *engraved* with the winner's name will be the top prize. (What engraved? Cup. *Engraved* is a participle modifying the noun *cup*.)

L.3 *VERB AND PARTICIPLE* When an *ing* or *ed* word is joined to a helping verb, it is regularly part of the verb.

410

The Indian pottery *discovered* near West Islip beach was probably buried there about four hundred years ago. (*Was buried* is the verb. *Discovered* is a participle modifying *pottery*.)

PRACTICE 1   Distinguishing between Verbs and Participles

Copy each sentence. Underline the subject once and the verb twice. Draw a line from every participle to the word it modifies.

EXAMPLE   The souvenirs labeled in French were made in England.
1. The elm growing in our yard was planted by my grandfather.
2. Any boy winning a race will be given a medal.
3. Finding the way clear, the cyclist sped along much faster.
4. Having looked everywhere for the tickets, I have given up the search.

PRACTICE 2   Finding Participles

In the following sentences find the participles. What noun does each participle modify?

BRANDEIS UNIVERSITY

1. Brandeis University, located in Waltham, Massachusetts, was chartered as a nonsectarian liberal arts university. 2. Founded by American Jews but welcoming students of any race or religion, Brandeis has no official chaplain. 3. Among the modernistic buildings erected on the 260-acre campus stretching along the Charles River are three chapels — one Jewish, one Catholic, and one Protestant. 4. Constantly exposed to ideals of freedom and social justice, students become eager for social action.

5. Stressing mental development rather than vocational skills, Brandeis quickly won recognition for scholarship. 6. The undergraduate school of arts and sciences, founded in 1948, was accredited in two years. 7. In 1950 a graduate school, offering degrees in fourteen areas of study, was established. 8. The biochemistry department, headed by a leading scientist, is one of the country's best. 9. Recognizing Brandeis' academic excellence, Phi Beta Kappa granted a charter in 1962. 10. Attracting eminent scholars to its faculty, Brandeis encourages experimentation.

L.4   *PUNCTUATING PARTICIPIAL PHRASES* Use a comma to set off a participial phrase at the beginning of a sentence.

A participial phrase is a participle with its modifiers and completers.

Excited by tales of a wealthy Indian civilization, the Spanish explorer Coronado led an expedition into the Southwest.

L.5   *INTERRUPTING PARTICIPIAL PHRASES* Use commas also to set off interrupting participial phrases. (Review pages 289–295.)

His expedition, having explored the region from California to Texas, found nothing but ordinary Indian villages. (The participial phrase interrupts the flow of the sentence.)

Coronado returned home, having failed in his hopeless quest. (The participial phrase interrupts the flow of the sentence. Why is there only one comma?)

L.6   *NO COMMAS* If a participial phrase does not interrupt the flow of the sentence and is not at the beginning of the sentence, omit the commas.

We saw two bear cubs perched in a hollow tree.

You will ordinarily use a comma in writing where there is a pause in speaking.

PRACTICE 3   Punctuating Sentences with Participles

As you copy the following sentences, insert the necessary punctuation. Prepare to give a reason for each mark you supply.

SLY FOX

1. Hearing a commotion outside the house I rushed to the window.
2. Our police dog having been tied to a chain was barking at a fox near his food.
3. Circling the dog warily the fox kept out of reach.
4. He walked again and again around the pole allowing the dog a few feet of room.
5. Having followed the fox around and around the pole the dog suddenly found his chain very short.
6. The clever fox pausing a moment for dramatic effect grabbed a bone no longer within reach of the dog and made off with it.

L.7   *DANGLING EXPRESSIONS* If a participle or other verbal is placed so that it seems to modify a word that it cannot modify sensibly, (1) get rid of the participle or other verbal, (2) place it near the word it modifies, or (3) put into the sentence some word for it to modify.

WRONG   Jack noticed two robins bicycling to school.
CURE 1   Jack noticed two robins as he bicycled to school.
CURE 2   Bicycling to school, Jack noticed two robins.
WRONG   Having waited up for the election returns, weariness overcame us.
CURE 3   Having waited up for the election returns, we were weary.

Eliminate dangling participles by using one of the three cures.

1. Leaping out of the water, the trainer fed the porpoise a fish.
2. Staggering under our heavy packs, every rock seemed a huge obstacle.
3. We admired the autumn foliage gliding along in our canoe.
4. Turning the pages, my eye was caught by a shiny red motorbike.
5. We saw a deer riding along in our new Volkswagen.

L.8 *USING PARTICIPLES*   Use participles to vary sentences and save words.

DULL   Rayon was invented in 1855. It was the first man-made fabric.
BETTER   Rayon, invented in 1855, was the first man-made fabric.

In each of the following there are two statements. Improve each by changing one of the predicate verbs to a participle. Punctuate correctly. The preceding example shows you what to do.

MIDDLETON AND CYPRESS GARDENS, SOUTH CAROLINA

1. Middleton Gardens are located not far from Charleston, South Carolina. These gardens have a two-hundred-year history. 2. Before the Revolutionary War, Henry Middleton realized the beauty of this spot. He planned the magnificent terraces and floral paths of this garden wonderland. 3. The camellias grow at many points in the park. They actually provide a tunnel for visitors. 4. The magnolia walk lines the east bank of Reflection Pool. The walk includes a gigantic crepe myrtle. 5. A bank of azaleas rises from the Rice Mill Pond. It has few equals anywhere else in the world.

6. Cypress Gardens are located on the Cooper River. They present an altogether different kind of beauty. 7. From just such a spot as this Francis Marion, the "Swamp Fox," operated. He carried on guerilla warfare with the British. 8. Visitors glide along in boats. They observe the magnificent shrubs and unspoiled wildlife of South Carolina. 9. Gigantic cypress trees tower above the visitor. They suggest an outdoor cathedral. 10. The reflecting waters provide color everywhere. They double the visitor's enjoyment.

W

Make up sentences using any five of the following participles. Perhaps you will be able to join all in a connected paragraph.

Warning. Do not use any as predicate verbs with helpers.

cheering	having scored	laughing
having won	being left	having spoken
running	falling	selling
discovered	trampling	having been bought

GERUNDS: VERBALS USED AS NOUNS

L.9 *GERUND* **Verbals ending in *ing* can be used as nouns. These verbal nouns are called "gerunds."**

The ancient Egyptians avoided *killing* any sacred animal. (*Killing*, a gerund, is the direct object of *avoided.*)

The Greeks probably learned from the Persians the custom of *burning* incense. (*Burning*, a gerund, is object of the preposition *of.*)

L.10 *GERUND PHRASE* **A gerund phrase is a gerund with its modifiers and completers.**

L.11 *POSSESSIVE PRONOUN WITH GERUND* **Use the possessive form of a pronoun before a gerund.**

Hank's parents don't approve of *his* going to movies on week nights. (Hank's parents don't disapprove of *Hank*. They disapprove of *his going* to movies on week nights.)

Madeline told us about *your* being elected secretary of the Record Club.

L.12 *USING GERUNDS* **Use gerunds to help express your thoughts smoothly and concisely.**

DULL   Kingfishers tunnel into the sides of riverbanks. They build their nests this way.

BETTER   Kingfishers build nests by tunneling into the sides of riverbanks.

PRACTICE 7 Using Gerunds   W

In each group of sentences combine the separate statements into one good sentence by changing one predicate verb to a gerund. The preceding example shows you what to do.

1. You can crack any metal. You must sound the proper note.
2. Larry Jones hit safely four times in a row. Then he struck out.
3. Bob Beckett worked every morning at the beach club. In this way he made enough money for his first year in college.
4. I have read all of John Dickson Carr's novels about Dr. Gideon Fell, and I chose one about his other detective, Sir Henry Merrivale.
5. Gabriel Fahrenheit made the thermometer more accurate. He substituted mercury for alcohol.

6. Rub paraffin on the shoe part of your ice skates. This will keep the leather from cracking.
7. We lost the first three games of the season. Then we beat Troy 44 to 8.
8. The octopus shoots out a cloud of black fluid. In this way it conceals itself from its pursuers.

INFINITIVES: VERBALS USED AS NOUNS, ADJECTIVES, AND ADVERBS

L.13 *INFINITIVE* An infinitive is a verb form ordinarily introduced by *to*. It may be used as a noun, an adjective, or an adverb.

The infinitives of the verb *to try* are: *to try, to have tried, to be tried, to have been tried.* (See Appendix.)

NOUN *To fight* bravely was the chief ambition of a young Spartan. (*To fight* is used as a noun, subject of the verb *was*.)
ADJECTIVE This year Central is the team *to beat*. (*To beat* is used as an adjective modifying the noun *team*.)
ADVERB We used a dozen Japanese lanterns *to light* the patio for the party. (*To light* is used as an adverb modifying the verb *used*.)

To is commonly omitted after *dare, feel, hear, help, let, make, need, see,* and *watch*, and sometimes after a few other verbs.

Petey helped his uncle *paint* the dinghy.
You needn't *bring* your costume until the dress rehearsal.

L.14 *INFINITIVE PHRASE* An infinitive phrase is an infinitive with its modifiers and completers.

L.15 *USING INFINITIVE PHRASES* Save words by substituting infinitive phrases for some clauses.

to
Pigs roll in the mud ~~so that they can~~ get cool on hot days.

PRACTICE 8 Using Infinitives

By using an infinitive phrase in each, improve the following sentences. The preceding example shows you what to do.

1. I hoped that I could complete my report by the end of Easter week.
2. The linemen practiced all morning in order that they might prepare for Bay Shore's powerful halfbacks.
3. Dad wants that you should clean out the cellar tomorrow.
4. Sir Joseph Lister was the first by whom antiseptic methods were used during surgery.

5. After twelve hours of snow Dad decided that he should invest in a light-weight aluminum shovel.
6. Ken straddled the fence in order that he might get a better view of the prize-winning Ayrshire cow.
7. Friar Tuck gave Robin Hood a ducking in the stream in order that he might cool Robin's hot temper.
8. Dad promised that tomorrow he would take us to the California Rodeo in Salinas.

L.16 *VERBALS IN SENTENCE PATTERNS* Any basic pattern (pages 462–468) may be varied by using verbals.

PRACTICE 9 Time Out for Review

On your paper number from 1 to 50. After each number supply the correct or never-questioned word, expression, or punctuation to complete the sentence.

BASEBALL IN DECEMBER

Pointing toward the 1 (christmas, Christmas) tree 2 (**,** *or* no mark) my brother Pete shouted, "Steve, look 3 (**.**" *or* **!** ") 4 (Laying, Lying) among the presents 5 (was, were) two baseball bats. 6 ("Their, "They're) Louisville Sluggers!" exclaimed Pete, stroking the smooth finish. "A player 7 (doesn't, don't) have 8 (any, no) trouble with a bat like this."

Louisville Sluggers 9 (**,** *or* no mark) as you probably know 10 (**,** *or* no mark) are a favorite of big-leaguers. 11 (Me and Pete, Pete and I) 12 (could, couldn't) hardly take our eyes 13 (off, off of) the bats, for we had never owned 14 (that, those) kind of bats. We 15 (was, were) thrilled at our 16 (parents, parents') choice of presents.

Taking a trial swing with his bat 17 (**,** *or* no mark) Pete almost 18 (knocked, knocks) over 19 (Mother's, Mothers) milk-glass vase. A moment later Mother 20 (came, come) into the room and 21 (saw, seen) Pete about to take another practice swing. Looking sternly at Pete and 22 (I, me) 23 (**,** *or* no mark) Mother said, "I'm afraid I'll have to call time 24 (**,** *or* no mark) boys. Please put 25 (them, those) bats away until the 26 (spring, Spring)."

"If you'll 27 (set, sit) 28 (calm, calmly)," said Dad, "I'll tell you a few facts about the Louisville Sluggers. 29 (Theyre, They're) made by the Hillerich and Bradsby 30 (company, Company) of Louisville 31 (**,** *or* no mark) Kentucky. The company keeps an up-to-date file of professional 32 (ballplayers, ballplayers') bat requirements. Ballplayers 33 (dont, don't) ordinarily use the same type of bat for long. Ty Cobb 34 (**,** *or* no mark) however, the winner of twelve American League batting championships 35 (**,** *or* no mark) used the same Slugger model for twenty-four years."

As we 36 (sat, set) listening to Dad, 37 (me and Pete, Pete and I) 38 (look, looked) longingly at our bats.   Knowing how eager we 39 (was, were) to try out the bats 40 (, *or* no mark) Dad said, 41 ("Lets, "Let's) go out and hit some balls.   We've 42 (a half, half) an hour till dinner."

Without a word Pete and I 43 (grab, grabbed) our jackets and 44 (follow, followed) Dad 45 (in, into) the snow-covered backyard.   Noticing 46 (Mother's, Mothers) astonished look 47 (, *or* no mark) Dad called out 48 (, *or* no mark) 49 ("It's, "Its) all right, Lilian.   50 (Weve, We've) decided to start the baseball season a little early.   Play ball!"

MASTERY TEST 11A   Correct Simple Sentences

In each of the following which word or expression in parentheses is the correct or never-questioned one?   On your paper write your choice after the number of the sentence.

1. A fallen tree was (laying, lying) across the trail.
2. I (can, can't) hardly wait for the results of that history test.
3. Theodore had never planted (that, those) kinds of flowers before.
4. *Inexpensive Vacations* (are, is) a book loaded with money-saving ideas.
5. The interior and exterior of that car (are, is) in excellent condition.
6. Karen (laid, lay) in her warm bed, wishing that it were Saturday rather than Tuesday.
7. We ate (good, well) after we had finished the seven-mile hike.
8. He (began, begun) to understand the importance of practice.
9. A good hunting dog (hadn't ought, ought not) to be spoiled like a household pet.
10. The town council (are, is) never able to agree without a fight.
11. The truck driver helped mother and (I, me) with the flat tire.
12. Everyone prepared (his, their) craft exhibit for the judging.
13. The clown opened the little car's doors, and out (jumped, jumps) fifteen tall men.
14. After the starter's bell the horses (came, come) charging out of the gate.
15. Between you and (I, me), there's no way we can walk to Trenton.
16. That is an (awful, extremely) bumpy road.
17. My grandfather once taught in a (university, University) in Texas.
18. Will you collect for the scholarship fund with Lucy and (I, me)?
19. After a half (an hour's, hour's) intermission the actors were ready to present their play again.
20. Neither Paul nor Harry (has, have) ever broiled a steak.
21. For this Saturday's game everyone needs to have (his, their) equipment in order.

22. I got the tickets (off of, from) my father's partner.
23. There (is, are) many tumbleweeds in and near Las Vegas, Nevada.
24. "Unusual Recipes" (is, are) a good title for your composition.
25. A former (mayor, Mayor) of Berlin was a visitor to our city.

MASTERY TEST 11B   Correct Simple Sentences

Follow the directions for Mastery Test 11A.

1. Only one player from each of the eight teams (was, were) chosen.
2. Would you like to take a walk with grandfather and (I, me)?
3. Vincent answered the difficult question (intelligent, intelligently).
4. Without a thought to the danger, Grace dived (in, into) the icy water to grab the child's arm.
5. Have you ever (gone, went) to an antique collectors' convention?
6. Mr. (Jone's, Jones's) spicy apple pie won a first prize at our county fair.
7. Did Hank Fortuna attend Southside (Junior High, junior high)?
8. One of the painters (is, are) an excellent trombonist.
9. The National Guard (came, come) to help the victims of the flash floods last year.
10. Why (don't, doesn't) he buy an inexpensive car for going to and from work?
11. We use (that, those) kind of spices to produce our famous mince pie.
12. At last night's school board meeting there (was, were) over one hundred citizens in attendance.
13. A lot of stamina and energy (are, is) required for mountain climbing.
14. Our purring cat was (laying, lying) contentedly before the roaring fire.
15. Can someone lend me (his, their) flashlight?
16. Neither the fifth grade nor the sixth grade (is, are) coming to the junior high open house this year.
17. My father will pick up Dave and (I, me) at exactly 7:30.
18. It's so dark that Ken (can, can't) barely see the goalpost.
19. Laura did very (well, good) in the 100-yard dash.
20. Jim set the table (expert, expertly).
21. They (hadn't ought, ought not) to go too near the beehives.
22. Somebody has left (her, their) sweater in the lobby.
23. Sam said he would meet us by the fountain in a half (an hour, hour).
24. One of the leading experts on pottery in the United States (is, are) my mother's cousin.
25. We once (grew, growed) wheat and corn on my family's farm.

31 *The Structure of Compound and Complex Sentences*

Spaghetti is usually considered a native Italian food. It actually comes from the Far East, though. Marco Polo brought the recipe back from the Orient. Spaghetti was unknown in Italy until then.

Too many simple sentences in a row can be boring. Now read the same facts expressed in grown-up style.

Spaghetti is usually considered a native Italian food, but it actually comes from the Far East. It was unknown in Italy until Marco Polo brought the recipe back from the Orient.

In the second version the simple sentences have been linked to form a compound sentence and a complex sentence. Good writing contains compound and complex sentences as well as simple ones.

COMPOUND SENTENCE

Study these sentences.

The American jay is bright blue with black and white markings.
His Canadian cousin is gray.

Each of these is a simple sentence with a subject and a predicate. The two sentences are related in thought, however, and can be connected like this:

The American jay is bright blue with black and white markings, but his Canadian cousin is gray.

The new sentence is a compound sentence with two independent clauses joined by the conjunction *but*.

M.1   CLAUSE   A clause is a group of words with a subject and a predicate. Clauses, like sentences, are constructed according to basic patterns (pages 462–468).

419

The large <u>claw</u> of the fiddler crab <u>looks</u> menacing, | but <u>it</u> <u>is</u> <u>used</u> largely for bluff. (The vertical line separates the clauses. The subjects are underlined; the verbs have two lines under them.)

M.2 *INDEPENDENT CLAUSE* An independent (or principal) clause usually makes sense when standing alone.

M.3 *COMPOUND SENTENCE* A compound sentence has two or more independent clauses.

The clauses of a compound sentence are usually joined by a coordinate conjunction.

M.4 *COORDINATE CONJUNCTIONS* Coordinate conjunctions connect words, phrases, and clauses of equal rank.

Be sure you use the right conjunction to express the relationship you suggest. Common coordinate conjunctions are *and, but, or, nor*.

Your nails and your hair are dead, *but* they grow from living cells. (*But* is used to suggest contrast.)

Leaves manufacture plant food, *and* other parts of the plant store the food. (*And* is used to suggest additional information.)

You told me, *or* I read it somewhere. (*Or* is used to suggest an alternate possibility.)

Denny didn't care for swimming, *nor* was he interested in any other water sport. (*Nor* is used to suggest a negative addition.)

Where there is no coordinate conjunction, a semicolon is used to separate the independent clauses.

Flotsam is floating wreckage; jetsam is wreckage on shore.

PRACTICE 1 Using Coordinating Conjunctions Effectively

In each sentence supply *and, but, or,* or *nor* to fill in the blank. Justify your choice. If two alternatives are possible, explain the difference when you use each alternative.

1. A sweet potato is a root, ＿＿＿ a white potato is a swollen stem.
2. Plants manufacture food in the light, ＿＿＿ they absorb their food during the evening hours.
3. The Cardinals may win the pennant, ＿＿＿ the Giants may beat them.
4. Most plants have roots, seeds, flowers, and fruit, ＿＿＿ the algae and fungi have none of these.
5. Wendy doesn't enjoy mystery novels, ＿＿＿ she does like westerns.

Diagraming Compound Sentences

1. The Plains Indians wandered from encampment to encampment, but the Pueblo Indians built permanent settlements.

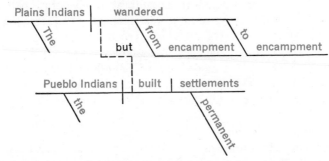

The two clauses are joined by the conjunction *but* to make a compound sentence.

To diagram a compound sentence,
1. diagram the two independent clauses;
2. join the predicate verbs of the independent clauses with a broken line; and
3. on the broken line place the conjunction joining the clauses.

2. Come to my house at noon; Dad will drive us to the game.

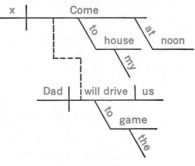

You (understood), indicated by *x*, is the subject of the first clause. Since a semicolon separates the independent clauses, there is no word on the coordinate conjunction line.

PRACTICE 2   Identifying Parts of Compound Sentences   D

Diagram the following sentences.
OR   As you copy the following sentences, enclose each clause in parentheses. Draw one line under a simple subject and two lines under a predicate verb. Write one of these abbreviations above every appropriate word to show how it is used.

p.a. — predicate adjective	**d.o.** — direct object
p.n. — predicate noun	**i.o.** — indirect object
p.pr. — predicate pronoun	**o.p.** — object of a preposition

FORT RALEIGH, NORTH CAROLINA

1. Does "Lost Colony" mean anything to you, or have you forgotten the name of the first settlement on Roanoke Island? (*Lost Colony* is one name.) 2. In 1586 Sir Walter Raleigh established this unfortunate colony in North Carolina, but the venture was a failure. 3. The settlers grew homesick, and the entire group finally returned to England.

4. The second colony included many families, and a new attempt at permanent settlement was made. 5. An English child was born in the colony, and the prospects for a permanent colony looked bright. 6. The colonists expected frequent help from England, but because of the war with Spain, no English ship came to the settlement for several years.

7. An English ship finally brought the island assistance, but the colony had completely disappeared. 8. Nobody knows the real story of the "Lost Colony," nor has anyone ever uncovered the fate of the missing settlers. 9. This area is now a national historic site, and visitors live for a moment in the distant past. 10. A museum at the site displays objects from the area, but the terrible secret of the lost settlers is still unsolved.

Which Is It — Simple or Compound?

You can always divide a compound sentence into two or more good sentences.

> The male pigeon sits on the eggs from about ten a.m. to four p.m., and the female takes the long night shift.

SENTENCE   The male pigeon sits on the eggs from about ten a.m. to four p.m.
SENTENCE   The female takes the long night shift.

> Penguins are good swimmers but cannot fly at all.

SENTENCE   Penguins are good swimmers.
NOT A SENTENCE   but cannot fly at all.

The second verb has no separate subject. The sentence is not a compound sentence but a simple sentence with a compound predicate, *are* and *can fly*.

SIMPLE SENTENCE WITH COMPOUND SUBJECT   The chestnut and the horse chestnut are not related.

SIMPLE SENTENCE WITH COMPOUND PREDICATE   Chestnuts taste good and are popular food in Europe.

SIMPLE SENTENCE WITH COMPOUND SUBJECT AND PREDICATE   Sixteenth-century explorers and traders discovered the horse chestnut tree and brought it back to northern Europe from Constantinople.

COMPOUND SENTENCE   The bark of the chestnut tree produces tannin, and the wood makes excellent fence posts.

PRACTICE 3 Compound Sentences, Subjects, and Predicates

Which two sentences are compound? Which two are simple sentences with compound subjects? Which two simple sentences have compound predicates? Which two have compound subjects and compound predicates?

EXAMPLE Along the quiet Caribbean are many reminders of the old Spanish Main, and ancient Spanish fortresses now slowly crumble in the warm tropical sun. — compound sentence

SAN JUAN NATIONAL HISTORIC SITE

1. At the western tip of San Juan, Puerto Rico, the sturdy walls and picturesque towers of Morro Castle stand as a reminder of Spanish influence in the New World.
2. Morro Castle and Florida's St. Augustine were once twin anchors in Spain's defense and harassed British and Dutch adventurers in the Caribbean.
3. From the walls of El Morro there are many beautiful views, but the most picturesque sight is the fort itself.
4. The thickness of the walls and the height of the towers always impress visitors and suggest the lonely grandeur of this fort.
5. Sir Francis Drake and his men once threatened the powerful fortress.
6. Your guide will point to a hiding place in the government house and tell a tale of concealment and panic at the approach of the feared Drake.
7. Drake never completed the attack but sailed off to his death elsewhere.
8. An army camp is stationed at the site, but the public can visit the historic fortress with a park ranger as guide.

Punctuating Compound Sentences

M.5 *COMMA* Use a comma to separate the independent clauses of a compound sentence if they are joined by *and, but, or,* or *nor.*

Mark Twain grew up in a small town in Missouri, and his boyhood experiences later furnished the basis for the adventures of Tom Sawyer and Huckleberry Finn.

In a short sentence the comma may be omitted.

In Denver the summer days are warm but the nights are cool.

M.6 *SEMICOLON* Use the semicolon between the clauses of a compound sentence if they are not joined by *and, but, or,* or *nor.*

In this use the semicolon is a weak period; a period is permissible. (Note the use of the semicolon in the preceding line.)

Flying squirrels don't really fly; they just glide from tree to tree.

Or: Flying squirrels don't really fly. They just glide from tree to tree.

Lincoln spent his childhood in Kentucky and Indiana; he did not move to Illinois until the age of twenty-one.

M.7 *TRANSITIONAL ADVERB* The following words are ordinarily used as transitional adverbs, *not* conjunctions: *also, consequently, furthermore, hence, however, moreover, nevertheless, otherwise, then, therefore, thus.* A semicolon is often used before a transitional adverb in a compound sentence.

Viking ships had oars as well as sails; thus they were not completely dependent on the wind. (Do not use a comma.)

STRUCTURE CLUES — CONJUNCTIONS AND TRANSITIONAL ADVERBS

1. A conjunction has a fixed place in the sentence pattern, ordinarily at the beginning of its clause. A transitional adverb usually moves freely in its own clause.

CONJUNCTION The reverse rockets fired, and the capsule decelerated. (*And* cannot be moved about.)

TRANSITIONAL ADVERB The reverse rockets fired; then the capsule decelerated.

Or: The reverse rockets fired; the capsule then decelerated.

2. A conjunction does not ordinarily begin or end a separate simple sentence. A transitional adverb frequently does so.

CONJUNCTION ~~But~~ The tree fell. (The conjunction *but* is not ordinarily used to begin a sentence.)

TRANSITIONAL ADVERB Nevertheless the tree fell. (The transitional adverb *nevertheless* may begin a sentence.)

TRANSITIONAL ADVERB The tree fell nevertheless. (The transitional adverb *nevertheless* may end a sentence.)

3. In speaking, a transitional adverb ordinarily receives more emphasis than a conjunction.

CONJUNCTION The wind blew, and we lost our sail. (*And* is not emphasized.)

TRANSITIONAL ADVERB The wind blew; thus we lost our sail. (*Thus* is emphasized.)

Punctuate the following compound sentences and give a rule for each mark inserted.   Do not mark this book.

THE CALENDAR

A. 1. Primitive farmers wanted some system to help them regulate their planting consequently they tried many types of calendars
   2. Through the years the need for an accurate calendar increased and different civilizations developed different calendars
   3. In an ideal calendar the spring equinox occurs on approximately the same day year after year but this goal is difficult to achieve
   4. In 46 B.C. Julius Caesar sponsored calendar reform the name of the Julian calendar pays tribute to his efforts
   5. The Julian calendar was very much like our own every fourth year was a leap year with an extra day
   6. The calendar problem seemed solved but the new plan had a grave defect
   7. This calendar assumes a year of $365\frac{1}{4}$ days but the measurement is about eleven minutes too long

B. 1. The extra minutes seem insignificant but over the years they led to a gradual change in the date of the equinoxes
   2. By 1580 the difference had grown to ten days and spring officially arrived ten days early
   3. Two years later ten days were just dropped from the calendar and at that time the Gregorian calendar was adopted in many European countries
   4. England accepted the new calendar in 1752 but by then the discrepancy had grown to eleven days
   5. George Washington was actually born on February 11 but we celebrate his birthday on February 22 because of the change during his lifetime
   6. In the Gregorian calendar years divisible by 400 are leap years but other years ending in hundreds are not
   7. The loss of three leap years every four hundred years balances the calendar therefore further adjustment of year length is not needed

M.8   *USE OF COMPOUND SENTENCE*   Use a compound sentence to express two similar ideas of equal importance.

If two ideas are not closely related, put them in separate sentences.

POOR   The earth has only one moon, and Jupiter is the largest planet.
BETTER   The earth has only one moon, but Jupiter has twelve.

PRACTICE 5 Recognizing Good Compound Sentences

The following ten sentences are compound. Five of them are good, because the halves express similar ideas of equal importance. Five are poor, because the halves are not similar or equal in importance. On your paper number from 1 to 10. Beside each number place **+** for a good sentence and **—** for a poor sentence.

1. The Arabian camel has one hump, and the Bactrian camel has two.
2. The Arabian camel has one hump, and a camel sheds its hair periodically.
3. The island of Puerto Rico was originally called "San Juan," and the city was called "Puerto Rico."
4. The island of Puerto Rico was originally called "San Juan," and it is roughly rectangular in shape.
5. The bobsledders leaned far to the left, and bobsledding is a dangerous sport.
6. The bobsledders leaned far to the left, and the sled sped safely around the dangerous turn at the midway mark.
7. During the night a blizzard struck the mountain village, and by morning telephone communication had been cut off.
8. During the night a blizzard struck the mountain village, and the previous winter had been quite mild.
9. The Tourist Trap looked expensive, but the wares were very reasonable.
10. The Tourist Trap looked expensive, and it is located in old San Juan.

M.9   *USING COMPOUND PREDICATE* For conciseness, convert a compound sentence into a simple sentence with a compound predicate if the subject of the second clause is a pronoun with the subject of the first clause as its antecedent.

COMPOUND SENTENCE   Dragonflies eat insects, and they help keep down the insect population. (*Dragonflies* is the antecedent of *they*.)
COMPOUND PREDICATE   Dragonflies eat insects and help keep down the insect population.

PRACTICE 6 Using Compound Predicates   **W**

Change each of the following sentences into a good simple sentence with a compound predicate.

1. The game of dominoes was invented many years ago by French monks, and it took its name from the first line of their evening service.
2. Some fictional characters have become almost real and they live on in people's imaginations.

3. Tommy Brummeloh hit a home run in the last inning and he sent the game into extra innings.
4. The leaves of the red maple turn a vivid scarlet in the fall, and they add a burst of color to a hillside.
5. I read Ellery Queen's latest novel, and I enjoyed it.

COMPLEX SENTENCE

Which clause can stand alone? Which cannot?

Medieval war horses, which had to bear the weight of knights in full armor, were chosen for strength and not for speed.

Medieval war horses were chosen for strength and not for speed is the independent clause. It has a subject and a predicate — war horses were chosen — and can stand alone as a sentence. Though the rest of the sentence also has a subject and a predicate — which had — this clause cannot stand alone. It is a dependent, or subordinate, clause.

M.10 *DEPENDENT CLAUSE* A dependent (or subordinate) clause is used like an adjective, an adverb, or a noun.

It depends on another clause and ordinarily does not make complete sense by itself.

ONE WORD	DEPENDENT CLAUSE
Stevie caught a *huge* trout.	Stevie caught a trout *that measured eighteen inches.*
We'll meet you *there.*	We'll meet you *where the town bypass leaves the main highway.*
Did you hear the *announcement?*	Did you hear *that Glee Club tryouts will be held next week?*

M.11 *COMPLEX SENTENCE* A complex sentence has one independent clause and one or more dependent (adjective, adverb, or noun) clauses.

The dependent clause is usually connected to the independent clause by a subordinate conjunction or a relative pronoun.

M.12 *SUBORDINATE CONJUNCTION* A subordinate conjunction connects a dependent clause with an independent clause.

These are commonly used subordinate conjunctions:

after	as soon as	in order that	that	whenever
although	as though	lest	though	where
as	because	provided	till	wherever
as far as	before	since	unless	whether
as if	how	so that	until	while
as long as	if	than	when	why

What does each italicized word do in the sentence?

1. The late nineteenth century was the period (*when* American genius turned its energy toward industrial progress). (*When* is a conjunction joining the adjective clause with *period.*)
2. [*If* a key jams], try powdered graphite as a lubricant. (*If* is a conjunction joining the adverb clause with *try.*)
3. Show me ⟨*where* the wild strawberries grow⟩. (*Where* is a conjunction introducing the noun clause.)

Note.   Throughout this book boldface parentheses **( )** will mark adjective clauses; brackets **[ ]**, adverb clauses; and pointed brackets **< >**, noun clauses.

PRACTICE 7   Supplying Subordinate Conjunctions   V

Provide an appropriate conjunction to fill each blank.

1. ____ it was pouring, we enjoyed ourselves in the picnic shelter.
2. ____ you would win, you must learn to fall.
3. Last summer we visited the town ____ I was born.
4. ____ you receive this letter, show it to Allan.
5. Did you know ____ a furnace thermostat is a kind of computer?

M.13   *ADJECTIVE CLAUSE*   An adjective clause, like an adjective, modifies a noun or a pronoun.

ADJECTIVE   Julie has an *antique* music box.

ADJECTIVE PHRASE   Julie has a music box with an interesting history.

ADJECTIVE CLAUSE   Julie has a music box that plays a theme from one of Mozart's symphonies.

Note that the phrase provides more information than the single adjective and that the clause provides information that a word or phrase could not provide.

M.14   *WORD VS. CLAUSE*   Do not use a phrase or a clause if a single word can do as well.   (See page 426.)

WORDY   The house which belongs to the Shorts lost several shingles in Tuesday's high wind.

CONCISE   The Shorts' house lost several shingles in Tuesday's high wind.

PRACTICE 8   Writing Concisely   W

For each italicized adjective clause substitute a single adjective. Write the new sentence with the adjective in proper word order.

1. The stoop, *which is made of wood*, is beginning to crumble.
2. Glenn Weed, our best miler, ran a race *that was very fast*.
3. We stopped and watched the puppies *that were playing happily*.
4. My brother bought a car *that is red in color*.

PRACTICE 9   Writing Effective Adjective Clauses   W

Expand each of the following sentences by substituting an adjective clause for each italicized adjective. Begin your clause with *who*, *which*, *that*, or *whose*. Underline the adjective clause. Be sure your clause provides information the single adjective cannot provide.

EXAMPLE   The Nantucket Islanders were *seafaring* men.
The Nantucket Islanders were men <u>who sailed the whaling vessels and merchantmen of years ago.</u>

1. Mr. Wickett was a *greedy* man.
2. On our trip to Catalina we took a *slow* boat.
3. The magazine had a *colorful* cover.
4. Mrs. Hoffman is a *careful* driver.
5. The chorus sang a *cheerful* sea chantey.

M.15 *RELATIVE PRONOUN* The relative pronouns *who*, *whose*, *whom*, *which*, and *that* attach adjective clauses to their antecedents — the nouns or pronouns modified.

A relative pronoun also acts as a subject, an object, a predicate pronoun, or a possessive modifier in its own clause. *That* is not always a relative pronoun; it is a relative pronoun when *who*, *whom*, or *which* can be substituted for it.

Bees *that do not live in colonies* are called "solitary bees." (*That* connects the italicized adjective clause with *bees*, the antecedent of *that*. It is also the subject of the verb *do live*.)

In each of the following sentences the dependent clause is in parentheses and an arrow is drawn from the relative pronoun to the noun the adjective clause modifies.

SUBJECT   Sir Arthur Conan Doyle, (who created the immortal detective Sherlock Holmes), was a doctor. (*Who* is the subject of *created*.)

DIRECT OBJECT   Edgar Allan Poe, (*whom* some people know only as a poet), was also the father of the modern detective story. (*Whom* is the object of *know*.)

OBJECT OF A PREPOSITION   Wilkie Collins, (to *whom* we usually give the credit for writing the first full-fledged detective novel), was originally a lawyer. (*Whom* is the object of the preposition *to*.)

POSSESSIVE   Mary Roberts Rinehart, (*whose* first mystery novel was published over fifty years ago), was one of the first women to write detective fiction. (*Whose* modifies *novel*.)

Sometimes the relative pronoun is omitted.

The Murder of Roger Ackroyd is one of the best books (*that* Agatha Christie ever wrote). (*That*, the relative pronoun, may be omitted.)

Some adjective clauses are introduced by *where* or *when*.

The coach showed pictures of Chavez Ravine, (*where* the Dodgers' stadium is located).

Diagraming Sentences with Adjective Clauses

1. Graphite, which is used in lead pencils, is a very hard form of coal.

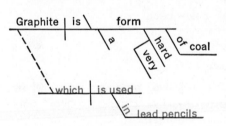

A broken line connects the relative pronoun *which* with its antecedent, *graphite*. Since slanting lines join modifiers to the words they modify, the broken line shows that the clause modifies *graphite*. Besides connecting an adjective clause with the word it modifies, a relative pronoun does a job in its own clause. Here *which* is the subject of *is used*.

2. The so-called flying fox is actually a large bat whose face resembles a fox's face.

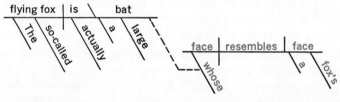

The relative pronoun *whose* modifies *face*. The broken line connects *whose* with its antecedent, *bat*. The possessive noun *fox's* is diagramed like an adjective.

3. Some wasps chew wood, from which they make paper houses.

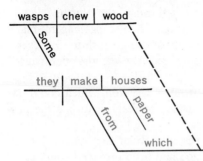

The relative pronoun *which* is the object of the preposition *from* and is connected with its antecedent, *wood*, by a broken line. The adjective clause modifies *wood*.

4. A journey by automobile was a daring adventure in the days when no paved highways existed.

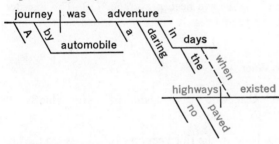

When, a conjunction connecting the two clauses, is placed on a slanting broken line between the adjective clause and the word it modifies.

5. There is one story I'll never forget.

```
There
    story | is
      \  \ |
     o \   \ |
      n \    \
  I| 'll forget|  \  x
        \
         n \
          e \
           v
            e
             r
```

The introductory word *there* is placed on a separate line above the independent clause. *X* stands for the omitted relative pronoun *that* or *which*.

PRACTICE 10 Identifying Adjective Clauses

Diagram the following sentences.

OR Write the adjective clause under the independent clause. Underline each simple subject once and the verb twice. Draw an arrow from the adjective clause to the noun or pronoun it modifies.

EXAMPLE In 1912 loss of the *Titanic*, which had been considered almost unsinkable, shocked the world.

In 1912 <u>loss</u> of the *Titanic* <u>shocked</u> the world

```
                      ↑
    | which had been considered almost unsinkable |
```

A NIGHT TO REMEMBER

1. The *Titanic* was proceeding speedily through the North Atlantic, where icebergs had been frequently reported. 2. The passengers, many of whom were famous, relaxed in the security of this great ship. 3. Several iceberg warnings, which might have encouraged renewed vigilance, caused no undue alarm.

4. An iceberg suddenly loomed in front of the ship, which could not swerve sharply. 5. The slight impact, which scarcely disturbed the passengers, had actually struck a fatal blow.

6. Many passengers who chatted casually about the impact did not realize their peril. 7. The lifeboats which had been provided could carry only a fraction of the passengers. 8. Some of the boats which were launched promptly were not filled. 9. The panic that overcame most of the passengers at the end might have been prevented. 10. The disaster, in which 1,513 persons lost their lives, is vividly described in *A Night to Remember*.

Who, Whom, Which, That, What

M.16 **WHO, WHOM** Use *who* and *whom* to refer chiefly to persons.

A Greek scientist *who* lived in the third century B.C. invented the first steam engine. Do you know *whom?*

M.17 **WHICH** Use *which* to refer to lower animals and to things and occasionally to collective nouns referring to persons.

Nightingales, *which* are never found in the Western Hemisphere, are nevertheless familiar to us through fairy tales and folk legends.
A catboat is a small sailboat *which* has a single mast and one large sail.
The army *which* defeated Napoleon at Waterloo was composed of British, Dutch, and German soldiers.

M.18 **THAT** Use *that* to refer to persons, animals, or things.

Any major league pitcher *that* can win twenty games a season is considered outstanding.
Lions *that* are raised in captivity are surprisingly tame.
The huge palaces *that* once belonged to the French kings have been turned into museums.

Notice that *two commas to set off* are not used to enclose adjective clauses beginning with *that*. These clauses do not interrupt the flow of the sentence. (See page 289.)

M.19 **WHAT** *What* never has an antecedent.

The buses *which* go to La Guardia Field leave from the East Side Air Terminal. (buses which; NOT "buses what")

PRACTICE 11 Using Correct Relative Pronouns

Correct the following sentences and give a reason for each change you make. One of the sentences is right.

1. *The Tempest* was probably the last play what William Shakespeare wrote.
2. The left fielder, which had caught the fly ball, threw to second for the double play.
3. The impala, who can easily leap thirty feet, is one of the most graceful antelopes.
4. The rescue of the exhausted swimmer was managed by the two lifeguards, one of which stayed on shore and carefully paid out the lifeline.
5. Two drum majors what stood in front of the gaily dressed band gave the signal for the start of the parade.
6. The bird that you saw outside your window this morning was a common starling.

M.20 *USING ADJECTIVE CLAUSES* Often a complex sentence with an adjective clause is smoother and more effective than two short sentences.

TWO SENTENCES Zebras resemble sleek domestic horses. They can be trained to pull carts.

COMPLEX Zebras, which resemble sleek domestic horses, can be trained to pull carts.

M.21 *PUNCTUATING ADJECTIVE CLAUSES* Use commas to set off an adjective clause that interrupts the flow of the sentence.

Such a clause, called "nonessential," merely adds information. It does not answer the question "Which one?" A person reading aloud usually pauses before and after a nonessential clause.

NONESSENTIAL Curling, which is a Scottish form of bowling, is played on ice. (The adjective clause interrupts the flow of the sentence. It does not answer the question "Which curling?" A speaker would pause before and after the clause.)

ESSENTIAL A sport that many Scotsmen enjoy is curling. (The adjective clause does not interrupt the flow of the sentence. It answers the question "Which sport?" A speaker would not pause before and after the clause.)

PRACTICE 12   Using Adjective Clauses to Improve Sentences

Using the ideas and most of the words in the two sentences after each number, write one good sentence with an adjective clause. Use correct relative pronouns. Punctuate your sentences correctly.

EXAMPLE   Hailstones are snowflakes or raindrops. These have been carried aloft into cooler layers of air.

Hailstones are snowflakes or raindrops which have been carried aloft into cooler layers of air.

A. 1. Some snowflakes are carried up into the air again and again. They acquire layers of ice.
   2. Many hailstones acquire several layers of ice. They will then be large and heavy.
   3. Hailstorms may strike unexpectedly in summer. They often destroy crops.
   4. A greenhouse may be demolished by a hailstorm. The storm may drop egg-sized stones on the glass.
   5. Threatening, heavy clouds obscure the sky. These often herald the approach of a hailstorm.

B. 1. The armadillo looks like an armored porcupine. It can roll itself into a smooth ball for protection.
   2. The original Ferris wheel was constructed for the Chicago Columbian Exposition in 1893. It was 250 feet in diameter.
   3. The coffee tree originated in Africa. It has since been introduced into Asia and South America.
   4. Ecuador lies astride the equator. It takes its name from that imaginary line.
   5. Because of its elevation Quito has an excellent climate. It lies only fifteen miles south of the equator.

ADVERB CLAUSE

M.22   *ADVERB CLAUSE*   Most adverb clauses modify verbs; some modify adjectives or adverbs.

ADVERB   Mary Lou got up *early.*
ADVERB PHRASE   Mary Lou got up *at dawn.*
ADVERB CLAUSE   Mary Lou got up *when the sun flooded her bedroom.*

Note again that the phrase provides more information than the single adverb and that the clause provides even more information.

PRACTICE 13   Studying Conjunctions in Action

In the following sentence use in turn each suggested conjunction. How does the meaning of the sentence change as each is used?

(——) I left, the noise began. (After, As, Because, Before, When, Whenever)

Diagraming Sentences with Adverb Clauses

1. Cut flowers will last much longer if they are kept in a cool place.

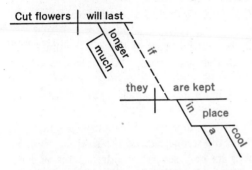

The slanting line shows that the clause *if they are kept in a cool place* modifies *will last*. The subordinate conjunction *if* is placed on the broken line.

2. Some of the Indian cliff dwellings in the Southwest are older than any of the medieval cathedrals in Europe.

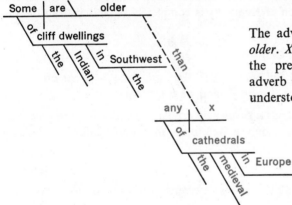

The adverb clause modifies *older*. *X* is used in place of the predicate verb of the adverb clause, *are*, which is understood.

PRACTICE 14   Identifying Sentences with Adverb Clauses   D

Diagram the following sentences.

OR   Write the adverb clause under the independent clause. Underline each simple subject once and a verb twice. Draw an arrow from the adverb clause to the word or words it modifies.

EXAMPLE   Though water is often used as boundary markers, water markers change.

water <u>markers</u> <u>change</u>
      ↑
| Though <u>water</u> <u>is</u> often <u>used</u> as boundary markers |

ODDITIES OF UNITED STATES GEOGRAPHY

1. When states claimed land, surveyors often used rivers for boundary markers.
2. Although rivers are convenient markers, they sometimes shift their courses.
3. If you look at a map of Illinois, you will find a small projection in the southwest portion.
4. Though at one time Illinois lay entirely east of the Mississippi River, the small area now lies west of that great river. (Consider *east of* and *west of* prepositions.)
5. Because the river in flood once cut a new channel, a part of Illinois remained west of the river.
6. When the Mississippi changed its course near Vicksburg, several acres of Louisiana land were left on the wrong side of the river.
7. When the Ohio River shifted its bed, several hundred acres of Kentucky were left on the Indiana side of the river. (Consider *several hundred* one adjective.)
8. Because the Mississippi River makes a loop near New Madrid, a ten-square-mile section of Kentucky is completely separated from the rest of the state.

Punctuating Adverb Clauses

M.23   *BEGINNING OF SENTENCE*   Use the comma to set off a long adverb clause at the beginning of a sentence.

> *Since in former times a cavalry officer supplied his own horses and paid for their upkeep,* only a well-to-do man could afford to join the cavalry.

The comma may be omitted after a short introductory clause.

> *If you like jazz* you'll like this new version of "When the Saints Come Marching In."
>
> *Or: If you like jazz,* you'll like this new version of "When the Saints Come Marching In."

Always insert a comma if there is any danger of misreading.

> After the horses had eaten, Jimmy and George led them to the stream to drink.

(If you read that sentence without the comma, you'll understand why the comma is required.)

M.24   *COMMA BEFORE CONJUNCTIONS*   Use the comma before these conjunctions: (1) *for, though, although;* (2) *as* and *since* when they mean "because."

The heroes of the Trojan War wore bronze armor, as iron and steel were unknown at that time.

Switzerland has never had a salt-water navy, since the country does not have access to any sea.

Don't leave a camera in the hot sun, for heat may damage the film.

PRACTICE 15 Punctuating Adverb Clauses

Punctuate the following sentences. Give a reason for each mark you use. Do not write in this book.

A. 1. Although Columbus made four voyages to the New World he never discovered the coast of the mainland
   2. Early settlers in Australia and New Zealand were homesick for there were no familiar animals in these new lands
   3. Although science fiction is often considered new the first story about a trip to the moon was written in the second century A.D.
   4. Ships sailing through the Panama Canal from the Atlantic to the Pacific travel from west to east as the Isthmus of Panama takes a considerable bend at this point
   5. As minute after minute the searching plane grew smaller in the distance the men on the life raft became more and more disheartened
B. 1. After he had called Jack left for school
   2. Before the chimes of Big Ben can be heard in the London streets they are heard in distant Australia
   3. Since the sound is sent over radio waves at 186,000 miles per second the sound of the chimes reaches Australia in a fraction of a second
   4. In 1900 an automobile trip was a challenging adventure for there wasn't a single mile of concrete road in the United States
   5. If you throw a pinch of spilled salt over your left shoulder for luck you are actually "bribing an evil spirit" not to harm you

PRACTICE 16 Using Complex Sentences

Change each *so* sentence into a complex sentence by putting one of the ideas into an adverb clause beginning with *as*, *since*, or *because*. Punctuate correctly.

EXAMPLE Plastic containers melt easily, and so you should never leave them on a radiator.
   Because plastic containers melt easily, you should never leave them on a radiator.

1. Southern California has a very warm climate, and so houses there are often built without furnaces.
2. Bobby wanted to give up his paper route for the summer, so Billy Crest took it over.

3. Dad enjoys orange-blossom time in Florida, and so we left for New Port Richey at the beginning of the Easter vacation.
4. The snow continued to fall without letup, so we decided to leave for home an hour before sundown.
5. The paint had begun to peel from the trim and the window frames, so Dad decided to paint the house.
6. We still had three days left of our vacation, so we decided to visit the Luray Caverns near Front Royal, Virginia.

NOUN CLAUSE

M.25 *NOUN CLAUSE* A noun clause is used as a noun.

NOUN We learned a surprising *fact* today.
NOUN CLAUSE We learned *that trees can become sunburned.*

A noun clause may take over the noun's duties in a sentence.

SUBJECT *Whoever took down this message* didn't write very clearly.
DIRECT OBJECT He said *that butterflies drink nectar from flowers.*
OBJECT OF A PREPOSITION Anne gave a talk on *how Seeing-Eye dogs are trained.*
INDIRECT OBJECT Tell *whoever calls* that I'll be ready at six.
APPOSITIVE Thomas Edison held firmly to his belief *that he would eventually find a suitable filament for the light bulb.*

Diagraming Sentences with Noun Clauses

Coach Davis told us that the Red Sox once scored twenty-nine runs in a single game.

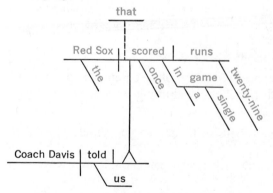

The noun clause is the object of the verb *told* and is placed on a platform above the line. The subordinate conjunction *that* introduces the noun clause.

In diagraming noun clauses first decide how you would diagram the sentence if a noun were substituted for the clause. Then place the clause on a platform above the line as in the example.

PRACTICE 17   Identifying Noun Clauses   **D**

Diagram the following sentences.

OR   Find the noun clause in each of the following sentences. Tell how the clause is used in the sentence.

1. What Paul did was certainly courageous.
2. I hope that you will come.
3. Does Karen know that she lost the frankfurter fork?
4. In music class today we learned that no American river is spelled *Swanee*. (Consider *Swanee* a predicate noun.)
5. Our science teacher told us that Adélie Land in Antarctica has average winds of gale force.

PRACTICE 18   Using Noun Clauses   **W**

Using a noun clause in each, write six sentences in which you give facts you have learned in school this year. Underline the noun clauses. Words like these are noun-clause makers: *knew, learned, discovered, showed, were informed, told, explained.*

EXAMPLE   Our fire warden told us *that an empty bottle in the woods can start a forest fire by magnification of the sun's rays.*

PRACTICE 19   Completing Sentences   **V**

Use your ingenuity. Complete each of the following skeleton sentences by adding colorful, specific words of your own. Tell what kind of subordinate clause each sentence has.

1. The pup that ————
2. That some persons ———— is certainly true.
3. Because ———— couldn't find ————, the rest ————
4. Although ————, we were not disappointed.
5. I never realized that ————
6. The librarian who ————

PRACTICE 20   Building Complex Sentences

Change a compound sentence or two sentences into a complex sentence by putting one of the ideas into an adjective, an adverb, or a noun clause.

EXAMPLE

TWO SENTENCES   Near the Potomac stands Mount Vernon. Here, in 1759, George Washington went to live with his bride, Martha.

COMPLEX   Near the Potomac stands Mount Vernon, where, in 1759, George Washington went to live with his bride, Martha.

MOUNT VERNON

A. 1. Take a trip to Mount Vernon. You will be taken back two centuries into the past.
   2. You approach through the visitors' entrance and suddenly you come upon a broad expanse of beautiful lawn.
   3. This is the bowling green bordered by majestic trees. These were probably planted by George Washington.
   4. Many smaller buildings are near the bowling green, but a visitor's eyes are immediately attracted to the mansion itself.
   5. This mansion is a unique historical monument, and so it has been restored as a national shrine.
   6. Many of the original furnishings have been brought back to the estate, and the interior takes us back to Washington's time.

B. 1. You sit on the porch of the mansion. You can look across the placid Potomac River winding its way below.
   2. Clothing, buttons, even shoes belonging to Washington and his family are displayed in the nearby museum. This was built in recent years.
   3. The smaller buildings include an icehouse, a smokehouse, a coach house, and a washhouse. These played an important part in the efficient running of so large an estate.
   4. The spinning house regularly employed twelve or more people. An attendant told me this.
   5. George Washington owned this beautiful estate from 1754 until his death in 1799. Because of his public service he could not live there for long periods.
   6. We think of the pleasant life George Washington gave up and then we can appreciate the extent of his sacrifices.

PRACTICE 21   Time Out for Review

As you copy the following sentences, correct all errors. For the three correct sentences write **C**.

CALIFORNIA

1. Since in our History class every student had their choice of a report topic, me and Paul Henderson have chose California.
2. It was he who first suggested learning more about that popular state.
3. Irving Stone, author of Immortal Wife had wrote for Holiday an exciting article about life in California.
4. Neither Paul nor I were aware of Californias long exciting history.
5. The first Europeans which visited California was led by Juan Rodriguez Cabrillo a Spaniard.

6. Mrs Nelson our teacher ask Paul and I have you read any books' about the settlement of California.
7. We didn't have no trouble finding Ramona a novel by Helen Hunt Jackson.
8. Paul and myself soon discovered that we gathered more information than we could possibly use.
9. Within the past few years the population of California has growed more rapid than that of any other State.
10. This here book, which I borrowed off of a friend, says that California is the third largest state in the Union.
11. On September 9 1850 said our teacher California become the thirty-first state to join United States.
12. Californias leading minerals are oil natural gas, sand, gypsum, salt, and gold.
13. Their is in California four national parks and many national monuments.
14. The fertile valleys lying between the Coast Range and the Sierra Nevada produce these varied crops: pears, asparagus, onions, melons, lettuce, grapes, and dates.
15. Although Dad grows melons, too, the cantaloupes from the Imperial Valley taste more sweetly than our's.
16. In the northwestern coastal areas the average rainfall in inches exceed seventy-five in the southeastern deserts the average is less than five.
17. Mt Whitney one of the highest points in United States is connected by scenic highway with Death Valley the lowest point.
18. One of the nations finest outdoor arenas are located in Pasadena, where each new years day the Rose Bowl football game attracts the attention of fans throughout the country.
19. "Does Columbia University or the University of California have the larger enrollment?" asked Paul.
20. "I seen that information in the *Information Please Almanac*," I replied, "but I cannot recall it.
21. "If your interested" I added "you'll find the book laying on the table near the window."
22. Our teacher said us boys done good in our report.
23. After class I said to Paul This Summer I'll be visiting my aunt and uncle out West.
24. My cousin Jack attends a High School in San Francisco, where he is studying English, Mathematics, Science, and Art.

32 *The Structure of Complete Sentences*

Jeff is dancing with Mary Lou is dancing with her sister.

There's something wrong here! Now read the words properly divided into two sentences.

Jeff is dancing with Mary. Lou is dancing with her sister.

The rise and fall of your voice in speaking tells your hearers where one sentence ends and another begins. In writing you need periods and capitals as signals to help your reader understand. Begin every sentence with a capital and end it with a sentence stopper (. ! ?).

DIAGNOSTIC TEST 12A Sentence Sense

Indicate by **0, 1, 2,** or **3** the number of complete sentences in each of the following. On your paper place a period between the number of the example and your answer.

EXAMPLES

    a. A line of dusty wagons rolling down the trail to Sacramento

    b. We hurriedly ran up the steps and entered the auditorium to our surprise the vast hall was empty

Answers a. 0 *b.* 2

The *0* indicates that *a* is not a sentence. The *2* shows that *b* is two sentences.

1. We spent almost all day fishing in the late afternoon a thunderstorm hit us the fish didn't bite again
2. Thousands of Chinese laborers built the transcontinental railroad and many died because of the difficult working conditions
3. The batter swung the ball arched into the air and vanished into the stands above the right fielder's outstretched glove

442

4. The firemen rescued the stranded cat the little boy was overjoyed that his pet was safe
5. The car skidding into a tree and turning over
6. Many cities in the United States have Spanish names Las Vegas means "the city of the plains" Los Gatos means "the place of the wildcat"
7. Late last month as my father was putting the car into the garage after a tiring drive from Baltimore
8. Who can forget the time that we picked three hundred boxes of blueberries in one day
9. The fishermen a hardy group who descended from people who originally settled in Nova Scotia
10. The lightning flashed and the thunder growled the gutters began to resemble a river

RUN–TOGETHER SENTENCE

N.1 *RUN–TOGETHER SENTENCE* If two or more sentences are written as one with a comma or no mark between them, the result is called a run-together sentence.

RUN-TOGETHER SENTENCE Do you have an extra tennis racket, mine is being restrung.

RIGHT Do you have an extra tennis racket? Mine is being restrung.

N.2 *MISLEADING CONNECTIVES* Some adverbs are often confused with conjunctions and used incorrectly to introduce clauses. The result is a run-together sentence.

Always check carefully a word group beginning with a word in the following list. These words are adverbs and cannot ordinarily join two clauses. (Review structure clues on page 424.)

also	furthermore	moreover	then
consequently	hence	nevertheless	there
finally	however	now	therefore
further	indeed	otherwise	thus

If you write a sentence using any of these adverbs in their transitional sense, punctuate your sentence as you would if the adverb were not there.

RUN-TOGETHER SENTENCE Herring spend most of the year in deep waters, then they migrate to the coast to lay their eggs.

RIGHT Herring spend most of the year in deep waters. Then they migrate to the coast to lay their eggs.

RUN-TOGETHER SENTENCE   Faster and faster the two trains raced down the
hills toward each other, finally they crashed with a roar like thunder.

RIGHT   Faster and faster the two trains raced down the hills toward each
other. Finally they crashed with a roar like thunder.

RUN-TOGETHER SENTENCE   Flamingos are usually pink, however, one rare
American variety is bright red.

RIGHT   Flamingos are usually pink. However, one rare American variety
is bright red.

PRACTICE 1   Correcting Run-together Sentences

Punctuate and capitalize the following. Be sure to place a capital
at the beginning and a period, an exclamation point, or a question
mark at the end of each sentence. In each simple sentence and in
each independent clause of a compound sentence or a complex sentence, draw one line under the simple or compound subject and two
lines under the predicate verb or verbs.

A. 1. Florence Nightingale was not happy in the idle luxury of her home
       even in her early years she wanted to help people
    2. I am coming to see you Saturday I hope you will be feeling much
       better
    3. Last week I went to a football game with the Youth Club we were
       supposed to leave the church at twelve-thirty
    4. How are you I hope you are all fine
    5. I've missed you since you moved away it's been very dull around
       here
    6. We fished for about two hours however I began to get tired and
       eager to go back
    7. My friend Sandi and I went in to New York to hunt for the thou-
       sand-dollar bill the radio show *Pulse* had hidden it somewhere in
       the city
    8. I started down the hill smoothly then the skis went completely out
       of control
    9. Did you really fall out of a tree and break your arm how in the
       world did that happen
    10. We stayed at the Desert Inn and found it very comfortable as well
        as beautiful how I hated to leave
    11. The "Screaming Woman" of the Australian countryside is really
        an owl it barks gruffly most of the time but at rare intervals emits
        ear-splitting shrieks
    12. Aunt Mary moved into her new apartment last Saturday her old
        apartment was a refrigerator on cold winter days
    13. Suddenly the creature behind us growled without bothering to look
        around Sally and I began to run

14. A medicine chest should be freshly stocked and neatly kept all medicines should be labeled correctly and any poisons should be clearly and conspicuously marked
15. Have you ever seen the ring around the constellation Lyra it looks like a smoke ring blown by a locomotive
16. The kiwi resembles everything but a bird its naked and useless wings are concealed beneath its thick hairlike body feathers
17. Wet your hair thoroughly with lukewarm water and rub in the shampoo with your fingertips taking care not to dig into the scalp with your fingernails after a couple of minutes rinse free of suds now reach once more for the shampoo and repeat the performance
18. The Indian called for water it was Deerslayer who got the water for him
19. The book told me many things about names there are at least 1,500,000 Americans named *Smith*
20. I have four brothers two of them are still in elementary school

B. 1. Last night Joanne and Dick came to the house about fifteen minutes later the rest of the crowd began to arrive
2. The studio couch wouldn't go through the hall finally we took it back downstairs turned it on its side and tried again
3. Would you like to come to visit me again this Thanksgiving let me know
4. My dog is very fussy about her food she refuses everything except meat and ice cream
5. I stepped back at John's warning the car missed me by a few inches
6. I worked in my father's lumberyard and had a lot of fun I had training in all kinds of measurement
7. We walked around the building for several hours by that time we were quite worn out
8. Norman and I performed a major miracle last week we took the brakes on his father's car apart and relined them
9. Stock-car races are exciting and full of surprises have you ever seen one
10. I must end this letter now and do my homework write me soon
11. On Saturdays my friends often come to my house we listen to records together
12. The quarterback took the pass from center suddenly he flipped the ball over the line of scrimmage
13. We reached Grand Canyon in the morning then we went to the floor of the canyon by burro
14. When the wood of the breadfruit tree is seasoned it resembles mahogany the natives of the islands in the Pacific make a strong cloth from its inner bark
15. My little cousin is taking concertina lessons I'll never know why

16. We were on our way to Mount Evans at 5:30 a.m. before we had gone five miles the left rear tire went flat
17. Andrew Jackson was born in a log cabin near the boundary of North and South Carolina as a lad of thirteen he fought in the American Revolution
18. In colonial America when a young man called on his best girl the two sat among the family and whispered to each other through a courting stick this was a wooden tube about eight feet long
19. Through an opening in the trees Rip could see the Hudson far below him lying on a grassy knoll he watched the river move slowly
20. For my birthday Dad gave me *Tales of Old-Time Texas* by Frank Dobie, it's a collection of yarns that mix history with folklore

PRACTICE 2 Punctuating and Capitalizing

Punctuate and capitalize the following paragraphs. Be sure to place a period, an exclamation point, or a question mark at the end of a sentence and to begin a sentence with a capital. There are fourteen sentences.

SNOWBOUND

If there's anything more fun than summer camping it's winter camping with or without snow last weekend my Girl Scout troop bivouacked at Snow Goose Lodge in the Cyamaca Mountains weeks before we had put our dads to work making barrel skis and cutting bamboo poles although none of us are Olympic material we were looking forward to a few practice runs on level ground weekends at the lodge are definitely not for the indoor girl among our usual activities are sledding rock collecting trail blazing and visiting the Ranger station and the fire-observation posts

This time Mother Nature took a hand in our fun no sooner had we reached the lodge than a blizzard broke while the storm raged we gathered around the huge stone fireplace keeping up our spirits with songs and tall tales on Saturday one of the girls discovered a record player and that night we produced our own "Sing Along" by that time some of us were secretly hoping we'd be snowbound until spring Monday morning however found us back at our desks in school the Forest Rangers knew of our whereabouts they showed up early Sunday afternoon and with two snowmobiles took us out over the drift-piled roads

SENTENCE FRAGMENT

N.3 *SENTENCE FRAGMENT* When a group of words that is not a sentence is written with a capital letter and a period, the expression is called a "sentence fragment."

A sentence fragment usually fails to tell who did something, what someone or something did, or what happened.

N.4   *CURING SENTENCE FRAGMENTS*   The two cures for sentence fragments are:
A. Attach the fragment to the preceding sentence.
B. Make the fragment into a complete sentence.

ATTACHED	MADE INTO A COMPLETE SENTENCE
A. One of the most ferocious eaters on earth is the piranha, a little fish of the Amazon River.	A. One of the most ferocious eaters on earth is the piranha. **This is** a little fish of the Amazon River.
B. In an attempt at exterminating the tiny monsters, Brazilian scientists have been using a violent poison, which the Amazon Indians have smeared on the tips of their darts for many years.	B. In an attempt at exterminating the tiny monsters, Brazilian scientists have been using a violent poison. **The** Amazon Indians have smeared this poison on the tips of their darts for many years.

Three Kinds of Fragments

Sentence fragments are chiefly of three kinds.

N.5   *NO VERB, NO SUBJECT*   A group of words without a verb or without a subject is a sentence fragment and should not be punctuated and capitalized as a complete sentence.

SENTENCE AND SENTENCE FRAGMENT   In cattle drives through piranha-infested waters, Brazilian farmers have always expected a loss.   At least one animal in every herd.

ATTACHED   In cattle drives through piranha-infested waters, Brazilian farmers have always expected a loss of at least one animal in every herd.

MADE INTO A COMPLETE SENTENCE   In cattle drives through piranha-infested waters, Brazilian farmers have always expected a loss.   **They have expected to lose** one animal in every herd.

Use the cure that produces the more effective result.   In the preceding examples the "attached" method produces a superior sentence, concise and grown-up.

PRACTICE 3   Correcting Sentence Fragments

After each of the following numbers there is a sentence fragment. Correct each fragment by using one of the two methods suggested.

1. Hobbyists seek the piranha for home aquariums and will pay a good price. At least seventy-five dollars for a single fish.
2. Cortland, New York, was once known as the "Carriage City." The home of the finest carriages ever made.
3. Cortland wagons and carriages were exported all over the world. Even to faraway lands like China and India.
4. A minority of drivers have the majority of accidents. According to a recent report by a leading insurance company.
5. The word *mortgage* originally meant a death pledge. A promise to repay a debt upon the death of a wealthy father.
6. Jet-engined aircraft require tremendous amounts of fuel. As much as eleven thousand gallons an hour.
7. Fortunately, jet engines can use kerosene. A cheaper fuel than high-octane gasoline.
8. An Israeli archaeologist has attributed many military successes to Joshua. The Biblical conqueror of Jericho.
9. We drove up the spur road through the forests to Timberline Lodge, halfway up the slope of Mount Hood. A skier's paradise with chair lifts, rope tows, a three-and-a-half-mile aerial tramway, trails three and four miles long, and open slopes unlimited.
10. The fourth night we stopped in a motel near Colorado Springs. Just at the foot of towering, snowcapped Pikes Peak.
11. For her first formal dance Gina bought a powder-blue dress with yards and yards of taffeta swirling in all directions. Also blue sandals.
12. A banged-up old bicycle with twisted handlebars and a broken saddle.
13. All of us like to have Clem throw for batting practice. A pitcher with a terrific fast ball.
14. A typical beef cow has a deep, wide body. With thick muscles, a broad neck, and short legs.
15. For my birthday Mother baked a coconut layer cake. Also a batch of blueberry muffins.
16. The day dawned bright and clear. The kind of day we all enjoy.

N.6 **VERBAL AS FRAGMENT** Participles, gerunds, and infinitives do not make statements, ask questions, or give commands and therefore are never predicate verbs. A verbal by itself can never take the place of a predicate verb. (Review pages 410–418.)

SENTENCE AND SENTENCE FRAGMENT From the top of the Ferris wheel I could see three merry-go-rounds. Spinning dizzily in the center of the carnival grounds.

ATTACHED From the top of the Ferris wheel I could see three merry-go-rounds spinning dizzily in the center of the carnival grounds.

MADE INTO A COMPLETE SENTENCE   From the top of the Ferris wheel I
could see three merry-go-rounds.   **They were** spinning dizzily in the
center of the carnival grounds.

SENTENCE AND SENTENCE FRAGMENT   We're going to Kansas City during
vacation.   To see our cousins.

ATTACHED   We're going to Kansas City during vacation **to** see our cousins.

MADE INTO A COMPLETE SENTENCE   We're going to Kansas City during
vacation.   **We're planning** to see our cousins.

PRACTICE 4   Correcting Sentence Fragments

In each of the following get rid of the sentence fragment by making it into a complete sentence or by attaching the fragment to
another sentence.   In each simple sentence and in each independent
clause of a compound or complex sentence draw one line under the
simple subject and two lines under the predicate verb or verbs.

1. I began to collect stamps about a year ago.   To learn something about
    the nations of the world.
2. At Freedomland we saw Gerry and Bill.   Riding high above us in the
    mine-bucket ride.
3. The old clam boat riding at anchor a hundred yards from shore.
4. Dad had our oak trees sprayed this spring.   To control the leaf miners
    that have seriously weakened the trees in recent years.
5. For nearly an hour we watched the gulls.   Soaring gracefully above
    the dock at St. Petersburg.
6. There are many exciting things to do at Niagara Falls.   For instance,
    taking a trip in the steamer *Maid of the Mist*.
7. Victoria hurried along the lower woods road.   Skillfully sidestepping
    puddles and fallen branches.
8. The *Chanticleer* staff met yesterday afternoon in Room 108.   To dis-
    cuss assignments for the Christmas issue.
9. I believe in eating a big breakfast.   Including orange juice, hot cereal,
    eggs, toast, and milk.
10. George Washington Carver studying peanuts and other crops and
    making discoveries that greatly helped farmers in the South.

N.7   *DEPENDENT CLAUSE AS FRAGMENT*   Many sentence fragments
have subjects and predicate verbs, but the subjects and verbs are
in dependent clauses.

SENTENCE AND FRAGMENT   You can't visit Yellowstone Park in the
winter.   Because it is buried under ten feet of snow.

ATTACHED   You can't visit Yellowstone Park in the winter because it is
buried under ten feet of snow.

FRAGMENT   Martha's Vineyard, which is an island off Cape Cod.
MADE INTO A COMPLETE SENTENCE   Martha's Vineyard is an island off
   Cape Cod.

PRACTICE 5   Correcting Sentence Fragments

Get rid of the sentence fragment in each of the following by making it into a complete sentence or by attaching it to another sentence. Then draw one line under the simple or compound subject and two lines under the predicate verb or verbs of the simple sentences and of all independent clauses in compound and complex sentences.

1. Certain birds don't come to our feeding station.   Unless we put out pieces of suet.
2. Lou Gehrig, whose courage and patience have remained a legend among ballplayers.
3. A stamp collector looked through his Canadian stamps and found a dozen Seaway commemoratives.   One of which had an inverted center.
4. Our family has owned a beagle, a retriever, and a setter.   Dogs which are frequently used for hunting.
5. From reading history I learned many interesting things.   For example, that James Buchanan was the only bachelor president.
6. Dad says he won't be talked into buying a station wagon.   Just because everybody else on Top Hill has one.
7. Ponce de León, the Spanish adventurer who went in search of the legendary Fountain of Youth.
8. On the trip to Washington I met an exchange student from Japan.   Who is now my pen pal.
9. The porcupine, which was once thought to throw its quills.
10. One of the lifeguards saw me and pulled me out of the water.   Just as I was going down for the third time.

Sentence Fragments in Conversation

Some sentence fragments are acceptable, especially in conversation.

QUESTIONS AND ANSWERS TO QUESTIONS   "Any Cokes in the refrigerator?"   "On the top shelf.   See them?"   "No."   "In back of the milk. Found one?   Good."   "Better put some more in, just in case."
EXCLAMATIONS AND COMMANDS   What a sunset!   To the rear of the bus, please.

Many professional writers use sentence fragments deliberately and effectively.

A husky howled from the bank, the last retort of a long day's argument. *An answering yelp from the opposite camp. Then silence.* — ANNE MORROW LINDBERGH

Perhaps your teacher will not object to your use of a sentence fragment now and then if you place an asterisk (*) before it and write "*Sentence fragment" at the bottom of the page. Pupils' sentence fragments are usually just bad writing. Be sure you know a fragment when you see it.

I like breakfast! Half a Bender melon from our own garden, rich golden yellow, ripe and sweet; a hot wheat biscuit upon which I spread a broad slice of my own comb honey, fresh from the hive, delicious to the taste. — DAVID GRAYSON

N.8 **SOUND AND SENSE** For a final check of sentence structure, read aloud what you write.

Your voice will often tell you where to put capitals and periods.

PRACTICE 6 Writing a Story   **W**

Does one of the following sentences remind you of an experience you've had? Make a good story of the experience to read to your classmates. Answer the questions "Who?" "When?" "Where?" "What?" in your opening paragraph. Arouse curiosity at the beginning and keep your audience in suspense. Give details that will help your classmates share your experience. Build up to a climax and conclude briefly.

After writing the story, look through it carefully for sentence fragments and run-together sentences. If you find any, correct the errors. Read the story aloud as a final check.

1. When the canoe tipped over, someone on the bank began to shout.
2. The little boy went tearfully to the policeman and said, "I'm losted."
3. The sky was leaden gray when we turned around to go back.
4. Since the path looked inviting, we decided to take it.
5. Puppies are one thing; kittens are a different problem.
6. Last Monday started out like any other school day.
7. Sometimes it's fun to be sick.
8. I was a new boy (or girl) in the neighborhood.

Indicate by **0, 1, 2,** or **3** the number of complete sentences in each of the following. On your paper place a period between the number of the example and your answer.

1. Sam is a very unusual boy who invents weird contraptions he is not dull
2. Bronco Crunch a linebacker for the Green Bay Packers always has an enormous breakfast of a quart of orange juice eight eggs a pound of bacon and half a loaf of toasted bread
3. Clouds of thick black smoke belching from the factory smokestacks screening the rays of the sun
4. As soon as he saw the wave approaching the captain spun the wheel to starboard
5. The volunteer firefighters are collecting money in town the funds will be used to purchase lifesaving equipment the citizens always appreciate their efforts
6. Before the first coat of wax is applied to the surface that has been sanded smooth with fine steel wool
7. Have you seen the plans for the new community center a place designed for meetings and local celebrations
8. We chose new stationery for our club plain white paper with the club's motto on it
9. Laura became fascinated by history reading book after book about the War of 1812
10. I need a new bicycle a ten-speed built along the lines of a British racer with such a bike I could get the exercise I need

As you rewrite the following, correct all the errors. Make each sentence fragment into a sentence. Divide each run-together sentence into two or more good sentences. For the two correct sentences write **C.**

FUN WITH WORDS

1. Have you ever noticed how humor often depends upon a tricky use of words? Like puns, for example?
2. Here's some examples of jokes what depend upon double meanings of words. (The key word is in italics in each story.)

3. The young girl setting in the witness stand certainly looked familiar to the judge.
4. "Haven't you already appeared as a witness in this *suit,*" asked the judge?
5. "In this old thing?" replied the boy in amazement. "Oh, no, this here *suit* is brown. The other was navy blue."

6. "Where's George, your daydreaming helper?" a customer he said to the proprietor of a small grocery store.
7. "I seen him only two days ago. He ain't fell and hurt hisself since, I hope."
8. "No," replied the owner, "He's just not working here as he use to."
9. "Have you filled the *vacancy* yet," asks the customer.
10. "When George leaves a job," replied the proprietor, "he don't leave no *vacancy.*"

11. Producer Gilbert Miller once brang to America a real popular london comedy.
12. Unfortunately, new york audiences didn't take very enthusiastic to the play.
13. About a week later the english playwright become anxious about the fate of his play and cabled new york, "how is it *going?*"
14. Miller cabled briefly, "It's *gone.*"

15. A overworked dentist was given orders by his doctor, "You should of took things easier. Cut down your work, or you're headed for a breakdown."
16. The next day a patient called and ask for a immediate appointment.
17. "I have broke a tooth," the patient said, "And want to see you right away."
18. "Sorry," replied the dentist, I have eighteen *cavities* to fill first.
19. With a grin he picked up his golf bag, then he went over the links.

20. Having trouble with his car, Gil had went to a garage.
21. The mechanic inspected the motor and said at last, "You wasn't getting full power. A cylinder is *missing.*"
22. "*Missing?* Impossible!" declared Gil. "I haven't never left the garage unlocked for more than a half an hour at a time."

23. For her birthday party the young hostess had baked all the cookie's.
24. At the party a guest confided to her neighbor, "Watch out! Them cookies on the tray is awful. They're as hard as granite."
25. "I know," replied her friend. "That's why Jennie told you to take your *pick.*"

33 *Structure for Style*

Study these two accounts of an exciting meeting between a boy and a wild stallion.

An inhuman scream suddenly shattered the stillness. It was a wild, terrifying call. The sailors stood still. They were stunned. The hairs on the back of their necks seemed to curl. A horse appeared beside Alec as if by magic. It was a giant black horse. His mane was waving like a flame. The horse screamed again. The sailors could see even at a distance that he was a tremendous horse. He was a wild stallion.

Alec flung his arms around the black's neck. He buried his head in the long mane. He called the horse "Black." He told him they were leaving together. He talked to the stallion soothingly, steadying him. He descended the hill after a few minutes. The horse hesitatingly followed.

Suddenly an inhuman scream shattered the stillness — a wild, terrifying call. Stunned, the sailors stood still, and the hairs on the back of their necks seemed to curl. As if by magic, a giant black horse, his mane waving like a flame, appeared beside Alec. The horse screamed again. Even at a distance the sailors could see that he was a tremendous horse — a wild stallion.

Alec flung his arms around the black's neck and buried his head in the long mane. "We're leaving together, Black — together," he said. Soothingly he talked to the stallion, steadying him. After a few minutes he descended the hill, and the horse hesitatingly followed.[1] — WALTER FARLEY, *The Black Stallion*

Walter Farley wrote the second account. Instead of writing eighteen sentences — all starting with the subject — he used nine sentences, only two starting with the subject. He quoted conversation directly and used two appositives. In some places he said in one word or phrase what in the first account it took a whole sentence to say.

[1] Reprinted by permission of the publisher, Random House, Inc. Copyright, 1941.

You may not become another Walter Farley, but you can improve your writing by learning to vary sentence beginnings, to streamline your sentences, to quote directly, and to use complex sentences.

SENTENCE VARIETY

O.1 *SUBJECT–NOT–FIRST SENTENCES* For variety and for emphasis frequently place a word or words other than an adjective before the subject. Thus you vary the basic patterns (pages 462-468).

Emphasis falls naturally at the beginning and at the end of a sentence. Notice the effective emphasis in these subject-not-first sentences:

ADVERB   Ordinarily we think of the cactus as a desert flower.

ADVERB CLAUSE   Although the cactus is associated principally with desert areas, cactus plants are actually widespread.

PARTICIPIAL PHRASE   Having studied the cactus all over the United States, Sir Oliver Leese has reported his unusual findings.

INFINITIVE PHRASE   To find a cactus plant, look around in your own state, unless you live in Maine, Vermont, or Alaska.

PREPOSITIONAL PHRASE   In every state of the Union, except the three mentioned, the cactus grows wild.

DIRECT OBJECT   This information we read in a *New York Times* news item.

Do not change the normal subject-first order if the change makes the sentence sound clumsy or unnatural.

UNNATURAL   On the subject of cacti Sir Oliver has written a book.

BETTER   Sir Oliver has written a book on the subject of cacti.

PRACTICE 1   Revising Subject-first Sentences

Improve the following sentences by putting something other than an adjective before the subject. Make your sentences smooth, natural, and effective.

EXAMPLE   The Great Dismal Swamp in Virginia and North Carolina is one of the strangest spots on earth because it is a land of unexpected sights and unusual sounds.

Because it is a land of unexpected sights and unusual sounds, the Great Dismal Swamp in Virginia and North Carolina is one of the strangest spots on earth.

THE GREAT DISMAL SWAMP

1. Few tourists stop to investigate the wonders of the Great Dismal Swamp, though they pass through sections of it on their way to Florida.
2. The Great Dismal, named by Colonel William Byrd two centuries ago,

is scarcely explored even today. 3. No roads or highways penetrate into the real depths of the swamp along the North Carolina border. 4. The vegetation throughout the area is unbelievably dense and vigorous. 5. A traveler must duck low in some places to see more than a few feet in any direction.

6. Attempts to use the rich soil for agricultural purposes have been given up, although many persons have tried. 7. George Washington, oddly enough, formed a company to drain the swamp. 8. Cotton plants grew to ten feet and produced blue and yellow bolls when they were started in the soil of the swamp. 9. The soil can actually catch fire because it is so rich in vegetable matter. 10. Fire pits form as a result of fires and add a weird trap for unwary travelers.

11. The Dismal Swamp, naturally enough, provides an ideal home for many kinds of wildlife. 12. The swamp would be a hunters' paradise if it were more accessible. 13. Animals, birds, fish, and snakes abound in the heart of the swamp. 14. Some hunters go in on foot to tap the resources of this wonderland. 15. They must be vigilant and stay with a skilled guide if they wish to return safely.

A string of subject-not-first sentences would be just as monotonous as a series of sentences with the subject first, but you are probably in no danger of carrying the good idea to extremes.

STREAMLINED SENTENCES

0.2 COMPACT WRITING Get rid of excess baggage by substituting, when possible, a word or a phrase for a sentence or a clause.

Pick out the words expressing the important ideas and with these words build a compact sentence.

Review pages 410–416, 419–441. (These are pages devoted to using verbals, using complex sentences, using compound sentences.)

WORDY The *name* of *Margaret* can be traced back. It *comes* from a *Greek* word. In the Greek language it *means "pearl."* (Three sentences, twenty-one words. The important words are italicized.)

COMPACT The name *Margaret* comes from a Greek word meaning "pearl." (Simple sentence, ten words)

WORDY The *army* that was commanded by *Washington* fought a battle at *Germantown* which resulted in a *defeat.* This was in the *fall* of *1777.* Then the army went and spent the *winter* at *Valley Forge.* (Three sentences, thirty-four words. *Valley Forge* is one word.)

COMPACT After a defeat at Germantown in the fall of 1777, Washington's army wintered at Valley Forge. (Simple sentence, fifteen words)

PRACTICE 2 Streamlining Sentences

By substituting a single word, a few words, or a phrase for each italicized sentence or clause, reduce each of the following to one compact simple sentence.

EXAMPLE Andrew Carnegie's parents were immigrants. *They came to America from Scotland.*
Andrew Carnegie's parents were Scottish immigrants.

1. Virginia City has a museum. *This is a historical museum and it contains relics from the old mining days.*
2. *A man who was a resident of Quebec* painted a street-light bulb black. *He wanted to stop the light from shining in his bedroom window.*
3. *In Caracas, Venezuela, there are prosperous beggars. They* imported beggars from other countries. *The imported beggars worked for the natives on a commission basis.*
4. The eye of the hurricane *is surrounded by whirling winds. The eye itself* is a place of calm air and bright sunshine.
5. *If you are interested in starting a butterfly collection,* you will need only two little items. *You will need a net and some chloroform.*

O.3 **DEADWOOD** Cut out deadwood. Don't say the same thing twice in different words.

"St. Louis Blues" is my favorite song, ~~and I like it better than any other song I know~~. (The words crossed out mean the same thing as *favorite*.)
~~In my opinion~~ I think football is a good sport to watch on television. (*In my opinion* duplicates *I think*.)
Carolyn whispered something to Billie ~~quietly in a low voice~~. (How else would she whisper?)

0.4 *VERY, RATHER* Avoid overusing words like **very** and *rather*. When these words are overused, they weaken statements instead of emphasizing (or intensifying) them.

It is ~~very~~ important to write your name legibly on the sign-up sheet.
I am ~~rather~~ fond of marshmallow sundaes.

PRACTICE 3 Cutting Out Deadwood

As you rewrite the following sentences, omit all useless words.

A. 1. Many city streets in downtown Boston are surprisingly narrow.
2. Teddy shouted in a loud voice, "Watch the second baseman!"
3. Lenny See is rather tall for his age.
4. It was last summer that I decided to become a journalist.
5. My very worst fault is my very quick temper and the way I fly off the handle.
6. Just pack the necessary things you'll need for an overnight hike.
7. The very narrow road took a very sudden turn.
8. Is the ferry to Breezy Point still running any more?
9. Please send me the following books listed below.
10. In my opinion I think a good pie is a lot easier to make than a good cake.

B. 1. Dogs can hear sounds that are inaudible to the human ear and cannot be heard by people.
2. I beg to inform you that the December issue of *National Geographic* magazine has not yet arrived.
3. Cal Markley, the new president of the Student Council, is very popular and is very well liked by everyone.
4. The book *Please Don't Eat the Daisies* is one book that had me laughing constantly every minute of the time I was reading it.
5. Chokecherries are rather bitter to the taste.
6. Before you go to bed look and make sure that all the windows and doors are locked.
7. My sister Lois is working at a job as an usher at the Colony Theater showing people to their seats.
8. It is very essential to take every advantage of the extra opportunities your school offers you outside of your daily class activities.
9. Sun Valley, Idaho, is a popular year-round resort in the Sawtooth Mountains, and many vacationers go there.
10. Can you ever forget the never-to-be-forgotten spill we took on the bobsled at Lake Placid?

O.5 *APPOSITIVES* To streamline your sentences, substitute an occasional appositive for a clause or a sentence.

An appositive saves words, makes a sentence more forceful, and adds important information briefly.

TWO SENTENCES Princess Anne is a big gray mare. She is the fastest horse at Muir's Stable.

APPOSITIVE Princess Anne, a big gray *mare*, is the fastest horse at Muir's Stable.

COMPLEX SENTENCE   The ibex, which is a species of wild goat, is highly
   prized by hunters.
APPOSITIVE   The ibex, a *species* of wild goat, is highly prized by hunters.

PRACTICE 4   Using Appositives

In each of the following substitute an appositive for one of the
sentences or for the dependent clause.

OUR NATION'S CAPITAL

A. 1. Every spring over half a million vacationing students visit
Washington, D.C., which is one of the finest tourist cities in the world.
2. Major Pierre Charles L'Enfant drew the plans for the city. He was a
French engineer. 3. All the streets and avenues begin at Capitol Hill,
which is a plateau eighty-three feet above the Potomac River. 4. Situated
on this plateau, the Capitol overlooks the other government buildings.
The Capitol is an impressive white sandstone building. 5. Three streets
running from Capitol Hill help divide the city into four sections. These
streets are North Capitol, East Capitol, and South Capitol. (Use dashes
to set off the three appositives.) 6. The fourth dividing line is an imaginary one extending from the Mall, which is a wide stretch of walks and
gardens.

B. 1. At the eastern end of the Mall is the Grant Memorial. This
memorial is the second largest equestrian statue in the world. 2. The
Washington Monument rises near the center of the Mall. The Washington Monument is a 555-foot shaft made of Maryland white marble.
3. West of the Washington Monument are the long Reflecting Pool and
the Lincoln Memorial, which is a temple-like building with marble columns forty feet high. 4. From nearby Potomac Park tourists can look
across the river toward Arlington, Virginia. Arlington was once the home
of Robert E. Lee.

5. Mount Vernon, which is another tourist attraction, lies fifteen
miles south of Washington. 6. This beautiful estate is the former home
and the burial place of George Washington. It is a national shrine.

PRACTICE 5   Streamlining a Theme

Make the following theme more effective by using some subject-
not-first sentences, by getting rid of useless words, and by using
appositives.

FRANKFURTER FAVORITES

The Pig and Whistle is a drive-in. It's at Oak Neck Beach. The
speciality of the house at the Pig and Whistle is the hot dog. Right now
I'd give anything to bite into one this minute.

I usually order the Dachshund. This is a king-size frankfurter. It's layered with sauerkraut. The sauerkraut is very mouth-watering and the servings are very generous. There is another favorite. It's the Chihuahua. This is a regular-size frank. It's smothered with chili sauce that's red hot.

I eat two or three Poodles after a very hard day riding the waves. These hot dogs are the very same size as the Dachshund. They're not served with sauerkraut though. They're served with chopped onions instead.

I munch my way through a Frank Kabob when I can afford it. This is a charcoal-broiled frankfurter. It's on a skewer. There are chunks of baked ham and juicy pineapple on the skewer too.

There's a hot dog in the Pig and Whistle's kennel for just about almost everyone.

0.6   DIRECT QUOTATIONS   Use direct quotations for clearness and forcefulness.

Do you like number 1 or number 2 better? Why?

1. "Any questions?" asked the guide after a tour of the Metropolitan Museum of Art.

"Yes," a little old lady said; "how do you get such a high finish on your waxed floors?"

2. After a tour of the Metropolitan Museum of Art, the guide asked the group whether there were any questions. A little old lady asked him how the Museum got such a high finish on the waxed floors.

0.7   COMPLEX SENTENCES   To add force and variety to your writing, occasionally substitute complex sentences for compound sentences. (Review pages 427–441.)

COMPOUND SENTENCE   Leonardo da Vinci was interested in flying, and he made many sketches of possible airplanes.

COMPLEX SENTENCE   Because Leonardo da Vinci was interested in flying, he made many sketches of possible airplanes.

PRACTICE 6   Telling an Experience   **W**

After studying the following example, write entertainingly about a first experience of your own — for example, your first report card, your first train (or other) ride, your first visit to the dentist or doctor, your first experiences in earning money or in learning to skate, ski, fish, dance, swim, or ride a bicycle.

As you revise your story, improve the sentences in the ways suggested. Then place before a sentence the figure 1 if you have put something other than an adjective before the subject, 2 if there is an appositive in it, 3 if it contains a direct quotation, and 4 if the sentence is complex. For example, the (1, 2, 4) before the first sentence of "Fishing at Night" shows that something other than an adjective has been put before the subject (1), there is an appositive (2), and the sentence is complex (4).

FISHING AT NIGHT

(1, 2, 4) Time after time I had heard my father and his friend Mr. King say that nothing could beat the night fishing from the jetties along the Jersey coast. (4) Imagine my surprise and joy one morning when Dad told me that I could go with them on their next trip. (2) Mr. King, a bachelor, wasn't too anxious to take me along, but summer was nearly over and Dad wanted me to have an experience I'd never forget. (1, 4) As it turned out, I won't forget. (1) Neither will Mr. King.

(1) After fussing all afternoon and evening with our equipment, we set out a little after midnight. (1) Arriving at our destination, we each unloaded our own gear from the car. (1, 4) When we came to the embankment leading to the beach, Dad and Mr. King slid expertly down the slope. (1, 4) Since I was in strange country, I followed rather cautiously.

(1, 4) As we trudged along the beach, my foot struck a partly hidden piling. I fell flat on my stomach with my face and reel buried in the sand. (1, 3, 4) As I scrambled to my feet and picked up the reel, Mr. King exclaimed, "Why, that's my reel!"

(1, 4) When we unloaded the car in the darkness, we must have switched rods. (1, 4) Since Mr. King had an expensive reel, it was heavily oiled for protection from the salt air. (4) The sand sifted into every opening and stuck as though the oil were glue.

(1, 3) "Are you all right, Paul?" Dad sounded concerned, but he was looking at the reel, not at me.

(1, 3) "Y-yes," I sputtered through a mouthful of sand. (1, 3) "Is the reel O.K.?"

(1) After one murderous look at me, the two men scooped up the equipment and headed for the car and home. (1) Without a word of instruction Mr. King handed me some toothpicks with cotton wrapped around them. (1, 4) As he took the reel apart I carefully wiped each of the fifty tiny cogs. It was now about one-thirty. The fifty parts seemed like five hundred. (1, 4) Just as the sun was coming up, we tested the assembled rod and heard the smooth, humming sound of a well-oiled reel. (1) Yawning, I staggered up to bed.

I have gone fishing many times since and have handled some expensive equipment. (1, 4) Whenever anyone takes a reel apart for oiling and I see all those tiny parts spread out, I get a little dizzy. — PAUL GORELICK, The Bronx, New York

34 *Sentence Patterns*

Patterns with chapter English deals sentence this.

There is something familiar about the preceding sentence, but the meaning is tantalizingly obscure. You recognize the words; yet the sentence doesn't make sense. Why not? It doesn't make sense because it doesn't fall into an English sentence pattern.

This chapter deals with English sentence patterns.

Now this sentence makes sense. What has happened? The words have been rearranged into a recognizable pattern.

Because millions of persons have been using English for hundreds of years, certain basic ways of expressing ideas have become fixed. Certain patterns have been developed. These patterns are as recognizable as the structure of a human hand.

PRACTICE 1 Rearranging Scrambled Sentences

Rearrange each of the following scrambled groups into a recognizable English sentence.

EXAMPLE

the enjoy baseball boys.
The boys enjoy baseball.

1. clock the nine struck.
2. tests passed his all Joe.
3. my forgot I homework.
4. hamburgers Americans most like.

Signal Words

Common English words like *a*, *the*, *my*, and *to* help establish the patterns we recognize. (See also pages 259, 366, 368–369, 370–371 and 372.) Without these signal words (or function words as they are sometimes called) many written messages would be difficult to understand. Note how the insertion of two signal words completely transforms the meaning of the following sentence:

Bud dropped the branch.
The bud dropped **from** the branch.

The Basic Patterns

There seems to be an almost infinite variety of English sentences, and many of them are extremely complex, but all of them are built according to a handful of basic patterns. When someone speaks or writes a sentence, he constructs it according to one of these patterns, and the position of each word in the pattern helps indicate its part in expressing the meaning of the sentence.

The sentences we speak or write are produced by changing, or transforming,[1] one of these basic patterns into the particular sentence that expresses our meaning.

Knowing how various kinds of thoughts are best expressed by various patterns is like knowing how the diverse parts of your automobile work. Your knowledge enables you to use the machine more effectively. Knowing several ways of expanding basic sentences will help you master the finer points of operating your language machine.

 PATTERN 1. S V **(SUBJECT • VERB)**

S V
Strangers came.

This sentence shows the SV pattern in its simplest form. Few of our sentences are so uncomplicated. As we expand basic patterns with modifiers (pages 352–365), we express our meaning more exactly and completely.

S V
⌐Fierce strangers⌐ came.

The modifier *fierce* adds a descriptive detail to the noun *strangers*. A noun with its modifiers is sometimes called a *noun cluster*. The noun modified is called the *headword* (page 352).

A noun cluster may grow in richness and complexity.

S   V
⌐Fierce strangers in huge iron war canoes⌐ came.

The bracketed words constitute one noun cluster with *strangers* as the headword. Note that the pattern is still **SV.** The sentence may be expanded in other ways.

---

[1] Some grammarians refer to this process as "transformation" and describe English grammar by working out the rules according to which such transformation can be made.

S   V

Strangers ⌐suddenly came ⌐.

The preceding sentence adds a modifier, *suddenly*, to the verb *came*. The verb with its modifiers is sometimes called a *verb cluster*. This time the verb *came* is the headword.

S   V

Strangers ⌐suddenly came to the lonely South Sea islands⌐.

Further expansion adds descriptive details to the verb cluster. Now let's combine the detailed noun and verb clusters into a single sentence:

S   V

⌐Fierce strangers in huge iron war canoes⌐ ⌐suddenly came

to the lonely South Sea islands⌐.

Despite the expansion of the original sentence, the pattern is still **SV**. We speakers of English are constantly devising detailed and varied sentences. Yet despite the seeming variety we use only a few basic patterns.

PRACTICE 2   Identifying the SV Pattern

Pick out subject and verb. Show that the pattern of each of the following sentences is **SV**.

1. The rain fell steadily for two days.
2. Suckers from the roots of an old chestnut tree grew along the trail around Big Meadow swamp.
3. A threatening mass of cumulonimbus clouds arose in the western sky before sunset.
4. Many azaleas bloom in March in the famous Middleton Gardens.
5. Eleanor arrived at the meeting a few minutes after eight.
6. Many unusual and scenic hikes start from the road along the Skyline Drive in Virginia.

PRACTICE 3   Writing Sentences with the SV Pattern

A. Write five two-word sentences, each containing the simple **SV** pattern.

EXAMPLE   Helicopters arrived.

B. Write five sentences with noun clusters and verb clusters, but retain the simple **SV** pattern. Do not add a complement (pages 366–

374). If you wish, you may expand some or all of the sentences you used in A.

         S   **V**

EXAMPLE Helicopters with food and medical supplies arrived at the isolated farm on the frozen prairie.

PATTERN 2. S V O (SUBJECT • VERB • DIRECT OBJECT)

              S   **V**   **O**

Birds eat insects.

The sample sentence shows the **SVO** pattern in its simplest form, but we are seldom satisfied with such brevity.

            S   **V**   **O**

|Many birds| eat |harmful insects.|

Now we have expanded the original sentence and formed two noun clusters, but we have retained the original **SVO** pattern.

        S   **V**   **O**

Birds |often eat| insects.

Now we have expanded the sentence by introducing an adverb to make a verb cluster (in brackets), but we have again retained the original **SVO** pattern.

The following sentences with their noun and verb clusters all demonstrate the **SVO** pattern.

      S   **V**   **O**

|A hairpin| |prevented| |the crash of an Australian airliner|.

       S   **V**   **O**

|The pilot| |cleverly short-circuited| |the electrical system|.

        S   **V**   **O**

|This procedure| |luckily freed| |the jammed nosewheel of the loaded airplane|.

For further study of the **SVO** pattern see rule H.1 and pages 366–367.

PATTERN 3. S V I O (SUBJECT • VERB • INDIRECT OBJECT • DIRECT OBJECT)

             S   **V**   **I**   **O**

Uncle sent me money.

     S   **V I**   **O**

My uncle in Mexico sent me some Mexican money.

For further study of the **SVIO** pattern see rule H.2 and pages 368–369.

PATTERN 4. S V N **(SUBJECT • VERB • PREDICATE NOUN OR PREDICATE PRONOUN)**

S   V   N
Books are safeguards.

  S   V   N
Books, **according to Andrew Jackson,** are safeguards **of our nation.**

S   V N
The winner **of the first race** was he.

For further study of the **SVN** pattern see rule H.3 and pages 370–371.

PATTERN 5. S V A **(SUBJECT • VERB • PREDICATE ADJECTIVE)**

S   V   A
Reptiles were dominant.

S   V   A

Huge reptiles were dominant **throughout the earth during the Mesozoic Era.**

For further study of the **SVA** pattern see rule H.4 and page 372.

PRACTICE 4 Identifying Sentence Patterns

Identify the pattern in each of the following sentences. Label the key words in each.

S   V   O

EXAMPLE Flounders change the size of their spots for camouflage.

1. Dinosaurs became extinct for a variety of reasons.
2. Some dinosaurs were rather gentle creatures.
3. Terry lent me his pen.
4. The Japanese have developed a half-inch camera.
5. Illinois became a state on December 3, 1818.

PRACTICE 5 Expanding Sentences

Expand each of the following sentences. Add modifiers but retain the basic pattern in each case. Do not, for example, add an object to an **SV** pattern. Label each key word.

EXAMPLE Ted sent us oranges.

S   V I

During his last trip to Fort Myers Ted generously sent us juicy Valencia

   O

oranges.

1. We enjoy bread.	6. Rooms were chilly.
2. Kittens play.	7. Stars are suns.
3. Kevin was cheerful.	8. Spectators applauded.
4. Dogs are companions.	9. Arnie gave me advice.
5. Mother gave us lemonade.	10. Snakes destroy rodents.

PRACTICE 6 Writing Sentences

Write ten vivid sentences based on events that happened to you during the past week. Use all five patterns. Be ready to identify each pattern and point out the key words.

OTHER EXPANSIONS

The patterns are varied in many ways. You have already noticed how noun clusters and verb clusters help expand ideas. Notice in the following examples how other devices provide additional variations. But note also that the basic patterns remain.

1. A compound element (page .274)

    S   V   O

Ellen and Harry joined the beach club and country club. (Still **SVO**)

2. A two-, three-, or four-part verb (pages 263–264) or other word (page 265).

    S   V

Vikings may have landed in the Western Hemisphere long before Columbus. (Still **SV**)

          S   V   O

The Bay of Fundy has spectacularly high tides. (Still **SVO**)

Other variations include inverted sentences (page 272) and verbs in the passive voice (pages 345–347). Native speakers of English handle these variations with ease.

3. An inverted sentence

Where have you been?

   S   V

You have been where? (When the sentence is arranged in subject-first order, it falls into the **SV** pattern.)

4. A verb in the passive voice

We were disappointed by John's performance.

This sentence is a transformation of a basic sentence (Pattern 2).

          S   **V**   **O**

John's performance disappointed us.

PRACTICE 7   Identifying Sentence Patterns

A. Identify the patterns of the sentences in Practice 15, page 268. Label the key words. Check in class before going on to B.

B. Point out the patterns in the practices listed below.

<table>
<tr><td></td><td>1, page 260</td><td></td></tr>
<tr><td>4, page 355</td><td>3, page 369</td><td>6, page 373</td></tr>
<tr><td>10, page 359</td><td>5, page 371</td><td>8, page 373</td></tr>
</table>

C. Point out the patterns in the practices listed below. If a sentence is inverted, rearrange it in natural order and identify the pattern in the rearranged sentence. Do not label sentences with passive verbs.

20, page 273   21, page 275   16, page 364   9, page 374

PRACTICE 8   Creating and Expanding Sentences

For additional practice in expanding sentences refer to the practices listed below. Create or expand sentences according to the directions. Identify the patterns you use.

<table>
<tr><td>2, page 260</td><td>3, page 354</td><td>2, page 368</td></tr>
<tr><td>5, page 263</td><td>6B, page 356</td><td>7, page 373</td></tr>
<tr><td>18, page 271</td><td>13B, page 361</td><td>10, page 374</td></tr>
</table>

35 *Spelling*

"Spelling is so difficult," says Myra Lewis, but she can remember, note for note, a complicated sonata. "I just can't learn to spell," says Dave Pollett, but he readily remembers the heights of the mountains in a nearby range.

If Myra and Dave gave to spelling a third of the energy they now devote to other feats of memory, they'd find this "difficult" subject much easier. You can become a good speller if you decide to master those words you misspell.

HOW TO BECOME A GOOD SPELLER

1. Know the meaning and the pronunciation of each word you study. When in doubt, look the word up in your dictionary.
2. Spend all your spelling time studying the words you misspell. If your teacher doesn't test you when he assigns a spelling lesson, have someone at home read the words to you as you write them. List in your notebook the words you miss. Circle or underline the spot that gave you trouble. Study each word until you can spell it correctly every time.
3. Add to your notebook list the words you misspell in themes, letters, and tests. STUDY, TEST; STUDY, TEST; STUDY, TEST until you've mastered the list. Review your list every two weeks. Refer to it when you check your written work.
4. Don't guess. If you're not sure you can spell a word correctly, look it up in the dictionary. If you can't find a word in the dictionary, ask your teacher to help you.
5. Observe words sharply. When you proofread your papers, look up every word that doesn't look right. Most poor spelling is pure carelessness.
6. Learn to apply these basic spelling rules: *ei-ie* (**P.7**); final *e* (**P.9** and **P.10**); final *y* (**P.13**); and doubling final consonants (**P.11** and **P.12**).

PRACTICE 1 Diagnosing Your Spelling Demons

Your teacher will dictate the following list of one hundred frequently misspelled words. Many of them are common words you use every day. Write in your notebook the words you miss. (Rule numbers are listed. Rule P.1 could apply to all of the words.)

100 SPELLING DEMONS

acquaint	disappear	meant P.5	stopped P.11
across P.2.1	disappoint	minute	stretch
all right P.5	doctor P.4.5	necessary	studying P.13
almost	does	ninety P.10	surprise P.2.2
always	doesn't P.6	ninth P.10	their P.14; P.15
among	every	noticing P.9	then P.3
appreciate	exception	occasion	there P.14
asked	excitement P.10	occurred P.5; P.12	they're P.6; P.15
athletic P.2.1	experience	piece P.7	thorough P.5
beautiful P.13	February P.2.2	pleasant P.5	through P.14
beginning P.12	finally P.2.2; P.8	principal P.14	to P.14
believe P.7	forty P.5	principle P.14	together P.5
benefit P.5	fourth P.5	privilege P.2.2	too P.14
boundary P.2.2	friend P.7	probably P.2.2	toward
business P.5	government P.2.2	quiet P.3	tried P.13
buy P.5	grammar P.4.2	realize	truly P.10
character P.5	humor P.4.5	really P.8	until
clothes P.3	immediately P.10	receive P.7	usually P.8
coming P.9	interesting	recommend	where
committee P.5	it's P.6; P.15	scene	whether P.14
decision	its P.15	secretary P.2.3	which
definite	know	separate P.5	writing P.9
describe	knowledge P.5	similar P.4.2	written
description	library P.2.2	since	your P.15
different P.12	lose P.3	speech P.5	you're P.6; P.15

HAVE A SYSTEM

P.1 *SEE–SAY–WRITE* Use the see-say-write method to learn to spell a word.

Repeat these steps three times for each word on your spelling list. After you have studied ten words in this manner, have someone dictate them to you. Give the words you still misspell the see-say-write treatment again. Continue the studying and testing until you learn to spell every word on your list.

1. See the word. Look at it carefully. Notice double letters: *committee;* hard spots like *cq, ai: acquaint;* endings like *ar* or *or: grammar, humor.* Close your eyes and see the word on a mental chalkboard. Open your eyes and compare your mental picture with the word in the book. See the mental picture again. Check.

2. Say the word. Pronounce the word distinctly. Say it by syllables: *char ac ter.* Compare what you hear with what you see. Notice silent letters: *scene;* different sound for the same combination of letters: *through, though.* Use the word in a sentence.

3. Write the word. Cover the book and write the word from your mental picture. Check with the book.

PRACTICE 2   Applying the See-Say-Write Method

Refer to your notebook list of words misspelled in Practice 1. Study one word at a time, using the method described under P.1.

Numbers for spelling helps in this chapter have been placed after some of the words in the demon list on page 470. If you have misspelled *friend*, for example, refer to P.7 for additional help in learning to spell this word.

SAY IT AND SPELL IT

P.2 *PRONOUNCE AND SPELL*   Clear pronunciation will help you to spell many words correctly.

The hard spots in the following groups of words are underlined. Listen closely to your pronunciation when you say these words.

1. Don't add an extra sound: once NOT "onct"; elm NOT "ellum."

across	drowned	film
athletic	entrance	pronunciation

2. Don't omit a sound: fam i ly NOT "famly"; quan ti ty NOT "quanity."

boundary	finally	library	probably	surprise
February	government	privilege	recognize	twelfth

3. Don't transpose sounds: apron NOT "aporn"; modern NOT "modren."

children	perhaps	prevent
perform	preserve	secretary

P.3 *WORDS OFTEN CONFUSED* Watch your pronunciation of these pairs of words that are often confused.

Be sure you know the meaning of each word.

accept an apology	a guilty *conscience*	*lose* your way
all *except* Pat	*conscious* of guilt	a *loose* noose
advice for batters	a simple *device*	*prophecy* of a witch
advise the team	*devise* a plan	to *prophesy* doom
breath of air	*formally* dressed	a *quiet* room
breathe deeply	*formerly* sang in the choir	*quite* sunny room
wear *clothes*		*then* I'll study
polish with *cloths*		sooner *than* Bud

The nouns *advice*, *device*, and *prophecy* are spelled with *c;* the verbs *advise*, *devise*, and *prophesy* have *s*.

PRACTICE 3 Using *Loose* and *Lose*

As you copy the following sentences, fill each blank with *loose* or *lose*. *Lose* (LOOZ) is a verb meaning "not to have any longer." *Loose* (LOOS) is usually an adjective meaning "not tight." Say the word aloud and then spell it correctly.

1. How could you ____ such a large carton unless the rope was ____ ?
2. Tie that ____ lace before you ____ your shoe.
3. Don't ____ your footing on those ____ stones.
4. A ____ steering wheel caused him to ____ control of the car.
5. If you let Squiffy run ____, you may ____ her.

PRACTICE 4 Using Words Often Confused

W

A. Copy the following paragraph, filling each blank with the letters for the word that will complete the meaning of the sentence.

Denny's (1) consci____ bothered him (2) qui____ a bit. He tried to (3) devi____ an excuse his mother might (4) ____cept. He was (5) consci____ that he had not followed her (6) advi____. How (7) th__n could he explain the condition of his good (8) clo____ (9) ____cept by confessing he'd been fighting again? He took a deep (10) brea____ and shuffled up the porch steps.

B. Use ten words from the above list in good sentences. You may use more than one of the words in a sentence.

OR If you would like to test your ingenuity, write a paragraph. Perhaps you would like to tell what happened when Denny faced his mother.

MAKE AN ASSOCIATION

The English language has such a variety of combinations of letters for different sounds that pronunciation may not always help you to spell words. After you've marked the hard spots for such words on your personal list, try one of these helps.

P.4 *SIMILAR HARD SPOTS* Group words that have similar hard spots.

If you always spell *labor* correctly, remember the *or* in *labor* when you spell *janitor*.

1. These words have *ai* in the last syllable.

bargain	captain	maintain
Britain	certain	villain

2. Note that the *ar* ending of these words sounds like *er*.

beggar	calendar	collar	particular	vinegar
burglar	circular	grammar	similar	vulgar

3. Only three words end in *ceed*. Remember *ex*, *pro*, and *suc*.

exceed	proceed	succeed

4. Five common words end in *el*.

angel	label	level	towel	vessel

5. The *or* ending of these words sounds like *er*.

author	elevator	humor	radiator	sponsor
aviator	error	janitor	rumor	successor
director	governor	mirror	senator	vigor
doctor	harbor	professor	spectator	visitor

P.5 *SPECIAL HARD SPOTS* Make up a sentence or a phrase to help you remember a hard spot.

all right	Two words like *all wrong*
answered	**Were** the letters answered yesterday?
benefit	Mr. **Ben E. Fit** opened the **benefit.**
business	I need a **bus in** my **busi**ness.
buy	When you **buy** something, you **pur**chase it.
character	**Char**les will **act** a **charac**ter from the Arabian Nights.
committee	2 *m*'s, 2 *t*'s, 2 *e*'s
courtesy	The judge in **our court** insists upon **court**esy.
familiar	I'd rather not be famil**iar** with a **liar.**

forty	**Forty** soldiers defended the **fort.**
fourth	We wrote **four th**emes last month.
knowledge	Do you **know** if the **owl** at the **edge** of the **ledge** has any **knowledge** of your presence?
meant	Put **mean** in **meant.**
occurred	2 *c*'s, 2 *r*'s
off	To do**ff** your hat means to take it **off.** (*Doff* means *do off.* *Don* means *do on.*)
pleasant	Nothing pleas**ant** about **ant**s at a picnic
separate	Doesn't **Pa rate** a se**parate** bunk?
speech	Don't spee**d** through your spee**ch.**
thorough	**O!** How **rough** her th**orough** scrubbing was!
together	We went **to get her** ticket **together.**

PRACTICE 5 Spelling from Dictation

Often you spell a list of words correctly. Do you spell these same words correctly when you use them in sentences? Prepare to write the following sentences from dictation. The words in boldface type you've studied in the lists for P.1 – P.5.

1. The **business** before the **committee** is the dance in **February** for the **benefit** of the **athletic** department.
2. **Separate** those **clothes** for **children** and put the coats with **loose** buttons on the **bargain** counter.
3. The **secretary meant** to **maintain quiet** in the **library.**
4. In his **speech** the **senator** proved that he had a **thorough knowledge** of the **government** of **Britain.**
5. Will the **pleasant professor finally proceed** with the **grammar** lesson?
6. The **visitor answered,** "The accident **occurred** at the **entrance** to the **elevator.**"
7. "That **error** caused us to **lose forty** yards," said the **captain.**
8. If he follows the **advice** of the **director,** Don **probably** will **perform** that **familiar** tune **all right.**
9. **Together** the **governor** and his **doctor** walked **across** the room.
10. Will this **particular villain succeed** in **quieting** his **conscience?**

LEARN A FEW RULES

Contractions

Contractions are used freely in friendly letters and in the conversational parts of stories.

P.6 *APOSTROPHE FOR OMITTED LETTERS* Put an apostrophe where one or more letters are left out in a word.

COULD N~~O~~T   COULDN'T

Don't add a letter and don't change the letters around.

could + n~~o~~t = couldn't   she + ~~wi~~ll = she'll
he + ~~i~~s = he's   they + ~~ha~~ve = they've
it + ~~has~~ = it's   we + ~~a~~re = we're
o~~f~~ + ~~the~~ + clock = o'clock   you + ~~woul~~d = you'd

EXCEPTION   will + not = won't

PRACTICE 6   **Forming and Using Contractions**   **W**

Write the contractions for the expressions printed below. Then write a short conversation in which you use at least ten of the contractions. Underline each contraction and punctuate correctly. (See pages 286–303.) Here is a sample beginning, using some of the contractions from the examples.

"It's been snowing all day," said Betsy, "and we're going skiing as soon as it stops. You'd better come with us."

"Dad won't let me," complained Trudy. "He's insisting that I do my homework."

are not	do not	I have	should not	we have
can not	has not	I would	that is	we will
did not	have not	is not	there is	were not
does not	I am	it is	they are	you are

ei and ie words

P.7 *EI, IE* Put *i* before *e*
           Except after *c*
           Or when sounded like *a*
           As in *neighbor* and *weigh*.

i before *e*	**except after *c***	**sounded like *a***
achieve	ceiling	sleigh
handkerchief	perceive	vein

EXCEPTIONS
1. **Neither** the **weird financier** nor the **foreigner seizes leisure** at its **height**.
2. *C* pronounced as *sh;* **ancient, conscience, efficient, sufficient**

PRACTICE 7   Spelling Words with *ei* or *ie*

As you copy the following sentences, supply *ei* or *ie* in each word with a blank.   Be ready to give a reason for your choice: (1) *i* before *e*, (2) *ei* after *c*, (3) *ei* sounded like *a*, (4) exception 1, (5) *c* pronounced *sh*.

1. The effic—nt cash—r couldn't bel—ve his fr—nd was capable of dec—t.
2. With a w—rd shr—k the f—rce highland ch—f began the s—ge of the anc—nt city.
3. The warehouse for for—gn fr—ght rec—ved more police protection after a r—gn of th—very.
4. During her l—sure my n—ghbor's n—ce always gets into misch—f that leads to gr—f.
5. What a rel—f to perc—ve that my h—ght and w—ght were normal for my age!
6. Can you conc—ve how a scientist will sh—ld himself while s—zing a p—ce of radioactive material for w—ghing?
7. The handkerch—f and the v—l rose w—rdly toward the c—ling.
8. N—ther the financ—r nor his n—ghbor could ach—ve rel—f of the s—ge.

Suffixes

A suffix is one or more letters added to the end of a word to change its meaning.

friend + s = friends   ask + ed = asked
joy + ful = joyful + ly = joyfully

P.8   *ADDING* LY   Don't lose a letter when adding *ly* to a word ending in *l.*

cheerful + ly = cheerfully   cool + ly = coolly

PRACTICE 8   Adding *ly*   W

Add *ly* to each of the following words without losing an *l*.   Then write sentences to illustrate the use of five of these *ly* words.

actual	continual	ideal	physical	successful
awful	cordial	natural	real	unusual
beautiful	final	occasional	respectful	usual

Final e

P.9   *FINAL E BEFORE VOWEL*   Drop final silent e before a suffix
beginning with a vowel.

larg(e) + est = largest   lov(e) + ing = loving
lik(e) + able = likable   scarc(e) + ity = scarcity

EXCEPTIONS
1. Adding *able* or *ous* to words ending in *ce* or *ge: traceable, exchangeable* (to keep the soft pronunciation of *c* and *g*)
2. Adding *ing* to words ending in *ie: die, dying; lie, lying; tie, tying* (to avoid double *i*)
3. *dye, dyeing* (to distinguish from *die, dying*)
4. *canoeing, hoeing, shoeing, tiptoeing*

PRACTICE 9   Adding *ing*

Can you spell all of the following words correctly? When you've
mastered them, build new words by adding *ing* to each. Be prepared
for a test on spelling the *ing* forms.

appreciate	come	encourage	lose	realize
argue	complete	excite	notice	receive
arrange	decide	hope	owe	separate
believe	describe	interfere	practice	surprise
choose	enclose	lie	purchase	write

PRACTICE 10   Adding *able* and *ous*

Form adjectives by adding *able* or *ous* to these words. What
do *able* and *ous* mean? Why do you drop or keep the *e*?

admire	change	debate	manage	outrage
advantage	compare	desire	marriage	peace
advise	conceive	endure	note	pore
believe	courage	excite	notice	service

P.10   *FINAL E BEFORE CONSONANT*   Keep final silent e before
a suffix beginning with a consonant.

acute + ness = acuteness   nine + teen = nineteen
amaze + ment = amazement   taste + ful = tasteful
lone + ly = lonely   voice + less = voiceless

EXCEPTIONS

acknowledgment	awful	judgment	truly
argument	duly	ninth	wholly

PRACTICE 11 Adding Suffiixes

1. What do the suffixes *ful, ly, ment, less, ness,* and *ty* mean? If you don't know what these suffixes mean, look them up in the dictionary.

2. Form adjectives by adding *ful* to these nouns:

| care | disgrace | hope | peace | use |

3. Add *ly* to each of these words:

accurate	definite	fortunate	mere	scarce
affectionate	entire	immediate	probable	severe
complete	extreme	loose	rare	sincere

4. Add *ment* to each of these words:

| achieve | amuse | arrange | excite | manage |
| advertise | announce | encourage | improve | require |

5. Add the indicated suffix to each word:

care + less	nine + ty	sense + less
change + less	polite + ness	use + less
coarse + ness	safe + ty	value + less

FINAL CONSONANT

How is the *o* pronounced in each of these words: *hop, hope?* What happens when you add *ed* or *ing?*

The next two rules will help you to spell over three thousand words.

P.11 *ONE–SYLLABLE WORD* Double the final consonant before a suffix beginning with a vowel if a one-syllable word ends in one consonant preceded by one vowel.

big + est = biggest   can + ing =.canning   sun + y = sunny

Here's how you apply the rule:

1. hop, hopping, hopped. *Hop* has one syllable. It ends in one consonant, *p*, preceded by one vowel, *o*. The rule applies.
2. hope, hoping, hoped. *Hope* has one syllable, but it does not end in a consonant. The rule does not apply. (What other rule does apply to *hope?*)
3. clear, clearing, cleared. *Clear* has one syllable and one final consonant, *r*, but *r* is preceded by two vowels, *e* and *a*. The rule does not apply in this case.
4. crawl, crawling, crawled. *Crawl* has one syllable, but it ends in two consonants, *w* and *l*. The rule does not apply.

PRACTICE 12 Doubling Final Consonants

List the following verbs in two columns, one for those ending in one consonant preceded by one vowel, and the second for all others. Then for each word write the present participle and the past tense.

EXAMPLES

Words Ending in One Consonant
Preceded by One Vowel   *All Other Words*
hum — humming, hummed   lurk — lurking, lurked

bare	dine	file	grip	hire	rot	step	sun
bat	drag	grab	help	plan	ship	stir	whip
beg	drop	grin	hem	plane	slip	stop	wrap

ACCENT ON LAST SYLLABLE Double the final consonant before a suffix beginning with a vowel if a word that is accented on the last syllable ends in one consonant preceded by one vowel.

Here's how you apply this rule:

1. reGRET, regretting, regretted. *Regret* is accented on the last syllable. The final consonant, *t*, is preceded by a single vowel *e*. The rule applies.
2. LIMit, limiting, limited. *Limit* is accented on the first syllable. The rule does not apply.

EXCEPTIONS When the accent shifts to the first syllable: *CONference* from *conFER*, *PREFerence* from *preFER*, *REFerence* from *reFER*. *EXcellent* from *exCEL*, however, has two *l*'s.

PRACTICE 13 Doubling Final Consonants

1. Add *ing* to each of the following words. In which do you double the final consonant? Why?

admit	control	forget	permit	shine
begin	defer	interfere	prefer	shop
commit	differ	occur	put	suffer
compel	dig	offer	refer	swim
confer	equip¹	omit	run	transfer

2. Add the indicated suffix to each of the following words. In which do you double the final consonant? Why?

cat + y	differ + ence	forgot + en	propel + er
confer + ence	drug + ist	infer + ence	rebel + ion
control + able	equip + ed	occur + ence	red + est
defer + ence	excel + ent	prefer + able	ton + age

¹ Here the *u* of *qu* is considered part of the consonant.

Final y

P.13 *FINAL Y* Change final *y* preceded by a consonant to *i* before any suffix that does not begin with *i*.

For the application of this rule in forming the plurals of nouns ending in *y* turn to page 307.

EXCEPTIONS
1. day, daily; lay, laid; pay, paid; say, said
2. Proper names: the Kirbys next door; two Tommys in my class

Now let's see how the rule works.

1. ally, alliance, allied — *Ally* ends in *y* preceded by a consonant, *l.* Change *y* to *i.*
2. ally, allying. *Ally* still ends in *y* preceded by a consonant, but the suffix, *ing*, begins with *i.* Keep the *y.*
3. alley, alleys. *Alley* ends in *y*, but the *y* is preceded by a vowel, *e.* Keep the *y.*

PRACTICE 14   Adding Suffixes to *y* Words

Build new words by adding the indicated suffix to the words in each of the following groups.   Which of the three explanations of how the rule works applies to each word?

1. To these verbs add *s* or *es* to form the third person singular of the present tense, *ing* to form the present participle, and *ed* to form the past tense and past participle.

EXAMPLE   bury — buries (1), burying (2), buried (1)

accompany	defy	enjoy	occupy	stay
apply	delay	hurry	prophesy	study
carry	deny	marry	reply	try

2. Add *er* and *est* to form the comparative and superlative of these adjectives.

chilly	friendly	happy	hungry	pretty
clumsy	gray	heavy	noisy	ugly

3. Make adverbs by adding *ly* to these adjectives.

angry	clumsy	happy	necessary	ready
busy	easy	hearty	noisy	steady

4. Write the new word.

accompany + ment	bury + al	likely + hood	mercy + ful
apply + ance	buy + er	lively + hood	merry + ment
beauty + ful	carry + age	marry + age	try + al

PRACTICE 15 Writing Contractions and Adding Suffixes

As you copy the following selection, write contractions for the words that are underlined. Add the suffix *en*, *es*, *s*, *ed*, *ing*, *able*, *ly*, *less*, or *ment* to words in parentheses. Let the meaning of the sentence guide you in choosing the suffix. Be prepared to explain why you drop or keep a final *e*, why you double a final consonant, or why you change a final *y* to *i* when adding the suffix.

MY PRIVATE EYE

The *39 Steps* is one of the most (grip)¹ (mystery)² I have³ ever read. I have⁴ (enjoy)⁵ it right from the (begin)⁶. That is⁷ why I am⁸ (hurry)⁹ home right now. I can (scarce)¹⁰ wait to get back to the book.

Last night after I had (study)¹¹ my assignments for today, I (try)¹² to finish it. (Occasional)¹³ Mom has (forgot)¹⁴ my (stay)¹⁵ up past bedtime, but not last night. Even the fact that she was (steady)¹⁶ (write)¹⁷ letters did not¹⁸ prevent her from (stop)¹⁹ long enough to say, "Lights out."

"Just a few more minutes," I (beg)²⁰. "I have²¹ just reached the most (excite)²² part."

"(Definite)²³ not," she (reply)²⁴. "To keep (physical)²⁵ fit, you must avoid (lose)²⁶ sleep."

(Decide)²⁷ from the tone of her voice that it was not²⁸ (advise)²⁹ to protest again, I left the room (immediate)³⁰, (carry)³¹ the book under my arm. (Natural)³² I (plan)³³ to read in bed. After (put)³⁴ on my pajamas and (arrange)³⁵ my pillows (careful)³⁶, I (slip)³⁷ between the sheets and again (occupy)³⁸ myself with Richard Hannay's efforts to solve the riddle of the thirty-nine steps. Suddenly Mom (whip)³⁹ the book out of my hand. I had not⁴⁰ even heard her (come)⁴¹!

42 43 44 45
I have just been (realize) that Mom's an (admire) sleuth herself. It
46 47 48 49
is (use) to try (commit) a crime around our house. There is no (deny)
50
she (usual) catches me.

KNOW THE MEANING

Homonyms

Homonyms sound alike but are spelled differently and have different meanings.

P.14 *HOMONYMS* Think of the meaning you wish to express and match the spelling to the meaning.

capital
capitol
The chief city of a state is the *capital*. You write proper names with *capital* letters, invest *capital*, and receive *capital* punishment. The building in which the legislature meets often has a dome and is called a *capitol*.

lead
led
Lead (lĕd), the name of the heavy metal, is often confused with *led*, the past tense of *lead* (lēēd): *lead* pipe, *led* the band.

principal
principle
The adjective is always *principal* — "*principal* speaker." The noun refers to a person — "your *pal*, the *principal*" — or to a sum of money — "*principal* and interest." *Principle* means "underlying truth" or "rule" and like *rule* ends in *le* — "a *principle* of freedom."

stationary
stationery
Stationary means "not moving" or "fixed." Something that is *stationary* stands still. Let the *er* in *paper* and *letter* remind you that paper for letters is *stationery*.

their
there
Their is a pronoun denoting possession — "*their* heir." *There* is an adverb — "here and *there*."

threw **through**	*Threw* is the past tense of the verb *throw*. *Through* means "from one end or place to another" or "to an end." "Tom *threw* the ball *through* the basket." "Are you *through* with the sports section?"
to **too** **two**	*To* is a preposition. *Too* is an adverb. *Two* is the number *2*. "Did the *two* girls row *to* the island *too?*"
weather **whether**	If the *weather* (condition of the atmosphere) is cold and blustery, I don't know *whether* (alternative) I should go.

PRACTICE 16 Spelling Correctly Words That Sound Alike

A. As you copy the following sentences, fill each blank with **too, to,** or **two.**

1. This morning Dad got up ____ late ____ eat breakfast. 2. Because it was ____ hot ____ rush ____ the station, he decided ____ take the bus. 3. After a minute or ____ he realized that he had left ____ hurriedly and had forgotten his ____ briefcases. 4. As he was ____ far along ____ go back, he waited, then phoned from the station. 5. I raced down with the ____ briefcases and an umbrella ____ but was ____ late.

B. As you copy the following sentences, fill each blank with **their** or **there.**

1. ____ goes the band! 2. Aren't ____ new red-and-gold uniforms beautiful! 3. ____ instruments are new too. 4. Although ____ were five other bands in the Pioneer Day parade, ____ wasn't another that could equal ____ marching or playing. 5. Where is ____ another school band as good as ours?

C. As you copy the following sentences, fill each blank with **principle** or **principal.**

1. As a matter of ____, the ____ refuses to interfere with the spring play. 2. Miss Johnson will assign the ____ roles. 3. Her guiding ____ is, "A tragedy is best read at home." 4. Her ____ reason for not choosing a tragedy is that we would all overact. 5. Last spring the ____s in *Julius Caesar* shouted themselves hoarse.

D. As you copy the following sentences, fill each blank with **lead** or **led.**

1. Who ____ the sight-seers through the ____ mine? 2. Did you know that ____ pencils are made of graphite? 3. I was ____ to believe

that ____ pipes are best. 4. ____ melts at a temperature of about 620 degrees. 5. Next we were ____ into the refinery, where huge kettles of ____ were boiling.

A. Show that you can match the meaning to the spelling by writing sentences of your own for the homonyms on page 482. Underline these words in the sentences you write. You may use two or more of the words in each sentence. If you're not sure of the meaning of a word, look it up in the dictionary.

B. Write sentences using the following words. Underline these words in the sentences you write. You may use two or more of the words in a sentence. If you're not sure of the meaning of a word, look it up in the dictionary.

| allowed | coarse | hear | hole | passed | scene |
| aloud | course | here | whole | past | seen |

Personal Pronouns and Contractions

P.15 *POSSESSIVES AND CONTRACTIONS* Be careful not to substitute the possessive forms *its, your, their, theirs,* and *whose* for the contractions *it's, you're, they're, there's,* and *who's.* The possessive pronouns aren't written with an apostrophe.

it's heavy BUT *its* weight   *there's* a plane BUT is it *theirs?*
they're driving BUT *their* car   *who's* singing BUT *whose* song
                    you're invited BUT *your* invitation

A. As you copy the following sentences, fill each blank with **its** or **it's.** Use *it's* wherever you can substitute *it is.*

1. ____ interesting to study the whooping crane. 2. ____ over five feet tall. 3. ____ wingspread is seven feet. 4. Except for ____ black-tipped wings, ____ plumage is white; ____ legs are black; and ____ bill is yellow. 5. ____ now one of the rarest birds in North America.

B. As you copy the following sentences, fill each blank with **their** or **they're.** Use *they're* wherever you can substitute *they are.*

1. ____ never going to make ____ train if they don't hurry. 2. I hear ____ taking ____ dog along. 3. ____ baggage is light, for ____ experienced travelers. 4. ____ spending two days in Longmeadow with ____ aunt. 5. ____ here; I just heard ____ car pull up.

APPENDIX

GRAMMAR Grammar is the study of language structure — how words are put together to make sense.

Long ago you learned to use the basic structures of English, but you still need practice in working with a variety of structures to improve your power of communication. Your knowledge of grammar can help you eliminate careless, inexact, pretentious English.

USAGE Usage is the study of how people use words in various situations to communicate effectively.

Usage concerns itself with language etiquette. At any given time you must be alert to the need for using currently acceptable forms. Skill in writing and in speaking depends partly upon knowledge of current usage. Your working knowledge of usage can help you eliminate inappropriate expressions, whether you are writing to a friend or writing a research report. There are certain occasions when light and breezy expressions like "Hi!" and "How're you doing?" are inappropriate.

An increasing mastery of both grammar and usage will give you an increasing mastery of the English language, adding vitality, exactness, and power to your written and oral expression.

RHETORIC Rhetoric builds on the principles of grammar and usage to produce writing and speaking that communicates effectively.

It deals with such matters as clearness (pages 131–41), emphasis (454–61), organization (131–32), unity (48–78), variety (454–61), and diction (27–29).

Additional Terms Used in a Study of Grammar and Usage

COMPOUND–COMPLEX SENTENCE A compound-complex sentence has two or more independent clauses and one or more dependent clauses.

That piece of paper has a watermark, but you may not notice it **unless you hold the paper up to the light.** (The dependent clause is in boldface.)

KINDS OF SENTENCES A *declarative sentence* makes a statement; an *interrogative sentence* asks a question; an *imperative sentence* gives a command or makes a request; an *exclamatory sentence* expresses strong or sudden feeling.

DECLARATIVE Postal administrations sometimes put watermarks in postage stamps.
INTERROGATIVE Have you noticed the crown watermark on that Bermuda stamp?
IMPERATIVE Lay these stamps upside down on a dark surface.
EXCLAMATORY How unusual those watermarks are!

CASE   Some pronouns change in form to show how they are used in a sentence. (*I* asked Mom to mail *my* coin collection to *me*.) This change of form is called "case."

NOMINATIVE CASE   I, we, you, he, she, it, they, who (subjects and predicate pronouns)

OBJECTIVE CASE   me, us, you, him, her, it, them, whom (objects of verbs and of prepositions)

POSSESSIVE CASE   my, mine, our, ours, your, yours, his, her, hers, its, their, theirs, whose

Nouns have only two case forms — the possessive (*Ellen's, year's*) and an ordinary form that is used for subjects, predicate nouns, and objects (*Ellen, year*).

GENDER   Nouns and pronouns are sometimes classified by gender.

MASCULINE   Mr. Swanson, gander, postman, he
FEMININE   Mrs. Swanson, mare, postmistress, she
COMMON   voter, squirrel, they
NEUTER   desk, book, it, they

A pronoun should agree with its antecedent in gender as well as in number. My father is taking *his* vacation in October.

MOOD   Mood is the way in which a verb expresses an idea.
The *indicative* mood is used to state a fact or ask a question.
The *imperative* mood is used in commands and requests.

INDICATIVE   Why *do* governments *put* watermarks in stamps?
Watermarks *may discourage* counterfeiting.

IMPERATIVE   *Read* this article for an explanation of watermarks in stamps and in other kinds of paper.

Although the subjunctive mood has been fading from the language, it is sometimes used to express a condition contrary to fact (untrue) or a wish.

SUBJUNCTIVE   If I *were* you (I'm not), I'd take biology next year. (Informal: if I was . . .)
I wish I *were* as skillful a cook as you. (Informal: I wish I was . . .)

The subjunctive is used after *as if* and *as though* and after *I move that, I ask that, I suggest that*, and the like.

I move that John present his magic show for the benefit of the children in Mercy Hospital.
To enjoy life, suggests Helen Keller, live every day as if it *were* your last.

NOMINATIVE OF ADDRESS   A nominative of address is the name of the person spoken to.

Jody, where is Rex's leash?

NOMINATIVE ABSOLUTE A nominative absolute is a noun or pronoun, modified by a participle, which has no grammatical connection with the rest of the sentence. The participle may be understood, as in the second example.

The *car* having broken down, we walked nearly a mile to the nearest garage.
The *meeting* in an uproar, the chairman rapped vainly with his gavel for silence. (The participle *being* is understood.)

OBJECTIVE COMPLEMENT An objective complement completes the verb and refers to the direct object. It is usually a noun, a pronoun, or an adjective.

Merchant Lyte called Johnny Tremain a *criminal*. (Called Johnny what? A criminal)
The boys thought Tom *generous* for allowing them to paint the fence. (Thought Tom what? Generous)

A verb which takes an objective complement in the active voice may, in the passive, take a predicate noun or a predicate adjective.

OBJECTIVE COMPLEMENT   In 1960 the voters elected John F. Kennedy *President* by a slender margin.
PREDICATE NOUN   John F. Kennedy was elected *President* in 1960 by a slender margin. (John F. Kennedy = President)
OBJECTIVE COMPLEMENT   The track coach considers Frank *versatile*.
PREDICATE ADJECTIVE   Frank is considered *versatile* by the track coach. (Frank = versatile)

Where possible use the active voice.

COGNATE OBJECT A verb regularly intransitive may take a cognate object, a kind of direct object similar in meaning to the verb.

Sing a *song* of sixpence.

SECONDARY OBJECT Verbs of asking take two direct objects, the name of the person and the name of the thing (called the *secondary object*).

Mr. Allen asked me two *questions* about Isaac Newton.
For review ask me these *questions* in citizenship education.

RETAINED OBJECT A verb which takes an indirect or a secondary object in the active voice may in the passive voice retain a direct object (called the *retained object*).

I was asked these *questions* in citizenship education.

ACTIVE VOICE, WITH INDIRECT OBJECT   Dad gave Mother an Indian necklace. (*Necklace* is the direct object; *Mother* is the indirect object.)
PASSIVE VOICE, WITH RETAINED OBJECT   Mother was given an Indian necklace by Dad. (*Necklace* is the retained object.)

CONJUGATION To conjugate a verb is to give its forms in order.

Conjugation of **TO CHOOSE**

PRINCIPAL PARTS

Present: *choose*   Past: *chose*   Past Participle: *chosen*

INDICATIVE MOOD

ACTIVE VOICE   PASSIVE VOICE

Singular	Plural	Singular	Plural

Present Tense

I choose	we choose	I am chosen	we are chosen
you choose	you choose	you are chosen	you are chosen
he chooses	they choose	he is chosen	they are chosen

Past Tense

I chose	we chose	I was chosen	we were chosen
you chose	you chose	you were chosen	you were chosen
he chose	they chose	he was chosen	they were chosen

Future Tense

I shall choose	we shall choose	I shall be chosen	we shall be chosen
you will choose	you will choose	you will be chosen	you will be chosen
he will choose	they will choose	he will be chosen	they will be chosen

Present Perfect Tense

I have chosen	we have chosen	I have been chosen	we have been chosen
you have chosen	you have chosen	you have been chosen	you have been chosen
he has chosen	they have chosen	he has been chosen	they have been chosen

Past Perfect Tense

I had chosen	we had chosen	I had been chosen	we had been chosen
you had chosen	you had chosen	you had been chosen	you had been chosen
he had chosen	they had chosen	he had been chosen	they had been chosen

Future Perfect Tense

I shall have chosen	we shall have chosen	I shall have been chosen	we shall have been chosen
you will have chosen	you will have chosen	you will have been chosen	you will have been chosen
he will have chosen	they will have chosen	he will have been chosen	they will have been chosen

IMPERATIVE

Choose and *be chosen* are the only forms.

INFINITIVES

ACTIVE VOICE	PASSIVE VOICE
PRESENT: to choose	to be chosen
PERFECT: to have chosen	to have been chosen

PARTICIPLES

PRESENT: choosing	being chosen
PAST: chosen	chosen
PERFECT: having chosen	having been chosen

GERUNDS

PRESENT: choosing	being chosen
PERFECT: having chosen	having been chosen

Note Progressive forms of the verb are regularly formed with the verb *to be* and the present participle — for example, *I am choosing, he was choosing.* Emphatic forms are formed with the verb *to do* and the present tense — for example, *I do choose, I did choose.*

MARKING SYMBOLS

A symbol placed at the beginning of a composition calls attention to a serious or a repeated error.

Ab Do not abbreviate. (159, 164–65, 288–89)

Act Change from passive to active voice. (345–47)

C Capital misused or needed. (20, 278–85)

Cl Clearness. Make your meaning perfectly clear. (131–34, 298)

D or ℐ Omit word or words indicated.

Gr Grammar. Correct the syntax. (317–418)

Inc Incomplete. Idea not finished. (134)

K Awkward or clumsy. Rewrite the sentence.

M Margin. (159, 163)

NS Not a sentence. Complete the independent clause. (446–50)

P Punctuation. (159–60, 164–65, 286–303, 411–12, 423–24, 436, 443)

QA Question not answered, or problem not solved.

S Sentence. Begin a new sentence at the point indicated. (443–46)

Sp Spelling. (469–84)

Sub Subordinate one of the statements. (433)

Syl Syllabication. Divide only between syllables. See the dictionary.

T Wrong tense. (330–34)

W Use a correct or a better word. Consult the dictionary. (20–34)

Leave more space between words.

∧ Supply the word or words omitted.

¶ Begin a paragraph here. (52–54, 114)

? Disputed or questioned statement.

X Find the error in the line.

INDEX

Page numbers of rules and rule numbers are in boldface.

* indicates a definition.

A, an, **379 (I.13)**
A, an, the, 352, **379 (I.14)**
A half, half a (an), **380 (I.16)**
A person, 324 **(E.12)**
Abbreviations, period after, **288 (C.5)**
Able and *ous,* adding, **477 (P.9)**
Accept, except, 32, **472 (P.3)**
Acceptance, note of, 161
Acrostics, 9
Active voice, **345 (F.16)***
  use of, **346 (F.18)**
Address
  envelope, 160, 166
  inside, 163, 164
  punctuating, 294
Addresses and dates, punctuation of,
  294 (C.15)
Adjective, **352 (G.2),*** 352–57
  a, an, the, 352, **379 (I.14)**
  appropriate, 29, 356
  comparison of, **376–78 (I.1–9)**
  confusion of, with adverb, 358–59,
    381–83
  diagraming sentences with, 354
  position of, in sentence, 353
  predicate, **372 (H.4)**
  proper, **283 (B.6)**
  recognizing, 404–5
  suffixes of, 353
  use of, **355 (G.3), 378–79 (I.10–15),**
    428–29 (M.14)
Adjective clause, **428 (M.13),*** 428–34
  diagraming sentences with, 430–31
  punctuating, **433 (M.21)**
  recognizing, 431
  using, **428–29 (M.14), 433 (M.20)**
Adverb, **357 (G.4),*** 357–62
  confused with adjectives, 358
  confused with conjunctions, **443 (N.2)**
  diagraming sentences with, 359
  errors in use of, 380–82
  not ending in *ly,* **359 (G.5)**
  recognizing, **405 (K.2)**
  useless, 360–61
  using, **360 (G.6), 380–82 (I.18–21)**
Adverb clause, **434 (M.22)***
  diagraming sentences with, 435
  punctuating, **436–37 (M.23, 24)**
  recognizing, 435
Adverbial noun, 407
Advice, advise, **472 (P.3)**
Affect, effect, 32
Agreement, **317 (E.1)***

of pronoun with antecedent, **396–401
  (J.8–12)**
  of verb with subject, **317–29 (E.2–12)**
"Ain't," **349 (F.22)**
All right, **473 (P.5)**
Alphabetical order
  in bibliography, 153
  in card catalog, 251
  in dictionary, 20
Amount, number, 32
Anagrams, 9
Analogy, 66
Anapest, 214
And, 111, 274, 293–94
  in a series, 295–96
Antecedent, **396 (J.7)**
  vague, **398–99 (J.11, 12)**
Any other in comparisons, **377 (I.7)**
Apostrophe
  in contractions, **475 (P.6)**
  with possessive, **310 (D.12)**
Appearance of letters, 158–59, 163–65
Appendix, 485–89
Appositive, **292 (C.10)***
  colon with, **302 (C.26)**
  commas with, **292 (C.10, 11)**
  emphasis by, **292 (C.12)**
  to streamline sentence, **458 (O.5)**
Appositive adjective, 293
Argumentation, 98
Arrangement
  of bibliography, 153
  of business letter, 163–65
  of card catalog, 251–54
  of dictionary, 20–24
  of encyclopedia, 247
  in explanation, 131–32
  of friendly letter, 158–59
  of library, 246–56
  of news story, 186–87
  of newspaper, 186
  of paragraph, 68–72
  in a report, 147
  of story, 112
Article
  repetition of, **379 (I.14, 15)**
  use of, **380 (I.16, 17)**
Associated words, 25, 42
At, by, **384 (I.24)**
At, in, **384 (I.24)**
At, to, **384 (I.24)**
Author card, 251, 252
Autobiography, writing your, 117–18

491

Supplementary
Practice Exercises

Supplementary Practice Exercises

Copy each subject and each verb (main verb plus any helpers). Draw one line under the subject and two lines under the verb.   If the sentence is in the inverted order, search out the subject and the verb. (Review pages 272–273.)   If the subject or the verb is compound, be sure to list both parts.   (Review pages 274–277.)

EXAMPLE   There are dragons and unicorns in my imaginary zoo.

dragons   unicorns   are

BIGFOOT AND THE UNICORN

1. For four thousand years people believed in the existence of unicorns.
2. There were many stories and legends about these handsome creatures.
3. A unicorn horn was once priced at the equivalent of five million dollars.
4. The horn actually came from a species of Arctic whale.
5. About two hundred years ago the unicorn myth was destroyed by the French naturalist Georges Cuvier.
6. A horn does not grow from the forehead of an animal.
7. The horn of the rhinoceros grows from the nose, not the forehead.
8. There is another favorite legendary animal, the dragon.
9. In Western mythology the dragon is a ferocious monster, an enemy to man.
10. In China, on the other hand, the dragon is a symbol of good luck.
11. Some living animals resemble dragons and show us "dragons" in action.
12. With a little of your imagination alligators and lizards become ferocious dragons.
13. There is another relative of the legendary dragon.
14. Throughout history sailors have supposedly sighted sea serpents and have provided vivid descriptions of them.

15. The most famous sea serpent is really a "lake serpent." (*Sea serpent* is one name.)
16. In the West Highlands of Scotland is a beautiful lake, Loch Ness.
17. In 1933 someone supposedly saw a sea serpent in the deep waters of Loch Ness.
18. After that, many persons also reported sightings of "Nessie," the sea serpent.
19. At the time of this book, however, no conclusive proof had yet been offered.
20. In the Himalayas there is the Abominable Snowman. (*Abominable Snowman* is one noun.)
21. Expeditions to the mountains have sought this elusive great ape.
22. In our own Pacific Northwest there is Bigfoot.
23. Bigfoot is supposedly a giant ape, like the Abominable Snowman.
24. Many people believe in the existence of Bigfoot and the Abominable Snowman.
25. Nessie, Bigfoot, and the Snowman must be considered animals of the imagination, however, until more proof is supplied.

PRACTICE 2　Completing Sentence Fragments

Ten of the following are sentences, and ten are sentence fragments. Copy the subject and the verb of each sentence. Change the sentence fragments to complete sentences. (Review page 277.) For every sentence underline the subject once and put two lines under the verb.

SPIDERS ON THE PAYROLL

1. A great deal of incorrect information about spiders.
2. You have almost certainly walked through a spider web on a spider path.
3. You may have been a little annoyed and have brushed the "dragline" aside.
4. Something unusual about this special filament of the spider web.
5. The dragline, one of the strongest substances for its thickness in the world.
6. Even steel is less strong.
7. For many centuries primitive people around the world have been using spider silk for lures and nets.
8. Using spider silk in even the weaving of small bags and ornaments.
9. Nan Songer Hook, an ingenious California scientist.

10. She and her husband operate a strange business.
11. Raising spiders for their webs and the silk from the webs.
12. They have tested more than 50 of the 2500 different North American spiders.
13. Three types were chosen for their silk.
14. The dread Black Widow, one of their most precious workers.
15. The Hooks do not look upon spiders as "ugly, creepy, crawly things."
16. Have admired spiders and appreciated their magnificent handiwork.
17. From their "spider factory" comes silk for many modern instruments.
18. The fine silk provides cross-hairs for certain types of microscopes.
19. Some silk only 1/50,000 of an inch in diameter.
20. Have proved again the usefulness to man of even the tiniest creatures.

PRACTICE 3   Capitalizing Sentences

In each sentence copy and capitalize the words that need capitals. Prepare to give the reason for each capital inserted.   (Review pages 278–285.)

THE UNITED STATES LOOKS TO THE TWENTIETH CENTURY

1. Let's turn back the clock to the year 1900 and look at the united states at the turn of the century.
2. The population had reached nearly 76 million, and the center of population was near columbus, indiana.
3. The united states had about ten miles of concrete pavement and fewer than 8000 automobiles.
4. The first well-organized automobile race was held at springfield, long island, on april 15.
5. The largest railroad in the united states, the new york central, controlled 10,000 miles of track.
6. On may 3 the annual kentucky derby was won by the favorite, lieutenant gibson.
7. England and the united states inaugurated tennis competition for the davis cup, a trophy supplied by dwight f. davis.
8. Casey jones, famous engineer in song and legend, died on april 30 at the throttle of his locomotive, the "cannonball," trying to save his passengers' lives.
9. The wright brothers, wilbur and orville, built their first full-scale glider and flew it at kitty hawk, north carolina.

10. Among rising young novelists of the day were writers like zane grey, edgar rice burroughs, rex beach, and theodore dreiser.
11. The novelist irving bacheller wrote *eben holden,* a book that became a best seller.
12. Among the powerful painters of the time was albert pinkham ryder.
13. His famous painting, *toilers of the sea,* is a ghostly sea scene.   (Titles of paintings are capitalized like titles of books.)
14. Mrs. finley j. shepard gave a quarter of a million dollars to set up the american hall of fame at new york university.
15. On january 1 of 1900, william mckinley was still president, but 1900 was an election year.
16. On june 21, the republican national convention nominated mckinley to run again.
17. As his running mate the delegates chose theodore roosevelt of new york.
18. At the democratic national convention in kansas city, missouri, the delegates nominated william jennings bryan to run for president, with adlai e. stevenson of illinois as his running mate.
19. In december, negotiations were completed for the purchase of the danish west indies, now the united states virgin islands.
20. It was not until 1917, however, that congress appropriated the money to buy the islands from denmark.

PRACTICE 4   Punctuating Sentences

As you write the following sentences, punctuate them.   Prepare to give a reason for each mark inserted.   (Review pages 286–298.)

GAZING INTO THE CRYSTAL BALL

1. I think Sandra you would enjoy this book about predictions
2. John Durant the author of *Predictions* has gathered hundreds of cartoons from long ago
3. Yes it is surprising how accurate some of the guesses were
4. Cartoonists were drawing giant airships municipal airports and the modern superhighway even before the end of the nineteenth century
5. A 1901 cartoon showed motorists with gas masks as protection against dust not as protection against fumes
6. By 1904 a rise in automobile accidents brought speed laws with a top limit of 20 miles an hour on country roads
7. Oh yes even the house trailer was pictured years before it came into existence

8. Sandra can you picture a 1908 hot-rod automobile with teen-agers in the seats
9. Drive-in church services surprisingly enough were pictured thirty years before they were first tried
10. Some cartoonists felt however that the airplane not the automobile would be the major means of transportation
11. A 1909 cartoonist a man of great imagination showed how rain-makers of the future might operate
12. Luxury penthouses those gardens in the sky were predicted as early as 1909
13. Air pollution our constant menace was clearly shown in a cartoon from 1908
14. Cartoonists predicted advertising on airplanes on natural wonders and even on the Statue of Liberty
15. Bicycles not automobiles were the great fad of the 1890's
16. One manufacturer put out a real curiosity a 13-seater
17. Cartoonists we are told predicted unrealistic growth for the bicycle
18. Other guesses quite naturally were wrong too
19. Cartoonists thought that telegraph wires not the automobile would jam the city streets
20. Fanciful ideas included floating cities transoceanic trolleys and football players in heavy armor

PRACTICE 5   Punctuating and Capitalizing Direct Quotations

As you copy the following sentences, punctuate and capitalize them correctly. Prepare to give a reason for each punctuation mark or capital inserted. (Review pages 298–301.)

QUOTATIONS FOR EVERY OCCASION

1. Do you enjoy reading quotations asked Carol
2. Renee replied yes I collect quotations here are some examples
3. A committee of one gets things done said Joe Ryan
4. Anatole France once said I prefer the errors of enthusiasm to the indifference of wisdom
5. To draw exclaimed Pablo Picasso you must close your eyes and sing
6. The bumper sticker on the car ahead of us said Lord grant me patience but hurry
7. If you are happy declares a proverb from Bali you can always learn to dance
8. This year said Harold S. May you might try spending your vacation somewhere near your budget

9. When you feel that you have arrived declared Yul Brynner you are dead
10. News is history shot on the wing said Gene Fowler
11. Nothing is often a good thing to say declared Will Durant and always a clever thing to say
12. Charles de Gaulle once exclaimed how can you be expected to govern a country that has 246 kinds of cheese
13. Conceit is God's gift to little men observed Bruce Barton
14. You're kept alive by a third of the food you eat said Earl Wilson the other two thirds keeps the doctors alive
15. Jay Chase said money can't buy love health happiness or what it did last year
16. A celebrity is a person who works hard all his life to become well known declared Fred Allen and then wears dark glasses to avoid being recognized
17. Lord prayed Michelangelo grant that I may desire more than I accomplish
18. Reverend Theodore Hesburgh of Notre Dame University declared the most important thing a father can do for his children is love their mother
19. One of the strongest characteristics of genius declared John Watson Foster is the power of lighting its own fire
20. It might be a good idea if the various countries of the world would occasionally swap history books declared Bill Vaughan just to see what other people are doing with the same set of facts

PRACTICE 6 Writing Plurals

Number your paper from 1 to 10 and write next to each number the correct plurals of the italicized words in each sentence. Review pages 304–310.)

ENERGY TO SPARE

1. Harold H. Hart likes to tell *story* of unusual physical *feat,* of *victory.* won against great odds.
2. On May 25, 1935, at the Big Ten conference *championship,* Jesse Owens of Ohio State University broke four world's *record* in about 45 *minute.*
3. In 1936 an Alaskan girl, Mary Joyce, traveled 1000 *mile* by dog sled all alone through *blizzard* and subzero *temperature* to arrive safely at Fairbanks.
4. In 1940 Irving Bauman husked 46.71 *bushel* of corn in 80 *minute.*

5. In 1941 Joe DiMaggio of the New York *Yankee* hit safely in 56 straight *game*.
6. Nearly two *year* later *torpedo* sank an English merchant ship, taking the *life* of all *seaman* aboard but one.
7. The survivor, like the *hero* of old, showed courage and stayed alive 133 *day* on a lonely, drifting life raft.
8. Track star Fanny Blankers-Koen, one of the speediest *woman* in the world, won four gold *medal* in the 1948 Olympics.
9. Age sets no *limit* on achievement, for in 1965 Karen Muir set a world's swimming record at the age of 12.
10. Older people may be *dynamo* of energy too: in 1968, at the age of 80, Clara Wise bowled a 209 game.

PRACTICE 7 Possessives

Number your paper from 1 to 10. Next to each number write the correct forms of the words in parentheses. (Review pages 310–315.)

1. After a (year) experience, Beatrix and Susan enrolled in the (woman) tenpin league.
2. (Beatrix) average of 150 was higher than (Susan), but Susan was improving rapidly.
3. (Beatrix and Susan) skills made many contributions to their new (team) success.
4. The (husband) interests were not always the same as their (wife).
5. The men liked to play basketball in the (boy) gym at the local school or occasionally go fishing in the (St. John) River.
6. (Paul) skill in fishing was much less than (Dan), and the results were sometimes embarrassing.
7. After an (hour) fishing, Dan might have three fish, while his (friend) pail would be empty.
8. Once, after a (day) fishing, Paul did not get his (money) worth, and Dan offered to share his catch with Paul.
9. Paul was reluctant to take advantage of his (partner) generosity, but after a (moment) hesitation he agreed with a chuckle.
10. "Take one of (you)," he declared with a (conspirator) wink, "and throw it to me, so I can honestly say I caught it!"

PRACTICE 8 Time Out for Review

As you copy the following sentences, capitalize and punctuate them correctly. Correct the errors in the use of plurals and possessives. (Review pages 278–316.)

THE GREAT ICE AGE

1. During a number of periods in the earths history great sheets' of ice formed over large portions of the earths surface
2. These glaciers as they are called covered portions of the land a mile high
3. The glacier in new york for example covered the tops of the catskill mountains
4. Yes the glaciers acted as rivers of ice and ground everything in the paths before them
5. They scraped up rocks stones and soil and deposited them farther south
6. The stones in robert frosts poem mending wall probably were brought down by the glacier
7. The glaciers great mass ground down the tops of hills and gouged deeper valley's
8. The canyons carved by rivers however are different from those carved by glaciers
9. States with extensive glacial erosion include new york ohio indiana illinois michigan wisconsin minnesota and iowa
10. A section of wisconsin oddly enough was surrounded by the glacier but not covered
11. At one time or other all the new england states were under ice
12. The great lakes were formed when the ice sheet withdrew
13. Minnesota and wisconsin have many lakes' because of the glacial melt
14. During the ice age mastodons mammoths and saber-toothed tigers lived in north america
15. After the retreat of the ice some animals remained and survived under most unusual conditions
16. A certain species of beetle went underground into caves and survived not without loss of pigmentation and eyesight
17. Will the ice age come again ask some scientists
18. Others ask is the earth now getting warmer or colder
19. Conflicting evidence along with uncertainty about short-term and long-term trends makes conclusions doubtful
20. Glaciers around the world meanwhile remind us of the appearance of these frozen rivers

PRACTICE 9 Agreement of Subject and Verb

In each sentence which verb is the correct or never-questioned one? On your paper write your choice after the number of the sentence. (Review pages 317–329.)

A BOOK OF CURIOSITIES

1. Roberta Kramer's *A Book of Curiosities* (are, is) filled with many unusual bits of information.
2. The spokes of a quickly turning wheel (are, is) lost in a blur.
3. Images imprinted on the human eye (last, lasts) for about 1/16 of a second.
4. Images in too rapid succession (blend, blends) together.
5. (Don't, Doesn't) a dark object look smaller than a light object?
6. A person dressed in bright colors (look, looks) larger and more visible than a person in dark clothes.
7. The holes in Swiss cheese (are, is) formed by air bubbles.
8. There (are, is) only four basic taste sensations: sweet, bitter, sour, and salt.
9. Each member of a family of six probably (have, has) a different sensitivity to taste.
10. Coffee, like many other beverages, (act, acts) as a stimulant.
11. There (are, is) advantages to employers in scheduling coffee breaks.
12. A number of workers (are, is) spurred on to greater productivity by the coffee break.
13. Salt in our bodies (tend, tends) to draw water from body tissues.
14. Excessive salt in our foods (make, makes) us thirsty.
15. There (are, is) sometimes individual variations in the songs of birds.
16. Heat, humidity, and smoke in a crowded room (give, gives) headaches to many persons.
17. The number of explanations (are, is) limitless.
18. One reason for the headaches (are, is) lack of oxygen.
19. In a room, neither marble nor wood (are, is) actually colder than the other, but the marble feels colder.
20. The marble table top, unlike the wooden legs, actually (conduct, conducts) body heat away rapidly.
21. Knots in a wooden board (are, is) harder and denser than the rest of the wood.
22. Where (are, is) the stars on a moonlit night?
23. The number of stars in the sky (are, is) a constant figure.
24. The brilliance of the moon's rays (blot, blots) out all but the brightest stars.
25. There (are, is) only about nine thousand stars visible to the naked eye.
26. (Are, Is) all these stars ever visible at one time?
27. On the clearest evening only about four thousand stars in the moonless sky (are, is) visible.
28. You (were, was) correct in remembering that half the sky is above the other side of the world.

29. Rainfall over large industrial areas (have, has) increased in recent years.
30. The countryside around the industrial areas often (get, gets) less rainfall.
31. Pollution particles in the atmosphere (provide, provides) a necessary ingredient for condensation.
32. (Don't, Doesn't) the rain in an industrial area contain acids?
33. (Weren't, Wasn't) you the one who told me about Cleopatra's Needle in New York's Central Park?
34. The hieroglyphics on the monument (have, has) been badly eroded after a hundred years in an industrial area.
35. In an industrial area every one of the buildings (show, shows) some effects of pollution.
36. Loud noises, as in industry, often (lead, leads) to impairment of hearing.
37. There (are, is) many good reasons for not playing music too loud.
38. Either Jennie or the twins (are, is) using *A Book of Curiosities* for a book report.
39. A number of other students (are, is) reporting on Robert Ripley.
40. (Were, Was) you able to find this book in the library?

PRACTICE 10   Tenses of Verbs

In each of the following which word or expression in parentheses is the correct or never-questioned one?   On your paper write your choice after the number of the sentence.   (Review pages 330–335.)

1. Laurie went up to the box office and (takes, took) out her money for the tickets.
2. There (use, used) to be fine apples on that old Baldwin tree.
3. For the past week we (had, have had) nothing but rain.
4. Juana insisted she (had seen, saw) the comet early this morning in the eastern sky.
5. Ever since we moved to our present house, my brother Rinkie (had, has had) his own room.
6. Mom and Dad closed the trunk and then (discovered, discover) Dad's suit on a chair.
7. Nedra (has lost, lost) her turquoise necklace on the bus coming home from Philadelphia.
8. When we received the telegram, we telephoned right away, but we learned that Michael (had already left, already left).
9. The boys saw a strange shadow moving toward them, and suddenly they all (lose, lost) their voices.

10. Some areas of coastal Peru (had, have had) no measurable rainfall for many years.
11. The weather broadcaster announced that there (had been, were) four tornadoes the previous day.
12. Jimmy Connors announced that he (decided, had decided) not to enter the tournament.
13. We picked cherries today from my favorite tree, which (has been standing, stood) in our yard for more than a generation.
14. In the lacrosse game on television Cornell was five goals behind Maryland, but suddenly the Cornell team (began, begins) to score.
15. We (had, have had) a red house for years, but this year my Dad wants to change the color, and he probably will.
16. When the teacher began distributing the papers, Greg wished that he (had studied, studied) a little more faithfully.
17. On November 8, 1970, Tom Dempsey (has kicked, kicked) a 63-yard field goal to win the game for the New Orleans Saints.
18. Sharon hit a looping ball over the second baseman's head and (made, makes) a crucial base hit.
19. For the past three weeks Ted (has been reading, read) James Michener's *Hawaii,* and he hasn't finished it yet.
20. The umpire ruled that the ball (had rolled, rolled) foul just before the first baseman picked it up.

PRACTICE 11 Principal Parts of Verbs

In each of the following which word or expression in parentheses is the correct or never-questioned one? On your paper write your choice after the number of the sentence. (Review pages 335–345.)

1. Last week Merry (began, begun) a book about chess and became captivated by the history of the game.
2. Bernard Gittelson has (written, wrote) a popular book on the subject of biorhythms, a study of the body's cycles over a period of days.
3. By the time we came back to our hotel in the lovely French town of Dinard, the tide had come in and the water had (risen, rose) more than ten feet.
4. My aunt always has the same greeting for me: "My, how you've (growed, grown)!"
5. Baron Lüchow, our dachshund, had (laid, lain) quite still for ten minutes—until his tormenter, our Siamese cat, came into the room.
6. My grandfather (came, come) to Manlius nearly sixty years ago.
7. Derek's balloon suddenly (burst, busted), frightening all of us out of our daydreaming.

8. Meg mentally rehearsed her speech about the high school play and resolutely (rang, rung) the doorbell.

9. Although Perry had never (spoke, spoken) more effectively, he thought, his father still wouldn't let him take the car to the football game.

10. After looking for nearly an hour, I found Joey (setting, sitting) on a park bench, watching a man feed the pigeons.

11. When my grandfather was young, he actually (knew, knowed) a veteran of the battle of Gettysburg.

12. By the time Dad picked us up on that windy corner, we had nearly (froze, frozen).

13. Until I discovered how to make broccoli soup, my family had never (ate, eaten) the stems of broccoli.

14. After Sandy left, Dino said his heart was (broke, broken), but he still managed to eat a huge dinner with a rich dessert.

15. Mr. Abernathy launched his small model of the *Monitor,* and it (sank, sunk) like a rock.

16. We had never (ridden, rode) in a double-decker bus until we went to London.

17. The high winds on Saturday (blew, blowed) down the billboard at the corner of Main and Prospect.

18. Until my sister showed me how to make a box kite, I had never (flew, flown) one.

19. The choir (sang, sung) that song in the key of *E,* but Ray seemed to be singing in the key of *off.*

20. At the time of George Sand few European women had ever (wore, worn) trousers.

21. In 1954 in Oxford, England, Roger Bannister (ran, run) the first four-minute mile.

22. My favorite sweater has (shrank, shrunk) and now fits my little brother.

23. Max picked up the ball, (threw, throwed) it over the shortstop's head, and allowed two runs to score.

24. Our school's guidance counselor has never (gave, given) me bad advice.

25. Ginnie left a note that said, "I have (gone, went) to Korvette's to buy some tennis balls on sale."

26. If I had (taken, took) piano lessons as a young child, I'd be able to learn guitar more easily.

27. The coach (did, done) his best to encourage the team at half time, but the second half was even worse than the first.

28. I (drank, drunk) a glass of papaya juice for the first time and found it refreshing and tasty.

29. Everyone in Tom's band was (swore, sworn) to secrecy.
30. Frank (came, come) to see my sister Loretta, but he helped me wash the dog.
31. Until last summer I had never (driven, drove) the tractor on my grandmother's farm.
32. Several climbers have (fallen, fell) on the steep slopes of Huntington Ravine.
33. Until the ghost's appearance, Hamlet had (bore, borne) his burdens with resignation.
34. My sister has (flew, flown) more than thirty hours in a Piper Cub.
35. Have you ever (swam, swum) out to the raft and back?
36. Mopsy crouched in perfect immobility and then suddenly (sprang, sprung) at the piece of paper I was slyly dragging in front of her.
37. Then she (dragged, drug) the paper halfway across the room.
38. By the time the team captains picked Russ, all the good players had already been (chose, chosen).
39. Hal, I think you've (tore, torn) your new shirt.
40. The pitcher, who had not had a hit all year, (swang, swung) at an outside pitch and hit it safely into right field.

PRACTICE 12 Recognizing the Parts of the Sentence

Copy the following sentences, skipping every other line. Underline the simple subject once and the verb (main verb plus any helpers) twice. Write **adj.** over every adjective and **adv.** over every adverb. (Omit labels for *a, an, the.*) Enclose each prepositional phrase in a pair of parentheses. (Review pages 259–275, 352–364.)

A GALLANT LADY

1. During the celebration of the Bicentennial in 1976, tourists flocked enthusiastically to many historic sites throughout the country.
2. The Statue of Liberty was visited by millions of people from the United States and many other countries. (Consider the *Statue of Liberty* one noun.)
3. The statue did not always stand at the entrance to New York Harbor.
4. It was generously given to the United States by the people of France.
5. The idea for the gift was first suggested in 1865.
6. Many years passed without progress.
7. In 1871 Frederic Bartholdi came on a visit to the United States.
8. The idea for the statue was born in that year.
9. The construction of the statue did not begin until 1875.

10. The face of Liberty was lovingly modeled after the face of Bartholdi's mother.   (Consider *Bartholdi's* an adjective.   See page 407.)
11. Financial problems unhappily led to delay after delay.
12. At the Centennial celebration in 1876 the arm and torch were proudly put on display.
13. In 1884 the statue was finally completed in Paris.
14. The dismantled statue was carefully packed in 214 crates.
15. It was shipped to New York on a French ship.
16. On October 28, 1886, the statue was formally accepted by President Grover Cleveland.
17. For many years hardy visitors vigorously climbed into the torch.
18. Nowadays curious climbers must stop at the crown.
19. One of the best views of the statue is from the base.
20. The statue is instantly recognized around the world and is associated with the United States.

PRACTICE 13   Parts of the Simple Sentence

Copy the italicized words in a column and number them from 1 to 50.   Then, using the abbreviations listed below, indicate the use of each word in the sentence.   Write the correct abbreviation to the right of each word.   (Review pages 366–374.)

s.s.—simple subject	**p.n.**—predicate noun
v.—verb	**p.a.**—predicate adjective
d.o.—direct object	**o.p.**—object of preposition
i.o.—indirect object	

EXAMPLE

The Olympic Games every four years *give* the *athletes* of the *world* a showcase for their talents.

give—**v.**   athletes—**i.o.**   world—**o.p.**

STARS OF THE OLYMPICS

1. In 1976 in Montreal many world's *records* were broken by superb *athletes* from many lands.
2. Their *achievements,* however, should not overshadow the achievements of *stars* of earlier years.
3. After a *gap* of 1504 years the Olympic Games were revived in *1896* at Athens.

4. Jim Connolly gave the *United States* its first gold *medal* in the first track event of the games. (Consider *United States* as one expression.)
5. The United States sent a ten-man *team* to that Olympics and won *nine* of the twelve gold medals.
6. In the Olympics from 1900 through 1908 Ray Ewry *won* ten gold *medals*.
7. *Ewry* had been a *victim* of polio!
8. The 1912 *games* were called the "Jim Thorpe *Olympics*."
9. Jim Thorpe was from the *United States* and of Indian *blood*.
10. He won the pentathlon and the *decathlon* and was considered the greatest *athlete* in the world.
11. In the 1932 Olympics Babe Didrickson *was outstanding*.
12. She *broke* world's *records* in three events.
13. She also *excelled* in *golf,* basketball, baseball, football, billiards, tennis, and swimming.
14. Jesse Owens *was* the *hero* of the 1936 Olympics.
15. The United States *sprinter* won a *total* of four gold medals.
16. During the tryout for the broad jump a friendly German team member gave *Owens* excellent *advice*.
17. The two men *became* fast *friends*.
18. In recent years many *women* have become outstanding *stars* of the Olympics.
19. Shane Gould of Australia *won* three gold medals for *Australia* in the 1972 games.
20. In the same Olympics Micki King gave the *United States* a *winner* in the springboard dive.
21. In the swimming *competition* Sandra Neilson, Melissa Belote, Catherine Carr, and Karen Moe were gold-medal *winners* for the United States.
22. In the 1976 winter Olympics in *Innsbruck,* Austria, Dorothy Hamill of the United States won a gold *medal* in figure skating.
23. She was unusually *cool* under *pressure*.
24. Please lend *me* that *article* about Olympic winners.
25. *I* was *interested* in some of the stars of yesterday.

PRACTICE 14   Using Adjectives, Adverbs, and Prepositions

In each sentence which word or expression in parentheses is the correct or never-questioned one? On your paper write your choice after the number of the sentence. (Review pages 375–387.)

1. Jennifer plays the zither (good, well), but Madeline is even better.
2. Marshall came out of the examination room looking (unhappily, unhappy).
3. After our beagle Mitzi broke out of the yard, she wasn't (anywhere, nowhere) to be found.
4. My sister Cheryl took (a half, half) a day off to take her driving exam.
5. In Florida (that, those) kind of heavy clouds usually brings rain.
6. (This, This here) Timex watch was a bonus for opening a new bank account.
7. Little Pat walked (unsteadily, unsteady) for a moment or two and then scampered off down the hall.
8. (Them, Those) luscious dark plums are the El Dorado variety.
9. The linebacker and (safety, the safety) were both fooled on that play by the Green Bay quarterback.
10. Jennie's sense of humor is livelier than the (twins, twins').
11. In my opinion walnuts taste (delicious, deliciously) in pound cake.
12. At its brightest, Venus illuminates our backyard as (good, well) as half a dozen flashlights.
13. In the dim light of the phone booth I (could, couldn't) hardly read the telephone number.
14. (That, That there) powerful horse is a Percheron, a work horse of unusual strength.
15. My cousin Herbie believes that (somewhere, somewheres) there is a job ready to spring out upon him and grab him.
16. While they last, lilacs smell more (fragrant, fragrantly) than almost any other flower.
17. Try (this, these) kind of light bulbs to cut down the glare.
18. Bill lived (at, in) Madison while he was attending the University of Wisconsin.
19. Sean bought a new blue blazer; he really looks (good, well) in it.
20. The celebration for (the United States, United States) Bicentennial was long and enthusiastic.
21. If you want to go to Friendly's after the matinee, it's all right (by, with) me.
22. In their recent match Evonne Goolagong's net game was stronger than (Chris Evert, Chris Evert's).
23. By the time Jughead had eaten, there (was, wasn't) scarcely anything left.
24. I borrowed the meat loaf recipe (from, off of) Giselle, but she had neglected to list the onion.
25. After only three lessons with Tim Gallwey, Pudge plays tennis (wonderful, wonderfully) well.

26. When one of our team scores, for a moment our coach speaks too (excited, excitedly) to be understood.
27. (Them, Those) tools should not be left on the lawn; they'll rust.
28. To be sure I had enough reading material for the train ride, I took a book and (a magazine, magazine).
29. Midge waited (a, an) hour in the dentist's waiting room before being asked to go in.
30. The Democratic National Convention in 1976 was held (at, in) New York City.
31. My brother and I disagree. He thinks honey tastes (more sweetly, sweeter) than maple sugar.
32. Of Sarah's two parents, her dad is the (more, most) easygoing.
33. (This, This here) cut watermelon looks redder and riper than the others.
34. Isn't (anybody, nobody) going to volunteer for the arrangements committee?
35. Mr. Muncey just returned from a trip to (Soviet Union, the Soviet Union).
36. I saw Seven-Up sold in a jug that held (a half, half) a gallon.
37. The center and (goalie, the goalie) were voted the game's outstanding players.
38. Helga didn't win the trip she tried for, but she said she really didn't want to go (anyway, anyways).
39. Mom always tries to speak (cheerful, cheerfully), even when she's depressed.
40. Haven't you found (a, no) pen pal yet?

PRACTICE 15 Using Pronouns

In each sentence which word or expression in parentheses is the correct or never-questioned one? On your paper write your choice after the number of the sentence. (Review pages 388–398.)

1. Let's keep the story of my failing the driving test a secret between you and (I, me).
2. Any girl who hasn't taken (her, their) swimming test by Friday will have to come in on the weekend.
3. Fran, let's you and (I, me) enter the women's doubles tournament at Walker Park.
4. (Us, We) members of the Camera Club entered five slides in the annual club competition.
5. Ginnie asked Andy and (she, her) to make the ice cream in the new mixer.

6. Every player on the boys' championship basketball team won (his, their) school letter.
7. For finding lost objects there is no one like Betsy or (he, him).
8. (He, Him) and Rick raise bees for extra money.
9. The girl on the summit of Imp Mountain is (her, she).
10. (She and I, Me and her) won the table tennis tournament in school.
11. Any pigeon that cannot find (its, their) way home from the release point is not a homing pigeon.
12. For making objects from scrap lumber, nobody is better than (he, him).
13. (Them, They) and the Retaliata twins have been chosen to lead the assembly sing.
14. Within the past year my younger brother has grown taller than (I, me).
15. The two students who won citizenship medals were (her, she) and Celia Racanelli.
16. (I and Gary, Gary and I) played Hank Weber and George Larkin in the final round of the tournament.
17. The president of the club called (us, we) officers by telephone and asked our advice.
18. Maggie admitted it was (her, she) in the clown costume at the Freshman Frolic.
19. Don't let the children hurt (themselves, theirselves) on the slippery floor.
20. (Them, Those) are the books I'll need for tonight's homework.
21. Dorie was given the award by the mayor (himself, hisself).
22. The meager supplies were divided (among, between) the four explorers as they set out for their base twenty miles away.
23. The lady we had helped at the picnic sent thank-you gifts to Abby and (I, me).
24. (Me and Tom, Tom and I) are school reporters for the *Bay Shore Sentinel*.
25. I hope that you will reserve two spots on the bus for (us, we) girls.
26. Every puppy in the pet store has had (its, their) shot for distemper.
27. When Bob Tuomey is in a good mood, no one is funnier than (he, him).
28. The last piece of pie was divided between Bella and (he, him).
29. Either Marilyn or Nancy will have (her, their) camera at the picnic.
30. Robin, Kate, and (I, me) enjoy craft work.
31. (Them, They) have won every golf tournament this year.
32. Let's you and (I, me) visit the Frick Museum this Saturday.
33. Neither the poodle nor the spaniel had (its, their) flea collar on.

34. After the party Mom assigned Dad and (I, me) to the mop-up detail.
35. For a clever retort there is no one as quick as (he, him).
36. (Rochelle and I, Me and Rochelle) are knitting an afghan for Ellen's birthday.
37. In the car, dressed and ready to go, were Nelson and (her, she).
38. Every player on the football team must have (his, their) ankles taped before going out on the field.
39. (Us, We) members of the Gourmet Club planned a Japanese dinner for the end-term party.
40. For help when you really need it, there is no one like Gwen or (he, him).

PRACTICE 16 Review of Usage

In each sentence which word or expression in parentheses is the correct or never-questioned one? On your paper write your choice after the number of the sentence. (Review pages 278–285, 304–316, 330–345, 375–398.)

1. Neither of the two girls (are, is) a member of the Canoe Club.
2. The official ruled that the game (ended, had ended) before the goal was made.
3. Jeremy says that (a half, half) a loaf may be better than none, but he prefers a full loaf.
4. Many buildings in the Soho district of New York (are, is) faced with cast iron.
5. Mr. Winchell sent Luella and (I, me) tickets for the Pendleton Roundup.
6. Ted saw the menacing shadow on the wall and (takes, took) off at full speed, only to discover later that the shadow was that of a fire hydrant.
7. When we returned from our Christmas trip to my aunt's, we discovered that the water pipes had (froze, frozen).
8. Mac (could, couldn't) hardly read the telephone directory, so he had the prescription for his glasses changed.
9. The Cougars played (good, well) for three quarters, but in the last quarter their game fell apart.
10. Panama, now one of the Central American nations, (was, were) once considered part of South America.
11. (Surprising, Surprisingly) enough, a city dog, on the average, lives longer than a country dog.
12. One three-thousandth of an ounce of a certain bacteria toxin (are, is) enough to poison the entire human population of the earth.

13. A high school principal in Oregon began the daily broadcasting of the names of absent students, and suddenly truancy at the school (dropped, drops) by 25 percent!
14. Mrs. Oliver told Cindy and (I, me) that a section of railroad track in Australia does not make the slightest turn in 328 miles.
15. I must admit that Dad (became, becomes) a little annoyed when I told him about the dent in the right fender.
16. Maria, you (was, were) chosen to represent our homeroom at the party caucus.
17. My brother Anthony married into a large family and now has five (sister-in-laws, sisters-in-law).
18. The coastal areas of the Pacific (northwest, Northwest) have a great deal of rain in winter.
19. Our old dog Rocky has (laid, lain) quite still in the sunlight for over an hour.
20. Some fine women tennis players are not much over five (feet, foot) tall.
21. After we had (shaken, shook) the tree, we gathered the fruit that had fallen.
22. (Us, We) members learned today that the four *H*'s in 4-H Club stand for *Head, Heart, Health,* and *Hands.*
23. The saltiest of all the world's lakes (are, is) generally conceded to be the Dead Sea.
24. I (could, couldn't) hardly believe that a baby rattler at birth is as poisonous as a full-grown snake.
25. The number of languages and dialects spoken in India (exceed, exceeds) 1650.
26. After a (week's, weeks) delay because of bad weather in Alaska, a letter from Judy finally arrived.
27. Each member of the Journalism Club (brang, brought) a guest to the celebrity luncheon.
28. The missing scarf was (laying, lying) across the arm of the old rocker on the porch.
29. We (have lived, lived) in Roanoke for four years, but we're moving to Blowing Rock next month.
30. Jack took Charlotte and (he, him) to the wrestling matches in Tampa.
31. Every girl on the Olympic swim squad won (her, their) position by hard work and self-sacrifice.
32. I must admit I (been, have been) too busy to write you as often as I should.
33. (Them, Those) honeydew melons are a bit too hard to be ripe.

34. A number of marigolds in the garden (was, were) still alive after the first light frost.
35. I (knew, knowed) that *e* is the most commonly used letter in English, but I didn't know that *s* begins more English words than any other.
36. Jamie's pet raccoon got away and was (nowhere, nowheres) to be found.
37. My favorite subjects in high school are history, math, and (spanish, Spanish).
38. It (doesn't, don't) seem possible that someone could print the Gettysburg Address on a human hair, but the feat has been done.
39. Years ago there (was, were) restrictions on beards in Rumania.
40. A permit issued by the proper authorities (was, were) needed before whiskers could be worn.

PRACTICE 17 Recognizing Parts of Speech

Copy the following sentences, skipping every other line. Then, using the following abbreviations, tell what part of speech each word is. Write the abbreviation above the word. Each sentence contains ten words. (Review pages 402–409.)

n.—noun	**v.**—verb	**prep.**—preposition
pr.—pronoun	**adv.**—adverb	**conj.**—conjunction
adj.—adjective		

EXAMPLE

n.	**adv.**	**v.**	**pr.**	**prep.**	**adj.**	**n.**	**prep.**	**adj.**
Mario	slyly	interested	me	in	these	bits	of	trivial

        n.
information.

1. The Icelandic language has not essentially changed for many centuries.
2. A painting by Matisse was hung backward in a museum.
3. The mistake was not discovered by anyone for a month.
4. Thousands of people had seen the painting and enjoyed it.
5. Chop suey was created in the United States and was unknown in China. (Consider both *chop suey* and *United States* one expression.)
6. The hummingbird, unlike other birds, can hover or fly backward.
7. A beam of light can fly around the world swiftly.
8. It makes the trip in a tenth of a second.
9. Dolphins always sleep cautiously with one eye open and alert.

10. A flea can accelerate with incredible speed for its size.
11. Certain tiny fishes in the Philippines are smaller than ants.
12. Indians in Panama can easily shave themselves with natural razors.
13. Unusual native grasses have edges of razorlike sharpness and strength.
14. The trunk of an elephant holds six quarts of water.
15. A female cod lays millions of eggs, but few survive.
16. The flag of Denmark is the oldest unchanged national flag.
17. A tiny curlew can fly nonstop for two thousand weary miles. (Consider *two thousand* one expression.)
18. A bolt of lightning once melted a lady's metal earring.
19. Another struck a zipper and welded someone into a sleeping bag. (Consider *sleeping bag* one expression.)
20. Timothy Fullerton wrote a book on trivia and called it *Triviata*. (Consider *Timothy Fullerton* one expression.)

PRACTICE 18   Punctuating Compound and Complex Sentences

Punctuate the following sentences.   Give a reason for each mark you use.   Do not write in this book.   (Review pages 286–302 and 419–437.)

BEES IN HIS BONNET

1. Although Will doesn't always remember jokes he told me one he had heard earlier today
2. This joke which is filled with a very special kind of nonsense runs something like this
3. Two men who had not met for many years ran into each other
4. Because they hadn't seen each other for many years they asked for all the news
5. I'm retired said Mr Collins but I'm very happy
6. What do you do with yourself asked Mr Wolf
7. Actually replied Collins I'm very busy for I am now raising bees
8. Do you live out in the country where you have plenty of room asked Wolf
9. No replied his friend I live in that big apartment house over there
10. Wolf who had been picturing Collins in a country estate looked puzzled
11. You raise bees in your apartment in an apartment house he asked incredulously
12. I don't use the entire apartment explained Collins I use only one room

13. A strange look came over the troubled countenance of poor Mr Wolf and he began to speak again
14. You raise bees in a room of an apartment he asked
15. Well said Collins hesitantly I may have misled you since I am using only one closet in the apartment
16. You raise bees in a closet Wolf blurted out
17. Collins looked a little sheepish and he began a further explanation
18. Actually I keep the bees in a hat box in the closet but I usually keep the door closed
19. How can you keep bees in a hat box exclaimed Wolf
20. The bees are in the hat box said Collins but I really keep them inside a plastic bag inside the hat box
21. This is too much exclaimed Wolf as he began to tremble with the story he had just been hearing
22. You can't keep bees in a plastic bag in a hat box in a closet of a room in an apartment
23. Why can't I innocently asked Collins who was beginning to be amazed at his friend's distress
24. The bees must have air and food and room to fly around in or else they will surely die explained Wolf with feverish intensity
25. Oh well said Collins with a resigned shrug it's only a hobby

PRACTICE 19 Sentence Sense

Indicate by **0, 1, 2,** or **3** the number of complete sentences in each of the following. On your paper place a period between the number of the example and your answer. Get rid of a sentence fragment by making it into a complete sentence or by attaching it to another sentence. Get rid of a run-together sentence by correctly punctuating and capitalizing it. (Review pages 442–451.)

THE GREAT MARTIAN INVASION

1. Probes by the *Mariner* spaceships bringing us closer and closer to the planet Mars
2. Pictures sent back by the spacecrafts have shown us what the Martian surface looks like but there are no traces of a civilization like the Earth's
3. Once people dreamed about life on Mars some astronomers talked about canals authors wrote books about supposed life on Mars
4. One of the most popular books a novel by H. G. Wells called *The War of the Worlds*

5. In this book Martians invade the earth they attack the unsuspecting earthmen everything falls before them
6. The world seems doomed however the Martians have a hidden weakness they die of a human ailment the common cold
7. Their bodies being unable to fight off the attacks of earth's bacteria
8. On September 30, 1938, a radio program called the "Mercury Theatre on the Air" presented a dramatization of Wells's novel *The War of the Worlds*
9. By coincidence the producer of the radio program was also Welles Orson Welles indeed there were times Orson Welles was sorry he had ever heard of the other Wells
10. The radio program was put on realistically as it turned out it was too realistic
11. For greater realism Welles moved the scene of the novel from England to the United States the landing of the Martians occurred in New Jersey
12. It was less than a year before the beginning of World War II people were on edge frightening news bulletins were not uncommon
13. The program started like a typical music program with an ordinary weather report to provide realism
14. Then came a special bulletin about some explosions on the surface of Mars thus the listeners were being prepared for the make-believe invasion to come
15. Listeners who tuned in at the beginning and knew that this was a play and not a real event
16. Some people half listen to programs therefore they catch only fragments
17. Other listeners flip dials and tune into the middle of programs
18. Announcers repeated four times that the program was make-believe not a real broadcast however many listeners failed to catch these all-important announcements
19. Because these listeners had only a confused knowledge of what was going on
20. They believed the invasion was real they were terrified they lost their judgment
21. All over the United States but especially in the East people in a panic making frantic telephone calls and rushing out into the streets
22. Telephone switchboards were jammed people became hysterical ambulances were called out
23. As far away as San Francisco men volunteering to help in the dreadful emergency
24. Some purely local events made the events seem more real indeed a local power failure persuaded listeners that all was over

25. The actors on the show little realizing the havoc their broadcast was causing
26. People's imaginations played tricks on them as more and more people thought they saw the glow of fires in the distance
27. While others thought they smelled poison gas.
28. Cars speeding away from the "danger areas" failed to stop for police cars and shouted warnings about the "invasion"
29. It was some time before calm was restored and people realized that the invasion was just a clever radio program
30. Surprisingly enough no one was seriously hurt nevertheless listeners who thought the invasion was real would never forget the broadcast as long as they lived

PRACTICE 20   Sentence Patterns

In each of the following sentences identify the pattern: **SV, SVO, SVIO, SVN,** or **SVA.** (Review pages 462–468.)

EXAMPLE

Ancient Americans played many ball games.   **SVO**

PLAY BALL—AZTEC STYLE

1. An article in *Natural History* told me a great deal about sports in the New World before the arrival of the Spaniards.
2. The ancient Americans used rubber balls in their games.
3. Rubber was a New World discovery.
4. European sports were usually tests of individual skill.
5. Team competition, on the other hand, was commonplace in early America.
6. Thus the native Americans gave Europeans the idea of team sports.
7. The Middle American ball game was a combination of basketball, volleyball, soccer, and jai alai.
8. Amateur and professional teams existed in those early years throughout Middle America.
9. The Spaniards marveled at the skill and endurance of these early players.
10. The games were unbelievably strenuous.
11. According to Spanish eyewitnesses, sometimes players died of exhaustion on the playing field.
12. The rewards for the winners were great.
13. Rulers gave the winners rich gifts.

14. A loss, unfortunately, might be fatal.
15. Sometimes unhappy rulers sacrificed to the gods the captain of the losing team.
16. The spectators at these matches were incredible gamblers.
17. These gamblers might lose houses and fields in one day.
18. A spectator might wager his entire fortune on a single game!
19. Rulers sometimes played for kingdoms.
20. Sports were indeed important to the people of pre-Columbian America.

PRACTICE 21   Review

Number your paper from 1 to 40.   Each of the following sentences is either correct or contains one error.   If there is an error, it will be found in one of the four underlined sections, labeled **A, B, C,** or **D.**   Find the error and write the letter (**A, B, C,** or **D**) after the number of the sentence.   Then write the correct form.   If there is no error in the underlined portion, write choice **E** (No error) beside the number of the sentence.

EXAMPLES

By noon Mattie <u>had wrote</u> <u>half</u> her report <u>on</u> solar heating.   <u>No error</u>
A   B   C   D   E
B—had written (*Had wrote* is incorrect.)

Gerard <u>had</u> two <u>months'</u> <u>experience</u> <u>as</u> club manager.   <u>No error</u>
       A   B   C   D   E
E (There is no error in the sentence.)

1. <u>At least</u> one of the quiz show <u>contestants</u> <u>were</u> chosen <u>from</u> the
   A   B   C   D
   audience.   <u>No error</u>
             E
2. The puppy <u>who</u> I considered the <u>liveliest</u> <u>was</u> bought by someone
            A   B   C
   else before I got back <u>to</u> the pet store with my money.   <u>No error</u>
                         D   E
3. <u>Whenever</u> Sigrid tells <u>us girls</u> about her summer in Oslo, <u>she</u> speaks
   A   B   C
   <u>enthusiastic.</u>   <u>No error</u>
   D   E
4. In a corner of the barn <u>among some old rags</u> <u>was</u> five beautiful <u>kittens,</u>
                          A   B   C
   <u>all</u> with long white fur.   <u>No error</u>
   D   E

5. The civilized nation <u>what</u> <u>has</u> the best life-expectancy statistics is
                   A **B**
<u>Sweden,</u> not <u>the</u> United States. <u>No error</u>
  C   **D**   **E**

6. The <u>giant</u> birthday card for Dolores <u>was</u> <u>carefully</u> lettered by Milton
     A   **B**   **C**
and <u>I.</u> <u>No error</u>
   D   **E**

7. <u>Even though</u> it became <u>quite late,</u> Jacqueline <u>held</u> onto her feeling
   A   **B**   **C**
that her brothers <u>would arrive</u> that evening. <u>No error</u>
            D   **E**

8. Georgie insisted <u>without hesitation</u> that she <u>saw</u> a golden eagle at
                 A   **B**
Brownlee's woods <u>the day before.</u> <u>No error</u>
  C   **D**   **E**

9. Mom <u>borrowed</u> a cake pan <u>off of</u> a neighboring camper and <u>made</u> a
      A   **B**   **C**
tasty chocolate cake <u>in the table-top oven.</u> <u>No error</u>
               D   **E**

10. Nils <u>always complains</u> <u>because</u> his room is smaller <u>than</u> his <u>sisters.</u>
     A   **B**   **C**   **D**
<u>No error</u>
 E

11. <u>Was</u> you <u>present</u> in the auditorium when the names of the science
  A   **B**
winners <u>were read aloud?</u> <u>No error</u>
  C   **D**   **E**

12. In the famous picture <u>of Whistler's mother,</u> <u>she</u> is <u>setting</u> <u>quietly</u> in
                    A   **B**   **C**   **D**
her rocking chair. <u>No error</u>
             E

13. *Chance, Luck, and Statistics* <u>is</u> the <u>title</u> of a book by Horace C.
                       A   **B**
Levinson, a clever, witty, and <u>informed</u> <u>author.</u> <u>No error</u>
                     C   **D**   **E**

14. Our neighbor <u>Mr. Gilliam</u> <u>has went</u> to the last three summer Olympic
            A   **B**
Games, and he plans to go to the <u>next,</u> <u>also.</u> <u>No error</u>
                     C   **D**   **E**

15. New York City and <u>Paris which</u> <u>are</u> <u>similar</u> in many respects, face
                A   **B** **C**
many of the same problems, <u>both social and financial.</u> <u>No error</u>
                     D   **E**

16. I discovered the <u>hard</u> way that <u>there</u> <u>is</u> many miles between Tampa
            A   **B** **C**
and Palm Beach, particularly <u>by</u> bicycle! <u>No error</u>
                 D   **E**

17. <u>Did</u> you really grow <u>them</u> vegetables <u>all</u> by yourself in that little
  A   **B**   **C**
<u>handkerchief-sized</u> garden? <u>No error</u>
     D   **E**

18. Even though I secretly admired his <u>ready wit,</u> I <u>could never</u> admit
                                                 A   **B**
    that Anatole is <u>cleverer</u> than <u>me.</u> <u>No error</u>
                    C   **D**   **E**

19. <u>Those</u> new <u>kinds</u> of tennis balls seem to last longer and stay <u>livelier</u>
     A   **B**   **C**
    <u>than the old.</u> <u>No error</u>
        D   **E**

20. Mom <u>has</u> <u>broke</u> <u>nearly</u> all her wedding dishes, but she <u>still</u> has two
           A   **B**   **C**   **D**
    chipped saucers and a battered soup plate. <u>No error</u>
                                           E

21. The <u>number</u> of new stamps issued by the United States Postal Service
        A
    <u>has</u> <u>sharply</u> increased this <u>year.</u> <u>No error</u>
    B   **C**   **D**   **E**

22. <u>Putting</u> on my wristwatch, the clock struck <u>one,</u> <u>reminding</u> me
    A   **B**   **C**
    <u>to reset</u> the time. <u>No error</u>
    D   **E**

23. <u>Neither Sheila nor</u> her <u>brothers</u> <u>is</u> <u>likely</u> to attend a college in
            A   **B**   **C**   **D**
    another state. <u>No error</u>
                E

24. <u>Each animal</u> in the San Diego Zoo <u>has</u> <u>their</u> <u>place</u> in the educational
    A   **B**   **C**   **D**
    program planned by the curators. <u>No error</u>
                                  E

25. <u>Let's</u> you and <u>I</u> plan a trip to historic Charleston this <u>spring</u> during
    A   **B**   **C**
    the <u>Easter</u> recess. <u>No error</u>
         D   **E**

26. Jack Palombo, among all my closest friends, <u>don't</u> care <u>much</u> for
                                          A   **B**
    the opinion of <u>others;</u> <u>he's</u> a real individualist. <u>No error</u>
               C   **D**   **E**

27. <u>Having trained</u> for <u>only</u> a month, Pete did <u>good</u> <u>to make</u> the cross-
    A   **B**   **C**   **D**
    country team. <u>No error</u>
                  E

28. <u>For me, peanut butter and jelly</u> is a <u>real</u> <u>treat,</u> but I like it on whole-
    A   **B**   **C**   **D**
    wheat bread. <u>No error</u>
                 E

29. For years Brian <u>was</u> the <u>tallest</u> of the two O'Hara boys, but in the
                   A   **B**
    past year Sean <u>has</u> <u>suddenly</u> shot past him. <u>No error</u>
                 C   **D**   **E**

30. We <u>especially</u> enjoyed the art by Rembrandt at the Metropolitan
       A

Museum of Art and <u>felt</u> we could <u>keep</u> looking at <u>them</u> for hours.
      B   **C**   **D**

<u>No error</u>
E

31. When <u>we reached</u> the small cave on the mountain side, Myra took
   A

  off her pack, <u>made a pillow of it</u>, <u>laid</u> her head against it, and soon
         B   **C**

  fell <u>fast asleep</u>. <u>No error</u>
    D   **E**

32. My family <u>lived</u> <u>in</u> Flat Rock <u>for the past ten years</u>, and we hope
      A **B**   **C**

  to <u>live here</u> for many more happy years. <u>No error</u>
    D   **E**

33. A battered old sweater is <u>my brothers</u> security blanket, <u>and he</u> wears
       A   **B**   **C**

  <u>it</u> at every opportunity. <u>No error</u>
  D   **E**

34. We had <u>no rain</u> for <u>nearly a month</u>, and the leaves of the rhododen-
     A   **B**

  dron <u>begin</u> to <u>curl, droop, and fall</u>. <u>No error</u>
    C   **D**   **E**

35. I learned <u>a amazing fact</u>, <u>that</u> <u>there</u> is a golf hole in North Carolina
      A   **B** **C**

  that is <u>745 yards</u> long and is a par 6. <u>No error</u>
     D   **E**

36. Every girl in the <u>girls' health education class</u> <u>has</u> taken <u>their</u> swim
        A   **B**   **C**

  test and passed <u>it</u>. <u>No error</u>
      D   **E**

37. <u>From a mountain peak in Costa Rica</u> one <u>can see</u> both the Atlantic
       A   **B**

  and Pacific Oceans, the only point in the Americas from which <u>you</u>
                        C

  <u>can see</u> both oceans. <u>No error</u>
  D   **E**

38. You <u>hadn't ought to</u> <u>be sorry</u> to see heavy dew <u>on</u> the grass in the
    A   **B**   **C**

  morning, for the dew <u>usually</u> foretells good weather. <u>No error</u>
         D   **E**

39. Benjy took the suitcases <u>from the porch</u> and began <u>stuffing</u> them <u>in</u>
         A   **B**   **C**

  <u>the already overloaded</u> trunk. <u>No error</u>
    D   **E**

40. I thought Sam <u>might</u> hurt <u>hisself</u> chopping wood with the two-headed
      A   **B**

  axe, so I lent him my wedges and hammer, <u>which</u> <u>are</u> much safer to
                 C **D**

  use. <u>No error</u>
     E